SPEECH, CRIME, AND THE USES OF LANGUAGE

SPEECH, CRIME, AND THE USES OF LANGUAGE

KENT GREENAWALT

New York   Oxford
OXFORD UNIVERSITY PRESS

Oxford University Press

Oxford   New York   Toronto
Delhi   Bombay   Calcutta   Madras   Karachi
Kuala Lumpur   Singapore   Hong Kong   Tokyo
Nairobi   Dar es Salaam   Cape Town
Melbourne   Auckland

and associated companies in
Berlin   Ibadan

Copyright © 1989 by Kent Greenawalt

First published in 1989 by Oxford University Press, Inc.
200 Madison Avenue, New York, New York 10016

First issued as an Oxford University Press paperback, 1992.

Oxford is a registered trademark of Oxford University Press, Inc.

Library of Congress Cataloging-in-Publication Data
Greenawalt, Kent, 1936–
Speech, crime, and the uses of language.
Includes index.
1. Freedom of speech—United States.
2. Criminal law—United States.
I. Title.
KF4772.G74   1989
347.302853   342.73'0853   88-28894
ISBN 0-19-505799-6
ISBN 0-19-507711-3 (pbk)

9 8 7 6 5 4 3 2 1

Printed in the United States of America
on acid-free paper

To Sasha
With love, and great appreciation for his gifts

Preface

The genesis of this book lies in an invitation more than a decade ago by the American Bar Foundation to write an article for the Samuel Pool Weaver Constitutional Law Essay Program. Having been supervising revisions to the Commentary to the Model Penal Code and teaching *Brandenburg* v. *Ohio*, a decision that provides constitutional protection for inflammatory public speech, I was intrigued by the relation between free speech and the traditional crime of criminal solicitation; and my proposal to write on that topic was accepted by the Essay Committee. Much of the work on the article, published as "Speech and Crime," 1980 *American Bar Foundation Journal* 645, was done while I was a Visiting Fellow at All Souls College in Oxford in 1979, where I became interested in the writings of J. L. Austin, John Searle, and others on different uses of language. In the course of the article, I commented on these authors but did not attempt to develop in detail the relevance of their insights for the subject of free speech.

After its publication, Erwin Griswold, under whom I had worked as one of three deputies in 1971–72 when he was Solicitor General, wrote me a generous letter about the article, but suggested that I might aim to reach a wider audience with a shorter, less intricate treatment. His letter was critical to my thoughts of returning to the broad subject. During the spring of 1983, when I was visiting at Northwestern University Law School, I was asked to participate in a symposium on freedom of expression. Having recently read an important opinion of the Oregon Supreme Court on free speech and criminal coercion written by Hans Linde, I decided to tackle the topic of threats. That contribution was published as "Criminal Coercion and Freedom of Speech," 78 *Northwestern University Law Review* 1081 (1983). A few years later, Leonard Levy, in correspondence, suggested that I try to have the original article on speech and crime published as a book.

With these encouragements about the significance of the work I had done and feeling that it left much to be said, I decided to develop more fully my views on the important but little discussed relation between free speech and the uses of language and to assess the import of that evaluation for controversial topics such as pornography, racial epithets, and symbolic speech. Thus, while the book draws from the earlier articles, it is substantially more comprehensive and systematic, and it treats many subjects in some depth that are only fleetingly mentioned in the articles. A good bit of the last part of the book considers particular constitutional standards, but the book aims to make a broader contribution to understanding of freedom of speech and to political and constitutional theory.*

Over the years a great many people have helped me in one way or another that relates to this book. Peter Durfee, Maria Patterson, Stephanie Rasines, John Orenstein, and Spencer Thal provided vital research assistance. Jamie Titus helped with proofreading. Iqbal Ishar, a law teacher from India studying in Columbia's doctoral program, has given invaluable and extensive editing and re-search help during the last stage of bringing a rough manuscript into shape for publication. He also proofread the entire manuscript and prepared the index.

Colleagues Harold Edgar and Benno Schmidt made very useful criticisms of drafts of the two articles. Benjamin DuVal, Charles H. Joiner, William Van Alstyne, and Toni Carey commented helpfully on the first article; and the second article benefited from remarks at the Northwestern Symposium and from a presentation before members of the University of Chicago Law Faculty. Charles Larmore made fruitful suggestions for the book about some theoretical problems, Vince Blasi subjected the second article and parts of the book to penetrating and thorough critiques, and Robert Amdur gave a similar critique to the entire manuscript of the book. Conversations and exchanges of manuscripts with Edwin Baker have done much to illuminate our differences and the grounds of my own position.

The typing of stages of the book has been by Rhonda Callison, up to the summer of 1987, Madelain Amare, Susan Blommaert, and Sally Wrigley, with some help from Sara DeSouza, Marla Johnson, and Lillian Hoffman. All of them have worked with patience and good humor in the face of difficult demands, and at critical junctures in the last year the amount and quality of work that has been accomplished in very short periods of time have been amazing.

During the summers of 1987 and 1988 my efforts were supported by the Samuel Rubin Foundation for the Advancement of Liberty and Equality through Law, allowing me sustained time for reading, thought, and writing. I am very, very grateful to all those who have aided me in these various ways.

During the editing of the manuscript by Oxford University Press, my beloved wife Sanja became ill and died. These months have reminded me in the most poignant way how my life, including my work as a teacher and scholar, has depended on her. Her constant love and support have been the anchor for everything else, and the prospect of trying to carry on without her close presence is still almost unimaginable.

New York   K. G.
November 1988

---

*The note style in the book is an amalgam of that used in legal scholarship and that used in the social sciences and humanities. The only aspect that may require explanation is that the page number following an article citation refers to the first page of the article, and that is the only page indicated when the reference is to the article in general.

Contents

I
COMMUNICATIVE ACTS AND FREEDOM OF SPEECH

1

Speech, Communication, and Crime

Freedom of speech is a crucial political principle in liberal societies, and, for countries with written constitutions, some guarantee of free speech is almost certainly to be found among protections of individual rights. But what is the "speech" that is to be free and protected? Does it coincide with the category of verbal and written utterances, or is it possibly narrower or broader in some respects? This book addresses critical aspects of that question in a systematic way.

The book, which has related theoretical and practical purposes, explores a three-way relationship among the idea of freedom of speech, the law of crimes, and the many uses of language. The most abstract theoretical aim is to show how a sound political principle of free speech is responsive to the varieties of communicative acts. Many acts of communication have never been thought to raise free speech problems at all—a phenomenon occasionally remarked[1] but rarely analyzed. I explain why many communicative efforts do not seriously implicate the values that lie behind freedom of speech, showing that categories developed in the philosophy of language, though not simply transposable into political principles, can illuminate the proper boundaries of free speech.

Although one of my aims is to explore why it is that some verbal and written communications plainly fall beyond any plausible reach of a principle of free speech, I concentrate more attention on communicative acts whose possible coverage within the borders of free speech is debatable, especially solicitations to crime and threats. How these acts should be treated is of considerable practical significance, and I claim that their character has often been misunderstood. Beyond considering whether these acts fall within the outer boundaries of free speech, I discuss standards for determining which acts within the outer boundaries may nonetheless be punished. The broad focus on how communicative acts relate to the justifications for freedom of speech matters also for other subjects that are less close to the center of my analysis, and I sketch many of those implications.

Freedom of Speech as a Political and Constitutional Principle

A principle of freedom of speech may be understood both as a political guide and as an actual or potential standard of constitutional law. Americans, of course, are familiar with freedom of speech as an aspect of constitutional law. The First Amendment of the American Constitution states that "Congress shall make no law . . . abridging the freedom of speech, or of the press," and language protecting speech and press is also found in state constitutions. The guarantees apply to the executive and judicial branches of government as well as to the legislature, and the Supreme Court has declared that the post-Civil War Fourteenth Amendment made the federal provision apply against the states. As a consequence, all government activity in the United States is subject to the federal constitutional constraint. Although the "press," understood as covering all printed material, probably had special significance for the drafters of the First Amendment and although contemporary claims are made that the press, in the sense of media like newspapers and television broadcasters, enjoys certain independent constitutional protections not available to citizens speaking their minds, for the most part the protections of speech and press are the same. I use the term "freedom of speech" to refer to freedom of speech and press, when I draw no distinction, and most of my references to the First Amendment concern the protections of these freedoms, not the important guarantees of free exercise and nonestablishment of religion which the amendment also contains.

The constitutional guarantee of freedom of speech reflects the important political principle that government should not suppress the communication of ideas. Indeed, this principle is frequently regarded as a cornerstone of liberal democracy. Even in a country without a binding written constitution, freedom of speech and press may be an accepted political norm.[2] Part of what this entails is that legislators, out of respect for freedom of speech and press, will restrain themselves from enacting otherwise attractive laws. In a country with such a political principle, freedom of speech will also probably be a legal principle of nonconstitutional status, affecting the interpretation of statutes and the development of judicial doctrines.[3]

This book is about free speech both as a political principle generally and as a constitutional standard in the United States. In the first stages of the study, I concentrate on the political principle, reserving for later the connections to constitutional law. To understand whether a political principle is sound, one needs to explore the claimed justifications for it. Here, the exercise reveals much about the importance of preserving freedom of speech when that objective conflicts with other values and about what counts as the "speech" that should ordinarily be kept free. Chapter 2 addresses the justifications for freedom of speech, and Chapter 3 considers the communications to which a principle of free speech applies. The chapters in Part II examine bases on which criminal liability is fixed for communications, to see whether those bases are in serious tension with freedom of speech. Those chapters bear directly on the choices of legislators, whether they are acting in countries without enforceable constitutional limits on legislative power or are trying to decide within a range permitted by enforceable constitutional limits.

The third part of the book develops the significance of the earlier chapters' conclusions for American constitutional law. Most questions about understanding and applying the political principle have at least potential relevance to constitutional interpretation, but the shift from freedom of speech as a political principle to freedom of speech as a constitutional principle demands further levels of analysis. Without developing a complete theory of constitutional interpretation, I suggest standards for understanding constitutional protections of individual liberty. I also address the more particular subjects of what should be considered "speech" within the meaning of the First Amendment and what particular tests the courts should employ to decide when criminal statutes impinging on speech should be held to be unconstitutional, as written or in their applications to particular situations.

Both in regard to a political principle and in regard to constitutional norms, I distinguish between the outer range of coverage and what should finally be regarded as protected speech.[4] Roughly, if communicative or other acts are beyond the range of coverage, their prohibition can be considered without regard to freedom of speech. If acts are covered by a principle of free speech, it does not follow that their prohibition is foreclosed; in certain circumstances the state's interest may be powerful enough to forbid acts that qualify as speech. Conceptual analysis alone cannot yield a practical distinction between the question of coverage and ultimate protection; that depends on sensitivity to the tasks of legislators and judges. An important ambition of succeeding chapters is to draw this distinction persuasively. One conclusion that emerges is that it would be futile, indeed absurd, to employ one single test to decide which of those acts initially covered by a principle of free speech should be regarded as finally beyond prohibition.

The book's order of presentation has the drawback that many of its subjects are analyzed three times: first in relation to general theory, next in relation to legislative choice about criminal statutes, and finally in relation to constitutional standards. Although I reduce repetition by references forward and backward, certain basic ideas are offered two or three times. This disadvantage seemed worth embracing in order to disentangle the treatment of general theory and legislative choice from constitutional analysis. A reader unconcerned with American constitutional law can assess the thrust of my main contentions without being trapped in details of constitutional argument. And a reader with strong views about American constitutional cases can consider my general approach, relatively unencumbered by prejudgments about right judicial results. That reader can then see whether disagreements with me over the latter emerge from different notions of a sound political principle of free speech or from different beliefs about how a constitution should be interpreted. Moreover, since many ideas presented here will be unfamiliar to most readers, the repetition itself may possess some value. By presenting the ideas in various degrees of abstraction and in more than one context and by putting all the basic themes about free speech on the table before the constitutional analysis commences, the book should afford readers a firmer grasp of just what my claims are.

Communications and Crimes

It remains in this introductory chapter to indicate just how pervasive is punishment of communications and how wide-ranging is the question whether such punishment raises serious free speech problems. Any sound principle of free speech reaches many government actions besides the law of crimes, but the core of the idea of free speech concerns limits on behavior that the state should make criminal. My discussion, while treating many issues regarding civil liability, mainly addresses criminal sanctions. Since many instances in which the law impinges on communication and many important constitutional cases involve criminal penalties, conclusions about the law of crimes are immediately important for determining how far speech will be free, and they have powerful relevance for a broader range of government restrictions. My emphasis is on verbal and written utterances, although at various stages I also explore other acts that aim to communicate some message.

Understanding of my overall topic is enhanced by a brief initial reflection on some of the ways in which communication figures in treating the actions of individuals as criminal. Here, as elsewhere in the book, I use the Model Penal Code as the primary source of references. Though not actually law anywhere in the United States, the Code has been widely influential in American penal-law revision, and its Commentary contains extensive citations to provisions in actual jurisdictions.

An examination of American criminal law reveals that a person may be guilty of a crime if he or she:

1. agrees with another to commit a crime;[5]
2. offers to agree with another to commit a crime;[6]
3. orders another to commit a crime;[7]
4. requests another to commit a crime;[8]
5. induces another to commit a crime (as by a bribe);[9]
6. threatens harm unless another commits a crime;[10]
7. carries out an ordinary criminal purpose by communicating; for example, by telling a blind companion on a mountain path that he can safely step to the right, while wanting to cause his death and knowing that a 2000-foot drop lies to the right;[11]
8. puts another in fear of imminent serious injury by physical menace;[12]
9. participates in a criminal endeavor by communicating; for example, by telling thieving friends the combination of the employer's safe;[13]
10. warns a criminal how to escape from the police;[14]
11. threatens harm if someone does not turn over his wallet, submit to sexual intercourse, or perform some other act he is free not to perform;[15]
12. offers to bribe someone or offers to receive a bribe for the performance of an act that should be performed, if at all, free of such inducements;[16]
13. successfully encourages someone to commit suicide;[17]
14. entices a child from custody;[18]
15. uses provocative or insulting language likely to cause angered listeners to commit crimes;[19]
16. engages in speech likely to lead those who are persuaded by its message to commit crimes;[20]
17. perjures himself or engages in other falsehoods with respect to officials;[21]
18. makes a false public alarm;[22]
19. acquires property or some other material advantage by deception;[23]
20. falsely pretends to hold a position in public service with an aim to getting someone else to submit to pretended authority or act otherwise to his prejudice;[24]

21. uses language or representations that are insulting or offensive in some way.[25]

All these crimes and others critically involve communication; yet many of the communications do not seem candidates for protection as privileged speech. What is the explanation? Much of the first two parts of this book offers standards for exclusion from and inclusion within a principle of freedom of speech and suggests reasonable grounds for prohibiting communications that fall broadly within the free speech principle. The journey of exploration involves a searching look at how orders, requests, offers, and threats function in our discourse.

Notes

1. See, e.g., F. Schauer, *Free Speech: A Philosophical Enquiry* 13 (Cambridge, Cambridge University Press 1982): "there are activities that are speech acts in the ordinary sense, yet have nothing whatsoever to do with freedom of speech. Making a contract is a good example, and so is perjury, verbal extortion, and hiring someone to commit murder for a fee." See also id. at 92, 102–3. For discussion of some communicative acts that may fall outside a principle of freedom of speech, see M. Nimmer, *Nimmer on Freedom of Speech* § 3.05 (New York, Matthew Bender Co. 1984); D. Farber, "Commercial Speech and First Amendment Theory," 74 *Northwestern University Law Review* 372, 387 (1979).
2. This is approximately the situation in Britain, although adherence to the European Convention for Human Rights binds that country to a written document that includes guarantees of free expression and is enforceable by a supranational tribunal.
3. See, e.g., E. Barendt, *Freedom of Speech* 30 (Oxford, Clarendon Press 1985). A similar role in respect to judicial action might obtain if the principle were announced in a written constitution but not judicially enforceable against the legislature.
4. See Schauer, note 1 supra, at 89, distinguishing between coverage of a right and protection of a right.
5. *Model Penal Code* § 5.03(1) (criminal conspiracy).
6. Id. § 5.02(1) (criminal solicitation).
7. Id. § 5.02(1); § 2.06(3)(a)(i) (liability for conduct of another).
8. Id. § 5.02(1); § 2.06(3)(a)(i).
9. Id. § 5.02(1); § 2.06(3)(a)(i).
10. Id. § 5.02(1); § 2.06(3)(a)(i).
11. Id. §§ 210.1(1), 210.2(1)(a) (criminal homicide and murder).
12. Id. § 211.1(1)(c) (assault). Physical menace would often though not always include verbal communication. See also id. § 211.3 (terroristic threats).
13. Id. § 2.06(3)(a)(ii).
14. Id. § 242.3(2)(3) (hindering apprehension).
15. Id., e.g., § 222.1(1)(b) (robbery); § 223.4(1) (extortion); § 213.1(a) (rape); § 213.2(1)(a), (2)(a) (deviate sexual intercourse by force or imposition); § 240.2(1)(a) (threats of officials); § 212.5 (criminal coercion).
16. Id. § 224.8 (commercial bribery); § 240.1 (official bribery). See also id. §§ 240.3–240.7.
17. Id. § 210.5(2) (soliciting suicide).
18. Id. § 212.4(1) (interference with custody).
19. Id. § 250.4(2) (harassment).
20. See, e.g., the Smith Act. Ch. 439, § 2, 54 Stat. 670 (1940). (See 18 U.S.C. § 2385.)

21. *Model Penal Code* § 241.1 (perjury); §§ 241.2–241.5.

22. Id. § 250.3.

23. Id., e.g., § 223.3 (theft by deception); § 224.1 (forgery); § 224.7 (deceptive business practices); § 213.3(d) (seduction by a false promise of marriage); § 230.1 (bigamy). Strictly, bigamy need not involve deception, but when one enters a bigamous marriage ceremony with the second spouse, the official performing the ceremony, at least, will almost always be deceived.

24. Id. § 241.9 (impersonating a public servant).

25. Id. § 250.2(b) (disorderly conduct); § 250.4(1)(3) (harassment); § 251.4 (obscenity).

2

Rationales for Freedom of Speech

This chapter explores the justifications for freedom of speech. If sound political philosophy supports something properly called a principle of free speech, there will be reasons why a government should be hesitant to punish verbal or written expression even when it has made a judgment that the expression is potentially harmful. The discussion in this chapter underlies the development of standards for determining which communications raise free speech problems and which may appropriately be suppressed, and it is also critical for the subsequent examination of constitutional issues.

Most of the chapter is devoted to particular justifications for free speech, but I deal first with some preliminary matters. I indicate why one can speak of a principle or principles of free speech only if there are bases for protecting speech that do not apply similarly to some substantially broader category of acts. Once the idea of a principle of free speech is clarified, I turn to the nature of justifications. Before providing an account of multiple justifications divided along consequentialist and nonconsequentialist lines, I suggest why no single justification is likely to be adequate and why the distinction between consequentialist and nonconsequentialist justifications is fruitful.

How a Genuine Principle of Freedom of Speech Compares with a Minimal Principle of Liberty and Broader Principles of Extra Protection

A principle of freedom of speech asserts some range of protection for speech. Given the uneven application of various reasons for free speech to different sorts of communications, there is some question whether one should speak of "a principle" or "principles" of free speech. For simplicity's sake, I adopt the singular form, but that form should not obscure the complexities of the subject.

Beyond a Minimal Principle of Liberty

A political principle of free speech is warranted only if reasons to protect speech go beyond the reasons for what I shall call a *minimal principle of liberty*. According to a minimal principle of liberty, the government should not prohibit people from acting as they wish unless it has a positive reason to do so. The ordinary reason for prohibiting action is that the action is deemed harmful or potentially harmful in some respect; driving a car 100 miles per hour is forbidden because people are likely to get hurt. Although sometimes the government may compel behavior in order to generate benefits rather than prevent harms,[1] I shall disregard that subtlety and concentrate on harm. What legitimately counts as "harm" is an important and controversial aspect of political theory,[2] but here I mean the term in an inclusive, nonrestrictive sense, including indirect harms, psychological harms, harms to the actor, and even harms to the natural order. Thus, as far as anything I say here is concerned, sexual intercourse between human beings and animals might be prohibited on the ground that it has deleterious indirect effects on family life, is psychologically bad for the people involved, or is intrinsically "unnatural."

Since governments have little apparent reason to prohibit action other than to prevent harm that the action may cause, an assumption that people should otherwise be left free comes very close to being an obvious principle of rationality for governance. A challenge to the principle is imaginable, but the theory of human nature and government it would represent would be most unattractive. Government control of perfectly harmless actions like whistling in one's room might be a technique to induce unquestioning obedience to government authority. In that event, the prohibition would be designed to prevent *some* harm, "unhealthy" independent civic attitudes, but the harm would be unrelated to acts of whistling or their effects.[3] Conceivably, such control of "neutral" matters may have a place in training techniques for highly disciplined subgroups, such as monastic orders or military personnel, but accepting its appropriateness for regulating the general class of citizens would be to embrace the kind of extreme totalitarianism suggested by fantasies like George Orwell's *Nineteen Eighty-Four*.[4] The alternative, which I call the minimal principle of liberty, is a fundamental premise of all "Western" governments and, in this modest form, is probably accepted as well by almost all authoritarian or dictatorial governments, whether of the right or the left.[5]

As far as speech is concerned, the minimal principle of liberty establishes that the government should not interfere with communication that has no potential for harm. To be significant, a principle of freedom of speech must go beyond this,[6] positing constraints on the regulation of speech which are more robust.

A principle of free speech could establish more stringent constraints than the minimal principle of liberty, either by barring certain possible reasons for prohibition or by establishing a special value for speech. The latter way is the easier to understand. If some human activities have special value, a good government will need stronger reasons to prohibit them than to prohibit other activities. If speech has more positive value than acts of physical aggression, for example, more powerful reasons will be needed to warrant its suppression. A related but more subtle point is that legislatures or other political actors may be prone in particular instances to undervalue certain kinds of acts; if that were true about speech, a principle of free speech might compensate for that tendency. In effect the principle would tell those involved in government that acts of speech should be assumed to have a higher value than they seem to have in the immediate context.

The second way in which a principle might give special protection to speech is by positing that the government is barred from employing certain reasons for prohibiting speech. Such a constraint might derive from a notion that particular reasons for prohibitions are at odds with how human beings should be regarded or with the proper role of government. Thus, it might be claimed that, because an aspect of the autonomy of human beings is that people should discover for themselves what is true, suppressing speech to prevent contamination by false ideas is impermissible. Or it might be said that the government cannot suppress political ideas that pose challenges to it, because one aspect of a legitimate government is that criticism of those presently in power may be entertained. The import of a "disqualifying" principle might be less extreme than total exclusion of a reason for prohibition. A reason might be viewed with great suspicion, but treated as a legitimate basis for prohibition if the case were sufficiently compelling.[7]

Using threads like these, a principle or theory of freedom of speech would claim that expression cannot be regulated on every basis that could surmount the minimal principle of liberty and satisfy ordinary prudential considerations regarding effective legislation.[8]

Some claims about the value of speech or about the inappropriateness of certain reasons for prohibition could be thought to be largely independent of wider assertions of political ideology, but many claims bear a distinctive relation to liberal political theory. A proponent of claims that involve a controverted liberal view of human autonomy and government might assert that the liberal view is fundamentally correct and should be embraced by all peoples or by all peoples at a certain stage of economic and social development; in that event, a complete defense of the claims about free speech would require argument for the superiority of the liberal perspective. Alternatively, one who advances liberal claims might assert that, since a particular society is grounded on liberal ideas, that society should act on their implications, at least in the absence of opposed premises for social life that are clearly preferable and attainable.

Because I aim to elucidate standards that could be endorsed by people who disagree about many fundamental matters, my account does not depend on a single systematic version of liberal political theory. But, doubting whether there is a better form of government for large developed countries and strongly believing that no other form is clearly preferable and attainable, I assume in this study that conclusions about freedom of speech that can be drawn from *basic premises* of liberal democracy are sound, without examining possible competing premises.[9] My reliance on basic premises does not mean that I accept without analysis every "liberal" idea; discrete arguments having to do with freedom of speech are scrutinized carefully.

Is There a Distinctive Principle of Free Speech?

A principle of freedom of speech does not itself flow from the conclusion that the minimal principle of liberty inadequately protects some liberties. We must still ask why—and whether—freedom of speech should be singled out, since a sound principle more robust than that of minimal liberty might apply to matters other than speech. Only the analysis of the justifications for speech reveals the full response to this query, but that analysis can be clarified by a number of preliminary points.

First, a principle of freedom of speech is certainly compatible with other principles that are more protective of liberty than the minimal principle. One might defend, for example, a distinctive principle of religious liberty or of family liberty. The scope of another liberty can overlap with liberty of speech; for example, assertions of propositions about religion are covered both by religious liberty and by freedom of speech.

Second, a principle that covers most speech may or may not cover all speech, and it may or may not cover only speech. Although it would be misleading to refer to any distinctive principle of free speech if the principle covered such wide areas that speech was only one small subcategory or if the principle covered only a little of speech, someone might talk roughly about a principle of free speech if the principle reached a few other activities besides speech or failed to cover all speech. Another conceptual approach, the approach I mainly employ, is to understand "speech" as including only and all of what is actually covered by a proper principle of freedom of speech, using some other term, like "communication," to cover the broader class of activities that may superficially resemble what is covered by the principle.[10]

Contrary to what has sometimes been supposed,[11] a distinctive principle of freedom of speech may be maintainable even if no reasons for liberty apply uniquely to speech.[12] An insistence on unique reasons disregards the possible complexity of justifications. Reasons of more general applicability may have special *strength* with respect to speech, or various reasons *in combination* may apply to speech in a way that is not true of other activities. In either event speech might warrant unique protection, though no single reasons for protection applied uniquely to speech. However, if the only good reasons for liberty of speech apply in the same strength to a much broader range of activities, no distinctive principle of free speech is defensible.

Third, some aspects of a principle of free speech may lie closer to more general claims of liberty than do others. As we shall see, the reasons for protecting speech apply with variant strength to different sorts of speech. Even within the domain of what counts as speech, some communications may deserve more protection, or protection for different reasons, or protection against different bases for suppression, than do other communications. A political principle of free speech need not and should not amount to a single rigid principle, having the same import for all kinds of speech. Indeed, a more precise portrayal might show a loose constellation of reasons, subjects, and subprinciples governing the protection of speech.[13] Some of these subprinciples might lie particularly close to principles governing certain nonexpressive activities. For example, as to communication whose main justification is that it provides an outlet for emotional release, we might think that the reasons behind protection would cover other activities by which people vent emotions, such as vigorous athletic activities. Yet other reasons covering other forms of speech might have no bearing for athletic endeavors.

Multiple Justifications That Are Consequentialist and Nonconsequentialist

What sorts of reasons justify acceptance of a principle that protects speech even when speech seems to carry a potential for harm which would warrant prohibition if all that were at stake were the minimal principle of liberty and ordinary canons of prudent legislation? Examining briefly the reasons commonly thought to be relevant, I conclude, in accord with now dominant assumptions, that many reasons do have force. In this chapter, I pay little attention to which sorts of communications the reasons cover, but much of the next chapter and the rest of the book are devoted to the thesis that the reasons taken together have little application to some kinds of communications and that, among communications to which the reasons do apply, the strength of any particular reason depends considerably on the nature of the communication. Before addressing the various reasons, I offer a few general remarks on the possibility of a single unifying reason for free speech and on the approach to classifying reasons that I employ.

Multiple Reasons or a Single Unifying Justification

Some have suggested in recent years that there is a single unifying justification for freedom of speech, at least as far as the law of the First Amendment is concerned.[14] One of two unpersuasive strategies is followed to give credence to this initially implausible proposal.

The first strategy is elimination. Various reasons for free speech are found to be applicable to things other than speech and, therefore, are presumed to be nonsupportive of a distinctive principle of free speech, whatever their relevance for some more general theory of liberty.[15] A single reason for free speech is left, and that is said to be *the* reason behind a principle protecting speech. (Were no reason left over, the assumption is that no principle of freedom of speech would be warranted.)

I have already said enough to indicate why such efforts must be viewed with great skepticism. A reason that applies to other subjects may apply with special intensity to speech; various reasons may coalesce in a unique way with respect to speech. The idea that any justification with broader relevance may be written off as not bearing on a principle of freedom of speech is erroneous and must be strongly resisted.

The second strategy for arriving at a single principle is inclusion.[16] A number of reasons are taken as having some merit, but this merit is then shown to contribute to some yet larger value. Suppose, for example, that maximizing individual fulfillment is taken as the overriding value behind freedom of speech, and one considers the claim that speech also promotes scrutiny of government misdoing. The linkage is that government wrongdoing interferes with human fulfillment, and the seemingly independent reason is then swallowed up in the broader reason.

The strategy of inclusion suffers some basic defects. One is that any reason broad enough to yield a plausible claim that it includes everything else is bound to be extremely general and vague. Such a reason will not provide a very helpful starting point for dealing with many actual social problems if citizens, legislators, and judges must descend quickly to the more specific "subsidiary" reasons whose implications are clearer. And a reason broad enough to swallow up all narrower reasons for free speech is unlikely to apply uniquely to speech; further exploration will be needed of why the reason undergirds a principle of freedom of speech rather than some wider robust principle of liberty.[17]

Another defect of the inclusive strategy involves an error that creeps in during the process by which narrower reasons are subsumed. No doubt, holding the government to account contributes to individual human fulfillment, but there may be other reasons, such as social justice, for responsible government. The value of free speech for accountable government may be underestimated if only the relationship to individual fulfillment is addressed. Putting the point more abstractly, the process of inclusion may distort the significance of more discrete reasons whose importance lies partly, but only partly, in what they contribute to the most general value. This distortion often occurs when people seek to bring multiple and diverse considerations under an encompassing value. For practical thought about most social practices, the distortion is best avoided by ackowledging a plurality of values.

Consequentialist and Nonconsequentialist Reasons

There is no single correct way of presenting the justifications that matter for a principle of freedom of speech. One can distinguish, for example, between reasons that focus on individuals and those which focus on society at large, between reasons that relate to speakers and those which relate to listeners or a broader public, between reasons that relate to the form of government and those which do not, between reasons that reflect optimism about human capacities and those which reflect pessimism, between reasons that concentrate on the positive value of speech and those which emphasize the untrustworthiness of government. Because the reasons for free speech are based on complex and somewhat overlapping elements, no basic division or multiple categorization can be wholly satisfactory.

I have chosen to distinguish between consequentialist and nonconsequentialist reasons. This approach too has its drawbacks, requiring, among other things, somewhat strained divisions between arguments concerning individual autonomy and between arguments concerning democracy. Nonetheless, this familiar way of distinguishing reasons for action is useful here, because it differentiates claimed reasons that are to be viewed in light of factual evidence and claimed reasons that rest more purely on normative claims.[18]

A practice has value from a *consequentialist* point of view if it contributes to some desirable state of affairs. Thus, to say that free speech contributes to honest government is to advance a consequentialist reason for free speech. The force of a consequentialist reason is dependent on the factual connection between a practice and the supposed results of the practice. A *nonconsequentialist* reason claims that something about a particular practice is right or wrong without regard to the consequences. Notable among reasons of this sort are reasons cast in terms of present rights or claims of justice: "Suppressing Joan's ideas is wrong because it violates rights or is unjust."

The relation between consequentialist and nonconsequentialist reasons is an enduring problem for moral philosophy. I shall offer a few summary comments to sustain the discussion that follows.

One philosophical position is that nonconsequentialist arguments are in some sense reducible to consequentialist considerations, that the only really good practices are those which produce desirable states of affairs, broadly understood, and that the better practice is that which produces better effects. On this view, it becomes an open question whether it is desirable that people should actually *think* in terms of effects. According to the most unqualified consequentialist position, citizens would ideally conceive moral problems in terms of consequences; but it is possible that overall better effects will occur if ordinary people accept some nonconsequential norms. For example, perhaps the most wholesome effects of truth telling will be produced if people think it is always inherently wrong to tell a lie.

Since I am engaging in practical thought about a particular social practice, what matters for this book is the critical perspective that members of a society would best adopt. Even if an outsider might rightly say that the best practice produces the best effects, even if in some ultimate sense nonconsequentialist reasons can be reduced to some form of consequentialist evaluation, a reason counts as nonconsequentialist here if it is the sort of reason to which citizens should give weight and if it is best cast for them in nonconsequentialist terms. In our culture many nonconsequentialist claims are conceived as having force, and few are confident that it would be helpful to banish those claims from practical discussion. I proceed on the assumption that nonconsequentialist reasons do have force for normative issues in moral and political philosophy.

On the opposite end of the spectrum from unmitigated consequentialism is the view that nonconsequential claims should dominate political and moral thinking, that what mainly is involved is according people rights and justice, and that calculations of consequences should play a decidedly secondary role. I am highly skeptical that any such priority can be established,[19] and I think freedom of speech affords an apt illustration of why such a priority is dubious in the evaluation of social practices. In any event, I assume that both sorts of consideration count and count significantly, that no collapse of one to the other or priority of one over the other works at the level of practical thought.

Having said this much, I should acknowledge that the line between consequentialist and nonconsequentialist claims is not always clear. Part of the problem is deciding where the intrinsic nature of the act stops and consequences begin. Is the fact that a listener will be misled an aspect of the nature of lying (there are unsuccessful lies, so not every lie actually misleads), or is the likelihood of someone's being misled to be counted as a common consequence of lying? A second concern is determining the kinds of consequences that matter for a consequentialist justification. Although consequentialist reasons are often linked to claims about overall welfare or preference satisfaction, I here count as consequentialist any claim resting on the production of future consequences, including a claim, say, that the recognition of rights or justice will be promoted in the future if particular practices are engaged in for the present.[20] A third difficulty, which emerges as more serious in the context of free speech, is the status of certain reasons that are cast rather vaguely. Suppose it is said that free speech conforms with a view that people should be rational. If the idea is that free speech actually helps make people more rational, it is consequentialist. If the idea is that a principle of free speech *treats* people as rational and that that is intrinsically appropriate, the reason is nonconsequentialist. I try to indicate which claimed justifications for free speech straddle consequentialist and nonconsequentialist reasons, and I try to identify the various elements.

Closely related to this third difficulty for classification is another: how to treat coherence arguments for free speech. Suppose it is argued that, given certain institutions or practices, having freedom of speech is required or at least is positively indicated. A full defense of such an argument requires reasons why the underlying institutions may be taken as starting points and reasons why free speech connects to the underlying institutions. Roughly, the reasons for the institutions might be cast in terms of justice or fairness ("only democratic forms of government are just"), in terms of consequences ("democracy better serves human welfare than other forms of government"), or in terms of social acceptance ("whether better or not, liberal democracy is our form of government and should be taken as a starting point for evaluation of practices like free speech"). The coherence reasons for free speech might be cast in terms of what the underlying institutions somehow imply ("to deny free speech is to refuse to treat people as democratic citizens") or in terms of how free speech serves objectives of the institutions ("representatives will make better decisions if speech is free"). The complexity here is that the reasons supporting the connection of free speech to the more underlying institutions may or may not be of the same kind as the reasons why the institutions may be taken as starting points for evaluation. In the classification that follows, I concentrate on the distinctive reasons for free speech. Since I am not developing a general theory of government, I do not explore why democracy may be warranted; rather, I examine how free speech connects to basic premises of democratic government.

Consequentialist Justifications

During most of the twentieth century consequentialist arguments have dominated discussion of freedom of speech, although the last two decades have seen a resurgence of nonconsequentialist arguments cast in terms of basic human rights and dignity.[21] Consequentialist arguments reach public and private life; they reach governmental and nongovernmental matters; they reach speakers, listeners, and others who are indirectly affected.

"Truth" Discovery
The Basic Justification

The most familiar argument for freedom of speech is that speech promotes the discovery of truth. Found in Milton's *Areopagitica*[22] and in eloquent opinions by Oliver Wendell Holmes[23] and by Louis Brandeis,[24] the argument is the core of John Stuart Mill's defense of freedom of speech in *On Liberty*.[25] Mill says that, if the government suppresses communications, it may suppress ideas that are true or partly true. Even if an idea is wholly false, its challenge to received understanding promotes reexamination which vitalizes truth. When Mill asserts that government suppression of ideas rests necessarily on a false assumption of infallibility, he overstates his case: suppression might reflect cynical skepticism about any truth, or a belief that, fallible as it is, the government is likely to judge more accurately than is a dissident minority; or a conviction that, true or not, some ideas are too destructive of a social order to be tolerated. But Mill's basic point that speech contributes greatly to the search for truth does not depend on whether suppression always represents a claim of infallibility. Mill's sense of truth is broad, covering correct judgments about issues of value as well as ordinary empirical facts and embracing knowledge conducive to a satisfactory personal life as well as facts of general social importance.

Although he does not assume that people will grasp the truth whenever it appears, Mill believes that, if voice is given to a wide variety of views over the long run, true views are more likely to emerge than if the government suppresses what it deems false. In this standard form, the truth-discovery justification combines a contained optimism that people have some ability *over time* to sort out true ideas from false ones with a realism that sees that governments, which reflect presently dominant assumptions and have narrow interests of their own to protect, will not exhibit exquisite sensitivity if they get into the business of settling what is true.

Often taken as an axiom in liberal societies, the truth-discovery justification is subject to a number of possible challenges: that objective "truth" does not exist; that, if truth does exist, human beings cannot identify it or cannot identify the conditions under which it is discovered; that, even if human beings can identify truth sometimes, free discussion does not evidently contribute to their capacity to do so; and that the way "free" discussion works in practice contravenes the open market of ideas that the truth-discovery justification assumes.[26] A searching answer to these doubts would require a systematic examination of notions of truth and evidences of truth and of human learning. I have to settle for a more modest response, but even this response makes my discussion of truth discovery much longer than my treatment of other justifications of free speech. This indulgence seems warranted by the need to understand how far these sweeping challenges really do threaten this most commonly offered rationale for free expression.

I shall examine each of the four challenges in turn, reserving for last the one most troublesome for the purposes of this book: the doubt that free discussion contributes to the discovery of truth.

Does Relevant Truth Exist?

Contrary to the blithe assertion that "the assumption of the existence of objective truth is crucial to classic marketplace theory, [and] almost no one believes in objective truth today,"[27] the truth-discovery argument can survive a substantial dose of skepticism about objective truth.[28] This is most obvious in respect to factual matters. Suppose no objective truth exists outside human experience or that the only truth for human beings is the set of propositions that serves them best or most fully conforms with their experiences at a given stage in history. These positions about truth do not deny that people can learn from evidence and argument or that in some sense they can be closer or farther from understanding what is true. Given all the ways in which available evidence suggests that the earth is round rather than flat and the usefulness of people's operating on that assumption, for example, we can say that someone who believes that the earth is round is closer to the truth than the person who believes that it is flat. Similarly, the person who thinks that many Jews were killed in Nazi concentration camps in

World War II is closer to the truth than the person who denies that such events took place. Whatever the ultimate status of the propositions that the earth is approximately a sphere and that many Jews were exterminated, virtually everyone accepts some notion of empirical truth which renders claims of truth other than wholly subjective or relative.[29] That is a sufficient beginning for the "truth discovery" theory.[30]

Claims of values pose somewhat greater difficulties, since the assertion that they are wholly subjective is not so plainly fallacious. I shall not pause here to defend my own belief that rational discourse can say a good deal about ultimate values,[31] but, whether or not this is so, rational discourse certainly bears on the coherence of value claims and on the elucidating and clarifying of the values of a culture and of individuals. Thus, for example, an American might have said during the 1950s: "Given the social history and racial attitudes of this country, acceptance of racial segregation in public facilities is in severe tension with a belief that people should be treated as morally equal." Propositions like these can be extremely important for how people try to resolve social problems, and one can say that such propositions may be true or sound without invoking an objective status for ultimate values. If the idea of truth is broadened a bit farther to include understanding by people of the claims of value that best suit them personally, then one could speak of "truth discovery" even in respect to claims of value and other matters as to which one doubted whether there was any *interpersonal* truth.

Can People Identify Truth and Regimes That Promote It?

I have used my examples to demonstrate that significant domains of truth exist even on relatively skeptical premises; the examples also show that many truths are accessible to people and that most people are somewhat open to evidence and argument about those truths. This is not to say that people can ever be *completely* sure of anything, but it is nonetheless reasonable for them to have a high degree of confidence about some propositions, for example, that "in the northern latitudes, January is usually colder on the average than July," that "people who are deprived of what they value the most often resent those who they think have deprived them." Even when a dominant theory is understood to be provisional, as is the case with many abstract scientific theories, there may be a high degree of confidence that certain conceivable competitors are false.

If so much is granted, any idea that people are wholly incapable of evaluating what sorts of social practices promote discovery of truth is untenable. If truth is a meaningful concept and people are capable of asserting many propositions of fact and value with confidence, they must have *some* basis for recognizing what social practices promote the discovery of truth. One approach is to look at various societies and historical periods to see when the discovery of truth has prospered. That obviously is most practical for the sorts of questions as to which an interpersonal truth is undisputed; we can examine whether belief in the earth's roundness happened more quickly where discourse was relatively free. On the other hand, assessing degrees of coherence about values or whether the values people accepted were personally suited to them is a daunting task in respect to other historical eras and cultures. The needed judgments are incredibly complex, and we are hard put to make the imaginative leap from our experience and values to those of other societies. In respect to values, personal experience may be of some help. Of course, experience is inevitably limited, and people are notoriously incapable of assessing much of their own experience objectively; moreover, they can barely guess what their own internal life would be like in a society with very different social practices. Still, they can ask themselves whether open discussion has enlightened or confused them, helped them to achieve a more coherent and personally satisfactory set of values or not. They can try to imagine what life would be like if certain ideas were not available, and they can draw from the experience of acquaintances who have been brought up in very different cultures, a rich source of enlightenment in a society with as many immigrants as the United States.

People can reasonably differ over the persuasiveness of available evidence connecting free speech to truth discovery. Judgments are undoubtedly subject to many of the uncertainties that infect psychology and the social sciences; certainly few judgments about the effects of social practices on the fate of truth can have the degree of confidence attainable about propositions like the roundness of the earth. Any sensible position probably must, as I suggest below, distinguish among kinds of truths, among communities in which discussion is free, and among degrees of suppression. But what is important here is that all the uncertainties and needed qualifications do not show that the question of whether free speech promotes truth is somehow beyond our capacities to consider. Relevant evidence and arguments do exist.

The Significance of Inequality in the Marketplace

Acquiring confidence that truth will advance in a regime of freedom would be simple if people rather quickly understood the truth when it was presented to them and if competing ideas had an equal claim on people's attention. Two worries that undermine such confidence are the inclination of people to believe messages that are already dominant socially or that serve unconscious, irrational needs, and gross inequality among communicators in the marketplace of ideas. Because its import for my study is much less threatening, I address the second worry first.

Standing alone, the inequality of those who seek to communicate supports a particular understanding of freedom of speech rather than a rejection of the entire concept.[32] If we assume that people are reasonably competent to sift claims of truth, then a process in which all relevant claims are provided with a fair hearing is plainly preferable to government suppression of apparent falsehood. If the problem with present social arrangements is that an aggregation of economic and social power so largely determines what the public hears that unfavored ideas have no chance to gain a foothold, then the government might make available new channels of communication or regulate existing channels to ensure more equal access. Conceivably, the latter approach would include restricting the frequency with which some kinds of messages were presented, but no message would be denied an outlet altogether. Such an approach to speech would emphasize fairness in the dissemination of messages rather than unrestricted liberty for those who want to communicate and hear, and movement toward that approach might drastically alter the freedom some media presently enjoy to present what they choose.

The important point for the main purpose of this book is that an equality-of-outlet approach to speech would have little impact on criminal penalties and civil liability for communications that are deemed harmful in themselves, that are penalized because they are believed in general to be undesirable. These are the communications on which I focus, and the arguments for suppressing them are quite different from the arguments for limiting communications that are wholly appropriate in moderation. There is a conceivable equality-based argument to the effect that the government is unable in practice to regulate the presentation of ideas in the interests of fairness and that the realistic alternatives are government suppression of ideas and domination by private centers. But, given the government's power to circulate ideas itself or make forums available,[33] using the more drastic remedy of prohibiting the expression of some ideas altogether would clearly be unwarranted.

Free Speech and Capacities to Discover Truth

The claim that people are persuaded to believe what is already dominant or what fits their irrational needs is a much more serious challenge to the truth-discovery justification for free speech. If people were incapable of really assessing claims of truth, then Mill's argument for free speech would falter at a critical point. We do know that people are able to learn some things from experience; if they find that each time they take the bus the trip takes over an hour and each subway trip to the same spot takes only twenty minutes, they come to realize they should take the subway when they are in a hurry. People also learn from communications of the experiences of others; out-of-towners told of the trips of residents will also understand that the subway is faster than the bus. But, perhaps, on deeper questions, people do not make reasoned judgments about competing positions but merely acquire reinforcement of views that conform with social conventions or serve their particular interests or unconscious desires. In that event, the "marketplace of ideas" praised by Holmes gives little promise of yielding truth even in the long run, particularly if the disproportionate influence of a few centers of private power over what is communicated is likely to be exercised in favor of dominant and comforting views.[34] In addressing this deep concern about reactions to ideas, I first clarify the critical factual question; I then suggest the need to consider various domains of truth and the audiences that assess them, and degrees of suppression.

The critical question is not how well truth will advance absolutely in conditions of freedom, but how well it will advance in conditions of freedom *as compared* with some alternative set of conditions.[35] Suppose one were highly pessimistic about the capacity of people to ascertain important kinds of truths, but believed that governments that suppress ideas almost always manage to promote falsehoods, and, further, that the propensity of officials to support falsehoods flows from the nature of government and is not corrigible. One might then support freedom of speech as being less damaging to truth than an alternative social practice. One's overall judgment on this subject must depend on a delicate judgment about people's responses to claimed truth, about the effects of inequality of private power over what is communicated, and about the soundness of government determinations about valid ideas.

A sensitive assessment requires subcategorization among domains of truth and audiences, and recognition of degrees of possible interference. Freedom of speech almost certainly contributes to understanding of truth in the physical sciences. Although some broad scientific questions are not now answerable with confidence, and most dominant theories are provisional and will probably not be accepted in some distant future, many important questions have fairly definite answers about which there exists a wide range of agreement.[36] There is also wide agreement that advancement in understanding among persons capable of assessing scientific claims is promoted by freedom of communication within the scientific community, that government intervention to suppress some scientific ideas in favor of others would not promote scientific truth.

For most scientific truths, ordinary people accept as accurate a view that is widely agreed upon among scientists. As to many subjects, people have no psychological investment in one account rather than another; but, even when the dominant appraisal is unsettling, the general public is likely to accept it so long as the subject is widely understood to be scientific, the virtually unanimous judgment of scientists is well publicized, and the judgment matters to citizens. This generalization is supported by opinions about the dangers of smoking. Though much uncertainty remains about causes and effects, disinterested experts now agree that substantial smoking poses a serious risk to health and life. This is a message that confirmed smokers were psychologically disinclined to accept, but nearly all smokers, in the United States at least, now believe it,[37] although the government has never forbidden communication of the competing message.[38]

Before a general lesson can be drawn about freedom of speech for scientific matters, we should consider the possibility that broad freedom is unnecessary, that only freedom within the scientific community is needed. When the scientific community is relatively united behind judgments, it might make sense to allow contrary views to be presented to scientists, but not to the general public, which would only be confused by opposing claims on matters it does not understand. But such a proposal would be very difficult to carry out within a generally open society. Many scientists teach at universities. Would they have to withhold dissident theories and the evidence for them from students in classes and from graduate students who help with research? Would students who have access be forbidden to disclose to other students? How would the government decide whether a view had become unanimous enough to warrant suppression of competitors? Who would decide exactly which expressions of views fell afoul of restrictions on broad publication? At the least such a regime would be extremely unwieldy and would require establishment of formal channels of communication among scientists, not accessible to the general public. By far the simplest way to ensure freedom of scientific communication within the community of experts is to have a general regime of free speech for science.

In domains other than the physical sciences, the grasp of truth is much less secure. For many value judgments, no one is a real expert, and for many interpretive judgments about complex historical and psychological questions, experts disagree about many fundamental questions. For subjects like these confidence in any advance of truth needs to be highly qualified, but these are also the subjects in which judgments by governments are least to be trusted. Accepting of dominant opinion and desirous of preserving its own power, a government deciding what historical, political, and moral ideas to suppress is bound to be affected by aims other than the disinterested pursuit of truth.

Owners and editors of newspapers and television stations and other private individuals with huge influence over the dissemination of ideas will also have their own objectives to pursue, but private influence is a far cry from outright suppression. No private enterprise can prevent others from speaking. On many points, those with private power will have different visions of the truth or will have reasons to present competing claims. Even when that is not the case, competing ideas may gain some access, say through radical professors' writing in academic journals, to some part of the public. Further, as already pointed out, if government intervention of some sort is warranted to redress an imbalance, regulation, as by the "fairness" doctrine for television and radio,[39] or government presentation of a competing point of view is less drastic than outright suppression. One could sensibly support extensive suppression only if one were very skeptical of the ability of people to deal with claims of truth and had a great deal more confidence in the government than in private institutions.

Given important matters of degree, a comparison between a regime of free speech and one of suppression is overly simple. Indeed, one might look at the question as being *how far* constraints on conversation[40] imposed by the government will serve the truth. For the government to promote particular messages, as the United States government has done with advertising of the dangers of smoking, is already to depart from a pure "marketplace" approach to speech. And, if the government prohibits some messages in some contexts, as it has done with broadcast advertising for cigarettes, and requires warnings of danger for advertising that is permitted, then the government is going farther and restricting speech. If one concludes that free speech generally is better than suppression for discovering truth, it does not follow that every kind of government restriction on speech will be harmful to understanding of truth. Suppose it were proposed that governmental suppression of scientific ideas is appropriate if and only if the following conditions are met: (1) there is virtual unanimity among scientists that the contrary ideas are correct; (2) the subject is one as to which government officials can be relatively dispassionate; (3) public misjudgments are likely; (4) public misjudgments will cause serious harm; and (5) suppression will extend only to communicators who have a dominantly commercial motive. It is at least possible that this and perhaps other modest limits on maximum freedom of speech will contribute to the promotion of truth; and this study adverts to that possibility in various contexts.

The Scope of the Truth-Discovery Justification

I need still to consider a final objection to the "truth discovery" reason as a justification for free speech and then to ask about the appropriate political force of the justification if its intrinsic validity is in doubt. The objection is that, even if the truth-discovery argument for liberty has some force, it has no special application to speech. Crudely put, the contention is that discovery of truth comes from experience as well as speech and that, if it is valid, the reason should protect all forms of liberty or many forms of liberty other than speech. As indicated earlier in the chapter, the wider applicability of a reason for protecting liberty would not necessarily undercut its relevance for a distinctive free speech principle; the reason might have a special intensity for speech or coalesce in a special way with other reasons in respect to speech. But "truth discovery" has traditionally been regarded as such an important support for free speech that it would be troubling if that support applied with equal force to many other activities.

To evaluate the claim that any truth-discovery rationale applies much more broadly, we need first to put it in a reasonably precise and plausible form. Occasional intimations that experience and communication may be substitutable, that one can learn from either,[41] are at most true only at the margins. Experience and communication are both necessary conditions of understanding. Without communicating in language to their fellows, men and women would be incapable of understanding much more than nonhuman animals; without some personal experience of life besides cognitive thought, most ideas would have no reality for most people. Only in reference to people who have already received substantial amounts of communication *and* had substantial experience apart from communication could we believe that more of one is a good substitute for less of the other. And even this proposition about substitutability requires substantial qualification. Any sensible thought about communication and experience must recognize that, for some domains of truth, personal experience has little to contribute and that, for others, communication can supply only a pale shadow of understanding; relatedly, though some forms of noncommunicative experience are highly valuable for understanding, other forms teach little about truth in any significant sense.

There are whole domains of knowledge that ordinary living hardly touches. An increase or decrease in my personal noncommunicative liberty will hardly affect my understanding of mathematics or of many aspects of the physical sciences. Of course scientific experiments involve a kind of experience, and experiments may be indispensable to learning of some scientific truths;[42] but no one individual can perform many complex experiments. For learning the fruits of experiments, even a scientist's overwhelming reliance will have to be on communications about experiments performed by others.

In respect to matters like history and politics the role of personal experience is more complex. Our personal lives give us a perspective against which to evaluate competing historical claims, but there are few pieces of ordinary living in which we might engage in order to increase our ability to assess plausible claims about particular historical events. Active involvement in local affairs may teach us a good bit about contemporary political life. "Travel" can contribute to a grasp of both historical and political truth. A trip to the ruins of Athens can enrich one's appreciation of the ancient Athenian civilization, and a trip to Nicaragua could enlighten perspectives on the revolutionary government there. It would be odd to think that either of these experiences would have much "truth" value without extensive communication as well, but if travel were forbidden, important sources for "truth discovery" would be foreclosed.

For some forms of understanding, particular personal experience is really indispensable. If the "truth" in question is how one *feels* when one falls in love, has an orgasm, or drinks a lot of alcohol, no amount of reading or discussing can make up for a lack of experience. If the government were capable of foreclosing a kind of experience and did so,[43] it would sharply inhibit appreciation of particular truths of that sort.

Other limitations on liberty touch experiences that have little to do with discovery of truth in any significant sense. Suppose the government is considering regulating the sale of alcohol, forbidding sales below and above certain prices. The experience of charging a certain price is not a significant avenue toward truth, and a truth-discovery rationale is no reason against the regulation.[44]

We may draw the following conclusions. There are some basic aspects of human understanding, or understanding within a certain culture, that cannot be fully appreciated without immediate experience. As to some other matters, partic- ular kinds of experience, such as experiments and travel, may be either indispen- sable or a substitute for listening to communications. Other liberties of action bear remote relation to discovering truth, and for many truths the acquisition of much learning depends almost entirely on communication.

The "truth discovery" reason is widely understood to reach activities like experiments and travel, which are properly seen as closely related to liberty of speech, and it also underlies solid arguments against forbidding highly significant forms of experience, as Mill recognized in his claim that the interests of human beings as progressive beings were served by acquaintance with a wide diversity of styles of life.[45] Still, the "truth discovery" reason has little to do with many liberties, and the connection between understanding and communication is powerful enough to warrant the conclusion that truth discovery is a very impor- tant reason for a distinctive principle of freedom of speech.

Practical Force in Conditions of Uncertainty

Having argued that the challenges to the truth-discovery justification for free speech are largely misconceived, I now briefly examine the proper place of that justification in the face of significant uncertainties about its force. One might say that no justification can stand unless supported by convincing evidence, but I am strongly inclined toward a different, more conservative, position that values cultural conti- nuity and is modest about powers of rational understanding. If a justification that remains coherent in its premises has long been assumed to support a settled social practice, then the justification is entitled to continued weight until the case against it is very strong. Since legal interpretation rightly gives effect to the justifications that lay behind the framing of legal norms, that conservative principle is certainly correct for reasoning within the law. Given the desirability of continuity of political institu- tions, discourse, and values, the principle is also appropriate for nonlegal political assessments. I have said enough to show at a minimum that the "truth discovery" reason for free speech is neither incoherent nor evidently fallacious. This is sufficient to warrant continued reliance on it in our culture.

Interest Accommodation and Social Stability

A good answer to many social problems depends not so much on discovery of "true principles" as on accommodation of competing interests and desires. Of course, no sharp line demarcates truth discovery from interest accommodation. Learning someone else's desires is discovery of one kind of truth, and even determining an optimal or acceptable accommodation of competing desires or interests can be seen as understanding a mix of relevant facts and values. And when social action (e.g., abolition of capital punishment) is based on an assessment of empirical information (e.g., that capital punishment does not uniquely deter) and a sound resolution of value questions (e.g., that retribution is an unacceptable basis for punishment), we can still think of the decision as working some kind of accommodation among affected interests. Still, a significant difference in approach remains between seeking to find "true principles" to resolve troubling issues like capital punishment and seeking to strike a sort of balance among conflicting desires, as in working out a schedule of household responsibilities.

Appropriate accommodations are more likely if those making decisions can assess desires and interests accurately, and communication serves this purpose. Few societies bar the expression of personal feelings and attitudes that contribute to acceptable accommodations in families and other small social units, but many societies proscribe public discussion of significant points of view, and they pay some price in their ability to estimate relevant sentiments within the community.

The interest-accommodation reason for free expression can be challenged on grounds similar to those advanced in respect to truth discovery. It may be said that free expression does not produce an adequate reflection of the spectrum of desires and interests. Because the desires of the rich, the powerful, and the articulate are given more voice than those of the poor, the powerless, and the inarticulate, decision makers, themselves mostly members of the favored group, get a false picture of what people generally want. The difficulty in respect to "real" interests goes deeper; so great is the control of culture by the privileged that the dispossessed lack even the ability to understand what their real interests are; thus the expression of their desires may not be a reflection of what they genuinely need.

No doubt this picture has much truth. In no society are desires and interests[46] assessed without distortion, and the distortion almost always favors the privileged classes to some degree. But what is the remedy, if any? Would matters be improved if the government suppressed the expression of certain desires and interests? For reasons indicated in connection with truth discovery, it seems highly unlikely that outright government prohibitions would produce a more accurate account of the desires and interests of citizens.

Failures of accommodation are often a source of social instability. Those who are resentful because their interests are not accorded fair weight are likely to be doubly resentful if they have been denied the opportunity to present those interests in the political process. If sufficiently frustrated, they may seek to attain by radical changes in existing structures what they have failed to get from officials within those structures. Though liberty of speech can often be divisive, it can, by forestalling this sort of frustration, also contribute to a needed degree of social stability.[47]

Exposure and Deterrence of Abuses of Authority

Closely linked to truth discovery and interest accommodation is a consequentialist justification that warrants separate mention because of its historical significance and central importance: free speech as a check on abuse of authority, especially governmental authority. The idea, powerfully developed by Vincent Blasi in a well-known article,[48] is that, if those in power are subject to public exposure for their wrongs in the manner exemplified by journalists' accounts of the Watergate scandal, corrective action can be taken. And if public officials know they are subject to such scrutiny, they will be much less likely to yield to the inevitable temptation presented to those with power to act in corrupt and arbitrary ways.

In major part, the justification based on exposure and deterrence of government abuse can be seen as a subcategory of the truth-discovery justification. When truths about abuse of authority are revealed, citizens or other officials can take corrective action. But an extra dimension of truth discovery is important here. In areas of human life involving choice, what people do is partly dependent on what they think will become known. Most particularly, persons are less likely to perform acts which are widely regarded as wrong and which commonly trigger some sanction if they are not confident they can keep the acts secret. Thus the prospect of truth's being discovered influences what happens; public scrutiny deters. Viewed from the perspective of interest accommodation, a free press that exposes wrongs affects the balance of sensitivity in the direction of the interests of ordinary citizens as compared with the interests of the officials themselves and of those to whom they feel especially aligned by mutual advantage or common feeling. Perhaps the benefits of exposure and deterrence reach beyond anything neatly captured by truth discovery or interest accommodation. Apart from truths it actually reveals and even when what it claims turns out to be inaccurate, a critical press affects how officials and citizens regard the exercise of governmental power, subtly supporting the notion that government service is a responsibility, not an opportunity for personal advantage.

It is worth mentioning that the ways in which exposures of abuse contribute to healthy government are not limited to liberal democracies. Even in relatively authoritarian regimes where ordinary citizens have little to say about who makes up the government, the threat of exposure can restrain officials from personal abuses of office. In fact, in some countries, such as Yugoslavia, where selection for office remains largely the responsibility of a single party and proposals for complete change of that social system are beyond bounds, press criticism of official inadequacies can be quite sharp.

Autonomy: Independence of Judgment and Considerate Decision

By affording people an opportunity to hear and digest competing positions and to explore options in conversations with others, freedom of discussion is thought to promote independent judgment and considerate decision, what might be characterized as *autonomy*.[49] This is the consequentialist argument that connects free speech to autonomy.

This claim, as I mean to consider it here, is not true by definition. If freedom of speech failed to bring the range of relevant considerations before people as effectively as would a structure of discourse controlled by government or if, despite opportunities to converse and exposure to various relevant points of view, people in a regime of free speech passively followed the opinions of persons in authority or decided on the basis of irrational passions, then freedom of speech would not promote autonomy in this sense. The factual premises of the claim about autonomous decisions are that, when all ideas can be expressed, people will be less subject in their decisions to the dictates of others, and that they will be encouraged to exercise this independence in a considerate manner that reflects their fullest selves. The supposition is not that freedom of speech will actually produce fully autonomous persons or even that it will produce people who are by some measure more autonomous than not; the claim is only that people will be *more* autonomous under a regime of free speech than under a regime of substantial suppression.

I shall not attempt to establish the claimed factual links. Any attempt to do so convincingly faces severe difficulties. It is very hard to compare degrees of autonomy among citizens of different societies, and whether a country enjoys free speech is only one of many relevant cultural factors. Moreover, it is possible that a certain kind of freedom lulls people into a passive acceptance of things as they are, whereas stark suppression forces them to focus on their values. In support of the dangers of the "repressive tolerance" of freedom, it is sometimes remarked that political discussions at the dinner table in countries tending toward totalitarianism have a liveliness that is lacking in liberal democracies. On the other hand, lively conversation is sometimes an outlet for those incapable of making choices that influence events, and the liveliness of ordinary conversation under the most oppressive regimes, such as Nazi Germany, was certainly not great. Matters of degree are important here, and confidence in generalizations must be modest, but I think we are warranted in believing that government control of communication usually tends to induce unreflective reliance on authority and that, if one regards societies in history, comparative autonomy of individuals is linked to relative freedom of opinion.

If one grants that free speech contributes to autonomy, there is still the question of why independence of judgment and considerate decision are good. It may be believed that those who decide for themselves and in a rational manner are acting in a more distinctly human and intrinsically better way than those who passively submit to authority; these personal qualities will then be valued for their own sakes. The qualities may also be means of achieving other values. For example, despite the burden of anxiety that often accompanies serious personal choice, many people can work out for themselves a style of life that is more fulfilling than what they could achieve by simply conforming to standards set by others. Both the valuation of autonomy for its own sake and the belief that it contributes to other satisfactions are aspects of traditional liberal theory.

Emotional Outlet, Personal Development, and Sense of Dignity

The practice of free speech enhances in various other ways the lives of those who seek to communicate. For the speaker, communication is a crucial way to relate to others; it is also an indispensable outlet for emotion and a vital aspect of the development of one's personality and ideas.[50] The willingness of others to listen to what one has to say generates self-respect. Limits on what people can say curtail all these benefits. If the government declares out of bounds social opinions that a person firmly holds or wishes to explore, he is likely to suffer frustration and affront to his sense of dignity.

Because communication is so closely tied to our thoughts and feelings, suppression of communication is a more serious impingement on our personalities than many other restraints of liberty; but some noncommunicative restraints, for example, those relating to sexual involvements or drug use, may equally impair personal self-expression in a broad sense. An argument based on the value of liberty as an emotional outlet and means of personal development is not restricted to speech alone. Indeed, it may reach widely and strongly enough to some other matters so that alone it would not warrant anything properly identified as a distinctive principle of free speech. But if a principle of free speech is supportable on other grounds, this justification does provide an extra reason why speech should not be prohibited and, as we shall see in subsequent chapters, may help determine what the boundaries of protected speech should be.

Liberal Democracy

I turn now to arguments from democracy, which have been said in a comparative study to be the "most influential . . . in the development of twentieth-century free speech law."[51] Given my basic division between consequentialist and nonconsequentialist justifications, I postpone for later sections claims that liberal democracy simply requires freedom of speech, whether or not speech contributes to the effectiveness of that form of government. Here, I consider the claim that free speech contributes importantly to the functioning of liberal democracy and to the values it serves.

This claim is largely reducible to reasons I have already discussed as those reasons apply to political discourse and decisions and to the participation of people in the political process. A liberal democracy rests ultimately on the choices of its citizens. Free speech can contribute to the possibility that they and their representatives can grasp truths that are significant for political life, it can enhance identification and accommodation of interests, and it can support wholesome attitudes about the relations between officials and citizens.[52] Government officials are especially to be distrusted in deciding what political messages may be heard, because of their interest in staying in office and in promoting the political ideas in which they believe. And government suppression of political messages is particularly dangerous because it can subvert the review of ordinary political processes which might serve as a check on other unwarranted suppression.[53] I have already mentioned the notion of unrestrained speech as a check on abuse of office; since citizens' votes are essential in a liberal democracy, the importance of their being informed of government misconduct is particularly great under that form of government. It has long been assumed, though it is perhaps hard to prove, that a better-informed citizenry will yield a better government and better political decisions.[54]

Whether participation in the political order is deemed uniquely important for people or one among many opportunities for realizing participatory values, that participation can be more autonomous if relevant information and arguments are available, and a regime of free speech may help develop the kinds of self-reliant, courageous citizens that Justice Brandeis holds up as an ideal in his opinion in *Whitney* v. *California*.[55] Finally, the healthy sense that one is participating as an equal citizen is enhanced if what one believes about politics can be communicated, and speech about injustice can help relieve frustration about an undesired course of political events.

Because a decent political process and informed decision–making by citizens are such critical aspects of a model of liberal democracy, and because government suppression of political ideas is so likely to be misguided, the application of a principle of freedom of speech to political affairs is centrally important. The sorts of underlying consequentialist reasons for freedom are not radically different for political speech from those for speech about nonpolitical facts and values, but these reasons take on extra weight when political matters are involved.

Promoting Tolerance

It has been suggested, in a thoughtful recent book by Lee Bollinger, that the main modern justification for a principle of free speech is its capacity to promote tolerance.[56] The basic idea is that if we are forced to acknowledge the right of detested groups to speak, we are taught the lesson that we should be tolerant of the opinions and behavior of those who are not like us. Almost certainly the core of Bollinger's claim is true; living in a regime of free speech helps teach tolerance of many differences, just as living in a regime of religious liberty helps teach tolerance of religious diversity. But it does not follow either that promoting tolerance is now the primary justification for free speech or that attention to tolerance should play the critical role in decisions whether to restrict speech.

If it is true that people in liberal societies have so internalized a norm of free speech that traditional justifications are no longer extensively argued and if the potential acts of suppression these justifications cover most strongly are not even attempted, that does not mean these justifications have somehow been supplanted by the aim of promoting toleration. And, even if Dean Bollinger is right that the tolerance justification has more force than any other for the extremist destructive speech of the Nazis, it is not the primary justification for many other forms of speech. Given the assumption that broad tolerance of how others live can be encouraged in different ways, it is doubtful that one would introduce and defend a principle of freedom of speech in the absence of other more basic justifications, and it is questionable whether a persuasive argument against particular suppression can be grounded mainly in the tolerance justification.[57]

Nonconsequentialist Justifications

Not all arguments for free expression rest on desirable consequences; some liberal conceptions of the relationship between state and citizen may suggest a liberty of citizens to express opinions which is independent of the likely consequences of prohibition. As the phrase "liberal conceptions" implies, these justifications draw more distinctly on characteristic value premises of liberal theory than do the consequentialist justifications, though embedded in many of the latter are common liberal assumptions about facts and values.

Social Contract Theory: Consent and the Private Domain

The Anglo-American tradition of liberal democracy has historically been linked to a theory of social contract, which grounds the legitimacy of the state in the consent of the governed and establishes significant limits on the authority of government. According to John Locke, whose views greatly influenced the revolutionary generation of Americans, the legitimate authority of government is based on consent and is limited to the protection of rights and interests that individuals could not adequately safeguard.[58] Individuals entering into a social contract consent to government power to secure their lives, liberty, and property, but they do not give the state authority to interfere in other domains. In his *Letter Concerning Toleration*, Locke employs this analysis to put control of religious beliefs and expressions outside the ambit of secular authority, but his conclusions have broader implications, reaching all states of mind and activities that do not threaten interference with the limited aims a government may permissibly have.

Locke apparently supposed that at some early age in history people actually entered into a social contract. That is implausible, but his theory can be interpreted in a hypothetical way, as indicating what form and purposes of government individuals leaving a state of nature would consent to. To be morally legitimate a government needs to take this form and pursue only the prescribed purposes. Even in this hypothetical version, the theory is now highly controversial, because it posits individuals outside of organized society with needs, desires, talents, and property. Such an approach pays insufficient regard to the extent to which human nature and human purposes are themselves determined by organized society, and it underestimates the positive contributions society and government can make to human flourishing. Still, the ideas that government should take a form to which people do or would consent and that it should do only those things which people need it to do (or which it is uniquely suited to accomplish) retain a powerful appeal in liberal societies. The implications of these ideas reach far beyond speech, but they have considerable relevance for speech as well.

I shall focus first on the conditions of consent. No doubt, valid consent to something can often be based on less than full information, but a problem arises when the authority that seeks consent also controls the available information. If someone asks my agreement to a course of action, then actively conceals much relevant information that would affect my judgment, my "consent" is of lessened or no effect. Under social contract theory, a government is legitimate only if it receives or warrants consent from the people under it. It may be debated exactly what conditions are required for valid actual consent or for the hypothetical consent of persons whose nature and social condition fit some model.[59] However, a claim of actual consent would certainly be undermined if information highly relevant to evaluation of the government was systematically suppressed; and rational actors in some idealized setting could not be expected to give valid consent in such circumstances and would be unlikely to approve in advance a regime that would conceal such information from actual citizens.[60] Thus, the idea that government should be of a kind that people would consent to and the idea that actual citizens should have the opportunity to consent to the legitimacy of their governments underlie a substantial argument against the suppression of political ideas and facts, even when a present majority approves that suppression.

I turn now to the notion of limited government. That notion most obviously constrains what can count as harms and as proper purposes for a liberal society. Suppressing expressions of belief simply to prevent mistakes about religion or aesthetics would not, for example, constitute a proper purpose. And the propriety of suppressing obscenity because it tends to make those who look at it unhappy would be doubtful, since liberal governments should not often be protecting individuals against themselves. Although I do not develop in this book any full theory about the limits of government, I do identify situations in which arguments about suppression of speech rest on contested claims about those limits.

Most claims in favor of prohibiting speech in modern Western societies do not rest on asserted harms that are controversial in this way, perhaps partly because critical assumptions about the limits of government are deeply entrenched. Usually the harm that is to be avoided by prohibiting speech is a harm that a liberal government undoubtedly can try to prevent. But questions about limits on governmental power may remain. These are more subtle questions about remoteness of cause and about the extent to which the government may interfere in a normally private realm to accomplish concededly valid objectives. To take an extreme case, imagine a proposal that, because the attitude of racial prejudice generates the social harm of racial discrimination,[61] the government should undertake compulsory psychological conditioning to erase that attitude from individuals who have it. Almost everyone would agree that such an interference with the private domain would be unacceptable, and many would say that the connection between private thought and harmful act is too remote or indirect to warrant social control,[62] even though the government's ultimate objective is appropriate.[63] Similar concerns would be raised if, instead of trying to control thoughts themselves, the government forbade all expressions of racial prejudice. The communication of attitudes would be regarded as closer to the private domain of having the attitudes than to the public domain of acting upon the attitudes in a socially unacceptable way.

In summary, we can think of the traditional idea of limited government as operating at two levels in respect to free speech: as setting some constraints on appropriate governmental objectives and as requiring that the connection between prohibited speech and social harm be reasonably direct. Although social contract theory cannot plausibly be thought to yield the conclusion that all communication must be left untouched by government prohibition, the theory may illuminate some inhibitions on government interference with private individuals.

Recognition of Autonomy and Rationality

Respect for individual autonomy may curb interference with expression. In my treatment of consequentialist justifications, I have already suggested how speech can contribute to the development of autonomous individuals. Here I focus on two related nonconsequentialist arguments for the view that the government should treat people as it would treat autonomous persons. Of course, every governmental prohibition of action interferes with free choice and, therefore, with the *exercise* of autonomy. If autonomy is to undergird a principle of freedom of speech, a notion of autonomy is required which has some special relation to communication and which helps draw lines between permissible and impermissible regulation.

The most straightforward claim is that the government should always treat people as rational and autonomous by allowing them to have all the information and all the urging to action that might be helpful to a rational, autonomous person making a choice. This claim focuses on the autonomy of the recipient of communication. As Thomas Scanlon has put it, an "autonomous person cannot accept without independent consideration the judgment of others as to what he should believe or what he should do."[64] As we shall see in more detail later, a principle that the government should always treat its citizens as autonomous would not necessarily lead to freedom for every kind of communication—outright lies and subliminal manipulation may not contribute to autonomous choice and might be restricted. But a strong version of a principle that the government must always treat citizens as autonomous by maximizing opportunities for informed choice would be powerfully protective of many kinds of speech.

The difficulty with the principle in this strong form lies in its implausibility. The government must protect citizens from social harms, and many fellow citizens do not act in a rational and autonomous way. If some communications are especially likely to lead irrational people to do harmful things, why must the government permit them access to those communications as if they were rational and autonomous, rather than protect potential victims of their irrational actions? Few suppose that compulsory commitment of insane people who are demonstrably dangerous to others is a violation of liberal government; we cannot rule out in advance the possibility that the government may regulate communications in a manner that takes account of frequent deviations from an ideal of autonomy.

Further, a deep ambiguity lurks in the concept of rationality and autonomy. Does a rational and autonomous person always act with appropriate regard for the interests of others, or might such a person pursue his own interests unjustly at the expense of others? I do not want to explore here the complex question of whether rationality and autonomy imply acceptance of all valid moral claims. If it is supposed that the rational autonomous person always acts morally, then such a person can be trusted with as complete information and as much urging to action as is possible. In that event the only worry about treating actual people as rational and autonomous is how far people fall short of being rational and autonomous. Matters are more complicated if it is supposed, to the contrary, that rational, autonomous people may freely choose to pursue their own interests immorally. In that case, if rational, autonomous people were given, for example, full information about how to engage in undetectable cheating on their income taxes, many would take advantage of the information by cheating. A principle ensuring full freedom of speech might thus lead to social harms that could be avoided if some information were suppressed. Of course, one might contend that the government's treating people as autonomous is more important than preventing the social harms that would result from full information, but a defense of that position would then be needed.

In an article[65] whose major thesis he no longer defends,[66] Thomas Scanlon developed a somewhat more complex claim about autonomy and expression. He took as a standard for the limits of legitimate government "the powers of a state . . . that citizens could recognize while still regarding themselves as equal, autonomous, rational agents."[67] In this form the claim in favor of treating people as autonomous is grounded in a version of social contract theory that asks what rational autonomous people would agree to. This extra step actually eliminates assurance that the government should treat people as autonomous and rational on every occasion. For the reasons that have just been rehearsed, rational autonomous people deciding on the general limits of government interference would want to protect themselves from harms wrought by irrational people and by rational, immoral people (Scanlon is quite clear that his notion of autonomy and rationality does not guarantee moral action). To protect themselves from those harms, rational autonomous people *might* agree to constraints that would inhibit to some degree the extent to which all citizens, including themselves, would have available information and advocacy that would maximally serve rational and autonomous choice.

In brief, if one asks what limits on government rational autonomous people would set, they might well conclude that the government should not always allow people everything a rational autonomous person would want to have in making a particular choice. And if one simply asserts a principle that the government should never act to inhibit conditions for rational autonomous choice, it is hard to see how that principle could be supported.

What may remain is a less rigorous standard, namely, a premise of liberal democracy that human beings are largely rational and autonomous and should be treated as such.[68] That a proposed prohibition would not treat people in this manner counts against it, and prohibitions that do not respect autonomy may call for especially careful review of possible justifications.

Dignity and Equality

A justification for free speech which is closely related to the points just made but which focuses on the speaker more than on his or her listeners is the idea that the government should treat people with dignity and equality. As a matter of basic human respect we may owe it to each other to listen to what each of us has to say, or at least not to foreclose the opportunity to speak and to listen. Under this view, suppression represents a kind of contempt for citizens that is objectionable regardless of its consequences, and when suppression favors some points of view over others, it may be regarded as failing to treat citizens equally.

How to take this argument depends on whether any infringement of liberty impairs dignity and on whether any infringement that is significantly selective impairs equality. Many actions that people would like to engage in must be restricted, and some of these restrictions, e.g., denying the right to practice medicine to those not certified in a prescribed way, are bound to be "selective." The concerns about dignity and equality may seem not to be specially related to speech but to be arguments, perhaps rather weak ones, in favor of liberty generally.

There may, however, be a tighter connection between restrictions on communications and affronts to dignity and equality. Expressions of beliefs and feelings lie closer to the core of our persons than do most actions we perform; restrictions of expression may offend dignity to a greater degree than most other restrictions; and selective restrictions based on the content of our ideas may imply a specially significant inequality. So put, the notion of affront to dignity and equality bears a plausible relationship to free speech, though it also reaches other forms of liberty, such as liberty of sexual involvement and liberty of personal appearance, which lie close to how we conceive ourselves.

The Marketplace of Ideas

I now summarily examine a mistaken or incomplete argument for free speech, the argument that suppression is wrong because truth should not be impaired and that what emerges from the marketplace of ideas simply counts as the truth under a liberal government.

The "marketplace of ideas" approach, so conceived, either is unpersuasive or must rest on some further unexpressed premises. Holmes's notion that the best test of truth is what is produced in the marketplace of ideas is sometimes taken as a version of the truth-discovery theory I have already discussed, namely, that there are things that count independently as the truth and that the chances of those being accepted by people are enhanced by a marketplace of ideas. On that account, whether free speech contributes to truth is a factual question, however hard to answer. The alternative way of regarding what Holmes said is that there really is no test of truth except what comes out of the marketplace, because there is no independent truth. On that interpretation, a normative claim is made that people should accept as decisive the results of a marketplace of ideas rather than the results of some other process. But, once the claim is so understood, the question arises, "Why should people accept those particular results?" If the answer is "Because we live in a liberal democracy," the next question is "Why does liberal democracy commit us to the results of a marketplace of ideas rather than, say, to the results of democratically determined suppression?" An attempt to answer that question returns us to the various justifications we have already considered. Unless an independent notion of truth is supposed, an argument that truth is what emerges from the marketplace of ideas does not yield distinctive support for a free speech principle.

The Import of the Justifications

The nonconsequentialist justifications, like the consequentialist ones, fall short of setting clear principles that can be confidently applied to decide what practices of suppression are unwarranted. What all these perspectives do provide, however, is a set of considerations, a set of standards for the relation of government to citizens, which help to identify which interferences with expression are most worrisome and which operate as counters, sometimes powerful ones, in favor of freedom.

Notes

1. This subject is complicated in ways that would demand examination were this not just a preface to a discussion of free speech. Parents may be directly compelled to confer benefits on their children. One argument for forbidding adultery is that it threatens families and the benefits children receive. Other acts might be compelled or forbidden in order that people develop regular habits of behavior that will lead overall to benefits for others. How far the last justification for control of adults is acceptable is something that may separate "liberal" societies from many others.

2. See generally J. Feinberg, *Harm to Others* (New York, Oxford University Press 1984).

3. This is what differentiates stopping whistling from stopping acts that themselves threaten harm over the long run.

4. G. Orwell, *Nineteen Eighty-Four* (2d ed., I. Howe ed., New York, Harcourt Brace Jovanovich 1982).

5. But a "nonliberal" government may be much more willing to forestall perceived indirect harms and to promote virtuous habits than a liberal government. See note 1 supra.

6. See F. Schauer, *Free Speech: A Philosophical Enquiry* 5–12 (Cambridge, Cambridge University Press 1982).

7. One might say, to illustrate with an example not involving speech, that any governmental justification for enforced segregation based on violence that might flow from hostility between members of different racial groups should be viewed with extreme suspicion, but that temporary racial segregation in a prison might be warranted after an extensive race riot in which prisoners have been killed.

8. I add this phrase because the costs of administration and other considerations may make it unwise to forbid much behavior that could be forbidden under a minimal principle of liberty.

9. The discussion that follows suggests what I consider the basic premises of liberal democracy. My views on that subject are developed in *Religious Convictions and Political Choice*, especially at 14–29 (New York, Oxford University Press 1988). I do not think that the basic premises of liberal democracy include extreme rationalism, extreme individualism, neutrality among ideas of the good, or exclusive reliance for political choice on shared premises and publicly accessible grounds for determining truth.

10. This is a fairly common approach, followed by Schauer, note 6 supra, at 89–92, among others. Chapters 3 and 9 of this book discuss governmental prohibitions of acts not designed to communicate messages when the reason for prohibition is to deter what observers will take as implicit messages. In such cases, a principle of free speech may affect the legitimacy of prohibition, although the acts viewed by themselves may not be speech. From this perspective, not all activities reached by the free speech principle count as speech, and the sentence in the text needs to be understood as referring to all actions that are covered by the free speech principle because of the nature of the actions themselves rather than the particular reasons for prohibition.

11. See, e.g., R. Bork, "Neutral Principles and Some First Amendment Problems," 47 *Indiana Law Journal* 1, 26–27 (1971).

12. See generally M. Redish, *Freedom of Expression* 1, 40 (Charlottesville, Va., The Michie Co. 1984).

13. See Schauer, note 6 supra, at x.

14. See, e.g., E. Baker, "Scope of the First Amendment Freedom of Speech," 25 *University of California in Los Angeles Law Review* 964–90 (1978); Bork, note 11 supra, at

20–26; Redish, note 12 supra, at 1–84. Since Redish includes within the broad value of self-realization both "the inherent value in allowing individuals to control their own destiny, and the instrumental value in developing individuals' mental faculties," id. at 30, it may be argued whether he settles finally on one or two values. A similar question may be raised about Baker, who talks of individual self-fulfillment and participation in change as key First Amendment values. Baker, supra, at 991. And because Bork is concentrating on an appropriate principle of constitutional law for the courts and rejects the "safety valve" function of speech because it raises issues of prudence inappropriate for the judiciary, he might consider that proposed reason for free speech as having a place in a justification of a political principle of free speech.

15. See, e.g., R. Bork, note 11 supra, at 25.

16. See, e.g., Redish, note 12 supra.

17. Redish acknowledges that his overall principle of "individual self-realization" covers more than speech, but he argues that communicative activities are especially likely to develop individuals' mental faculties, are less likely to be harmful than other courses of conduct, and, in any event, were given special protection by the adopters of the Bill of Rights. See M. Redish, "Self-Realization, Democracy and Freedom of Expression: A Reply to Professor Baker," 130 *University of Pennsylvania Law Review* 678, 684 (1982).

18. It is likely that many nonconsequentialist claims rest on deep factual assumptions about human nature; so in this respect the distinction between consequentialist and nonconsequentialist reasons is less sharp than the text indicates. I address this problem in relation to a "natural duty" to obey the law in *Conflicts of Law and Morality* 159–86 (New York, Oxford University Press 1987).

19. I try to show the implausibility of any clear priority in one context in id. at 207–25.

20. In id. at 213–20, I discuss this category of reasons in more detail.

21. For excellent modern discussions, see T. Emerson, "Towards a General Theory of the First Amendment," 72 *Yale Law Journal* 877–86 (1963); J. Feinberg, "Limits to the Free Expression of Opinion," in J. Feinberg and H. Gross, eds., *Philosophy of Law* 217–32 (3d ed., Belmont, Calif., Wadsworth Publishing Co. 1986); T. Scanlon, "Freedom of Expression and Categories of Expression," 40 *University of Pittsburgh Law Review* 519 (1979).

22. J. Milton, *Areopagitica* (London, for Hunter & Stevens 1819).

23. *Abrams* v. *United States*, 250 U.S. 616, 624, 630 (1919) (dissenting opinion).

24. *Whitney* v. *California*, 274 U.S. 357, 372, 377 (1927) (concurring opinion).

25. J. S. Mill, *On Liberty*, in *Three Essays* 22–68 (World Classics ed., London, Oxford University Press 1912) (1st ed. of *On Liberty* 1859).

26. See generally Baker, note 14 supra, at 965–81. See also B. DuVal, "Free Communication of Ideas and the Quest for Truth: Toward a Teleological Approach to First Amendment Adjudication," 41 *George Washington Law Review* 161, 191–94 (1972).

27. S. Ingber, "The Marketplace of Ideas: A Legitimizing Myth," 1984 *Duke Law Journal* 1, 25.

28. See T. Emerson, "Colonial Intentions and Current Realities of the First Amendment," 125 *University of Pennsylvania Law Review* 737, 741 (1977): "The essential point is that the process is necessary for reaching the best social decision, regardless of whether ultimate values are conceived in absolute or relative terms." See also Schauer, note 6 supra, at 18–26.

29. In *The Structure of Scientific Revolutions* (2d ed., Chicago, University of Chicago Press 1970), Thomas Kuhn takes a relatively skeptical position about the nature of scientific theories, but he does not deny that, within a given paradigm, answers to "puzzles" are correct or incorrect, he does not deny that in choosing among possible paradigms observations and experimental conclusions are highly important, if not completely determinative, and he does not deny that later theories are generally better at solving puzzles

than the earlier theories they replace. On Kuhn's view of science, there are more than sufficient indicia of objective judgment to make justifications for free speech relevant.

30. See H. Wellington, "On Freedom of Expression," 88 *Yale Law Journal* 1105, 1130–31 (1979).

31. Though I think rational discourse can say much about ultimate values, I also believe many fundamental conflicts in values are not finally resolvable on rational grounds. *Religious Convictions and Political Choice*, note 9 supra, gives a fairly comprehensive account of my sense of the limits of reason.

32. See D. Richards, *Toleration and the Constitution* 216–24 (New York, Oxford University Press 1986); L. Tribe, *Constitutional Choices* 194–98 (Cambridge, Mass., Harvard University Press 1985), suggesting a more equality-focused approach to the First Amendment.

33. It may, of course, be argued that a principle of freedom of speech largely denies government the power to tell private media what to communicate. My point here, however, is that, if the unfairness of the marketplace is raised as an objection to free speech altogether, accepting a version of free speech that allows such regulation makes much more sense than assuming that there is no principled barrier to complete suppression of some ideas. For a critique of a "market failure" model, see Baker, note 14 supra, at 981–90.

34. See Baker, note 14 supra, at 976–80; Ingber, note 27 supra, at 26.

35. This is true at least if some minimum threshold is exceeded. If truth advanced terribly under any conditions but slightly better under freedom, perhaps it would be all right to forget about truth and concentrate on other objectives.

36. See Kuhn, note 29 supra.

37. At least they believe it on the general and abstract level. Quite possibly many smokers do have a "hunch" which is not rationally based that *they* will not be seriously hurt by smoking.

38. The example is a less than perfect illustration because the government does restrict cigarette advertising on television and radio and requires the printing of a warning on advertisements and on packages of cigarettes.

39. According to the fairness doctrine developed by the Federal Communications Commission, broadcasters had to present sides of a topic fairly. An adjunct of the doctrine was that people attacked had a right to respond. (A parallel provision required equality of time for political candidates.) The Supreme Court upheld aspects of the fairness doctrine against a First Amendment challenge in *Red Lion Broadcasting Co.* v. *Federal Communications Commission*, 395 U.S. 367 (1969), but in the second Reagan administration the commission decided to drop the requirements imposed by the doctrine.

40. I should note that there is a big step from believing in "constrained conversation" in the sense of thinking that citizens and officials in a liberal society should not rely on certain kinds of arguments to believing that the government should mandate constraints.

41. See, e.g., Schauer, note 6 supra, at 57, doubting that communication is a necessary condition for intellectual self-fulfillment. See also Baker, note 14 supra, at 975.

42. An outright ban on experiments with human embryos, for example, would impede discovery of some scientific truths.

43. Governments can forbid drinking alcohol, but they cannot forbid falling in love (though they might create conditions that would make falling in love less common).

44. Knowing how it feels to break the law may be a significant experience, but that experience can occur only if liberty is curtailed and is thus not a reason against regulation. Knowing how it feels to set one's own price rather than be restricted may be a significant experience, but a person can have both experiences only if there is both regulation and liberty; so the experience of liberty cannot underlie a "truth discovery" argument against any particular regulation, unless regulation is otherwise pervasive.

45. See Mill, *On Liberty*, note 25 supra.

46. I accept the basic premise that real interests may differ from desires, but I do not defend the premise here or worry about just how the two things may diverge.

47. Since too much stability is undesirable, especially in the face of serious injustice or outmoded practices, it is very hard to estimate any ideal mix of stability and ferment or to say exactly how free speech affects an existing mix.

48. See V. Blasi, "The Checking Value in First Amendment Theory," 1977 *American Bar Foundation Research Journal* 521, providing both an account of this rationale for free speech and an argument about its implications.

49. See Richards, note 32 supra, at 167–69. The role of free speech in protecting those who "speak out against . . . existing institutions, habits, customs, and traditions" is stressed by Steven Shiffrin, *The First Amendment, Democracy, and Romance*, Ch. 2 (to be published).

50. See generally Baker, note 14 supra, at 966; Emerson, note 21 supra, at 879–80; Redish, note 12 supra, at 20–30. As these writings reflect, consequentialist arguments in respect to personality development and autonomy are not sharply distinct.

51. E. Barendt, *Freedom of Speech* 23 (Oxford, Clarendon Press 1985).

52. See generally A. Meiklejohn, *Political Freedom* (New York, Harper & Brothers 1960).

53. This, it seems to me, is the main reason why the fact of a majority vote to suppress is not sufficient. Even a majority should not be able to undermine the conditions for a fair political process. See, e.g., J. Ely, *Democracy and Distrust* 105–36 (Cambridge, Mass., Harvard University Press 1980).

54. This conclusion does not itself depend on a presumed equality of all citizens. Even if some citizens could not vote, as women in the past could not vote, or if citizens had weighted votes, there would still be strong reasons for each citizen to be as fully informed as possible.

55. See V. Blasi, "The First Amendment and the Ideal of Civic Courage: The Brandeis Opinion in *Whitney* v. *California*," 29 *William and Mary Law Review* 653 (1988).

56. L. Bollinger, *The Tolerant Society* (New York, Oxford University Press 1986). The book leaves some doubt about how far more traditional justifications that lie in the background still have force and how far the tolerance justification applies to matters other than dissenting and extremist speech. For a thorough and perceptive review of the book, see V. Blasi, 87 *Columbia Law Review* 387 (1987).

57. See P. Schlag, "Freedom of Speech as Therapy," 34 *University of California in Los Angeles Law Review*, 265, 281–82 (1986). One of the great strengths of Bollinger's book is its illuminating analysis of the dimensions of tolerance. Since too much tolerance, as Bollinger recognizes, presents social dangers of its own, the use of tolerance to decide whether to suppress is troublesome.

58. John Locke, [Second] *Treatise of Civil Government* and *A Letter Concerning Toleration*, ed. Charles L. Sherman (New York, D. Appleton-Century Co. 1937) (1st eds., London 1690 and 1689, respectively). Garry Wills, in *Inventing America* (Garden City, N.Y., Doubleday & Co. 1978), suggests that the influence of the less individualist Scottish "common sense" philosophy was greater than has been commonly realized.

59. As in the original-position analysis of John Rawls. See J. Rawls, *A Theory of Justice* (Cambridge, Mass., Harvard University Press 1971).

60. In considering possible hypothetical consent one needs to think of two stages of consent. The first involves the conditions under which the hypothetical actors consent, the second the conditions under which real people consent in an actual political order. For the first stage, it is hard to imagine any model that permits actively misleading hypothetical actors about actual facts (although they may be in *ignorance* of certain facts, especially

relating to their own personal talents and position). But it is conceivable that actors deciding in hypothetical "presocial" conditions might knowingly consent to live in a political regime that would then engage in active suppression of important political ideas. They might do so, for example, if their judgment (as hypothetical rational beings) was that actual people are so irrational and destructive that necessary social solidarity can be achieved only by the government's rigidly controlling opinion. The sentence in the text assumes that their factual judgment would not lead the hypothetical actors to confer on the government such unbounded power over ideas.

61. I am assuming here (what not everyone accepts) that a liberal government can properly prevent "private" racial discrimination in housing and employment.

62. To be more precise, one would need to distinguish children from adults and educational from coercive efforts to influence thoughts. The government's latitude in respect to school children is greater in some respects than its latitude in respect to adults. Even for adults, education to influence thoughts may be warranted. What is objectionable is coercive effort to invade the "private domain."

63. Edwin Baker's "liberty model" for free speech, note 14 supra, at 964, might be regarded as in part an elaboration of an idea of limited government, although Baker does not subscribe to social contract theory.

64. T. Scanlon, "A Theory of Freedom of Expression," 1 *Philosophy & Public Affairs* 204, 215-16 (1972).

65. Id. The article and its claimed connection between freedom of speech and autonomy are perceptively criticized in R. Admur, "Scanlon on Freedom of Expression," 9 *Philosophy & Public Affairs* 287 (1980).

66. See Scanlon, note 21 supra.

67. Scanlon, note 64 supra, at 215.

68. Two writers who place great emphasis on respect for autonomy are David Richards, note 32 supra, at 85, 169, 183; and Edwin Baker, note 14 supra, at 991.

3

The Boundaries of Speech:
What Actions and Restraints
Are Significantly Reached by
Justifications for Free Speech?

This chapter focuses on what counts as "speech" for a principle of freedom of speech and is, thus, an introduction to all the chapters that follow. I proceed on the premise that the principle of special protection for speech covers mainly behavior to which its underlying justifications apply (though the principle may also come into play when the government has certain objectionable reasons for restricting behavior that itself might not qualify as speech). The chapter first explores the connection between the justifications for freedom of speech and the coverage of a principle of free speech. It then turns to claims of fact and value, communications that the justifications for free speech plainly cover, and examines whether such claims may nonetheless fall outside a principle of free speech if they are false, have narrow practical purposes, have no political content, are made in private, or remain uncommunicated to others. Next is a brief treatment of artistic expression and of actions that are not communicative in the ordinary sense; that discussion addresses the application of a principle of free speech when the government seeks to deter messages even if the acts prohibited do not otherwise qualify as speech. The rest of the chapter is devoted to "situation-altering" utterances and "weak" imperatives. I argue that communications whose dominant purpose is to accomplish something rather than to say something are not reached by a principle of free speech or are reached much less strongly than are ordinary claims of fact and value.

The Basic Relationship between "Speech" and Justifications
for Freedom of Speech

The discussion in the last chapter presupposed an intuitive sense of what counts as speech, sufficient to sustain arguments for special protection. Here I develop a purposive approach to the concept of "speech" which draws a tighter connection between the justifications for freedom of speech and what qualifies as speech.

Roughly, speech or expression has to do with communication. We might initially suppose that all oral and written communication constitutes speech, along perhaps with nonverbal artistic endeavors. Classification would indeed be simplest if all standard acts of communication, and no others, were covered by the justifications for freedom of speech. Unfortunately, some acts that aim at expression, like public burning of one's draft card, do not involve standard forms of communication, and some ordinary communications are reached barely, if at all, by the justifications for free speech. This absence of fit between standard communications and the reasons for freedom of speech poses both a problem of terminology and a practical problem about the application of a principle that restrains interferences with speech. The terminological problems for a political principle or for constitutional law are best faced after the questions of practical application are clarified.

Imagine a society in which freedom of speech operates as a political principle, a principle understood to be supported by the justifications explored in the last chapter. The principle is used by legislators to check their own tendencies to regulate and by citizens to criticize legislative actions and proposals. In what situations would the legislature and informed citizens give weight to the principle? The most straightforward approach would be to use the principle only in cases to which the justifications that lie behind the principle apply. The principle might be employed even though what is involved is not communication in some ordinary-language sense, and the principle might not be employed every time something is communication.

For reasons of efficiency, however, legislators and others who use the principle might do so without seeking a perfect fit between justification and practical applications. If it were arduous to determine the exact reach of the justifications, and if legislators were confident that the justifications reached the overwhelming majority of communications and little else, they might treat the principle as applying to all communications and only communications, though recognizing that a degree of imprecision was involved.

A related reason for accepting some crudeness in categorization would be lack of confidence about one's ability to do better. Legislators might entertain uncertainty about their understanding of the reach of the justifications. Recognizing that much of the point of the justifications for protection is to counter tendencies of political leaders to suppress ideas at odds with their own, sensitive legislators could believe that even their ability to perceive the reach of the justifications for free speech is tainted and that they should accord protection to forms of communication even when they are dubious that the justifications for protection are relevant. This view would be reinforced if the legislators thought that a mistaken suppression of speech was a much worse wrong than a failure to adopt a desirable prohibition of communicative activities.[1]

Even a legislator confident that the justifications for free speech apply only to certain sorts of communication might doubt whether they yield either clear legislative categories or standards usable by those administering the law. For example, a legislator who believes that outright lies are not covered by the justifications, but is skeptical that others can tell when a person is lying, might decide to protect communications regardless of whether they are truthful or not.

Although the search for appropriate practical standards might lead one sensibly to treat the range of a principle of free speech as somewhat different from what one sees as the direct reach of the underlying justifications, I show in this chapter that gross discrepancies exist between the category of verbal and written communications and the category of what is covered by justifications for free speech. Given these discrepancies, any assumption that all communications are covered by a principle of free speech would be ludicrous. Although some concessions to uncertainty and administrative difficulty are apt, use of the principle for legislative purposes needs to be tailored in an intelligible way to the justifications for the principle.

If one thinks only of legislative restraint and public criticism, the related terminological question is not critically important. Shall one say that "speech" consists of those actions to which the principle of freedom of speech properly applies, or shall one say that the principle fails to cover some speech and covers some things that are not speech? The choice may matter for rhetorical force, but as long as everyone is clear about how the term "speech" is being used, either option could avoid confusion.

When we look at constitutional interpretation, the questions of practical application and terminology have extra dimensions. In respect to practical applications of a free speech principle, one difference is that judicial standards of inclusion and exclusion must be standards that courts can handle in principled constitutional adjudication.[2] An additional factor that might be yet more significant is the authoritativeness of the constitutional text itself. Conceivably the Constitution protects a class of actions that is narrower in some respects and broader in others than what a persuasive political principle of free speech reaches. Perhaps, for example, the free speech and free press clauses simply protect all communications, whether or not they are reached by the underlying justifications for free speech. If, as I shall try to show, this particular supposition is implausible, it still may be that appropriate strategies for interpreting the constitutional document will yield an imperfect fit between what is constitutionally subject to protection and what is reached by the justifications for free speech.

For purposes of legal interpretation, the terminological question is shaped by the constitutional language and is highly important. When what is forbidden is abridging "the freedom of speech, or of the press," it is hard to say, at least in the absence of an impermissible legislative aim, that a given action is protected unless it counts as speech or is an activity of the press. And although one might say that "the freedom of speech" does not necessarily reach all speech, it is easier to conclude that all that "really counts as speech" is somehow within the ambit of protection.

I assume that both the political principle of freedom of speech and the constitutional protection should be developed in a purposive way. The application of a free speech principle should pay close attention to the range of justifications, and the cleanest terminological approach is to treat as "speech" what falls directly within those justifications or what, for reasons of efficiency and uncertainty, should be treated as if it fell within those justifications. In Chapters 10 and 12 I outline a general approach to constitutional interpretation which supports this strategy for judicial implementation of the First Amendment.

Although what I have said thus far in this section suggests that the justifications either apply or do not apply, matters are, as I indicated in Chapter 2, much more complicated. For some communicative actions, certain justifications may apply but not others, and when a justification does apply, it may do so with more or less force. The extent to which legislative action should be constrained by a political principle of free speech will depend in part on which justifications apply and how powerfully. In constitutional adjudication, similar attention to coverage and weight is at least possibly appropriate; but the question whether courts should actually declare that some forms of speech are more deserving of protection than others is reserved for the last part of the book. In the rest of this chapter and in following chapters, I do not restrict myself to whether the justifications for free speech apply at all; I make some comments about which justifications apply and with what force.

Assertions of Fact and Value

When we think about communications evidently covered by the justifications for freedom of speech, what immediately come to mind are assertions of fact and value. Although much of this book is about communications that do not fit into this category, the discussion there depends on understanding of why claims of fact and value should ordinarily be free. Furthermore, some common questions about the protection of claims of fact and value require consideration in their own right. Among these questions are: the place of private communications, the status of acts that are designed to assert facts or values but do not involve verbal or written communication, the relevance of insincerity or selfish motives on the speaker's part, the place of assertions of fact and value that are dominantly aimed at producing specific, often immediate, action, and the importance of the conditions under which the audience receives what is asserted.

General and Particular Assertions of Fact and Value as Clearly Covered

A free speech principle most obviously covers factual propositions of a general sort, those asserted in statements such as "Physical objects have gravitational force," "Rapid inflation causes social instability," and "The human personality survives death."[3] Claims about general facts are critical for people's understanding of the world they inhabit, for their choices about how to live, and for their decisions on public issues. The truth-discovery justification applies strongly to general factual statements, and suppression of such statements would undermine independence of judgment and personal development. Many general claims about facts are important to the considered appraisal of government on which consent must rest; a government that recognizes autonomy and dignity will allow speakers to express and listeners to hear such claims about facts.

The same justifications for free expression reach more particular factual assertions, such as "The Soviet Union tested a nuclear device yesterday," or "Your wife has a lover." Some specific factual claims, such as the claim about Soviet testing of a nuclear device, have wide public significance, but even facts without such significance can be highly important for individuals. Typically, certain individual facts will be critical to decisions about how to act on particular occasions, and beliefs about particular facts are a large part of the basis on which we formulate or accept general propositions.

Among statements of particular facts are assertions of wants to be adjusted in social processes ("We wish to earn five dollars an hour"), indications of personal attitude ("I love Mozart's music"), and statements of feeling ("I'm angry"). Interests of social adjustment, development of personality, and emotional release, respectively, provide important reasons for protecting these kinds of statements.

A principle of free speech also reaches general and particular evaluations. General claims, like "Love is the greatest good" or "Capital punishment is unjustified," and particular claims, like "You should not lie about this to Mary," are bases on which people consider what situations and practices are desirable and how they should behave. If one believes, as I do, that all or many value statements are in some sense true or false, the reasons for protection will look closely similar to those which apply to factual assertions. But, even if one is radically skeptical about the truth or falsity of claims of value, good reasons exist for extending protection to them. For practical policy, the difficulty of disentangling fact from value is one barrier to assigning variant levels of protection to claims of fact and claims of value. A term like "heroic" incorporates both factual and value elements, and in context an evaluative term like "good" ("this is a good car") may be translatable into a number of factual claims.[4] But even if one could distill pure or nearly pure statements of value, strong reasons would exist for protection. As far as personal dignity and emotional release are concerned, freedom to express one's judgments of value is as important to speakers as freedom to indicate views about facts. And evaluations are important to listeners as well. People who make choices about personal and public matters must obviously rely on evaluations as well as factual conclusions, and listening to what others have to say helps them discover values to which they can subscribe. Government suppression of talk about values circumscribes the process of self-discovery, perpetuates institutions that otherwise would no longer win knowing acceptance, and frustrates the desire of people to converse with others about matters that concern them deeply.

I have now established basic premises about the coverage of general and particular assertions of fact and value. We shall subsequently see how those premises bear on uses of language whose claim to coverage is less secure but which relate in some significant way to talk about facts and values; now I address possible limits or qualifications regarding the application of a principle of free speech to such talk itself.

Communications That Are Nonpolitical or Private or Both

Is a principle of freedom of speech limited to political or public speech or speech of general concern? The discussion up to now has mixed examples of political and nonpolitical speech, speech in private and public contexts, and speech of general and limited concern, reflecting my view that no such limit is appropriate. Here I explicitly address these problems in relation to a principle of free speech for legislators and citizens, reserving for Part III of the book the claim of prominent scholars, including Alexander Meiklejohn and Robert Bork, that the First Amendment should be interpreted as touching only speech that relates to political subjects.

In respect to whether both political and nonpolitical speech warrant protection, little more is needed than a reminder of what Chapter 2 says. Liberal democracy requires that citizens enjoy broad freedom to engage in political evaluations, for example, that racial discrimination is unjust, and to express beliefs about politically relevant facts, for example, that inflation causes instability or that a judge has been bribed. Further, an element of a principle of free speech is distrust of official judgments that speech warrants suppressing, and this distrust may be most acute for political speech. But a conclusion that a principle of free speech reaches only political utterances hardly follows. Most of the justifications we have considered cover all domains of human concern, and no one can suppose that distrust of government extends *only* to explicitly political speech. Politics is not hermetically sealed off from other human concerns. Speech that is not explicitly political often has political implications; and, independent of these, legislators may be tempted to satisfy popular outrage by suppressing unfashionable views about sex or religion or other matters. A broad political principle of free speech reaches claims of fact and value relevant to all human concerns.

Similarly, and contrary to the suggestion that "Typically, the acts of expression with which a theory of 'free speech' is concerned are addressed to a large (if not the widest possible) audience,"[5] an acceptable principle reaches private as well as public communication. Whether communication is public or private can sometimes make an important difference, as I suggest in subsequent chapters, but it is worth stressing that the reasons for free speech plainly cover much private communication. The only explanation why anyone could have supposed otherwise is that modern liberal governments are rarely tempted to proceed against private assertions of fact and value.

For most of human history, the main source of beliefs and attitudes has been conversation with family members and close acquaintances; in this age of public education, television, and newspapers, private conversation remains both a primary expressive outlet for individuals and a significant source of insight. Many people are still more deeply influenced in what they believe about facts and values by the opinions of a narrow circle of intimates than by mass publications. As Steven Shiffrin has said, "the private daily communications of millions of individuals profoundly affect public opinion."[6] For almost everyone, restrictions on public discussion would be much more tolerable than effective restrictions on private communications. We need only think of eras, when religious heretics were persecuted for beliefs privately held and privately expressed and of thoroughly totalitarian countries like Nazi Germany in which "antisocial" statements in the home were highly dangerous, to recognize how much greater the impairment of liberty is in such climates than under regimes, like some of those now in Eastern Europe, in which the practical boundaries in private discussion are very relaxed, though fairly stringent restraints apply to public speech. A principle of free speech reaches intimate communications as well as those intended for a large audience.

A conceivable theory of coverage would limit a principle of free speech to speech of some general concern, including speech about aesthetics, morality, science, and so on, as well as speech about politics, but excluding personal matters, such as "Your boyfriend is considerate" or "Your sister's work is incompetent." The idea would be that free speech is about general discourse relevant to the larger society. Such a view is more plausible than a limitation either to political speech or to speech in public, but it is still flawed. The line between speech of general and personal concern is too blurred to support a total exclusion of the latter. More important, people obviously care deeply about personal matters, and most of the reasons for liberty of speech about general concerns apply directly to talk about personal subjects as well. Further, our understanding of personal matters greatly affects our views about many subjects of general concern. A political principle of free speech reaches private subjects as well as those of broad concern.

Although the analysis is a bit more complicated, the practical conclusion for private conversation and speech about personal matters is the same for the most private speech: "communications" to oneself in drafts, diaries, tapes, or spontaneous verbal expressions that are either not intended or not yet intended for any other audience.[7] Reasons for freedom involving the development and dignity of the speaker plainly apply. Self-communication is for many people an emotional outlet and an indispensable means by which thoughts are developed. Although no audience benefits directly from self-communication, the experience of academics writing notes for teaching and drafts of scholarship attests that self-communication is frequently an indispensable preliminary stage for communication to others. Were self-communication less protected than speech for others, one might be in the strange position of having to utter thoughts to an audience if one were to utter them at all. In ordinary circumstances, it would be anomalous to give less protection to self-communication than to communication to others.

If the protected status of self-communication is unquestionable, its proper categorization requires care. If self-communication does not really count as *speech*, someone might worry that a principle that protects it must be a more general principle that protects liberty or privacy. What such a worry fails to grasp is the crucial respect in which self-communication differs from other private acts. It lies somewhere between pure thought and speech to an audience. The idea that people should not be punished for thoughts alone is one of the most fundamental for liberal society.[8] Thought unaccompanied by action is the most private of private domains, and without free thought free speech is inconceivable. Frequently, linguistic formulation of ideas in thought precedes communication to others. Whether thoughts are spoken or written as a preface to interpersonal communication or are intended to remain indefinitely for oneself, an act of self-communication goes beyond mental processes, but does not yet reach others, and thus occupies the space between pure thought and ordinary communication. One might conceive of protection of self-communication as deriving from a principle of freedom of thought more fundamental even than a principle of free speech, but henceforth I shall simply assume that the principle of free speech embraces it, along with communication in private to other persons.

Motivations and Objectives

Assuming that a principle of free speech covers general and particular assertions of fact and value, political and nonpolitical, public and private, I now inquire whether special qualifying conditions make the justifications for free speech inapplicable or radically weaken their force. This section treats the speaker's motives and objectives; the next section addresses falsehood, insincerity, and the state of the audience.

I begin with the speaker's motivations. Does it matter whether the speaker is disinterestedly trying to disseminate truth for its own sake or for the sake of the listener, or is, instead, seeking to promote his own selfish goals? Motives are usually mixed; often a speaker's statements consciously serve some element of his self-interest to a greater or lesser degree. In any event, in respect to most justifications for free speech the speaker's motives for saying what he truly believes are not intrinsically relevant. The truthful or sincere assertion of a belief, e.g., that Republican foreign policy is misguided or that the bank president is embezzling funds, informs the listener, whether or not the speaker has a selfish purpose. However, when the speaker's overwhelming motivation for a statement is his own tangible interest, as when a seller describes the qualities of an article to a potential buyer, there may be special reason to distrust his judgment and sincerity. Dominantly selfish motivation may matter in drawing precise lines of suppression and protection, but it certainly does not render a principle of free speech inapplicable.

If motives are not usually crucial for free speech, perhaps the immediate objectives of speaker and listener, what they intend a communication to achieve, make a difference. Some assertions of particular facts and values are so closely and exclusively linked to narrow practical aims that the justifications for free speech are remote. Each time I use the Columbia gymnasium I am given a different lock, and the attendant tells me what three numbers to use for opening the lock. His communication does truly inform me of a fact, the combination that will open this particular lock, but it has little to do with speech. The significance of what occurs is almost identical to that of his handing me a key for the lock. In a certain context if I say, "The breeze from the window is making me cold," that may amount to a request to someone to shut the window.[9] Racial and religious epithets typically convey some assertion of fact (about the group to which someone belongs) and value (that the group is degraded in some way), but sometimes they may be uttered in order to start a fight or simply to hurt.

To argue that a principle of free speech has little or nothing to do with such communications, one would draw upon their immediately practical objectives. The argument against the relevance of a free speech principle is strongest when information disclosed is so narrowly specific that no significant subject of discussion or learning is involved. If what is said has more general relevance than a lock combination, then the reasons for free speech apply, but they apply less strongly if speaker and listener care only about an immediate practical objective and not about any increase in general understanding or expression of personal feelings or attitudes.

Falsehood, Insincerity, and Audience Conditions

How far do the justifications for free speech apply to false and insincere statements? Of course, one aspect of the justifications is distrust that those who adopt
or administer legal regimes of suppression can adequately ascertain what is true
or false and when a person is sincere, but some statements are demonstrably false,
that is, can be shown to be false to any rational person who surveys the evidence,
and occasionally statements that are not obviously false are obviously insincere.
The demonstrably false statements include general assertions like "Water turns to
ice as the temperature rises" and specific assertions like "Richard Nixon completed his second term as president." A person's lack of sincerity can be established when he repeatedly assents to a proposition, but asserts the contrary on a
single occasion when that serves his interest.

So long as listeners have the capability to sift claims of truth and falsehood,
even obviously false claims can have some value in the search for truth. As Mill
points out, exposure to falsehood can help people to understand the truth better
and take it more seriously. Still, the contribution to understanding that most
demonstrably false statements make is highly limited.

For justifications that focus on the speaker, it matters what the speaker
believes to be true. If a speaker is stopped from making a false statement that he
or she believes to be true, the immediate sense of affront to dignity will likely be as
great as if the statement were actually true, and suppression is less likely to change
the speaker's opinion than open dialogue. Possibly in retrospect if a speaker
comes to understand the untruth of his beliefs, he will then judge interference with
his speech to have been less an affront to dignity and autonomy than he thought
at the time, but justifications that involve impact on speakers apply almost as
strongly to believed statements that happen to be false as to statements that are
true.

If belief in truth is critical for some justifications that focus on the speaker,
one must take account of intermediate cases between firm belief in truth and firm
belief in falsity. A speaker might believe that a statement is probably false though
possibly true, or probably true though possibly false. What can be said generally
is that some justifications for protection decline as the likelihood of falsity in the
speaker's mind increases.

These brief comments help introduce the fundamental question whether the
reasons for free speech reach statements a speaker knows are false only to the
slight degree that exposure of listeners to ordinary falsehoods may increase their
discernment of truth. Is there an appropriate place in human discourse for
outright lying, and does that place have to do with the values of speech? I shall
consider three substantial arguments in support of a view that outright lies do
involve values of speech, but first I mention a practically important line-drawing
problem.[10]

Much speech employs hyperbole and parody. Things are said that neither
speakers nor listeners take to be literal assertions of truth. A baseball fan who
calls an umpire a "crook" is typically not seriously contending that, for corrupt
motives, the umpire is intentionally favoring one team. In the rough and tumble
of politics, loose accusations are often not to be regarded at face value. Discourse

would be impoverished if people always had to speak what they believed was literally true, and such discourse would make heavy emotional demands on those who expressed themselves. Freedom of speech certainly covers patent exaggerations and other nonliteral uses of language.

Distinguishing outright lies from nonliteral statements is often not easy. A lie involves the speaker's asserting something which he intends to be taken to be true but which he knows or supposes to be false, but, without examining the speaker's mind, one may not be able to tell exactly what, if anything, the speaker was intending to assert as literally true. For many of the reasons for free speech, what the audience thinks is being asserted will matter. If lies are assertions of truth which the audience understands in the manner intended by the speaker and which the speaker knows to be false, it is not easy to suppress lies without also reaching some misunderstood hyperbolic and other nonliteral uses of language.

One argument that outright lies themselves have value as speech is that lies serve as an emotional outlet. Some people vent their hostility or scorn or express their affection for other people by lying about them; lies can produce emotional satisfaction for the liars. This argument compels us to probe more deeply the emotional-outlet reason for speech. After all, a great many actions, including sexual acts, dance, athletic endeavors, and instances of physical aggression, can be outlets for one's feelings. If much action is valued partly because it expresses emotions, that reason may support liberty for broad categories of action rather than, or in addition to, special protection for speech.[11]

The need for emotional outlets has particular relevance for speech only if communications of feelings and of the attitudes that underlie feelings are among the actions that have the most intense emotional significance for people. Sometimes verbalization suffices less well to express extreme emotion than a more active physical act, and for many people, some other acts—one thinks especially of sexual acts—are generally more important emotional outlets than ordinary communicative acts. Nevertheless, it is plausible to suppose, though I shall not try to adduce the relevant psychological data, that communicative acts expressing one's feelings and attitudes are among the most important emotional outlets for most people, and this is a reason for affording these acts wide latitude. At least for ordinary people, outright lies do not play a similar role; most people feel an emotional release from expressing what they feel, not by lying about what they really feel or think.[12] Thus, the emotional-outlet argument for free speech does not apply with anything like the same force to lies as to sincere utterances.

A second argument for protecting lies is that they can often be an opening gambit in the search for truth. Suppose that a person suspects that a widely held belief is false. He may want to find out what others think without admitting his own present opinion—"Of course I don't believe that Janet would take money from the bank, but I heard someone say she did. What do you think?" In some conversations, initial deception is undeniably a way of moving forward to admitting unpopular truths.

A third, and troubling, argument for protecting lies is that someone may speak literal falsehoods in order to reveal what are honestly held to be deeper truths. Suppose that a racial incident occurs on campus and is followed by an ordinary process of investigation. A concerned black student feels that the administration and the white students exhibit a pervasive hostility and insensitivity toward blacks, but she cannot point to actual occurrences that will convey the reality to those who have not suffered it. She therefore claims particular acts and omissions which would be striking manifestations of discrimination but which she knows have not literally occurred, believing that only when others suppose that acts like these have occurred will they truly understand the hostility to the concerns of blacks on campus. In this instance, the student supposes that the only effective way to convey a deeper truth is to state a literal falsehood. To take a more mundane example, a man may feel that only by lying to his wife that a previous act of adultery had not occurred can he genuinely convey the love and concern he has for her. Perhaps one of the most common political uses of this technique is to claim that an official under criticism really intends or wants unacceptable outcomes, when all one really believes is that the official is indifferent to whether those outcomes occur.[13]

It is arguable whether social discourse would be improved if people eschewed all outright lies. Occasional lies may be needed to shield listeners from pain ("No, I don't think you are ugly") or to mislead dangerous persons ("The person you want to shoot is no longer in the house"). Barring such exceptions, my own belief is that the insidious effects of untruths intended to be taken literally are so damaging that we would be better off if people refrained from them. But certain values of speech do have *some* application to lies, and when prohibition of lying is considered, the possible expressive value of lies needs to be considered.

In speaking of insincere and demonstrably false statements, I have so far concentrated on factual assertions. Claims of value cannot be demonstrably false in the manner of ordinary facts, but a person can make demonstrably insincere claims of value. If Felicia tells Henry and others that Henry's wife Wanda would be justified in divorcing him and then, for $500, tells Wanda that no divorce is ever justified, Felicia has tried to manipulate Wanda by an insincere assertion of value. Since a serious claim of value involves an implicit assertion that one believes in the claim being made, an insincere claim of value involves a factual misrepresentation of one's own state of mind, one sort of lie. Like outright lies about facts, insincere claims of value are reached less strongly by many of the justifications for free speech than are sincere assertions, but some justifications do touch insincere assertions to some degree. For example, insincerely telling someone that no divorce is ever justified might be a means to express hatred of the person wanting a divorce or might be an opening gambit in exploring when divorce really may be justified.

Finally, I address what I call *predictable audience response*. As will become clear in subsequent chapters, this concern touches communications other than statements of fact, but I here consider it in that context. Many justifications for free speech presume that members of an audience can accord reasoned consideration to what is said, that they have some ability to sift truth from falsehood and to act on the basis of that sifting. To the extent that those assumptions are implausible the reasons for protecting speech are weakened.

In extreme cases a message may not be addressed to rational faculties at all, or listeners may be incapable of assessing the accuracy of assertions before they must act on them. Subliminal messages that listeners are not aware they are receiving may exert influence without any screening by their rational judgment. In the popular example of "shouting 'fire' in a crowded theater," the audience may have to react before it is able to tell whether the message is true.

More frequently, the audience's incapacity is less absolute. Listeners may be capable of checking the accuracy of a claim, say about the benefits of a product, but lack the practical means or inclination to do so. At other times, listeners, such as members of a highly charged mob, are in an emotional state that renders reasoned consideration very unlikely. When an active response is likely to precede deliberation or to result from a largely nondeliberative process, reasons for free speech are weakened.

A more subtle point is what I shall call the *residual effect* of some falsehoods. Suppose outrageously scandalous behavior is attributed to Paula, a prominent political figure. The claims are thoroughly rebutted two months later and are understood by all members of the audience to have been rebutted. Nevertheless, in the future when memories have dimmed, the mention of Paula's name triggers vague feelings of unease and distaste. At some level of consciousness, the connection of Paula to scandal has not been completely dislodged. Such residual effects challenge at some deeper level the completeness of "truth discovery" even under the best of audience conditions.

How far does this point about residual effects threaten what I have said about the truth-discovery justification for free speech? First, we need to remember that conscious awareness of what is actually true matters a great deal; a social practice that generally promotes that awareness should not be scrapped because of some occasional and unfortunate residual effects at subconscious levels. Second, the magnitude of residual effects and the harm they cause vary tremendously according to subject matter. If the word "Vikings" triggers in me certain warm feelings because I was told in childhood wonderful things about the Vikings which I now suppose are false, no one is much injured. Perhaps we can conclude that, for most kinds of statements, the possibility of residual subconscious effects is not a significant argument for punishing initial falsehoods, but when residual effects are likely to to be both powerful and seriously damaging to living persons, they may affect the proper treatment of false statements.

Artistic and Other Communication That Is Not in Words

Much communication does not involve linguistic utterance. One thinks, for example, of sculpture and painting, photography, ballet and modern dance, and instrumental music, as well as communication by recognized symbols such as Morse code. One might initially suppose that these are covered by a principle of free speech simply because they involve communication, but I have assumed that a form of communication must be covered by the justifications for free speech if it is to deserve special protection. How far these justifications cover such instances of nonlinguistic communication is a question whose complexity is much greater than its practical significance for this study, a significance limited mainly to restrictions of obscenity. For this reason, discussion here will be relatively brief.

The possible grounds for including such nonlinguistic expression within a principle of free speech concern the facts and values the expression conveys, the government's reasons for suppression, and the importance of communication that does not assert facts or values. Initially I treat grounds for protection that focus on the expression of facts and values as facts and values have so far been presented.

Messages about facts and values are often a significant aspect of nonlinguistic forms of communication.[14] This is, of course, obvious about visual or auditory symbols, like Morse code, which substitute in some clear way for words or ideas. But the point applies to much else. News photography is a telling way to transmit information; great art of the Middle Ages portrayed events of religious significance and held out a conception of how life should be lived;[15] much dance tells a story. If verbal and written statements of fact and value warrant protection, so also do these pictorial and artistic representations. And in this respect whether events are portrayed as historical or fictional does not matter, since fictional representations typically reflect some understanding of life and how it may be lived.

Once one realizes that much pictorial and artistic communication conveys understandings about facts and values, one faces the problem of how to distinguish what does convey such understandings from what does not. Exactly what messages count? Must they be in the mind of the creator? Must they at least be perceived as being an aspect of the work by members of the audience? Much highly abstract art might be thought either to have "no message about life" or to involve a kind of rejection of prevailing social values. Instrumental music is one of the most nonrepresentational of the arts, but some instrumental music tells a story, and other music seems to express an attitude toward life. Unless composers say what they are getting at, grasping their intent may be impossible, and it is unclear whether a composer's conscious intent should count more than his or her subconscious feelings or the audience's sense of what the work signifies. If listeners not only feel emotionally inspired but perceive truths about life in a Mozart symphony, should it matter for a principle of free speech that all Mozart was consciously trying to do was write the best music he could?

That aesthetic expression reflects in some subconscious way its creator's attitudes about life and generates attitudes in the audience is probably not enough alone to qualify it as speech. After all, virtually all our actions reflect our attitudes and feelings in some way, and people observing various forms of behavior may glean lessons about life. One thinks of the sport of boxing, for example. The way participants fight will indicate something about how they think or feel, and observers may think a fight poignantly portrays aspects of the human condition in microcosm. Yet one would not suppose that a proposed ban on boxing would raise a problem of free speech. That much behavior has an "expressive aspect" that touches on facts and values for actors and witnesses may be a reason for a general principle of liberty of action, but it fails to establish a distinctive basis for protecting aesthetic expression as speech.

Perhaps in two respects a tighter connection exists between purely aesthetic expression and messages of value than I have yet acknowledged. Every work of art may be said to represent at least an aesthetic judgment, such judgments being part of the domain of value, and a judgment about the proper place of the artist in society, precisely the sort of judgment that has given rise to suppression of abstract art in some totalitarian societies, where artists are expected to reinforce some approved vision of social life. An abstract work of art does "express" judgments about aesthetic merit and the artist's place, implicitly rejecting alternative aesthetic standards and the position that an artist should always do work with particular social meaning.

Against the supposition that these narrower connections between art and message bring art within the justifications for free speech, it may be responded that many activities reflect judgments about excellence and about appropriate roles. The professional boxer's movements show what he perceives to be competent boxing and reflect his view that making one's living in a sport where the object is to hit someone else is morally acceptable. Since many nonartistic activities carry as clear implications about roles people should occupy as do abstract works of art, the claim of a distinctively tight connection between art and ideas about social role seems implausible. Moreover, the strength of a free speech justification for nonlinguistic activity may depend partly on how easily the message could be conveyed in ordinary language. A person need not actually create a work of art to express a view that artists can pursue aesthetic excellence for its own sake.

The claim of a particularly close connection between act and message seems more compelling in respect to aesthetic ideals themselves. An artist may be hard put to describe in words what would satisfy his aesthetic sense; there may be no good substitute for actually producing and showing the work. Perhaps it is easier to separate an account of most other sorts of excellences from active efforts to achieve them. If this is so, the link between an expression of a standard of value and work done according to that standard may indeed be tighter for artistic activity than most other human endeavors.

A different response to the challenge that much nonrepresentational art does not assert facts and values is to focus on the possible reasons for government suppression. The principle of free speech may apply whenever the aim of the government is to suppress a message about values. Since a government would have little interest in suppressing abstract art and instrumental music[16] other than because of implicit messages, the idea that a principle of free speech can be invoked by the government's reason for prohibition is an important idea for art, with potential broader implications that deserve a summary examination.

The implications concern both the coverage of a principle of free speech and what, terminologically, is to count as "speech." I suggested early in Chapter 2 that one aspect of a principle of freedom of speech might be to foreclose, or render highly suspect, certain reasons for prohibitions. A government might entertain reasons of the suspect sort for forbidding activities whose initial status as "speech" is doubtful (as I have so far assumed about abstract artistic expression) or which pretty clearly do not initially qualify as speech. As an example of the latter, we might consider the act of committing suicide. That, taken by itself, is not a communication in any straightforward sense;[17] yet it is an activity that conveys strong implicit messages, and the government might ban it partly on those grounds. More specifically, legislators might take the following position: "Whatever we may think about suicide by mature people determined to end their lives because life has become too painful, the effect of suicides on impressionable immature people who may follow the example of others is too serious to permit anyone to take his or her own life." Does the principle of free speech come into play when the government's aim is to suppress some message an act communicates? If so, should the conclusion be conceptualized as: (1) whatever the government thinks of suppressing because of its message becomes "speech"; or (2) the principle of free speech applies to activities that are not themselves "speech" but are prohibited because of concern about message?

The substantive question about the reach of a free speech principle might be put most broadly as whether a legislature should always hesitate to prohibit acts if its reason for doing so is the harmfulness of some message that acts convey. When the message is an aspect of what the actor is trying to do and is understood by the audience as such, we can say comfortably that the act communicates the message and that the free speech principle is relevant. Thus, the free speech principle applies to abstract art if part of what the artist is trying to do is support an aesthetic ideal, if members of the audience understand that, and if the government considers suppression for that very reason.[18] The harder situation is one in which the actor has no message to communicate—he simply commits suicide out of desperation with life—but the government wants to foreclose others' being influenced by some implicit message they may find to the effect that life generally is not worth living and that suicide is appropriate. Liberty of the speaker *as speaker* is irrelevant, because the actor is not trying to convey a message, but justifications for free speech that focus on audience concerns apply when the government interferes to prevent some people from drawing personal lessons from the feelings and actions of others. If free speech considerations bear to a degree on the "example" reason for prohibiting suicides, it does not follow that a prohibition is wrong overall. There are independent reasons for stopping suicides, and the danger of "examples" may be so great that any free speech considerations are overridden. The strength of those considerations may depend partly on the conditions of audience response, particularly whether those affected are likely to give reasoned consideration to the "message" they perceive or to engage in irrational imitative reactions.

The best terminological approach is to draw a distinction based on the actor's aims. When the actor intends to communicate a message of fact or value to an audience, the act is at least partly speech and should be considered "speech" insofar as the government's interest is with the message itself.[19] When the government wants to suppress a "message" that the actor is not trying to convey, a principle of free speech is implicated in respect to an activity that is not itself speech. (The reader should note this minor exception to my approach of making "speech" correlate with the reach of a principle of free speech.)

How do these more general observations apply to aesthetic expression? If the analysis is sound, a principle of freedom of speech comes into play when an artist wants to convey a message of fact or value or when the audience's receipt of some unintended message is the possible basis for prohibition. If my terminological suggestions are followed, a government's aim to suppress a possible message is not by itself enough to turn aesthetic expression into "speech."

It is time now to address the fundamental question whether something critical is being missed when aesthetic expression is considered in light of claims of fact and value. Because, apart from representations considered offensive, such as pornographic photographs, modern liberal governments are not inclined to suppress aesthetic expression without regard to the facts or values it conveys; the status of aesthetic communications that ostensibly have no clear factual or valuational message and are so understood by members of the audience is of limited practical importance. Nonetheless, the argument that these communications themselves should be protected as speech is worth a brief look.

Art undoubtedly involves communication as a primary aspect; the artist tries to communicate something to an audience that looks or listens. Communication is not just an incidental byproduct of aesthetic expression, as it is of many other acts. Saying in general terms just *what* is communicated may not be easy for nonrepresentational art, but there is an expression of feelings, moods, and aesthetic tastes. Drawing from proponents of different perspectives on aesthetics, John Finnis has written of art as the "creation of forms symbolic of human feeling."[20] He says that the "idea" in art is not a message or doctrine, but "the symbol of feeling, whose sensuous quality is in the service of its vital import and whose unique power lies in the fact that it is an abstraction, a symbol, the bearer of an idea."[21] If the fundamental nature of aesthetic expression is not well captured in terms of assertions of fact and value, we need to ask whether the justifications for free speech cover what such expression does communicate. Some points are obvious. Nonrepresentational art has nothing directly to do with exposing government abuse. Although part of the point of some abstract art and atonal music may be to help liberate people from rationality and encourage a rebellious spirit, much art has little to do with promoting independent judgment about choices in life, other than choices of what art to see or listen to. Justifications involving personal development, outlets for emotional feeling, and the dignity of the speaker have considerable force.[22] More controversially, although the truth-discovery justification does not apply in a simple way, we may apprehend ourselves, our fellows, and our world more fully if we experience the deepening of feeling that art can produce.

This is not the occasion to attempt a full examination of how a principle of freedom of speech relates to aesthetic expression, but, for purposes of this study, we can rest with the following propositions. A great deal of nonlinguistic aesthetic expression, like linguistic expression, does assert facts and values. What is fundamentally conveyed by aesthetic expression is of great human importance even if it does not concern facts and values. Many of the arguments for free speech apply to what art conveys, but perhaps the line between the value of art and the value of some noncommunicative experiences is less sharp (many experiences express and deepen feeling) than the line between the value of ordinary speech and the value of noncommunicative experiences. Because of the significance of what art conveys for both artist and audience, because of the difficulty of deciding whether particular art is meant to assert facts and values, and because government suppression of art has often been aimed at the ideas implied by art, aesthetic expression should be treated as a form of "speech" for purposes of a political principle of free speech.

One final point here remains. Not every work that is produced in the same medium as art is necessarily art. Although some photographs and moving pictures will involve the "creation of a form symbolic of human feeling," not every photo or movie will do so. It, thus, remains an open question whether everything produced in the media associated with art should be considered "speech" for the purposes of a principle of free speech. This is a double question about what is conveyed by nonaesthetic uses of the medium, and about the possibilities of drawing distinctions. This question is raised again in the treatment of pornography.

"Ordinary" Behavior That Communicates Facts and Values

That all behavior impliedly "expresses" something about how people look at the world is not enough to make every action "speech", but there is a subcategory of "ordinary" behavior that falls very close to verbal and written communication. Some ordinary acts are dominantly intended to communicate a message and are understood as such. If a young man burns his draft card, it is almost certainly because he wants to express his rejection of the draft or of some war in which the country is engaged.

When the significance of such acts is evident, they are covered by a principle of freedom of speech. A legislature should strongly resist forbidding such acts *because* of the message they convey, but, even if the legislature has reasons for prohibition that do not relate to the message, the fact that the acts are dominantly communicative remains a reason for leaving them free. Now, one possible response to this conclusion is that, so long as verbal and written communication is allowed, no one really *need* engage in "symbolic" speech and that, therefore, what is often called "symbolic" speech does not warrant protection. The grain of truth in this response is that the importance of one kind of expression does depend in part on what other expressive outlets are available, but that is hardly a basis for affording *no* protection to speech through ordinary acts. Often symbolic speech is more effective than verbal speech, but in any event people should usually be free to communicate in the way that feels comfortable to them. If a legislature is considering a restriction directed at acts of symbolic speech, the principle of free speech constitutes a barrier.

Usually the legislative choice will not be posed so starkly. The question may be whether to prohibit a class of acts *some* of which are mainly or largely expressive. A ban on public nudity is an example. Sometimes people appear nude in public places mostly to make some moral or political point; sometimes these reasons *accompany* a sense that it is simply more pleasurable to be nude in certain settings, say while sunbathing; sometimes feelings of comfort or pleasure will stand alone. If a legislature considering a prohibition recognizes that a substantial percentage of the acts covered are meant to communicate a message, it should consider itself constrained by the principle of freedom of speech.[23]

Once a decision to prohibit has been made, a further question arises whether to except instances that are dominantly communicative. Much depends on how damaging the prohibited acts themselves are and how easily the communicative instances may be identified. I pay some attention to this problem as one of legislative choice in Chapter 9, and in Chapter 19 I consider possible constitutional protection for behavior that is ordinarily punishable but is undertaken for expressive purposes.

Situation-Altering Utterances

Having discussed kinds of communications that are not in linguistic form but have a substantial claim to be within the reach of a free speech principle, I now turn to what may be viewed as the other side of the coin: verbal and written utterances whose aim is something other than expression in any of the senses yet considered. As is conveyed by the slogan of philosophers of language, "the different uses of language," [24] the point of many communications is neither to transmit information nor to assert values. Without categorizing all the ways language is used, I here examine some major uses which are common subjects of criminal statutes and which do not dominantly involve claims of fact or value, in order to see whether these uses are reached by the justifications for free speech. The terrain divides itself into two large categories: what I call *situation-altering* utterances, on the one hand, and requests and encouragements, or what I call *weak imperatives*, on the other. With some strain, all my examples might be pressed into the "situation-altering" category, but to do so would be to obscure how requests and pure encouragements differ critically from the other uses I discuss.

Although the categorizations in the rest of this chapter may be unfamiliar to many readers who are trained in law, they help put in abstract and explicable form intuitions that have underlain adoption of bases for crime which have not been questioned from the perspective of free speech. By showing the good sense behind many traditional assumptions, the observations also serve to justify what may otherwise appear to be intellectual neglect. The examination of particular crimes that occurs in subsequent chapters offers a test of the abstract discussion; readers who find distinctions I draw initially unconvincing can consider them more fully in the light of actual legal norms. That more specific examination also affords the opportunity to work out important matters of detail passed over in this first presentation.

Situation-Altering Utterances: In General

Utterances are often a means for changing the social context in which we live. When members of a couple say the crucial "I will" in a marriage ceremony, their utterances alter the legal status of their relationship; legal rules and principles frequently determine circumstances in which communications by officials or ordinary people change legal relations. Other utterances alter situations according to nonlegal conventions. Rules governing a game, for example, may provide that certain utterances by participants or referees have consequences for the game, e.g., "I bid three hearts" or "You're out." [25] In each of the examples so far a particular utterance has worked a direct change in someone's status according to institutional standards of some sort;[26] even more commonly utterances can alter one's normative obligations, what one should do in the future. The conventions of language and of ordinary social morality make certain utterances, such as promises,2[27] count as far as one's moral obligations are concerned.[28]

My essential claim—a central claim for this book—is that utterances of these sorts are situation-altering and are outside the scope of a principle of free speech. Such utterances are ways of doing things, not of asserting things, and they are generally subject to regulation on the same bases as most noncommunicative behavior. I explore that claim in this chapter, in connection with a variety of situation-altering utterances, namely, exercises of official authority, agreements, promises, orders, offers, manipulative inducements, and manipulative threats. In the course of the discussion, I enter some qualifications to the assertion that the principle of free speech does not reach these utterances, and I suggest complexities which are developed further in chapters dealing with specific crimes.

I begin by making some general remarks about the category of situation-altering utterances and by offering a preliminary defense of the idea that these really are significantly different from assertions of fact and value.

The central idea about situation-altering utterances, as I have said, is that they actually change the social world in which we live. Modern recognition of the importance of this use of language owes a great deal to J. L. Austin, who coined the term "performative utterances."[29] My thesis about the nonapplication of the principle of free speech might be regarded as a thesis about utterances that are performative, but good reasons support choosing the alternative term "situation-altering" instead. The explication of these reasons helps emphasize that my aim is not just to replicate categories important in the philosophy of language.

My first reason for using the term "situation-altering" is that, especially for readers not familiar with work in the philosophy of language, it conveys the critical characteristic of these utterances more sharply than the term "performative."

The second, related, reason is that Austin's term "performative" has much wider application than the uses of language I discuss. It is true that many of his early and striking examples, such as the wedding vow and the christening of a ship, have the situation-altering aspect on which I concentrate. But Austin also includes among performative utterances "I apologize" and "I bid you welcome,"[30] and he speaks of "conclude" and "argue" as being performative verbs.[31] These utterances do not change the world in the significant way that I claim characterizes situation-altering utterances, and in any event they would rarely be likely candidates for legal prohibition. The category of utterances I discuss is, accordingly, much narrower than Austin's category of performatives.

The third reason for my choice of terms lies close to the second. As Austin's work progressed, he grew increasingly skeptical of any sharp distinction between performative utterances and "constative" utterances which make ordinary claims to truth; he urged that utterances generally have both a "locutionary" sense or meaning and an "illocutionary" force, and he may ultimately have doubted that there remained a distinctive class of performative utterances.[32] Whether a distinguishable class of situation-altering utterances exists is critical for my endeavor. Contending that, despite significant line-drawing problems, there is a class that is sufficiently distinguishable for social policy and constitutional law, I prefer to employ a term that does not suggest to readers of Austin that the category ultimately fails tests of distinctiveness.

My broadest reason for choosing the term "situation-altering" is to mark the fact that I am neither working directly in the philosophy of language nor claiming that work done there has some neat application to problems in political philosophy and constitutional law. The relationship is more subtle. I draw from efforts in the philosophy of language that have relevance to a principle of free speech, but the central analysis must lie in the domain of political and legal philosophy, and conclusions must be based on reasons that are significant for those fields.[33] The choice of a term other than Austin's signals that I propose something other than simple adoption of distinctions developed in the philosophy of language.

Before I consider particular types of situation-altering utterances, I respond to three general arguments that deny that any viable distinction relevant to social policy exists between situation-altering utterances and assertions of fact and value. The three arguments, which are further explored when I treat particular kinds of situation-altering utterances, are that situation-altering utterances do make claims of fact and value, that explicit assertions of fact and value have performative aspects and alter the world, and that, in any event, given the vague and equivocal uses of language, no line intended for practical application to natural uses of language can be drawn.

In order to assess the distinction between situation-altering utterances and assertions of facts and values, I need to make a little clearer the grounds of the distinction. Any assertion of fact or value, if believed and not merely repetitive of what the listener already thinks he knows,[34] alters the listener's understanding of the world he inhabits. But what such assertions do is to enlighten listeners about what in some sense is already there. That is clearest about facts. If a doctor tells George he has measles, she gives him information about what is already present; her comment does not itself change the actual circumstances of George's life. In ordinary life, people regard values similarly, as something that exists outside themselves which they may appreciate more or less fully. My own view, based partly on religious premises, is that this "naive" perspective is fundamentally accurate,[35] but that is highly controversial. Rehearsing the vast array of positions about fundamental values is not necessary here, so long as it is understood that typically assertions of moral and political values make some claim to universality and appeal to considerations independent of the speaker's statement of the considerations. Thus, to say "You shouldn't torture this prisoner because torture is always wrong" claims something about torturing in general[36] and does not depend for its persuasiveness on its being asserted by the particular speaker.[37] Even if such claims are thought to have no intrinsic objectivity and are regarded only as appeals to sentiments of the listener, they appeal to reasons that in some respect already exist in the listener's universe.[38] Thus, with some roughness, we can speak of assertions of fact and value as making claims about what already exists in the listener's world.[39]

Situation-altering utterances purport to change that world. In most of the examples I discuss they actually alter the normative world,[40] shifting rights or obligations or both. My promise does not merely reflect what I am bound to do; it *generates* an obligation to do something.[41] Understanding that situation-altering utterances are not merely reflections of states of mind is critically important. A promise can create an obligation even if the maker, right from the start, has no intent to keep it;[42] a jury's unanimous verdict of "not guilty" exonerates an accused from legal liability even if some jurors are convinced that guilt has been proved beyond a reasonable doubt and vote as they do only so they can get home to their families.[43]

With this clarification, we are ready to consider arguments to the effect that the basic distinction between situation-altering utterances and assertions of fact and value collapses. First, it may be argued that situation-altering utterances do involve assertions of fact and value, even if they are only implicit. If I say "I will" as a participant in a marriage ceremony, for example, I imply that I am in such a ceremony, that I am not already married, that I accept the idea of marriage and the prospect of a close connection with my new bride. No doubt, these implicit assertions and others may be gleaned from my utterance, but such implicit assertions may be drawn from virtually any behavior—a point I have already made in the discussion of artistic expression. If I participate in a tennis match, I could be said to "imply" that I understand I am in such a match, that I think tennis is worth playing, that I find the rules acceptable. Further, if we focus on opportunities for communication, whatever one wants to communicate about facts and values can typically be asserted much more straightforwardly by means other than a situation-altering utterance. Because the "performative" aspect of most such utterances so entirely dominates any implicit claims of fact and value and because similar implicit claims are present in virtually all noncommunicative behavior, we need not alter our conclusion that a principle of free speech does not apply to situation-altering utterances as it applies to claims of fact and value.

Does this conclusion need to be qualified for situation-altering utterances that have a significant truth dimension? Often authoritative judgments rest on assumptions about facts and values. The umpire's call of "out," the jury's verdict of "guilty," and the faculty's vote of tenure all change the world, but each is grounded on a judgment about what already exists, a judgment that may be right or wrong, sound or unsound.[44] For those sorts of situation-altering utterances, the assertions of fact and value are more central. Although free speech may have little to do with the judgments made, even in some settings where truth discovery is an aim, in other settings it may be relevant. Firing umpires because of inept calls raises no free speech problem, and whatever is worrisome about disciplining jurors for mistaken verdicts has more to do with the integrity of the criminal process than with free speech, but disciplining state university faculty members for unsound votes on tenure would present a serious issue of freedom of speech.[45] When situation-altering utterances have an important truth dimension, proposals for punishment based on the unsoundness of the judgments may raise free speech problems, but, since the criminal law rarely, if ever, imposes liability on this basis, this theoretical possibility is not of much practical importance.

Another kind of situation-altering utterance that makes a significant claim about facts is one that demonstrates intensity of belief. We can imagine Janet marrying Harold to prove that she cares for him deeply, but a much more common example is betting. Sometimes when an initial assertion about facts,

"Barry Goldwater's running mate was William Miller," is disbelieved, the speaker will offer to bet to show how confident she is ("Well, I'll bet you $10 he was"). If no one could ever bet, this particular device to demonstrate one's certainty about a judgment would be eliminated. Still, most offers of bets are not made in order to show this sort of confidence. Since a prohibition on betting would exert only a slight effect on people's ability to express the certainty of their opinions, the betting example does not yield a very strong argument for treating situation-altering utterances like statements of fact, and we can rest with the generalization that a free speech principle does not reach situation-altering utterances.

The second broad argument for the collapse of the distinction between situation-altering utterances and ordinary assertions of fact and value is that assertions have a significant performative aspect and also alter the world. This argument is not telling, both because an important difference remains in the way in which the two kinds of utterances change the environment and because my main thesis about treatment of dominantly situation-altering utterances would not be undermined by a conclusion that assertions often have secondary situation-altering aspects.

Since much of the justification for free speech is that communication alters the listener's understanding of the world, that alone is plainly not sufficient to tie assertions of fact and value to situation-altering utterances. The something more that might be claimed to erode the distinction is that a speaker's *statement* is itself situation-altering, or that it changes the conversational context, or that it triggers more important shifts in what the listener may or must do.

An assertion of fact and value does involve the speaker's stating something. Austin himself suggests that "I state" is performative language,[46] but surely it cannot be critical whether the speaker says "I state" (or "I contend" or "I argue") or merely makes a point directly. Statements have a performative aspect; the world *has changed* to the degree that the speaker has now stated something he had not previously stated in that precise context. But because this change *alone* works no significant change in the environment anyone else inhabits, it hardly touches the distinction between assertions and situation-altering utterances.

A speaker's statement usually does more; it alters the social context for listeners, affecting what would be an apt response. If you say to me, "It certainly is hot today," I may respond in a number of ways: "You're right," "It sure is," "I think it was even hotter yesterday," "Yes, and the humidity makes it very uncomfortable." But what I cannot politely say is "It certainly is hot today." Your statement alters the conversational context in a way that makes inapt what previously would have been an appropriate remark. This much may also be conceded, but subtle changes in the conversational context are still far removed from the significant alterations in the social environment that situation-altering utterances accomplish.

A more substantial matter is the fact that the stating of information can significantly alter what the listener may or must do. With some frequency, the giving of the information effectively renders a listener liable for what he might previously have done freely or gives him a freedom he previously lacked. A striking example involves liability imposed for reckless or negligent behavior.[47] Suppose I plan to engage in action that is risky for reasons I cannot be expected to be aware of; e.g., I am planning to drive my bus on a street that will shortly be inundated by a yet unreported, unexpected, flash flood. If I am then told about the flood and I drive my bus there anyway, I will be liable for injuries to passengers; if I had not been told I would not be liable. It is indeed a pervasive aspect of the law that one's liability depends on what one knows or can be expected to know. Thus, it is obvious that new information, statements of facts, can affect legal liability.

In *this relation* between assertions of fact and normative context, the source of information is fortuitous, and information is given by someone not in order to affect legal or moral liability but to provide the basis for a sensible decision. The information about the flood might have come over the radio or from someone else; what matters for possible liability is the knowledge I obtain from the utterance, not that a particular person told it to me.[48] A situation-altering utterance is quite different; a change in understanding in the listener's mind is not what is critical, what matters is the utterance itself.[49] Whereas the person who tells a driver about the flood aims to affect his action, with any possibility of liability being derivative, the direct purpose of many situation-altering utterances is to change normative relations. Of course, sometimes warnings are given to stubborn persons without much expectation that their behavior will be influenced, and a sign that says, "This pool is dangerous and unguarded," may be designed mainly to relieve the owner of liability for accidents. Such statements do come close to situation-altering utterances,[50] but one cannot generalize from them to the character of typical assertions of fact and value.

On some occasions the making of a statement of fact may more directly require responsive action. When the doctor tells me about my physical condition, I may have an obligation to pay her. Here, the particular doctor's statement of the information is critical, perhaps the last act that gives rise to my obligation to pay. But one of the many things people may be hired to do is to provide information, and what gives rise to the requirement of payment is the performance of requested services. That these happen to involve statements of information does not turn the statements into situation-altering utterances. The nature of "You have measles" is not changed by the doctor's being paid for her diagnosis; the statement would be the same if she were examining a relative for free. That the giving of information engenders a normative obligation does not make the statements themselves like situation-altering utterances.

Even if someone thought that the preceding analysis was unconvincing and that assertions of fact and value generally do have a significant situation-altering character, that would not matter greatly for my thesis about the treatment of situation-altering utterances. Since the primary issue is the reach of the reasons for free speech and since these reasons largely concern assertions of facts and values, whether statements dominantly asserting facts and values are also situation-altering is much less important than whether dominantly situation-altering utterances assert facts and values. Thus, my earlier argument about the nature of dominantly situation-altering utterances is more decisive than these last remarks about assertions.

Finally, I mention a concern about vagueness and equivocation which underlies an argument for the view that in practice no legal distinction should be drawn between statements of fact and value and situation-altering utterances. As Austin stresses about performative utterances generally,[51] the line between situation-altering utterances and statements of beliefs and feelings is by no means sharp in natural language. "I promise" is situation-altering. "It is my present intention to go but I make no commitment" is a statement of fact. "I am intending to go" could, given tone of voice and context, be a promise, a statement of fact, or a kind of commitment weaker than a promise.

The line-drawing worry can best be explored in the context of specific kinds of situation-altering utterances. I do not want to minimize the difficulties. Indeed, sensitivity to them is an essential ingredient of legal approaches responsive to a principle of free speech. Nonetheless, I claim—and believe the concrete examples establish—that there are enough circumstances in which utterances are dominantly and clearly situation-altering to support the distinction and the practical differences in treatment that follow from it.

I now address the major categories of situation-altering utterances that I discuss in the rest of the study.

Agreements and Promises

As my examples have shown, agreements and promises are among the most important situation-altering utterances. These are commonly understood to affect one's moral obligations even if they are not legally binding.

When two people have agreed to do something, each has undertaken an obligation toward the other to perform the task, an obligation that did not exist before the agreement was made. Typically the parties understand the agreement as an intermediate step toward the accomplishment of a goal or goals to which they subscribe. The mutual commitment represented by the agreement serves, in a sense, to lock them on course.[52] If an agreement is to perform a good or a morally indifferent act, virtually everyone assumes that the agreement has genuine moral force. Whether or not an agreement to perform an evil act has genuine moral force, the agreement will usually be viewed by the people who have made it as having such force, and it will also accomplish a change in their expectations and perceived responsibilities. Even if no participant thinks he has put himself under any real moral obligation, the fact of agreement renders each vulnerable to counterresponses for failure to act, responses that would not have been likely to occur or be perceived as appropriate in the absence of agreement.

It is possible that a systematic moral and political theory would include some principle of freedom to agree, the idea being that autonomous individuals should have an opportunity to alter their relations if they choose. That such a principle would include liberty to agree to engage in acts that are independently criminal seems most unlikely, but freedom to agree to do what is otherwise not wrongful, say raise prices, might be covered. In that event, a legislature should restrain itself from attaching criminal or civil liability to agreements to do what is not itself wrong. I am not concerned here to examine the existence and force of any claimed right to agree. If such a principle about free agreement exists, it may be an aspect of or closely tied to freedom of association, but it is not an aspect of a free speech principle. When criminal or civil liability follows from agreement, whether the agreement is to do what is independently wrong or not, no free speech problem is raised.

There is an exception to this conclusion. If the agreement itself concerns speech, then the subject of the agreement makes a free speech principle relevant. Thus if a contract is made between the government and employees of the Central Intelligence Agency stipulating that the employees will submit to the agency for review all their future writings about their work for the agency, that contract certainly does present a serious free speech issue.[53]

In addition to this exception, I need to add a clarification and a qualification to the basic claim that a free speech principle does not reach words of agreement. The clarification is that I am talking only about agreements as commitments to action, not acquiescences in judgment about what is true or desirable; the need to draw such a distinction between commitments to action and acquiescences in judgment raises a worry about equivocation and vagueness and presents a practical problem for applying a free speech principle. The qualification to my claim is that when agreement goes beyond acquiescence in judgment but remains very weak, I believe a principle of free speech does have relevance.

These points are well illustrated by variations on the following example. A group of young men in their last days of high school are deciding whether or not to submit to the draft. Some of the group have firmly decided not to serve, and one of these says, "Let's see how many of you agree with us not to serve." Steven responds with the words, "I agree." Are Steven's words to be taken as a real commitment to the others that he will refuse to submit, or is he merely agreeing in the sense of stating that he presently agrees in principle with that position and presently intends not to serve? In the latter event, his comment is not an agreement in the sense that matters here; rather it is a judgment of value (about the morality of refusing to serve) and a statement of fact (concerning his present intentions). Steven's actual comment may be ambiguous about whether he is genuinely undertaking a commitment to the others. Any regulation of agreements must pay close attention to such possible ambiguities.[54]

Suppose that Steven and the others assembled understand his words as a kind of commitment, but all also understand that, by the time each of them is actually subject to the draft, considerable time will have passed, and most of them will not be in close contact with other members of the group. All really understand that whatever is *undertaken* at this evening's meeting will itself be a very weak influence on choice at the time of decision. Such "agreements" are significantly different from those in which each participant is genuinely depending upon the other participants' performing the actions to which they have all committed themselves. Here, each understands that a genuine change of heart or a failure of courage may lead to shifts in what someone is willing to do, and others will not regard such a shift as a serious betrayal of a commitment. The import of these relatively weak agreements is less sharply demarcated from that of expressions of value and fact than is the import of strong agreements in which the action element powerfully dominates. In Chapter 4 I shall argue in more detail that these *weak agreements* are covered by a free speech principle.

Agreements involve mutual promises, but situations can also be altered by unilateral promises. Since a promise must ordinarily be communicated and is without force if the person for whose benefit it is intended forthrightly refuses to accept the promised benefit or the promise to confer it, even unilateral promises normally involve at least passive acceptance by a recipient. However, the shift in obligations goes in only one direction. The individual who promises creates new social obligations for himself and confers social claims on others. The analysis of how unilateral promises relate to a principle of free speech is the same as for agreements. And similar problems arise about promises to restrict speech, ambiguous language, and weak commitments. Perhaps the line between promises and statements of intention is even thinner in many circumstances than the line between such statements and agreements. One thinks, for example, of political candidates or employers who make "promises" to voters or employees. A sharp restriction on such promises would impair freedom of discourse.

Offers and Permissions

Offers may be of agreement or of some other sort. An agreement requires at least two people. In an ordinary conversation leading to an agreement, one person typically offers to undertake a commitment if the other agrees. Although not all agreements proceed in two definite steps of offering and accepting, most probably do, and clarity about the status of uses of language that permit another party to complete an agreement is important. The completion of the agreement, of course, binds both parties. But what of the offer that ends up being refused or is overtaken by events before the other party has a chance to respond? Is an unsuccessful offer within a principle of free speech?

The offer itself significantly changes normative relations by empowering the recipient to alter the substantive normative obligations of both persons, something he would not otherwise have been in a position to do. When A makes an offer of agreement to B, he thus changes his normative relations with B by conferring a power upon B. A's utterance is situation-altering and outside the reach of a free speech principle.

Not all offers call for eventuation in agreement. I consider below manipulative inducements, indications that one will do something the other person wants if that person performs a certain act, but we might also include as a variety of offer a permission that indicates a favorable disposition toward an act that would usually be wrongful. Suppose A says to B, "Go ahead and hit me, I wish you'd try it." Here, A does not invite agreement; he directly invites action. What A's offer does is eliminate an otherwise applicable normative restraint on B's act. A's comment does more than indicate his present state of mind; it changes the normative situation by rendering B's striking permissible, at least as far as A is concerned.[55]

Orders, Permissions, and Exercises of Official Authority

Situation-altering utterances frequently arise out of relations of authority. If a person with authority directs a subordinate to perform an act, the second person has a new duty to perform. In some settings, usually involving government officials, a directive may actually impose a legal duty to do an act that one previously had no duty to perform. A soldier has a duty to obey orders, and a willful failure to obey a superior's order is itself a crime. Most other officials do not actually commit crimes if they fail to obey, but the receipt of an order can often privilege behavior that would otherwise be illegal.

Even when orders have no legal power, they may have force in social morality and under narrower conventions. In the classroom, for example, a student who is called upon is supposed to respond, and, if he does not, he has failed in one of his responsibilities as a student.

Orders typically include permissions, but sometimes permissions stand alone. A person in authority permits an action that would otherwise be inappropriate: "If you want to take tomorrow off, that will be all right." Like orders, permissions change the normative structure in which the recipient finds himself; like orders, they are situation-altering.

For our purposes the tests of "orders" and "permissions" are not the language in which they are cast but their understood significance within the conventions governing the particular relations of authority. In many organizations, the explicit language of orders is rare, but certain "requests" coming from superiors may be effective directives to act. That is the critical standard for an order: whether what the superior says in reality imposes a new responsibility on a subordinate.

Often some official statement or document is a necessary precondition for other things to occur. When, in verbal or written form, an official utters the necessary words, a person's situation is altered; she may now practice medicine, drive a car, or be put in prison. We may view most exercises of official authority of this type as involving some mix of permissions and orders; certain people are allowed to do things they would otherwise not be allowed to do, such as practice medicine, and other people, typically other officials, are implicitly directed to recognize the privilege and what flows from it. An official's power to utter the words that count as an authoritative act is not covered by the justifications for free speech. If the legislature decides to terminate or sharply curtail particular exercises of authority, no principle of free speech is implicated. However, as I have indicated in respect to verdicts and grants of tenure, exercises of official authority not infrequently have an important truth dimension. Regulation on the basis of whether or not an official judgment has been sound might raise free speech concerns.[56]

Manipulative Inducements and Threats

The analysis of the kinds of utterances I now discuss is a bit more complicated, because in form these utterances are statements of what will happen in the future. Suppose that Tammy says to Victor, "If you hire Judy, I'll stop doing business with you," or "If you hire Jim, I'll increase my business with you." The first statement is a conditional *threat*, the second an *inducement*.[57] Tammy may intend the conversation to lead to an agreement with Victor about whom he will hire. Such an agreement would be outside the range of a free speech principle for reasons already explored, and the earlier analysis of offers bears on the status of the inducement, if not the threat,[58] even if Victor does not agree. But Tammy may not expect an agreement; she may expect to wait and see what Victor does and then to respond accordingly. It is conditional threats and inducements that do not look toward agreement on which I concentrate here.[59] ("Pure," or unconditional, threats are discussed in Chapter 5.)

If Tammy is merely telling Victor what will happen under certain conditions, her utterances are factual predictions and fall within the justifications for free speech. We can see that this is so most clearly by imagining that a mutual friend of Tammy's and Victor's says to Victor, "You know Tammy hates Judy so much that I am pretty sure she will stop doing business with you if you hire Judy." This *warning* conveys information that may be highly relevant for Victor's choice, the kind of particular factual information that is definitely reached by the justifications for free speech. If Tammy herself does the informing, it is hard to see how the value of the speech diminishes. The relevance for Victor is not lessened, and, in the circumstances, making the warning will constitute at least as much of an outlet for Tammy as it would for the mutual friend. If Tammy tells Victor that her natural reaction to possible behavior of his would be negative, then her *warning threat* is covered by the reasons for free speech. The same is obviously also true if Tammy's natural reaction would be to confer some benefit on Victor and she tells him so, what I shall call an *advisory inducement*.[60]

But not all inducements and threats are of this type. Many are *manipulative*. Suppose that Tammy wants Victor not to hire Judy away from Tammy's own firm. If Victor had already hired Judy or if Tammy was certain Victor would hire Judy whatever Tammy said, she would not cease her profitable business with Victor. But she wants to influence Victor's behavior and thinks the threat may work. Similarly, her inducement of increasing business if she wants Jim hired may be something she would not do if she was sure Victor would hire Jim anyway. What is critical in both instances is that the proposed alteration in the normal course of events is a product of Tammy's wish to affect Victor's behavior. I call these *manipulative threats* and *manipulative inducements*.

Most manipulative inducements amount to promises or something close to promises. If Tammy says simply, "I'll increase my business if you hire Jim," she has committed herself to do that if Victor acts accordingly. But not every inducement of this sort is a promise. Tammy *might* carefully say, "It is my present plan to increase my business if you hire Jim." Tammy may still be able to influence Victor's behavior without making a genuine commitment herself.

A person who threatens does not promise the unpleasant consequences. A threat does not involve a commitment *to* the person threatened.[61] Tammy has no obligation to carry out the threat if Victor hires Judy.

A manipulative threat, even though it does not involve a promise and even when it does not seek agreement, is situation-altering. No doubt, Tammy's threat is a statement about future consequences, false if she is bluffing, true if she acts on unsuccessful threats as a matter of "integrity" or to show her strength of will. Still, the consequence she threatens is one she has dreamed up solely to affect Victor's behavior. If she could not communicate her threat, she would see no point in carrying out her threatened behavior. The future facts that she threatens have come into existence only as part of a plan to get Victor to act as she wishes. Only Tammy's actual making of the threat sets in place the conditions for the threatened consequence to occur. The threat, therefore, is not a communication about what will occur in any event; it is a critical element in generating those occurrences. The communication is essentially not an effort to inform, but an effectuation of a change in Victor's environment. It is genuinely situation-altering, and in a significant way.

No doubt, some of the reasons for free expression based on self-disclosure do apply to such utterances, but they probably do not apply with greater force than to agreements, promises, orders, and to many nonverbal actions. Further, this is an instance in which a straightforward disclosure of one's feelings is usually possible; so the special expressive value for being able to threaten is highly marginal.

Thus, I conclude that ordinary manipulative inducements and threats, whether or not they seek agreement, are situation-altering and not within the reach of a principle of free speech. On the other hand, the principle does cover warning threats and advisory inducements. The practicality of drawing this line is discussed in subsequent chapters.

It is worth indicating here, however, that the term "ordinary" manipulative inducements and threats is meant to exclude those which are merely apparent or fleeting or highly emotional. Verbal threats or inducements coupled with demands or requests may amount to less than meets the eye. Apparent threats are often rhetorical, neither seriously intended nor meant to be taken as such. One must cut through the linguistic form of such "threats" to the actual message that the actor intends to convey, often a strong expression of outrage. Even when threats are genuinely made, they sometimes reflect powerful emotions. Many people resort to serious threats when they are upset; the person threatened knows that when heads become cooler the intent to carry out the threat will cease. Of course, the emotions could be otherwise expressed, but constraining spontaneous discourse is undesirable, and the law should not be too strict about proper modes of communication. Free speech is significantly implicated when threats or inducements carry with them powerful expressions of emotion or strong views about the rightness or wrongness of possible behavior by the person threatened or induced.

Weak Imperatives: Requests and Encouragements

I now discuss requests and encouragements, which I group together as "weak imperatives." My claim is that these are reached more significantly by a principle of free speech than situation-altering utterances, but less significantly than assertions of fact and value. Here, I defend placing of them in an intermediate category, explaining how they differ from situation-altering utterances and from assertions of fact and value; and I argue that a principle of free speech has some force with respect to them.

Requests and encouragements are similar to most of the situation-altering utterances I have considered in being designed to produce action by someone else, but simple requests and encouragements, if not accompanied by inducements or threats or made in circumstances where a positive response is obligatory, do not accomplish a significant change in normative relations or other aspects of the listener's environment.

No doubt, if you say to me, "Please shut the door," your request does itself alter the normative situation to a degree, since if I refuse to accede to such a request I show more disrespect for you than if I were aware that you (remaining silent) would like the door shut and I leave it open. But a request's situation-altering element is typically much weaker than the element in agreements, offers, orders by those in authority,[62] and manipulative threats or inducements. With some imperatives, the situation-altering element is completely absent. Suppose a marathon runner has slowed to a walk and a spectator shouts, "Come on, Number 503, don't stop now." The encouragement may affect the runner, but not because she perceives any duty to the spectator.

Like situation-altering utterances, requests and encouragements certainly imply assertions of fact and value. If you say, "Please shut the door," you imply that the door is open, that a human being can shut it, and that you have some reason for wanting it shut. We have already seen that the presence of some implications of fact and value is not alone enough to bring an utterance within a principle of free expression; but since requests and encouragements do not effect a powerful change in normative relations, the influence they exert on an audience may often not be sharply distinct from the influence exerted by expressions of opinion.

Indeed, perhaps the most troubling problem about weak imperatives is determining whether they are really distinguishable for our purposes from assertions of fact and value. This problem can be viewed as raising three separate questions: (1) In their typical instances, are requests and encouragements really like assertions of fact and value? (2) At the margin, are there instances in which a relevant distinction ceases to exist? (3) Are requests and encouragements usually so intertwined with assertions of fact and value that it is pointless practically to distinguish them? These questions, which I address preliminarily here, are the subject of extensive analysis in the context of the treatment in Chapter 6 of criminal statutes punishing encouragements to crime.

In relatively pure form, a request or encouragement differs from an assertion of fact or an assertion of value. The purpose of saying "Please shut the door" or "Kill him, Jack" is not to convey some truth, but to get something done.[63] Whatever information is implied could be communicated more straightforwardly; so the weak imperative plainly differs from ordinary factual statements. The relationship between requests and encouragements and claims of value is more complicated and more controversial. If, as I believe about the claims of moral and political values with which I am most familiar, some form of objective truth is at issue and the truth is subject to human recognition, however imperfect, the truth dimension of claims of value renders them quite distinct from simple imperatives, even if it is also the case that value statements have important prescriptive elements, since the truth concerns what people should do.

A somewhat more serious problem arises if someone contends that value statements are really only prescriptions for action by others. Analysis here depends a bit on precisely what claim is made. A plausible position should acknowledge that people generally, if wrongly, assume an objective dimension to ethical statements;[64] in that event, it is hard to argue that the reasons for free speech do not reach ethical statements. Because one central aspect of those reasons is the need to protect claims about what can truly be said, the reasons reach sincere mistaken claims of objective values. Suppose, instead, the claim about the prescriptivity of value statements is that, upon modest reflection, everyone would see that prescriptions are all that ethical statements really amount to. Even on this view, a substantial difference exists between assertions of value and simple imperatives. As I suggested earlier, a value statement typically invokes some universal claim, appeals to the considered judgment of the listener, does not purport to *alter* the sorts of factors that are relevant to decision, and does not rest its force on happening to be asserted by a particular speaker. Both simple requests and encouragements are quite different. They do not appeal to preexisting factors relevant to decision making. The force of a request is to introduce a new element, and a simple encouragement injects the force of the speaker's personality toward a particular result. Neither involves a universal claim or appeals to a considered judgment,[65] and their force depends on their being uttered by the speaker. Perhaps it is an illustration of a number of these points that whatever claims of value are put to the listener *could* have been discovered by him in a book by an author writing in a different place and time.[66] It takes a great strain to imagine a genuine request or encouragement coming from such a source.[67] As I indicated in Chapter 2, the nature of moral and other value assertions renders them subject to the reasons for free speech, whether or not such assertions are or are believed to be about objective truth. Simple imperatives are much less subject to those reasons.

If typical weak imperatives are different from typical assertions of fact and value, nevertheless in practice many assertions of fact and value function like imperatives, and explicit assertions of fact and value are often intertwined with imperatives.

Evaluations are often employed to produce specific action, and in ordinary usage there may be no practical difference between "Joan, please shut the door," and "Joan, it would be good to have the door shut."[68] Even the factual assertion, "The breeze from the open door is making me cold," may in context amount to a request to shut the door.[69] In Chapter 6, I will investigate in more detail the implications of a free speech principle for assertions of fact and value that slide toward simple imperatives.

The common intertwining of assertions of fact and value with requests and encouragements is also significant. Requests, and especially encouragements, are often accompanied by explicit evaluations or statements of fact. Even if in theory one can disentangle imperative elements from assertions of fact and value, it is doubtful that speakers should have to draw that fine line. Perhaps speakers can communicate their beliefs without urging specific actions, but broad ideas are illuminated by specific applications. When the speaker tells young men definitely not to volunteer for the armed services because the country is fighting an immoral war, she has shown with clarity the practical consequences of her moral beliefs and she has evidenced their intensity. She might be able to indicate those specific consequences and her own intensity while falling short of actually encouraging a course of behavior, for example, by saying that she would have an utter abhorrence of participating in the killing of innocent persons and that she regards joining the army as morally reprehensible. But pushing people to communicate in this manner creates a twofold difficulty. As the speaker comes closer to communicating all the beliefs about fact and value that would be contained in an encouragement, she comes closer to making that encouragement. And speech that matters is less free if ordinary persons must pick their words with exquisite care. If communications had to meet strict standards of correct formulation, people would be hesitant to speak their minds, and what they did say would be less expressive of their personalities, less valuable as emotional release, than the utterances that would come to them more naturally in the absence of constraint. Because requests and encouragements are designed to induce action and because much of what they impliedly communicate about facts and values could be otherwise communicated, they lie at the margin of a principle of free speech, but such a principle cannot disregard them altogether. Much of Chapters 6 and 15 is devoted to working out the implications of these generalities in the context of criminal solicitation statutes.

The general discussion in this chapter about the reach of a principle of free expression is now complete. This discussion underlies both the analysis in Part II of grounds of criminal liability and free speech and the constitutional analysis that occupies Part III.

Notes

1. See F. Schauer, *Free Speech: A Philosophical Enquiry* 139 (Cambridge, Cambridge University Press 1982). One will be particularly likely to take this view if one thinks that the nonconsequential justifications of free speech make it a moral or liberal political right and thinks, further, that denials of rights are more serious wrongs than failures to promote the general welfare.

2. I refer here to standards of sufficient clarity to permit consistency over time and guidance to lower courts and officials. I do not mean at this point to make any controversial claim about just how "principled" constitutional decisions should be. General standards for constitutional adjudication are discussed in Chapter 10.

3. Some may doubt that the last of these three assertions truly involves a factual proposition, on the ground that we have no way of telling whether it is true. The assertion is not evident nonsense; we have some vague idea of what it might mean for our personalities to survive our deaths. The statement, thus, qualifies as factual even if not subject to any verification, but there is, in any event, at least the possibility of verification after death, and presently available evidences and arguments, though inconclusive, do bear on the likelihood that the assertion is true.

4. For example, about the state of the engine, degree of comfort, etc. See generally R. Hare, *The Language of Morals* 112–13 (New York, Oxford University Press 1964).

5. T. Scanlon, "A Theory of Freedom of Expression," 1 *Philosophy & Public Affairs* 204, 206 (1972).

6. S. Shiffrin, "Defamatory Non-media Speech and First Amendment Methodology," 25 *University of California in Los Angeles Law Review* 915, 932 (1978).

7. For an illuminating discussion of self-communication and private communication and why they warrant copyright protection, see J. Newman, "Copyright Law and the Protection of Privacy," 12 *Colum.-VLA Journal of Law & the Arts* 459 (1988).

8. Lest it be supposed that government is incapable of punishing thoughts alone, I

should note that by lie detectors, truth serums, or torture governments can learn what people believe and punish them for it. In prosecutions for heresy, it was not a defense that one had never expressed to others one's heretical beliefs.

9. See John Searle's discussion of indirect speech acts. J. Searle, *Expression and Meaning* 30-48 (Cambridge, Cambridge University Press 1979).

10. Difficulties in distinguishing truth from falsity, of course, pose another line-drawing problem. That problem is addressed in concrete contexts in Chapters 7 and 18.

11. Even if the emotional-outlet reason has a much broader reach than speech, it could still *help* to justify special protection for speech when other reasons for special protection apply.

12. As Melville Nimmer, *Nimmer on Freedom of Speech* 2-45 (New York, Matthew Bender Co. 1984), has said, "When I express ideas which I do not believe to be true, I am not in any real sense expressing my *self*, and abridgement of such expression is not abridgement of self-fulfillment." However, it must be recognized that a lie about what one thinks (e.g., that *X* is a cheater) can sometimes express what one truly feels (hatred of *X*).

13. Many of these instances may lie at the borderline of hyperbole, since what the speaker says may not be taken to be meant as literally true.

14. See Schauer, note 1 supra, at 109-10.

15. Much of this art contains symbols whose significance was widely understood.

16. I believe it was Plato who thought that flute music was too exciting for people, but we do not imagine many modern governments suppressing instrumental music on that basis. Of course, loud instrumental music may be regulated to protect others from being exposed to offensive noise.

17. Of course, suicides are sometimes accompanied by written messages, and sometimes suicide is committed largely to express a strong message to particular individuals, but often a person committing suicide is not consciously focusing on the effect of the act on others.

18. See Nimmer, note 12 supra, at 1-51; Schauer, note 1 supra, at 110-11.

19. See Nimmer, note 12 supra, at 3-44, 45.

20. J. Finnis, "'Reason and Passion': The Constitutional Dialectic of Free Speech and Obscenity," 116 *University of Pennsylvania Law Review* 222, 232 (1967). See also H. Kalven, "The Metaphysics of the Law of Obscenity," 1960 *Supreme Court Review* 1, 16 ("beauty has constitutional status too").

21. Finnis, note 20 supra, at 236.

22. See M. Redish, *Freedom of Expression* 57 (Charlottesville, Va., The Michie Co. 1984).

23. If the percentage of instances of communication is very slight, the principle would have little bearing.

24. See J. L. Austin, "Performative Utterances," in *Philosophical Papers* 233 (3d ed., J. Urmson and G. Warnock eds., Oxford, Oxford University Press 1979).

25. When games are played in formal settings and the rules are official, the law may stand behind them in some remote way. If, for example, it were contested in court which of two professional teams actually won a game or if a defendant who had been called a "cheater" sued for libel, the court would acknowledge the importance of the judgments of designated referees. Those judgments (or the review of them by higher officials within the sport) would ordinarily be final, but, in answer to a claim that all relevant officials had blatantly misapplied the rules for some ulterior purpose, a court might ask whether the officials had attempted to apply the rules in good faith or whether the officials' interpretation of the rules deviated from the bounds of reasonableness. To that limited extent, the court would need to pay attention to the rules that govern the playing of the game, just as in other cases it might be called upon to pay attention to the rules of a private club.

26. In an illuminating "Taxonomy of Illocutionary Acts," John Searle treats as "declarations" speech acts in which the state of affairs represented by a proposition is brought about by utterance of the proposition. See Searle, note 9 supra, at 16–18.

27. In Searle's categorization (see note 9 supra, at 14), these utterances count as commissives. As the signing of a legal contract shows, a commitment to act in a certain way in the future can alter one's immediate status under conventional standards.

28. I do not mean to imply that the obligation that flows from a promise is *only* one of social morality. To the contrary, I assume that, given the desirable practice of promising, a promise ordinarily also generates an obligation according to sound principles of critical morality.

29. See generally J. L. Austin, *How to Do Things with Words* (2d ed., J. O. Urmson and M. Sbisà eds., Cambridge, Mass., Harvard University Press 1975); Austin, *Performative Utterances*, note 24 supra. See also M. Furberg, *Saying and Meaning: A Main Theme in J. L. Austin's Philosophy* (Oxford, Basil Blackwell & Mott, Ltd. 1971); J. Searle, *Speech Acts: An Essay in the Philosophy of Language* (London, Cambridge University Press 1969); P. Strawson, *Logico-Linguistic Papers* 149–69 (London, Methuen & Co. 1971); H. Grice, *Logic and Conversation* (unpublished lecture notes from William James Lectures at Harvard 1967).

30. See Austin, *How to Do Things with Words*, note 29 supra, at 79.

31. Id. at 85.

32. The later chapters of *How to Do Things with Words*, adopted from the notes Austin used for a series of William James Lectures at Harvard and from his notes for Oxford lectures, reflect these doubts. See generally G. Warnock, "Some Types of Performative Utterance," in Isaiah Berlin et al., eds., *Essays on J. L. Austin* 69 (London, Oxford University Press, Clarendon Press 1973).

33. For such an endeavor in respect to commercial speech and the First Amendment, see D. Farber, "Commercial Speech and First Amendment Theory," 74 *Northwestern University Law Review* 372 (1979).

34. Of course, sometimes hearing what we already believe increases our confidence in the truth of the proposition asserted.

35. I also believe that rational consideration can settle many, though by no means all, questions of value.

36. This aspect of universality would be present even if it were said only that torturing was wrong under certain specified conditions.

37. I do not foreclose the possibility that the listener properly assigns some weight to the general moral sense of the speaker. It is rational to give some deference to "moral authorities," who have proved their good moral judgment in the past. Nevertheless, the statement quoted in the text, like most moral claims, does not itself invoke any special moral authority of the speaker.

38. An appeal to a reason the listener has not yet accepted will almost certainly be cast in terms of other, deeper, reasons that the listener does accept. If it is said that moral arguments are merely rhetorical devices to get people to engage in particular actions, the short answer is that they are not so regarded by listeners or by speakers.

39. I mean to include here predictions about future events, which, except perhaps in the instance of predicted miracles, are based on conclusions about what exists at present.

40. For formal changes of names and the christening of ships, the only "normative" change is the relatively insignificant one of what it is proper to call someone or something. Much more significant exceptions for my purposes are some inducements and threats, discussed later in the chapter.

41. If someone promises to do what he is already morally bound to do, the promise creates a new *source* of moral duty and may strengthen the overall duty.

42. See Austin, *How to Do Things with Words*, note 29 supra, at 9–11.

43. What has occurred if one is not even aware of what one is doing is more complicated and will depend on convention. It is clear legally that one can make a contract if one is really "joking" but everyone else reasonably thinks one is serious. Whether someone has *really* promised if there is no intent to promise is more doubtful, though morality, as well as law, would impose some responsibilities arising from the reasonable reliance of others.

44. See id. at 140–45, showing how what Austin calls "verdictives" slide toward truth or falsity, and arguing that with respect to many matters something more subtle than a simple judgment of truth or falsity is needed. See also Searle's observation that the class of "declarations" overlaps with the class of "assertives" and that the assertive aspect of an utterance claims something about the world as it exists, whereas the declarative aspect alters the status referred to by successful performance of the declaration. Searle, note 9 supra, at 17–20.

45. Although in this book I concentrate on government suppression, I assume that principles of free speech can also have application to the actions of private organizations, including private universities.

46. Austin, *How to Do Things with Words*, note 29 supra, at 91.

47. Action is "reckless" if the actor is aware of the risk that makes the action unwarranted; action is "negligent" if a reasonable person would have been aware of the unwarranted risk.

48. Of course the reliability of a source matters. And certain information, coming from a person in authority, may be tantamount to an instruction not to act in a particular way.

49. It is true but not relevant here that, to be effective, most situation-altering utterances do have to be understood by the person to whom they are addressed. See id. at 116–17.

50. "Swim at your own risk" would be a closely analogous message that would be genuinely situation-altering if by that message an owner could shift responsibility to the swimmer.

51. See id. at 32–33, 79.

52. Sometimes an agreement may be little more than a coordination of future plans, e.g., to play tennis, with each party having the option to withdraw for virtually any reason. What each person has really committed himself to do may be to show up at the agreed-upon time *or* give his partner sufficient advance warning that he will not be there.

53. See *Snepp* v. *United States*, 444 U.S. 507 (1980).

54. The worry is less serious if the reasons for suppression are so strong that they could override the ordinary free speech reasons to protect statements of intention, but, even in that event, unless such statements are themselves explicitly made criminal, there remains a concern with giving people fair warning about what kinds of "agreements" are criminal.

55. There is a somewhat tricky problem. It might be argued that, as far as A is concerned, A's state of mind counts more than his permission. If A wants B to try to hit him, perhaps B's attempt is not wrongful even if A never gives the permission. This conclusion is probably incorrect. Even if A wants to be hit, he may feel that B's doing so is taking an inappropriate, wrongful, liberty. In any event, as far as other people are concerned, it is A's actual giving of permission that matters, if it is thought that the normative constraint against striking can be eliminated or weakened. (One who thought that permission only mitigates the wrong would regard permission as weakening but not eliminating the normative constraint.)

56. A legislature's sharp curtailment of official power to act, based on previous unhappiness with the views that previous exercises of power had reflected, might also implicate a free speech principle.

57. Roughly, an inducement represents a proposed positive alteration in the normal course of events, a threat a negative alteration. The exact line between them, an intriguing subject in its own right, is not critical for our purposes.

58. There are two complexities here. First, there may be a question whether Tammy's inducement reaches a stage at which an agreement can be closed by Victor's acquiescence. Perhaps what is present so far is only an "invitation" to Victor to make an offer, which will then be closed by Tammy's acquiescence. In Chapter 4 I explore this subtlety concerning preliminary remarks that look toward eventual agreement but do not yet constitute an offer. In the law of contracts, deciding whether an offer has actually been made can sometimes be very important.

The second complexity is the asymmetry between the threat and the inducement in respect to whether Tammy is making an offer of agreement. The ordinary nature of an offer is that it allows the recipient by his acceptance to bind the person making the offer. If Tammy wants an agreement and is willing to increase her business with Victor, then Victor by agreeing to hire Jim obtains Tammy's commitment to increase business. The situation is murkier with the threat. If Tammy is clearly committing herself to *continue* her present business with Victor if Victor does not hire Judy, then her threat does afford Victor an opportunity to ensure a new commitment from Tammy. It may strain ordinary language a bit to call this an "offer," but it has the situation-altering character of an offer. But suppose Tammy's position is this: "If you hire Judy, I'll stop doing business with you. If you agree not to hire her this source of concern will be eliminated, but I make no commitment about where my business will go in the future." Now in a sense Victor "gets" nothing from his agreement, but he may still be willing to agree, in order to forestall Tammy's anger, and he may be pretty confident that Tammy will continue her business with him if this difficulty is overcome. On this version, Tammy's threat does not commit her to anything; so it lacks the situation-altering quality of an ordinary offer. Exactly how best to characterize a conditional threat when it looks to agreement is not of great practical importance, given my conclusion, in the text following, that even most threats that do not look to agreement are outside a principle of free speech. I shall return to these complexities in Chapter 5 in discussing the criminalization of threats.

59. It is fairly frequent for the person making a threat or inducement to hope that he will achieve *either* agreement followed by the desired action *or* the desired action in the absence of agreement.

60. Interestingly, we have no word in English that parallels the word "warning" for situations in which one person informs another of benefits that will occur if he acts in a certain way. I choose the term "advisory inducement" to emphasize that one person is telling another what would happen in the natural course of events.

61. Except that often a commitment is made *not* to impose the unpleasant consequences if the victim of the threat complies, a subject to which I return in Chapter 5.

62. There may be cooperative endeavors in which requests are easily filled and where it is understood that everyone will fill everyone else's requests. In that setting a request by an equal may have a situation-altering force like an order. If someone at the dinner table asks me to please pass the salt and if the salt is within my reach and no one else's, I really have no option.

63. See Searle, note 9 supra, at 13–14, discussing "directives" as aimed at getting the world to fit one's words.

64. I think that John Mackie, in *Ethics: Inventing Right and Wrong* (New York, Penguin 1977), shows convincingly that people do make that supposition.

65. However, a request or encouragement may be made in circumstances where one expects a considered judgment; in that event the force of the request or encouragement may be to carry some independent weight in how the judgment is made.

66. Of course, it may be extremely unlikely that the value claims could be tailored to a precise factual situation faced by the listener.

67. An author might use the rhetorical device of pleading with readers, "Please, don't ever lie," or might give them encouragement to "Be strong in the face of evil," but I do not count these as true requests and encouragements.

68. See generally Searle, note 9 supra.

69. This statement does differ from a simple imperative in explaining why I want the door shut, but sometimes the explanation will be so obvious that the simple imperative will convey it equally well, though implicitly.

II
CRIMES AND COMMUNICATIONS

4

Agreements, Offers, Orders, and Criminal Implementation

This and the next five chapters explore the relationship between a political principle of free speech and bases for criminal punishment. Though I do not systematically explore civil liability for expression, free speech considerations constrain the imposition of such liability as well as criminal penalties. Much that I say in relation to the law of crimes also applies to possible decisions by legislatures or courts[1] to make people pay civil damages or subject them to injunctions. Occasionally, I comment specifically on civil liability, and for a few subjects that is the main practical relevance of my analysis.

The discussions in this part of the book mainly follow this pattern. I first introduce a particular basis for criminal liability. If the liability is of a standard sort, found in most common law jurisdictions, I usually provide the relevant language of the Model Penal Code. Its formulations, many of which are followed in a large number of American jurisdictions,[2] often distill in a somewhat more systematic way grounds that previously controlled under imprecise statutes that were interpreted and applied in accord with common law notions of criminal liability.[3] After indicating what the law provides, I suggest the reasons why criminal liability is imposed. This explication is brief when the reasons are obvious. I then consider reasons for not imposing liability or for limiting liability, roughly distinguishing reasons that arise out of general concerns about criminal sanctions from reasons that peculiarly concern free speech. I ask whether a legislature considering a form of liability should worry about free speech, and, if so, what responses to that worry are reasonable. To illustrate points, I occasionally mention the facts of constitutional law cases during these discussions. A systematic treatment of constitutional principles is reserved for Part III, but much of what is said in this part bears closely on the ensuing constitutional analysis.

This chapter considers agreements to commit crimes, offers, which usually but not always seek agreement, orders, and communications as means of implementing crimes. For the most part, the conclusions drawn here, in contrast to those of succeeding chapters, are fairly straightforward, and the analysis is correspondingly less detailed.

Agreements to Commit Crimes

Agreeing to commit a crime is itself a crime, the crime of *conspiracy*. Under the old common law, criminal conspiracy also included agreeing to perform undesirable acts that were not themselves criminal, but the modern tendency is to limit the ordinary crime of conspiracy to agreements to perform criminal acts, with special criminal liability for a few other agreements, like agreements to set prices. Under the Model Penal Code, a person is guilty of conspiracy with someone else if, with the purpose of promoting or facilitating the commission of a crime, he agrees that one or both of them will commit the crime or agrees to aid in the planning or commission of the crime.[4]

Conspiracy is a separate crime, usually somewhat less serious than the substantive crime the participants have agreed to commit. If the crime is committed as planned, conspirators who have not directly performed the criminal acts are commonly guilty as *accessories*, with the same liability as those who perform the acts. In some jurisdictions, conspirators are automatically liable for substantive offenses committed pursuant to the conspiracy; the Model Code has a separate formulation for accessorial liability[5] which is more limited in its coverage and which does not catch remote conspirators who have made no contribution to the commission of particular crimes. In many jurisdictions, a person may not be convicted of a conspiracy unless there has been an overt act in pursuance of the conspiracy; the Model Code continues that requirement except for the two most serious categories of felonies.[6]

In reaching back to the stage of initial agreement, plus a single, possibly insignificant, overt act, conspiracy law contrasts strikingly with the law of *attempt*, which governs the commencement of liability for a person acting alone. Suppose I intend to burglarize an apartment. I tell friends and make preparations, including renting a car for the evening. Although standards among states vary, I do not actually commit any crime until I am a long way toward entering the apartment.[7] Doubts that one can reliably tell when a crime is seriously intended largely underlie this traditional principle that criminal liability does not attach at early stages of preparation. Sometimes it will not be clear whether activities amount to preparations for a crime, but even when a person is definitely preparing to commit a crime, he may not yet have decided to go through with it (as a child may walk out to the edge of the diving board before she decides whether to jump). Behind these doubts about intent lies the idea that persons who may yet decide to withdraw should not be treated as criminal. Some people who have definitely decided to commit crimes change their minds before performing the final act (as a child confidently intending to jump may reconsider when she gazes at the water from the end of the board).

There is a threefold explanation why conspiracy liability long precedes the point at which behavior would amount to an "attempt" to commit the substantive crime. The existence of an agreement is thought largely to undercut worries about evidence of criminal intent. The agreement also shows that the purposes of participants are firmly fixed and makes changes of mind less likely. In addition, organized criminal activity is believed to generate particularly great harms. Since

why criminalize conspiracy

agreements to commit crimes are widely understood to pose a serious danger, the punishment of such agreements seems apt.

There are many concerns about conspiracy liability, but most of these have little to do with freedom of speech. The idea that conspiracy liability reaches back too far into the stages of preparation is occasionally heard, but the main objection to modern use of conspiracy charges is that the prosecutor gains unfair procedural advantages, being able, among other things, to use the acts and words of one conspirator against another.[8]

Agreements to commit garden-variety crimes have never been supposed to raise free speech problems. Putting aside unusual situations, mostly in respect to price fixing or other commercial activities, in which "agreement" may be discerned in conscious parallel behavior,[9] agreements to commit crimes are, like other agreements, based on verbal and written utterances. Existing law and the commentary that surrounds it implicitly assume what I urged in the last chapter: that words of agreement representing serious undertakings to commit ordinary crimes are not the sorts of communication to which a principle of freedom of speech applies.

Two "free speech" concerns about "agreements" raised in Chapter 3 do have relevance for conspiracy liability. One concern is that words of "agreement" may be ambiguous as to whether the speaker is just acquiescing in a point of view—in which case his utterance is covered by a principle of free speech—or is genuinely undertaking a commitment to act. For ordinary conspiracy liability, either statutory language or judicial interpretation should require clear evidence of a serious commitment to act.[10]

The second concern involves what I have called "weak agreements." Recall that I posited an "agreement" by a group of young men not to submit to the draft. Even if the undertaking to act is clear—because the men have signed a statement promising not to submit—the sense of commitment to other signers may be relatively weak, and the signers may not be *depending* on each other. Since each signer has the purpose of promoting illegal draft resistance and agrees to engage in prohibited conduct, the agreement is fairly clearly covered by language like that of the Model Penal Code, but, at least in the context of this example, that result is subject to challenge. As I explained in Chapter 3, punishing such agreements, which are not sharply demarcated from assertions of fact and value, impinges to a degree on a principle of free speech. It may be argued that the evil of the agreement is great enough to warrant punishment anyway, but, when the crime is to be committed openly and does not injure other persons, the government could reasonably wait and rely on punishment of those who actually commit the substantive crime.

A legislature adopting a conspiracy provision cannot focus carefully on each substantive crime and the various ways in which it might be committed; given the need of the legislature to generalize, we can perceive three possible approaches to the concern about weak agreements. The first approach would limit the legal scope of "conspiracy" generally to situations in which participants in the agreement have common plans or genuinely rely on each other's acts. Such an approach would exclude the "weak agreement" of these young men intending to engage in draft refusal at a later time. For their agreement, not imposing criminal penalties may be desirable, but this general approach would also render noncriminal a "weak agreement" by the same young men each to kill a member of a minority group in secret. Perhaps "weak agreements" to commit such serious crimes are never made, or are highly unlikely to be acted upon if they ever occur, but immunizing such agreements does give pause. The second approach is to leave the law as it stands, on the theory that weak agreements to commit openly crimes that lack victims are unusual and rarely prosecuted and that legitimate concerns about free speech can comfortably be left to the exercise of prosecutorial discretion.[11] The third approach is to add further complexity to the law of conspiracy by providing that, for open and victimless crimes, but only for those crimes, a common plan or genuine reliance is required for conspiracy liability.

If one focuses on legislative choice, each of these resolutions has a good bit to commend it. Though I favor the last approach, I recognize that it may introduce an undesirable level of refinement to deal with a problem of limited practical significance.

This completes my discussion of conspiracy in this chapter. I have not yet treated conspiracies to commit crimes in which the main element of the crime agreed upon is communication. That problem is postponed until after discussion of major crimes involving communication; it receives brief consideration in Chapter 6 and is the subject of Chapter 20 in Part III.

Offers of Agreement and Other Offers

Describing the criminal law relating to offers is complicated by the variety of kinds of offers that are prohibited. In Chapter 3, I identified offers to enter agreements, offers that remove normative constraints, and offers that induce action without any intermediary agreement.

Offers in all three categories can amount to *criminal solicitation*, which American jurisdictions make a crime, usually, like conspiracy, graded lower than the underlying substantive offense. Under the Model Penal Code, a person is guilty of solicitation if he "commands, encourages or requests" another person to commit a crime or engage in conduct that would establish his complicity in a crime.[12] Since seeking to enter a conspiracy with someone encourages that person to engage in criminal conduct, an offer to agree to commit a crime is a form of criminal solicitation. Offers not meant to eventuate in agreement also constitute solicitations. If Alan invites Betty to commit a criminal act against himself, say putting a fatal drug in his drink, he encourages a crime. Similarly, Alan is guilty of solicitation if he offers to confer a benefit on Betty for performing a criminal act against someone else: "I'll give you $500 if you burn Peter's house."

In addition to the general crime of criminal solicitation, some specific crimes involve offers that may or may not be meant to lead to agreements. Most notably perhaps, the crime of bribery covers someone who "offers" to give a government official money as a consideration for a decision, and it also covers a government official who "solicits" such consideration.[13] What the bribed government official decides usually would not, standing alone, be criminal; the underlying substantive wrong is the official's deciding under the influence of the bribe.

For crimes generally,[14] whether the law should reach back prior to an agreement or any act moving toward a crime and subject people to liability for unsuccessfully trying to induce others to act criminally, is a serious question, but this question does not often concern freedom of speech. As I suggested in the last chapter, when someone seriously offers to make a strong agreement or waives a normative constraint in his favor (e.g., as against killing him), the offer is situation-altering; it is not a use of language that the principle of free speech covers. Of course, what I have said about clear evidence of real agreement and agreement that looks to genuine mutual reliance, applies to offers of agreement; no offer should be punished unless the agreement that might follow from it should be punished.

Analysis of offers that do not look toward agreement and do not waive constraints is a bit trickier. But, in ordinary circumstances, double grounds will exist for considering an offer to be a situation-altering utterance outside the reach of a principle of free speech. Typically, an offer will amount to a promise, or at least some sort of commitment, to pay the money or confer whatever other benefit one has proposed as an exchange for the criminal act one hopes the listener will perform. Such commitments are situation-altering. Secondly, the vast majority of offers that are made criminal involve manipulative inducements. The person who offers to benefit someone else who commits a crime or decides a dispute in a desired way would not confer the benefit if he was assured that what he wanted to happen would happen without his inducement. When a "proposed benefit" is created only to produce the result wished for, the announcement of the benefit by the person who has created the benefit does not fall within a principle of freedom of speech.[15]

One can imagine "offers" that are not promises and do not involve manipulation in the sense I have discussed, and free speech considerations do bear on these. Suppose that Rachel has been seriously insulted by Sam and that a mutual acquaintance, Tom, has asked Rachel to hire him (Tom) for her advertising agency. Rachel says she doubts that she needs someone but will probably hire Tom if he beats up Sam. Now, were it true that Rachel, in any event, would be so pleased if Tom attacked Sam that she would gladly hire Tom out of gratitude, she is *only* informing Tom of her "natural reaction" to a possible assault by him on Sam. She merely makes a factual prediction of what would occur even without her communication to Tom. Having this knowledge in advance might influence what Tom will do, but Rachel's reporting of what her "natural reaction" will be falls broadly within the justifications for free speech. (This claim is further examined in Chapter 5, on Threats.)

What relevance does this slender class of "advisory inducements" involving natural reactions have for the treatment of offers under the criminal law? Although an argument *might* be made that such reporting of what will occur anyway is not really an "encouragement" or an "offer" within the meaning of relevant statutory sections, the present criminality of statements about benefits to be conferred almost certainly does not turn on whether the inducements are manipulative or simply reports of what would happen anyway. And concerns about honest statements of likely future behavior are probably not sufficient to warrant legislative re-examination of what offers are made criminal. Powerful public reasons exist to discourage all inducements of criminal behavior and of choices by officials made to secure extrinsic benefits for themselves. The effect of an inducement on the potential actor does not depend on the state of mind of the speaker about what he or she would do anyway. The expressive interest is slight in letting someone say ahead of time, and to the very person whose behavior might be affected, how he would react positively to criminal actions or to an official decision in his favor. Further, only very rarely will tangible inducements to people to commit crimes or to officials to decide in the desired way be neither promissory nor manipulative. Outsiders will often find it virtually impossible to identify these "natural" nonpromissory inducements. Legislatures sensibly proceed on the assumption that the great majority of offers of tangible benefits are promissory or manipulative or both; difficulties in identifying particular counter-instances combine with substantial reasons for punishing even the counter-instances to counsel against any exemption for "advisory inducements."

What I have said thus far about offers leaves one narrow set of circumstances to be examined. We can imagine a legislature deciding that a certain kind of undesirable act, say maiming oneself or engaging in sex in return for money, should not be the subject of criminal punishment, but that such acts should be kept to a minimum by forbidding agreements or offers to strangers to perform such acts. As a general matter it may be unwise to forbid people from making offers to encourage acts that are legal, but, if my claim is correct that most of the offers I have discussed do not count as "speech," a principle of free speech imposes no significant restraint on such prohibitions. In this setting, where the act encouraged is not criminal, it is arguable that the rare genuine advisory inducements should be excepted from criminal penalties. However, as the treatment of warning threats in Chapter 5 indicates, probably the line between manipulative and advisory inducements is too elusive of practical administration to be made directly in a statutory formulation.

Orders (and Related Imperatives)

Orders to commit crimes are undoubtedly one form of criminal solicitation, and the Model Code language explicitly reaches someone who commands another to commit a crime.[16] Chapter 3 has explained that orders are situation-altering because directions from a person in authority to a subordinate change the normative context for the subordinate. Even if an employee knows that what her manager has ordered her to do is a crime, say the mislabeling of products, she is aware that, according to informal norms governing the firm, she may be expected to comply and that she may be in for trouble from the manager if she does not comply. Orders clearly belong among whatever encouragements to crime are forbidden; the person who issues a serious order to a subordinate has at least as much responsibility as the subordinate for the resulting crime the subordinate performs, and usually the supervisor bears more responsibility.

Since someone who orders another is not engaging in expression, but is attempting to have his way through power or authority, a political principle of freedom of speech is no impediment to forbidding undesirable orders. And this conclusion holds even if the order is to do an undesirable act that could constitutionally be made criminal but has not been. The significance of free speech comes into play only in ensuring that a communication is a genuine and serious order (or some other utterance not reached by free speech) rather than a hyperbolic expression about facts and values.

Two troublesome borderline cases are "requests" from supervisors and "orders" unrelated to the domain of authority. If a supervisor suggests that an employee commit a crime at work, what matters is not the supervisor's exact language, but whether the employee conceives herself and reasonably conceives herself to be under some duty or strong pressure to comply. If the supervisor demands a crime unrelated to work, that should not be viewed as an "order," but if the employee reasonably expects penalties at work if she fails to act, the supervisor's utterance is a threat of the sort dealt with in the following chapter.

Implementation and Nonpurposeful Assistance

Words are often used in the commission of crimes that do not themselves necessarily or even usually[17] involve communication. Rather infrequently such crimes are committed by means of a communicative act alone. If on a dark path a woman holding the only flashlight tells her companion to "step to the right," knowing that the abyss lies in that direction, then she has committed murder when her companion plummets to his death, although all she has done is speak. Her liability would be the same if instead of uttering an imperative she had said, "The solid ground is on your right," a (false) statement of fact.

Much more commonly than people commit noncommunicative crimes "purely" by communication, they cooperate, by talking, in the commission of crimes that involve noncommunicative acts. If A and B have agreed to burglarize an apartment, B may stand as a lookout, and B's only act (other than standing in the required location) may be to tell A whether someone is coming. If A plans to steal money from a safe in a bank, B's only participation may be to provide A with the combination to the safe. B's participation in both crimes involves making assertions about particular facts.

The reasons of ordinary penal policy for covering communicative efforts to carry out ordinary crimes are obvious, and the criminal law sensibly draws no distinction between communicative and other acts. Although assertions of fact generally fall within a principle of freedom of speech, what these sorts of factual statements contribute to the general understanding of listeners is minimal, and the justifications for free speech that apply to speakers do not reach communications that are simply means to get a crime successfully committed. The relevance of free speech is so slight in respect to such highly specific information related to an immediate practical purpose that it can be disregarded here.

If the means of committing a crime were so complex that the main actors had to learn a great deal before they could accomplish it,[18] their instruction might include more of relevance for freedom of speech, but these instances are rare, and, when they occur, the reasons for prohibition outweigh the speech interests.[19] A legislature can simply assume that whatever communications of fact are made exclusively to implement a particular criminal purpose should be treated like any other participation in a criminal endeavor.

The issue of the outer edges of liability for helping criminal endeavors raises a more interesting problem, on which a principle of free speech has bearing when the help consists of providing information. I have thus far discussed only cases where the person who helps others shares their criminal purpose. One approach is to limit accessorial liability to such people;[20] another possibility is to extend that liability to persons who think what they do will in fact aid a criminal endeavor though that is not their purpose; a third approach, followed in some recent American codes, is to create a separate, lesser crime for those who provide such assistance to serious crimes.[21]

If either the second or third alternative is adopted, determinations must be made how far to extend the ambit of liability—whether to reach aid of any kind or only significant aid, whether to reach only those who believe they are probably providing aid or also those who recklessly or negligently provide aid. Should the kinds of aid to be punished include any aid, including, say, the sale at an ordinary price of some common commodity like gasoline, or be limited to significant aid not easily available elsewhere? Since it seems unwise to punish someone who renders ordinary services even when he knows the recipients of the services have a criminal purpose, liability should be restricted to significant aid. Public discussion of the limits of criminal assistance has concentrated on situations when a person believes that his acts will help those committing a crime. I also focus on that, commenting briefly at the end on the implications of a free speech principle for those who consciously disregard an unjustified risk that their acts will aid a crime or who are unthinkingly careless in a way that aids a crime.

Commonly, the critical issue about criminal facilitation does not implicate freedom of speech. Suppose Janice says to Fred, who owns a very fast car, "I'd like to borrow your car tonight, I'm going to move some drugs." Fred responds, "Listen, I don't like what you are doing at all and I want no part of it, but since you are a friend you can take the car if you want." Fred is knowingly facilitating the crime. Fred's lending his car raises no problem of free speech. Of course, Fred will communicate his permission, but the utterance is clearly situation-altering and so outside the reach of a principle of freedom of speech.

For other circumstances, a principle of free speech has some relevance. Suppose Janice asks Frank, an experienced truck driver, which roads are most closely patrolled by police, and Frank, again disavowing the planned crime, provides the information Janice wants. Frank's facilitation consists of asserting specific facts, and free speech has some bearing on his giving of information. It is only a minor impairment of freedom to tell people they cannot provide information they *want* to be used for a crime. It is somewhat more serious to tell them that, even if they have no such purpose, they must keep their mouths shut. A speaker may conceivably think a communication has significant value for the listener beyond the listener's immediate purpose, but, even if the speaker does not think that, perhaps a recognition of the speaker's autonomy should include allowing him ordinarily to say what he believes to be true to his acquaintances, regardless of the use he thinks they plan to make of it.

A further argument against such liability is the problem of determining facts accurately and the effect of the resulting uncertainty on people who speak. If people become aware that they can be treated as criminal for providing information they believe will aid a crime, they may hesitate to give information when they think there is some modest chance of criminal use, not trusting that prosecutors and jurors will always be discerning about perceptions of relevant probabilities.

The implications for free speech are serious enough to warrant careful attention to the problem of communications that facilitate. My own sense is that a legislature may appropriately accept whatever curtailment of expression is involved in a prohibition on facilitation that the actor believes is likely, and I do not think a legislature should bother to distinguish communicative facilitation from other sorts of assistance. However, a principle of free speech provides a powerful reason why liability should not extend to all negligent or reckless acts of communication, that is, to situations where the speaker is wholly unaware of the use to be made of what he says or thinks there is only some modest risk it will be used for a criminal purpose.[22]

This chapter has shown that many traditional bases for punishing communicative acts do not, with a few fairly narrow exceptions, present substantial questions involving freedom of speech. The next two chapters tackle more troublesome issues.

Notes

1. When legislatures consider statutes imposing civil liability, their choice should be affected by a principle of free speech in much the same way as when criminal provisions are involved. In countries with a tradition of respecting free speech but no enforceable constitutional guarantee, courts developing civil liability will and should be influenced by a principle of free speech.

2. The basic criminal law in the United States, in contrast to some other federal countries, is provided by individual states, with federal law covering only crimes that have some relation to national government. This means that in order to indicate with authority what is "the law in the United States" on conspiracy or murder, one must review the law of fifty states, the federal government, and the District of Columbia and Puerto Rico (which have their own codes). The Commentaries to the Model Code have extensive references and citations both to the preexisting law and to modern Code revisions, and are a good starting point for readers who are interested in more detail about American criminal law.

3. For a long time in the United States, the bases for criminal liability have been dominantly or exclusively statutory, with few or no "common law crimes." But a typical pattern has been statutory definitions of crimes whose significance must be filled in by courts according to common law principles. And with some frequency these statutory crimes have been subject to certain "common law" defenses not embodied in statutes. Within the last two decades, a majority of states have undertaken systematic criminal law revision and now have codes that are "unified" and more precise. But many states still follow the older pattern.

4. *Model Penal Code* § 5.03(1).

5. See id. § 2.06(3).

6. See id. § 2.06(3).

7. In respect to attempt, the Model Code formulation was consciously chosen to be less strict than many of the leading cases, requiring only that an act be "a substantial step in a course of conduct planned to culminate in . . . commission of the crime"; to be substantial a step must be "strongly corroborative of the actor's criminal purpose." Id. § 5.01(1)(c), (2).

8. It is actually a complicated question how far this and other advantages are limited to conspiracy cases. Many of the same prosecutorial advantages could be gained by charging people as accessories. See Comment to id. § 5.03.

9. Conscious parallel behavior can occur in the absence of commitment. Oligopolists A, B, and C may keep their prices at the same high level, recognizing that if any one cuts prices to increase sales, the others will do the same and all will lose profits. Such pricing might be sustained for a long time without the officers of any of the three companies feeling committed to anyone else to maintain the price.

When such parallel behavior can be criminal, an interesting question arises about information given by the officers of one company to the officers of another about future pricing plans. If it is clear that no commitment is involved, what is involved are statements of facts. But divulging those particular facts to those particular listeners would probably be regarded as helping to maintain existing practices of parallelism or to encourage the establishing of new ones. Factual disclosures that support criminal behavior are discussed later in this chapter; disclosures that encourage criminal behavior are discussed in Chapter 6.

10. As note 9 suggests, words that fall short of a commitment to act may nevertheless be criminal on some other ground.

11. In the United States, at least, prosecutors clearly have the authority not to prosecute acts that are technically criminal. The little-used practice of private prosecution in England renders matters less straightforward there.

12. Id. § 5.02. The language of the section is more precisely rendered in Chapter 6.

13. Id. § 240.1(1). See also id. §§ 224.8(2)(3) (commercial bribery), and 240.3–240.7 (other inducements to affect official or political action).

14. As to some particular crimes, including bribery, there can be little question of the wisdom of punishing offers. If only successful bribes were punishable, enforcement would be so difficult that the disincentive to offering bribes would be slight.

15. The same conclusion would apply whenever the benefit is "announced" by an agent of the "creator" to the person that the creator hopes to influence.

16. *Model Penal Code* § 5.02(1).

17. I exclude at this point crimes in which force or a threat of force is used to achieve results. The "threat" will usually involve verbal or written utterance, though it need not. These crimes are treated in the next chapter.

18. For example, one actor might give others substantial instruction about how the real estate industry operates as part of a plan to swindle people in real-property transactions.

19. The reader may understandably wonder whether for any cooperative scheme this discussion has a practical point, since those whose part is to communicate will almost always have agreed to commit the crime, will be liable as conspirators and therefore will be liable as accomplices if the crime is carried out. However, if one seriously entertained the idea that factual disclosures made in pursuit of a criminal purpose did not warrant punishment, one might begin to wonder whether either conspiracy or accomplice liability should be pegged to such action if it was clear from the start that an actor's only role was to communicate facts (as in the lookout example). Thus, it is important to establish that aiding by giving factual information does warrant punishment.

20. The Model Penal Code adopts this approach. See § 2.06(3). According to early drafts people would also have been punished for "knowingly substantially" facilitating commission of an offense. The language was dropped after a discussion and vote by the American Law Institute. The American cases are divided in respect to whether, under traditional common law notions, such knowing and substantial facilitation makes one an accomplice.

21. See *New York Penal Law* §§ 115.00, 115.01, 115.05, 115.08 (criminal facilitation).

22. I discuss the problem at somewhat greater length in K. Greenawalt, "A Vice of Its Virtues: The Perils of Precision in Criminal Codification, as Illustrated by Retreat, General Justification, and Dangerous Utterances," 19 *Rutgers-Camden Law Journal* 929, 942–48 (1988).

5

Threats

This chapter considers threats. Deciding exactly what threats should be made criminal is harder than deciding what offers should be made criminal, and a principle of freedom of speech has more evident relevance to the difficult cases. One reason for this is the phenomenon of pure, or unconditional, threats. No one supposes that one person's telling another that he plans unconditionally to benefit him should be criminal; but it is a serious question whether one person should be allowed to tell another that he plans to kill or maim him. The second reason why analysis of threats is both harder and more important is the judgment that in many situations in which inducements are acceptable people should be free of the kind of pressure that conditional threats involve. Most notable, for our purposes, is the inclination to punish some threats that neither seek nor threaten behavior that is an independent legal wrong. I begin my discussion with a treatment of pure threats and then turn to conditional threats. Sometimes threats are addressed to third persons or to a public audience with the expectation that the subject of the threats, or his employees, will become aware of them, but I shall focus in this chapter on the simpler case where the audience of the speaker is also the subject of the threat.

Pure, Unconditional Threats

A *pure* or *unconditional threat* is a threat that does not present the subject of the threat with a way to escape the threatened harm. Convinced that Victor has broken off an affair with her sister in an extremely cruel and hurtful way, Tammy approaches Victor on the street and says, "One of these days I'm going to kill you for what you did to my sister."

No general provision of the law makes threats like this criminal or even actionable under the law of torts, although various standards reach some threats. Under the Model Penal Code, one is guilty of assault who "attempts by physical menace to put another in fear of imminent serious bodily injury";[1] one is guilty of making a "terroristic" threat if one "threatens to commit any crime of violence with purpose to terrorize another, or to cause evacuation of a building . . . or otherwise to cause serious public inconvenience, or in reckless disregard of [such] a risk";[2] one is guilty of harassment if one taunts another in a manner likely to provoke a violent response.[3] Various federal statutes make it a crime to convey certain threats by mail or interstate commerce[4] or to threaten the life of the president.[5] In some cases, courts may grant civil recovery against those who have made threats, on the theory that they have inflicted mental distress.[6] Tammy's oral threat to Victor, a private citizen, is plainly outside the federal statutes. Since it does not put Victor in fear of imminent serious bodily injury and is unlikely to provoke a violent response by Victor, it amounts to neither assault nor harassment under the Model Code. Perhaps it at least risks terrorizing Victor, so a strained argument may be made that it is a terroristic threat.[7] Conceivably it is tortious, though it is probably so only if Victor actually suffers severe mental distress, if Tammy intentionally inflicts that distress or is highly reckless about its occurring, and if in the circumstances Tammy's behavior is judged truly outrageous.

How far the law should punish unconditional threats is troublesome. Since many threats are made in a flush of emotion that will dissipate and since sometimes threats operate as a psychological alternative to immediate physical assault, the failure to make criminal all threats of serious harm is understandable, but when a person threatens in a manner indicating a firm purpose to carry out the harm, something particularly likely when a threat is in writing, the person threatened can be extremely disturbed. And serious threats, especially those directed at prominent figures, may call forth extensive social resources to prevent fulfillment.[8]

Freedom of speech has some bearing on the treatment of pure threats.[9] Since these threats involve particular assertions of fact, what one plans to do on some future occasion, they fall within the broad range of communications to which a principle of free speech applies. Spoken threats typically involve an outpouring of emotion; so the emotional-outlet reason for free communication has special force with respect to them.

Despite the relevance of freedom of speech, a legislature could reasonably decide to make it criminal for a person with apparent firmness of purpose to threaten a specific legal wrong grave enough to be likely either to cause substantial emotional disturbance in the person threatened or to require the employment of substantial resources for investigation or prevention. Finding the appropriate language to reach just these threats is no easy task.

Conditional Threats

I turn now to the more complicated subject of *conditional*, or coercive, *threats*, which involve the threat of a harmful consequence that a person can avoid by performing a particular act. For the typical conditional threat, the threatened consequence is said to be avoidable by the victim's act, but occasionally the consequence is said to turn on an outcome that is only partly within the victim's control: "Unless I am made the vice-presidential candidate, I'll expose your drug problem" (said to a close adviser of the nominee for president). I shall disregard this variation and address the standard case. Varieties of conditional threats are made criminal in ways and on grounds I summarily describe. In contrast to the order for most other subjects, I then address the complex and disputed relevance of a principle of freedom of speech, before considering reasons for limiting punishment of conditional threats that do not relate to speech. Because of the interest of the questions involved and because they provide an illuminating test of major aspects of my broader thesis about the significance of uses of language, I enter into subtleties that a person with overriding practical objectives might avoid, but this largely theoretical discussion yields conclusions which are employed, along with aspects of ordinary penal policy, to suggest sensible legislative approaches to conditional threats.

Conditional Threats under the Criminal Law

I begin with conditional threats that are designed to get the person threatened to commit a crime.[10] If T (the threatener) threatens to harm V (the victim) in some way unless V commits a crime, T's threat is immediately criminal, and T will be liable for the crime committed if V acts on the threat. Though these conclusions are clear, precisely how to characterize the grounds of liability may vary among jurisdictions and depend on exact circumstances. Under the Model Penal Code, the threat would probably constitute a kind of "command" or "encouragement" to V to commit the crime and would therefore be a form of criminal solicitation.[11] If T's only planned conduct is to threaten V, T may be liable under the Code's definition of attempt, which includes doing anything with the belief that it will cause a particular criminal result without further conduct on one's part.[12] If V commits the crime subject to the threat, T will be liable as an accessory, either, depending on the magnitude of the threat and on V's motivations, as someone who has solicited V or as someone who has caused an innocent person to engage in criminal conduct.[13]

Just as bribes are designed to get officials to act on inappropriate bases, threats can also aim at obtaining decisions that are not disinterested. Officials who decide subject to threats may not be committing a crime, but the process of decision is unfair to those affected and is a kind of social wrong. The criminal law punishes threats in circumstances when bribes are also forbidden; the Model Code has a section directed mainly to threats of officials.[14]

Many ordinary crimes involve threats to innocent victims to get them to perform acts that are not independently wrongful. For crimes in which a determinative element is forcibly doing something—acquiring property, gaining entry to a building, or having sexual relations—a verbal threat of force can satisfy the element of forcibleness. Often that is explicit. The Model Code, for example, treats as robbery, threatening "another . . . with immediate serious bodily injury" or with immediately committing a serious felony;[15] and the definition of rape includes compelling someone to submit to sexual intercourse "by threat of imminent death, serious bodily injury, extreme pain or kidnapping."[16] If such a threat is unsuccessful, a person is guilty of an attempt to commit one of these specific crimes. For many other crimes, it is implicit that a plausible threat can satisfy a required element. For example, under the Model Code, kidnapping includes unlawfully removing someone or confining him in isolation,[17] and an element of false imprisonment is restraining another unlawfully.[18] These could undoubtedly be accomplished by a threat of force that coerces another to go or stay where he is directed.

The threats covered by the crimes of extortion, blackmail, and criminal coercion are much broader. Under the Model Penal Code, in a section that includes the traditional crime of blackmail, a person commits extortion if he obtains another's property by threatening, among other things, to inflict bodily injury or commit a crime, to accuse anyone of a crime, to expose a highly embarrassing secret, or to inflict any other harm which would not benefit the threatener.[19] The crime of criminal coercion, which covers a similar though somewhat narrower range of threatened harms, including committing a crime, accusing anyone of a crime, or exposing embarrassing secrets, has an embracive definition of purposes that the threatener may have: "with purpose unlawfully to restrict another's freedom of action to his detriment."[20] The definitions of the crimes of extortion and criminal coercion are notable in making it criminal to threaten some kinds of conduct, such as reporting a criminal act or disclosing an embarrassing secret, which it might be perfectly legal, perhaps even desirable, actually to perform.

As far as ordinary penal policy is concerned, the major question about coercive threats is the status of threats to do what one lawfully can do unless the victim does what he lawfully can do. The question is well captured by the classic instance of blackmail: Tammy threatens to disclose Victor's affair to his wife (something Tammy is free to do) unless Victor pays Tammy $1,000 (something Victor is free to do). No threatened, promised, or demanded action here is, standing alone, illegal. Although virtually everyone seems to suppose that blackmail should be made criminal, there is disagreement about the reason why: Is the aim to prevent immoral liberties,[21] to protect privacy,[22] to prevent information about someone's past from being used as an income-producing asset,[23] to avoid "private enforcement" of legal rules,[24] to avoid uneconomic activity,[25] to forestall institutionalized efforts to exploit the gains to be derived from blackmail,[26] or to prevent those who threaten from using an informational leverage that is not properly theirs?[27]

Since I am interested mainly in the relation between free speech and criminal communications, I do not undertake a careful analysis of these various theories or their practical implications, but understanding of the merits of the theories is aided if the instances of blackmail are broken down. Sometimes it would be socially desirable that disclosure occur, as when Tammy is aware of a serious crime that Victor has committed. In such an instance, allowing blackmail would give people aware of crimes a strong incentive to "settle" with the perpetrator instead of going to the police. That would be undesirable. On other occasions disclosure would be socially undesirable but not illegal. There are many embarrassing secrets whose disclosure (especially by a comparative stranger) is more likely to be destructive than helpful. Although Tammy, a remote acquaintance, is legally free to disclose a past affair of Victor's to his wife, this kind of tattling is ordinarily wrong, and the law should neither reward a willingness to tattle by allowing Tammy to profit from it at Victor's expense nor encourage people to spend their time and energy seeking such information. When the harm and benefit of disclosure are about evenly balanced, allowing blackmail would encourage the person aware of the secret to decide whether to disclose on the basis of personal profit, not considering what is morally right or socially best. That this is the kind of decision that should not be made for profit is suggested both by the theory that the blackmailer misuses someone else's leverage[28] and by the theory that this sort of knowledge should not serve as an income-producing asset.[29]

The categories I now develop from the perspective of free speech have some relation to these theories of penal policy, but I shall not attempt to trace the connections systematically.

Conditional Threats and a Principle of Free Speech

The analysis of conditional threats and free speech builds on the distinction between situation-altering utterances and ordinary assertions of fact and value, and particularly on the idea of manipulative threats, developed in Chapter 3. I suggested there that the critical element of a threat is an assertion of fact, one's planned future behavior if the victim of the threat fails to do what one wishes, but that a careful analysis of the nature of threats is quite complex.

Many threats imply a promise that one will not do the threatened act if the victim of the threat complies. Thus, the statement, "I'll burn down your store if you do not give me $1,000," may join an *assertion* that one will burn the store if the money is not forthcoming with an implicit *promise* that one will not burn the store (in the near future) if the money is paid. If I am right that promises are clearly situation-altering and not within the range of a principle of free speech, it may be thought that the promissory element eliminates worry about the relevance of free speech. But that would be mistaken in the many situations where the promise is to do only what one already has a duty to do and is generally expected to do; there the law's concern is not with the promise to refrain from harm but with the statement about doing harm. The point is illustrated by the following variation: "I don't promise anything if you give me $1,000. I may decide to burn your store anyway because I don't like you, but I will certainly burn it if you don't pay me the money." Elimination of a promissory element does not render this communication more acceptable than its predecessor. Although I consider, below, a significant class of instances in which the promise to refrain is highly important, the possible application of a principle of free speech must often be judged against the assertion of the threatened harm.

As to that, I claimed in Chapter 3 that a vital distinction exists between "manipulative threats" and what I am calling "warning threats." The manipulative threat involves the creation of prospective harmful consequences in order to achieve one's objective. Here is another example:

> Tammy knows that Valerie has had a secret abortion, and that Valerie's parents are adamantly opposed to abortion. Tammy has no objection to abortion and feels no obligation to report to Valerie's parents. In fact, she would never dream of telling them if she did not see a chance to benefit herself. She threatens that she will tell Valerie's parents unless Valerie gives her $1000. Tammy now plans to carry out the threat if Valerie does not comply.

If Tammy was unable to threaten Valerie she would not plan to tell Valerie's parents. Her conditional willingness to tell Valerie's parents comes into being only in connection with the threat. My claim is that, when a fact is "created" like this in a serious effort to coerce, the communication is genuinely situation-altering and is not covered by the main justifications for free speech.[30]

Not all conditional threats are manipulative. Some indicate what would otherwise be natural responses.

> Tom knows Victor is committing adultery. Tom's view is that a spouse should be told about such behavior if it continues, and he thinks he should tell Victor's wife, Nancy. But he knows Nancy will be upset and would not tell her if he was sure Victor was going to stop. Tom tells Victor truly that he will inform Nancy unless Victor stops.

In this instance, Tom's planned response does not depend on the threat. If he were unable to communicate with Victor he would go ahead and tell Nancy unless Victor ended his affair.[31] He acquaints Victor with a factual probability that exists independent of the threat,[32] altering Victor's perception of the world but not his external environment.[33] As I suggested in Chapter 3, had the warning of Tom's intention come to Victor from someone else, the warning would clearly fall within a principle of free speech; that the informing here is done by Tom himself is not crucial to that principle, which thus covers "warning threats" of natural responses.

The distinction between manipulative and warning threats must deal with an intermediate circumstance. Suppose that what Tom threatens, to tell Nancy about Victor's adultery, is a natural response for him, but Tom decides he will forgo that response in return for some separate advantage for which he may be able to bargain. Tom says to Victor, "I'll tell your wife about your adultery unless you hire me." Here the plan to inform Nancy is a natural response to the adultery, about which Tom informs Victor. But Tom's willingness not to respond in that way in return for being hired has a different status. Tom probably is implicitly promising not to tell Nancy if Victor hires him; the promise is situation-altering and outside a principle of free speech. Even if Tom stops short of a promise, his expressed willingness not to tell, if given *in return* for being hired, is manipulative. Tom is not protecting Victor because Victor *happens* also to be his prospective employer; he is protecting Victor *in exchange* for the job. The threat, thus, actually changes Victor's situation, because Victor can now achieve something by hiring Tom that he could not have achieved without Tom's communication to him. In this critical aspect, then, the threat is situation-altering.[34]

If the threat in this form combines a situation-altering element, either a promise or manipulative willingness to forgo a natural response, with an assertion of fact regarding the natural response, which aspect predominates? Since the aim of the communication is to get Victor to act in a way that will lead Tom to forgo his natural response and since his expressed willingness to do so is manipulative, we can treat the threat as essentially manipulative[35] and outside the reach of a principle of free speech.

This analysis yields greater precision about warning threats. We may take a warning threat, to which a principle of free speech applies, as requiring both threatened action which is a natural response to the behavior of the person threatened and a willingess to forgo that action which is also a natural response to hoped-for behavior by the person threatened. Both these requirements are met in the initial example of Tom's warning Victor that he will tell Nancy; even if Tom had not been able to communicate with Victor, he would have told Nancy if the affair continued and not told Nancy if he knew Victor had broken it off.

We are now ready to consider a troubling variation on the "hire me" threat which meets these requirements of naturalness and which poses a substantial test for the soundness of my approach to conditional threats. Suppose Tom, out of feelings of loyalty and fear, would never inform on a prospective employer. In that event, Tom would not tell Nancy about Victor's affair if Victor had independently offered to hire him. Thus his threatened response, to tell Nancy if Victor does not hire him, and his willingness to forgo the response, not to tell if Victor does hire him, are both "natural," and his threat is a true warning threat, according to everything I have said. Since this threat hardly seems benign, its proper treatment is the source of some difficulty. My suggestions on that subject are included in my comments on sensible approaches to criminalizing threats, a topic for which the basic categorization of manipulative and warning threats provides only a faltering first step.

An important preliminary to this effort is to compare my own approach with another that has been offered to explain what kinds of conditional offers and threats are protected by a principle of free speech. Edwin Baker has proposed that any conditional threat or offer that is "coercive" is outside the range of free speech; other threats and offers are protected speech. For Baker "coercive" is a critical term that summarizes a conclusion that a threat or offer is not covered by a principle of free speech.

Professor Baker's approach helps confirm most of my practical conclusions, and before I elaborate on our fairly significant theoretical differences, it is worth stressing what we share. Against the view that serious conditional threats are really like other forms of communication, such as disclosures of dangerous facts or encouragements to act, to be judged by some free speech standard that requires a high likelihood of harm and imminence of harm,[36] Baker and I agree that, typically, something about their character puts them outside of a free speech principle, regardless of their likely success or the imminence of what is threatened. Moreover, what Baker believes to be the feature that disqualifies a threat from protection coalesces in most cases with what I think is the disqualifying factor, and, even in virtually all instances when I believe a free speech principle initially *applies* and Baker does not, what he regards as of central relevance is something I think counts in the final judgment whether a prohibition is permissible. Thus, the practical outcome of applying Baker's approach falls much closer to my own suggestions than to the practical implications of the view we both reject: that conditional threats are just another kind of speech. Nevertheless, the differences between us are illuminating.

Understanding of Baker's approach is enhanced by a brief sketch of his theory of free speech. He is one of those who think a single value lies behind freedom of speech: the value of individual liberty to fulfill oneself and participate in change.[37] Central in determining the application of a principle of free speech is whether a communication amounts to coercive speech that interferes with the decision-making autonomy of individuals.[38] Speech can be coercive if the speaker restricts a person to options worse than the person had a moral or legitimate right to expect or if the speaker "employs means that she had no right to use for changing the threatened person's options."[39] Coercion relates, for Baker, to the impropriety of the pressure the speaker uses.

Baker's approach to free speech aspects of conditional threats differs from mine in focusing on the appropriateness of the kind of pressure placed on the subject of the threat rather than on the relationship between the communication and an already existing state of affairs.[40] Relatedly, Baker's notion of coercion,[41] or unacceptable pressure, needs to be tied to a full account of autonomous action in a good society,[42] whereas my approach does not require wholesale resolution of the correct extent of liberty of action. It will help clarify the narrower point of disagreement to consider first the more general one.

Baker believes that a theory of free speech should not accept as given what is presently legally permitted[43] or (I assume) what is presently permitted by dominant social morality. In order to decide whether communication should be protected, one has to make a normative judgment about proper domains of liberty; whatever speech would be allowed under a society with proper domains of liberty should be viewed as protected speech. My own approach suggests various boundaries of speech that legislatures, and courts, should protect, essentially independent of the way many other particular issues of liberty are resolved.[44]

This approach enjoys two fundamental and related advantages. No doubt there is a place for a comprehensive theory about state regulation of liberty, including regulation of expression,[45] and a legislator deciding narrowly on speech relating to some activity might be influenced by his or her own view that the activity, now prohibited, should be free. However, other legislators who think an activity itself deserves prohibition will hardly be persuaded to permit communication relating to it on the ground that the original prohibition violates correct notions of autonomy. If one can develop a distinctive principle of free speech that is not dependent upon a single social theory, it can substantially unite people who may disagree about many other social issues.[46] This more modest approach can be of greater assistance to legislatures and courts which are presented with general free speech arguments and which are not likely to try to reexamine and resolve every other principle about domains of liberty along the way. The more ambitious theory that ties free speech to an overall account of autonomy, however illuminating and sound, risks practical irrelevance unless the general account of autonomy is already reflected in social institutions or constitutional norms.

The following examples highlight my difference with Baker and the defense of my less ambitious approach. I use offers here rather than threats because our theoretical disagreement is the same for both and is more sharply evidenced in respect to offers. Suppose Olive says to Lee, "I will give you $200: (1) to make love to me; (2) for a pint of your blood; (3) for your hair; (4) for a semen sample." As I understand Baker's position, if a society with a proper view of autonomy would allow any of these commodities to be sold for cash, then the offer of cash for that commodity does not put improper pressure on the listener and is part of free speech. Thus, if our society criminalizes prostitution but a good society would not, a prostitute's efforts to solicit business should be considered protected speech. My approach allows the status of the speech to be resolved independently of the propriety of penalizing the resulting transaction. I think it is an unhelpful argument in a society in which prostitution is a well settled crime to say that a prostitute's offer to a potential customer to have sex now is protected *speech* *because* prostitution itself should really be allowed as an exercise of individual autonomy.[47]

Baker's position could be revised to meet this objection by using present law and social morality as the main determinants of improper pressure and claiming that improper pressure, so determined, is the critical element for whether threats and offers fall within the principle of free speech.[48] That position would still contrast with my own, which is that, for initial categorization, what matters for a principle of free speech is whether a threat (or offer) is manipulative or warns (or advises) as to what will occur in any event.

In terms of abstract categories, Baker and I disagree about some manipulative and some warning threats. When manipulative threats and offers do not involve improper pressure, Baker regards them as covered by free speech, and I do not. When warning threats and advisory inducements do involve improper pressure, I regard them as covered, and Baker does not.

As I examine cases in which the two approaches converge and diverge, it is important to re-emphasize that the practical consequences of our disagreement are not great, both because I think propriety of pressure is directly important to what *finally* should be punished and because my sense of warning threats and advisory inducements correlates fairly closely with Baker's ideas about proper pressure.

Many threats in our social life are both manipulative and acceptable. Suppose a university pays higher salaries to scholars it is trying to attract or is afraid to lose than it pays to equally competent scholars it regards as securely in the fold. For family and collegial reasons, Paula would prefer to stay at the university at her present salary rather than go elsewhere at a higher salary. But she thinks she should be paid more. She threatens to leave unless her salary is raised. If this pressure is proper according to prevailing standards, the threat will not be consciously prohibited by a legislature.[49] My approach, which treats the threat here as a situation-altering utterance outside a principle of free speech, relies on general reasons for liberty of action to explain why the threat should be legally permissible, whereas Baker ties protection to free speech.

Tammy's threat to tell Valerie's parents about Valerie's abortion unless Valerie pays her $1,000 provides a good example of a manipulative threat which has traditionally been punished and which Baker and I agree should be so. According to Baker, Tammy seeks to make Valerie "a puppet of her will";[50] she undermines Valerie's autonomy. In most instances of what I call manipulative threats that society is likely to prohibit, Baker and I converge in the opinion that reasons of free speech are not relevant.[51]

Disclosures of natural responses will usually not involve what Baker considers improper pressure. If Tom reports his inclination to tell Nancy, Victor's wife, about Victor's affair unless he breaks off the affair, Baker's analysis is that Tom uses "speech directly to make the world correspond to [his] substantive values . . . and does so without disrespecting the listener's integrity."[52] Tom is not using improper pressure[53] because "the 'threat' seeks the listener's help in pursuing the same values that the speaker's threatened behavior itself would further."[54] Most of what I call warning threats will be of just this sort.

Exactly which warning threats Baker thinks are not reached by a principle of free speech is a bit murky. When a speaker's threat is driven by crude feelings or purely selfish interests, it lies beyond the scope of free speech for Baker even if the speaker reports a natural reaction. Thus, if Nancy says to Victor, "I warn you that I am a vindictive person and I will make our children's lives miserable if you continue your affair," that is unprotected for Baker even if Nancy is truly reporting her natural feelings and highly probable natural reaction. Similarly, if Tom says to Victor, "Hire me or I'll tell Nancy about your affair," Baker would say the comment is outside free speech even if Tom is naturally disinclined to inform on a prospective employer. Apparently Baker's conclusion would be the same if the threatened action would implement some *value* quite different from that served by the listener's performing the desired action: "I'll tell Nancy about your affair unless you donate $3,000 to famine relief."[55] I think (with less confidence) that Baker's conclusion would be the same even if the desired and threatened actions served the same values but the demanded act was somehow disconnected from the threatened act, "I'll tell Nancy unless you donate $3,000 to the Society for Discouraging Adultery."

The examples in the last paragraph press on the question of why it should be so crucial for *free speech* that the speaker's threatened action seek to implement values in a way closely connected to the behavior that the threat seeks to elicit. From the listener's point of view such a threat may be every bit as impairing of freedom of action as it is if the speaker's aims are selfish; Victor may much prefer paying Tom $1,000 or hiring him to having to break off the affair or having Nancy told. And if Victor does not share Tom's values, believing that secret affairs are necessary for healthy marriages, he may regard his autonomy as being unjustly interfered with in any event. From the speaker's point of view, whether he is describing the world as he understands it is more central to liberty of expression than whether he is aiming toward a good or legitimate objective. My own approach stresses the value of people's being able to tell other people what are the conditions of their existence. If communication does that, without sharply changing those conditions, I claim that the reasons for free speech apply, *at least to some degree*.

A critical weakness of Baker's position is illustrated by reference to a third party, Olive, who tells Victor what Tom is likely to do. I have assumed that, if Olive informs Victor about likely consequences not within her control, her warning is definitely within the range of free speech. But that is not so clear under Baker's approach. Suppose Olive would like Tom's present job, and she tells Victor truthfully that Tom will probably inform Nancy about Victor's affair unless Victor hires Tom. Because Olive's purpose is to get Victor to act to her advantage under the pressure of Tom's inclinations, it appears, from what Baker says about coercive threats and his broader theory, that Olive's comment might not be within a principle of free speech.[56] For me, that possibility is strong confirmation that impairment of autonomous decision in the sense Baker understands it is *the key* neither to free speech and conditional threats nor to free speech more generally.

Which Conditional Threats Should Be Prohibited?

This extensive detour exploring Baker's challenging alternative approach provides a good introduction to the complexity of drawing appropriate lines for prohibited conditional threats. One must consider the outer limits of appropriate criminal sanctions, the values of free speech, and the need to draft succinct statutory language that gives fair warning and does not require impossible findings of fact.

If I am correct that the difference between manipulative threats and warning threats is important for a principle of freedom of speech, that does not mean that simplistic conclusions about what to allow and what to prohibit follow. Many manipulative threats should be permitted, some warning threats will generate enough social harm to warrant prohibition, and the difficulties of determining whether a threat is manipulative or warning cast serious doubt on the wisdom of ever using that distinction directly in statutory drafting. In order to emphasize the *limited* direct practical import of the distinction between manipulative and warning threats,[57] I begin the discussion of legislative formulations with matters that plainly do not call for drawing that distinction.

The first, and obvious, point is that a legislature must be careful not to criminalize too many threats. Minor threats, including manipulative threats, are a common part of social life, and many perform a significant commercial function. Frequently, in bargaining situations, one party threatens to take action, for example, forgoing a sale at a modest profit or engaging in a strike, that both parties realize is disadvantageous to that party but more disadvantageous to the other party. It would be wholly inappropriate for the criminal law to reach all those minor threats.

Legislative formulations vary in their sensitivity to the critical problem of breadth of coverage. Although the demands embraced by the criminal coercion section of the Model Penal Code are expansive: "with purpose unlawfully to restrict another's freedom of action to his detriment," the section circumscribes the category of threatened harms[58] so that typical minor threats are not covered. Some state provisions have been drawn considerably less carefully and have reached acts for which a criminal sanction is plainly inapt. The Supreme Court of Oregon concluded that the language of that state's provision, which included threatening "any harm which would not benefit the actor,"[59] would reach threats like: "If you don't quit making love to my wife, I'm going to tell your wife," and "Change your opinion, or I shall dissent and expose your complete ignorance of this area of the law."[60]

The problem of minor threats can also arise with extortion provisions. The judgment underlying the Model Code section on that subject was that because the only forbidden purpose is obtaining the property of another, the category of threats should be broad, including inflicting "any other harm which would not benefit the actor."[61] The logic is that the wrongness of trying to get another's property by threat does not depend on the sort of threat. But this catchall approach is literally too extensive even for threats to acquire property. Suppose I have a lovely tree on my land which is much admired by my neighbor and which blocks her view of an ugly factory. I ask my neighbor if I can have a bicycle her child has outgrown, and, without explanation, she refuses. Feeling that this is unreasonable, I respond, "If you don't give me the bike, I'll chop down my tree to spite you." In ordinary terms, I want to acquire property and this is a harm to the neighbor that does not benefit me; it seems covered by the Model Code's extortion section. Of course, no such case will be prosecuted, and a judge might manage to interpret the Code language not to include choices about what I do with my own land. Nevertheless, the example well illustrates the worry that general inclusive language risks extending the criminal law too far in respect to conditional threats.

I now turn to some kinds of conditional threats that should be criminal, whether they are manipulative or warning. When a threat to use physical force effectively substitutes for the actual use of physical force, as it can for robbery or rape, it should clearly be treated as criminal. And conditional threats to use serious physical force in the future should be criminal, even if the threatener is naturally inclined to use such force. If a private lender threatens to break the legs of someone who has not repaid him on time, there are decisive reasons why punishment should not turn on what the lender would do if unable to communicate the threat.[62] Most vitally, breaking legs and the fear of having one's legs broken are bad enough that society can try to discourage communications that engender some incentive to perform that action; prohibiting the threats may help people curb their leg-breaking inclinations.

Though conditional threats to commit serious crimes clearly warrant punishment, I am doubtful whether every threat to commit a minor crime should be covered by a criminal coercion statute. Suppose that someone tells a store owner that unless he hires a particular individual, demonstrators will block the store's entrance in an undeniably criminal way. Or that a person writes to the I.R.S., "If you don't give me my refund, I won't file in future years." It seems unlikely that the criminal law should intervene at the stage of such threats, rather than await the possible occurrence of the threatened action.

When the threatened conduct itself does not involve a crime, but the threat is designed to lead the person threatened to commit a serious crime, the threat should ordinarily be punishable; it now is, under rules regarding attempt, solicitation, and accessorial liability, and, in some circumstances, criminal coercion.[63] Since a person's *failure* to commit a crime rarely invokes a spontaneous hostile response, threats designed to get others to commit crimes will almost always be manipulative, but even warning threats of natural reactions that can coerce people to commit serious crimes should be punished. Again, I am doubtful about less serious crimes and modest threats. If a person says, "Unless you join us in this (illegal) teachers' strike, I'll stop our cooperative teaching endeavors," his communication should not be criminal.

So far my practical recommendations have not had to draw upon the distinction between manipulative and warning threats, but I now pass on to the more troublesome issues of coverage when a conditional threat neither threatens nor elicits a serious independent crime. In respect to these, notably including threats to disclose embarrassing secrets, the line between manipulative and warning threats has more potential significance.

My basic position is that manipulative threats, like "Pay me or I'll tell your parents about the abortion," should be regarded as potential subjects of criminal sanctions, whereas ordinary warning threats like, "Stop the affair or I'll tell your wife," should be understood as having speech value and should generally be left free. But this position requires qualification in respect to both kinds of threats. Some manipulative threats, as Chapter 3 indicated, are not serious, and others, the products of intense temporary emotion whose venting has value as expression, will quickly lose their force. Manipulative threats should not be punished unless they convey a firm determination to commit the threatened action.

In at least two special kinds of circumstances in which warning threats predict action on legally inappropriate grounds, the threats need not be regarded as potentially protected speech. Some warning threats, though not threatening a crime, constitute direct legal wrongs, violations of the substantive rights of the person threatened. Suppose the committee deciding on new members in a cooperative apartment engages in discrimination against blacks. A member of the committee tells a black woman seeking to apply, "Don't try for an apartment in our building; if you do, we'll find some basis to deny the application." The threat here may be of a "natural response" in my sense, but telling a potential applicant that you will discriminate is already to engage in a form of discrimination.[64] The failure to apply that the threat may induce is directly at odds with the purpose behind a ban on discrimination. Such a threat to discriminate in denying the application should not be treated as a more serious legal wrong than the discriminatory denial itself, but the threat should not be treated as privileged.

A threatened action can be an abuse of authority, wrongful in a sense different from its being independently a legal wrong. Suppose a police officer says she will issue a speeding ticket unless one donates $25 to the Police Benevolent Association. She may be permitted to encourage donations to the P.B.A., and she may have discretion to decide whether to issue the ticket or not, but she lacks the right to make her own issuance of the ticket turn on a failure to donate.[65] By stating her willingness to rely on unwarranted grounds, she invites her victim to cooperate in her reliance on these grounds. Threats of this sort will usually be manipulative,[66] but, even if the officer's threat is a "warning," because she does not arrest speeders who have spontaneously contributed to the P.B.A., her telling the speeder she is willing to abuse authority is already an abuse of authority which may be punished.

When these, and perhaps other, exceptions do not apply and warning threats neither threaten nor seek a criminal act, the interest in free speech is strong enough, I claim, so that such threats generally should not be punished.

We now face the question of how this conclusion might be acted upon by a legislature. The exemption for warning threats might be imported directly into a legislative formulation or employed as a judicial technique of interpretation for general statutory language. Alternatively, although the categories of forbidden threats would be enumerated without respect to the distinction between manipulative and warning threats, the legislative decision about which threats to cover could be informed by an inclination to avoid categories in which a substantial percentage of threats would be warnings of natural responses. For reasons to follow, not least the immense difficulty of distinguishing manipulative and warning threats in practice, the second alternative is preferable.

Were a legislature to try to implement my thoughts about manipulative and warning threats in a direct way, it could introduce the following sorts of qualifications to a criminal coercion provision and perhaps to an extortion provision as well.

No communication should be considered a forbidden effort to threaten under this section if either:

1. the communication does not convey a firm determination to commit the threatened action; or
2. (a) the threatened action and the willingness to forgo that action involve natural responses to behavior of the subject of the threat, and
   (b) the action that is sought is not criminal, the threatened action is not a felony against a person or property, and the communication does not itself involve an abuse of authority.[67]

Under a provision such as this, "natural response" could be defined, or interpreted, to refer either to people generally or to the particular person making the communication. Were the focus on the individual involved, some unpalatable threats would end up uncovered and the line-drawing requirement would be highly onerous. Both points can be illustrated by Tom's threat to Victor: "Hire me or I'll tell Nancy about your affair." If Tom thinks husbands should generally be informed but would never inform on a prospective employer, both the threatened act and the willingness to forgo it are natural for him, not dependent on his making the threat. My conclusion that free speech does have relevance for this case is troubling, because before Tom's warning Victor might have been exceedingly unlikely to hire Tom and because it may well be inefficient, personally demeaning, and conflict-promoting for people to choose employees in order to avoid disclosures of embarrassing secrets. If a principle of free speech is implicated here, the sacrifice of freedom involved in making the threat criminal is slight, since all Tom is prevented from doing is telling a single person at a single point in time what his specific inclinations are.

As Tom's threat to Victor reflects, distinguishing manipulative from warning threats will sometimes be very difficult. Even if all the facts, including the state of mind of the threatener, are known, manipulative and warning elements may be intertwined in ways that resist easy classification. And often the relevant facts will be hard to ascertain. Threateners will not always know whether a threatened response is natural; a response may jump into someone's mind as he reacts to a disturbing situation or an unexpected opportunity, and he may not be sure what he would have done if he had had to react without being able to make the threat. Even more often an outsider will be uncertain whether a response is natural or manipulative for a threatener. Who is to say whether Tom *generally* would report adulteries of prospective employers? A legislative formulation that made that precise question the critical inquiry for the vast majority of cases would be unfortunate.

If any legislative line is to be drawn between manipulative and warning threats, it should be in terms of the reasons of people generally, not those of particular individuals, and, if the legislature itself creates no exemptions for warning threats, a court might reasonably say that nothing counts as a "threat" if the harmful consequence it proposes would represent a natural response for many people.[68]

The alternative way to proceed is not to employ explicit legislative or interpretive judicial distinctions between manipulative and warning threats. The Model Code's criminal coercion provision is illustrative. It limits itself to threats generally regarded as illegitimate, and creates a broad affirmative defense that covers any actor who believes that a criminal accusation that he has threatened to make, or a secret he has threatened to reveal, is true, and who has a purpose limited to compelling the person threatened to behave in a way reasonably related to the circumstances.[69] Such an approach sensibly exempts most otherwise covered threats that one could defend as a reasonable part of our social life. It also happens to remove from coverage the vast majority of warning threats of natural responses. The few warning threats that remain covered might be viewed as appropriately punishable, despite their expressive value, because they involve improper pressure or because the line between manipulative and warning threats is regarded as too hard to draw in practice.

Given the infrequency with which warning threats will actually be prosecuted, legislatures should not themselves try to draw the line between manipulative and warning threats, instead displaying the kind of sensitivity for categorization found in the Model Code. What is appropriate interpretation will depend on statutory language, but, faced with flexible language, judges should avoid reading provisions to cover common threats of natural responses.

It is worth explicitly re-emphasizing the course of this chapter, one that is at least atypical for legal scholarship. I have been drawn to and have defended a line between manipulative and warning threats as being of fundamental importance for understanding what threats a principle of free speech reaches. I have suggested that this distinction should enrich understanding of which threats are appropriately subjected to criminal sanctions. But I have finally concluded that the line is probably not one that should be of direct legal significance for statutory language and *its* interpretation (though I shall argue in Chapter 14 that in some circumstances a constitutional outcome should depend on the distinction). We should not be surprised that the best distinctions for every relevant practice do not always track those of clearest theoretical importance, although legal scholars, including myself, feel most comfortable when they perceive congruence between the two.

Notes

1. *Model Penal Code* § 211.1(1)(c).
2. Id. § 211.3
3. Id. § 250.4(2). The reach of harassment over the telephone includes many threats, but is much broader; § 250.4(1). One is punishable who with a purpose to harass "makes a telephone call without purpose of legitimate communication." See also *United States* v. *Lampley*, 573 F.2d 783 (3d Cir. 1978); *Gormley* v. *Director Conn. State Dept. of Prob.*, 632 F.2d 938 (2d Cir. 1980), certiorari denied, 449 U.S. 1023 (1980).
4. 18 U.S.C. § 875(b)(c).
5. 18 U.S.C. § 871.

6. See generally *Hall* v. *May Dep't Stores Co.*, 292 Or. 131, 637 P.2d 126 (1981); 1 *Restatement of Torts* (Second) § 46.

7. Against this interpretation is the title of the relevant section and much of its language, which connotes mainly threatened terroristic acts like the planting of bombs, etc.

8. Given a single threat of a particular seriousness, say to kill, the most extensive resources are likely to be expended to protect a major political figure who may not even be aware of the threat and whose psychological reaction, if he or she is aware of the threat, is likely to be less intense than the reaction of an ordinary citizen.

9. As my analysis in the following section indicates, free speech has more to do with pure threats than with conditional threats of the same harm. Language in one case might be understood to assert exactly the reverse, though the wording leaves it unclear exactly what threats are being compared. *State* v. *Spencer*, 289 Or. 225, 611 P.2d 1147 (1980).

10. For this purpose, it is not relevant that the threatened person may actually have a defense of duress if he does what would otherwise be a criminal act.

11. *Model Penal Code* § 5.02(1).

12. Id. § 5.01(1)(b).

13. See id. § 2.06(3)(a)(i), (2)(a). If the threat were grave and the crime minor, *V* might be an innocent person; if the crime were grave and the threat minor, *V* would not be innocent.

In fact, under the Model Penal Code, Section 2.03 on what is commonly referred to as "causation" would also make *T* directly liable for criminal results, but that section is unusual in the extent to which it imposes direct liability for acts that lead others to act in a criminal way.

14. Id. § 240.2. There is no section explicitly analogous to Section 224.8 on commercial bribery, but presumably a threat to get a commercial agent to breach his duty to act disinterestedly would be regarded as criminal coercion or extortion, discussed below, or possibly as a form of bribery.

15. See id. § 222.1(b)(c).

16. See id. § 213.1(1)(a).

17. Id. § 212.1.

18. Id. § 212.3.

19. Id. § 223.4. The exact category of secrets covered is "any secret tending to subject any person to hatred, contempt or ridicule, or to impair his credit or business repute."

20. Id. § 212.5. The category of secrets covered is the same as in the extortion section. See note 19 supra.

21. See A. Goodhart, *Essays in Jurisprudence and the Common Law* 175–89 (Cambridge, Cambridge University Press 1931).

22. See J. Murphy, "Blackmail: A Preliminary Inquiry," 63 *Monist* 156–57 (1980).

23. H. Ball and L. Friedman, "The Use of Criminal Sanctions in the Enforcement of Economic Legislation: A Sociological View," 17 *Stanford Law Review* 197, 205–6 (1965).

24. W. Landes and R. Posner, "The Private Enforcement of Law," 4 *Journal of Legal Studies* 1, 2 (1975).

25. R. Coase, "Blackmail," 74 *Virginia Law Review* 655 (1988). D. Ginsburg, "Blackmail: An Economic Analysis of the Law" (Nov. 4, 1979) (unpublished manuscript).

26. R. Epstein, "Blackmail, Inc.," 50 *University of Chicago Law Review* 553 (1983).

27. See J. Lindgren, "Unraveling the Paradox of Blackmail," 84 *Columbia Law Review* 670, 680–701 (1984); J. Lindgren, "More Blackmail Ink: A Critique of *Blackmail, Inc.*, Epstein's Theory of Blackmail," 16 *Connecticut Law Review* 909, 922–23 (1984).

28. However, for many embarrassing secrets of the past, no one may properly have leverage.

29. Even if some knowledge about a person's past is properly used by others for income, as in writing a biography, this particular kind of use of this particular kind of information may be improper.

30. As to blackmail, see Comment, "Coercion, Blackmail and the Limits of Protected Speech," 131 *University of Pennsylvania Law Review* 1469, 1478 (1983) ("The blackmailer uses the threat of communication only as a sanction to obtain property"). Sometimes, as Chapter 3 indicates, manipulative threats are not seriously intended or, although seriously intended at the moment, reflect an emotional outburst rather than a considered plan of action. In either event, the reasons for free expression have stronger relevance because the main import of the threat is to express deep-seated feelings.

31. Whether Tom would carry out the response without the threat may not be the precise test of a warning threat. If Tom has a strong natural inclination to tell Nancy but also believes you should never inform on someone before he has had a warning to stop, the threat probably qualifies as a warning threat, even though Tom would not tell Nancy if he lacked the chance to talk to Victor.

32. It may be that Tom tells Victor that he will inform Nancy unless Victor promises to break off the affair. Though this threat initially seeks a promise, rather than just an end to the affair, it is still a warning, because if Victor independently promised a concerned Tom that he would end the affair, Tom would refrain from informing Nancy.

33. The ability to make a warning threat and receive a response will often affect the timing of what one does after the threat, but I assume that this effect on the timing of the "natural response" is not critical for free speech purposes.

34. If one takes the "natural response" of informing Nancy as the *ordinary* course of events, one might view this aspect of Tom's communication as a kind of offer of something favorable for Victor in return for a benefit to Tom. So viewed, the communication is in part a manipulative inducement which, as urged in Chapters 3 and 4, lies outside a principle of free speech because of its situation-altering character.

35. The point may be clarified by analysis of an ordinary offer. If I offer you $2,000 to paint my house, the clear implication is that I will not pay you unless you do that. My "natural response" not to pay you unless you do something for me is not a dominant aspect of the communication.

Although what I say in the text comfortably fits the example there and most others that come to mind, one can imagine a communication in which the "manipulative" element is not a dominant aspect: "I'll tell Nancy unless you stop or you donate all you own to the poor," said by Tom, who thinks Victor's making such a donation is highly unlikely but would be so wonderful that Tom would be willing to forgo his natural response in return.

36. See, e.g., *People* v. *Rubin*, 96 Cal. App.3d 968, 977–78, 158 Cal. Rptr. 488, 492 (1979), certiorari denied, 449 U.S. 821 (1980).

37. See E. Baker, *Scope of the First Amendment*, 50–55 (to be published by Oxford University Press 1989). Here and in following references citations are to proofs that are not yet final.

See also E. Baker, "Scope of the First Amendment Freedom of Speech," 25 *University of California in Los Angeles Law Review* 964 (1978). Given the two elements of liberty Baker emphasizes, his account may be viewed as based on two values rather than one.

38. Baker, *Scope of the First Amendment*, note 37 supra, at pp. 55–57. See also Comment, note 30 supra (following Baker's approach for instances when the listener is forced to choose between two things to which he has a right but rejecting the approach for some instances of blackmail).

39. Baker, *Scope of the First Amendment*, at p. 56.

40. For Baker, my own focus on the quality of the communication itself draws an unpersuasive distinction between situation-altering utterances and other utterances, id. at

pp. 62–63, and resonates with a misguided "market place of ideas" theory of free speech, id. at p. 62. I have, of course, offered a pluralistic account of the justifications for free speech and believe that the "truth discovery" reason is only one basis, albeit an important one, for concentrating on assertions of fact and value, but Baker is correct that I give much more importance to statements of ideas than he does.

41. Baker's sense of "coercion" appears to be broader than mine. Considering the example of a slave who has worked in the field being given a choice to work in the home, Baker assumes that an "offer," an improvement in possible states of affairs, can still be "coercive" if it involves improper interference with someone else's choice. Id. at p. 57. I assume that one is coerced only if what the speaker states indicates more unpalatable options than previously existed (or than the listener thought previously existed) or if the *particular choice* the speaker gives to the listener restricts freedom against a baseline of what justice requires.

Baker's illustration provides an indication of his sense of "coercive" and what I think is its flaw. He says the master's offer to work in the house rather than the field is "coercive" if the slave would not have accepted the offer under just conditions. Since no one would be able to put such a constrained choice to anyone else under just conditions, the offer in Baker's view is coercive. But then so must be almost any offer a master makes to a slave, e.g., "Which hut would you like to live in?" "Would you like me to keep your grown children on the plantation?" etc. I think this terminology effectively erases any distinction between masters who offer slaves more free choice and those who offer less. I would prefer to say something like this: "Of course, the slave's working in the house is *coerced* because a whole range of choices required by justice was foreclosed, most importantly the option to leave the plantation as a free person, but, within the bounds of the slave system, the choice to work in the house *rather than* the field was uncoerced since the master made clear that the slave could do whichever he wanted and this increased the slave's range of choice."

Standing alone, this difference about "coercion" is terminological. Though Baker's rhetoric of coercion helps suggest that all improper influence is tied to coercion in some significant way, his point about the boundaries of free speech does not depend on the term. And I could accommodate Baker's premise that any "coercive" offer or threat is outside a principle of free speech by specifying that the distinction between manipulative threats and inducements, on the one hand, and warning threats and advisory inducements, on the other, is crucial to what counts as coercive. In short, to understand our substantive disagreement, one must get beyond our different uses of the term "coercive."

42. Baker indicates this by talking of options that the listener had "a moral or legitimate right to expect" and by defending an approach that "more overtly requires reference to normative considerations" than taking existing law as the starting point. Id. at p. 57.

43. Id. at p. 58. Baker claims that such an acceptance is circular.

44. I do not mean that in all aspects a principle of free speech will be wholly detached from other principles of liberty, and it may be that a determination whether a particular sort of communication should be protected, say pornographic photographs, will be closely tied to other claims of liberty, say how to treat "self-regarding acts."

45. It is highly relevant here that Baker's notion of what counts as acts that are *themselves* speech is much more expansive than mine. See E. Baker, "Unreasoned Reasonableness: Mandatory Parade Permits and Time, Place and Manner Regulations," 78 *Northwestern University Law Review* 937 (1983); and Commentary, in id. at 1025–30 (including my critique). Indeed, our difference over what generally counts as speech may be *the central* basis for our disagreements over conditional threats.

46. Even when people agree on generally applicable standards for free speech, they may disagree about particular outcomes, because they disagree about how to classify

borderline cases or because they give different weight to concededly relevant values. Often such disagreements will reflect divergences over more general social theory.

47. Of course, if prostitution should be allowed by legislatures or held to be a constitutionally protected activity, it may follow that offers should be allowed, but I consider the critical question then to be liberty to engage in prostitution, not free speech.

48. I do not want to imply that Baker would welcome this revision, which almost certainly departs too far from what he thinks is fundamental in free speech theory.

49. A legislature might, of course, mistakenly reach too far with general language, as may well have happened in Oregon. See text accompanying notes 59 and 60, infra. If free speech considerations are tied to proper pressures as closely as Baker supposes, possible unconstitutionality would provide an extra reason for a legislature to be careful not to go too far.

50. Baker, *Scope of the First Amendment*, note 37 supra, at p. 60.

51. Our agreement would be greater if presently prevailing standards about autonomy were taken as the test of improper pressure, rather than what would be permissible pressure in a good society.

52. Id. at p. 38.

53. I have my doubts here concerning the values of autonomy in a good society and their relevance, for Baker. If reporting affairs would be regarded as a serious wrong in a good society, I am not entirely clear whether Tom's belief that reporting is morally right saves him from using improper pressure. In this part of his discussion, Baker focuses on the values of the speaker, but I am uncertain how this relates to his earlier more general treatment of conditions of coercion.

54. Id. at p. 40.

55. An example like this is highly unlikely to involve a warning threat, though it is conceivable that Tom would not inform on someone he regarded as generous to the poor. In any event, since Baker draws no distinction between manipulative and warning threats, the example is a fair test of how he draws his line of improper pressure.

56. As far as I am aware, Baker does not explicitly address such self-interested warnings by third persons; so I am uncertain whether he would actually reach this conclusion.

57. I say limited *direct* practical import, because it is my belief that the manipulative feature of most serious threats that have traditionally been made criminal helps to explain why those threats have seemed appropriate for punishment.

58. See *Model Penal Code* § 212.5(1) (committing a crime, accusing someone of a crime, exposing a highly embarrassing secret, taking action as an official or causing such action). See also the affirmative defense discussed in the text below.

59. *State* v. *Robertson*, 293 Or. 402, 414, 649 P.2d 569, 577 (1982).

60. Id. at 418–19, 649 P.2d, at 580.

61. *Model Penal Code* § 223.4(a).

62. Sorting out which threats of lenders to break legs are manipulative and which are warning would be highly onerous, and, even if a lender demonstrably does break the legs of those he is incapable of warning, the whole scheme may be manipulative, designed to produce maximum rates of repayment by other borrowers. The same might be said about threatened retaliation against those who give information to the government and are protected by statute. See, e.g., *United States* v. *Velasquez*, 772 F.2d. 1348 (7th Cir. 1985), certiorari denied, 475 U.S. 1021 (1986); *United States* v. *Wilson* 565 F. Suppl. 1416 (S.D.N.Y. 1983).

63. Coverage for criminal coercion depends on the nature of the threatened conduct.

64. Compare *Pittsburgh Press Co.* v. *Human Relations Comm'n.* 413 U.S. 376 (1973) (gender-specific want ads); *United States* v. *Gilbert*, 813 F.2d 1523 (9th Cir. 1987) (threats to adoption agency placing black and Asian children).

65. If she has a clear duty to arrest in the circumstances or if arrest is the usual practice, what will be involved will be an *offer* to commit an illegal act, an offer essentially similar to an offer to accept a bribe.

66. In circumstances like this, further, a stated willingness not to arrest in return for payment will usually be a situation-altering promise that falls outside the domain of free speech.

67. I am assuming that communications that involve noncriminal violations of substantive rights, as in my housing-discrimination example, will be covered in the statutory provisions establishing those rights.

68. It would be implausible to say that nothing is a "threat" if it is a natural response for the speaker. A vindictive killer's statement, "Don't leave me or I'll kill you," does amount to a "threat."

69. *Model Penal Code* § 212.5(1).

6

Encouragements to Crime

This chapter considers utterances that encourage other people to commit crimes. Chapters 4 and 5 dealt with agreements, orders, offers, and threats, which also can constitute forms of encouragement; I now mainly address a contrasting class of utterances that are not significantly situation-altering: weak imperatives and assertions of fact. I begin with explicit urgings to commit particular crimes and then turn to kinds of "encouragements" which in some way are less direct.

Direct Urgings to Particular Crimes

By a *direct urging* to commit a particular crime which is not an order, offer, or threat, I mean a statement like "Please beat up my sister's boyfriend for me," or "I implore you not to register for the draft." As I indicated in Chapter 3, such imperatives are often intertwined with assertions of fact and value and may strongly reflect ideas of fact and value even when these ideas are not expressed. Uttering such imperatives can also afford an emotional outlet. Because their main objective is to get something done, simple encouragements and requests are not as strongly within the justifications of freedom of speech as typical statements of fact and value, but the justifications apply more to these weak imperatives than to situation-altering utterances. These premises are the basis on which the more focused discussion here proceeds.

Criminal Law Policy

The crime of "criminal solicitation" covers requests and encouragements to commit crimes. These are made criminal in themselves, and, if the person solicited commits the crime, the person who makes the solicitation is an accomplice, even when no agreement precedes the crime.[1] I explore arguments for liability, problems about coverage based on general concerns about the use of criminal sanctions, relevant arguments about free speech, and the boundaries of reasonable legislative accommodation.

Under the Model Penal Code, a person is guilty of criminal solicitation if with the purpose of promoting the commission of a crime "he commands, encourages or requests another person to engage in specific conduct that would constitute such crime."[2] Since this language does not require a threat or an offer, plainly the request to beat up a sister's boyfriend and the urging not to register for the draft are covered.

If it is objected that punishment should be imposed instead on the actor who commits the substantive offense, the answer is that the solicitation section does not relieve that actor of liability, that the person who solicits a crime has a definite criminal intent, and that urgings to crime may cause some crimes to be committed that would not otherwise occur. The solicitor is a wrongdoer because he aims for a criminal result, and the punishment of solicitation may reduce to some degree the numbers of solicitations and substantive crimes committed as a consequence of them. These are good reasons for employing the criminal sanction.

There are, however, some counterarguments that can be made without regard to the values of speech. I noted in Chapter 4 that the usual point at which criminal liability begins is fairly late in the process leading up to final commission of the crime. Like the law of conspiracy, the law of solicitation reaches back to a much earlier stage. That may seem justified on the ground that the solicitation itself reflects a firm criminal purpose and may be the last action that the person making it plans to undertake, and with some frequency the person who solicits will be cleverer and have a more dominant personality than the person he solicits. But this justification slides over two troubling aspects: the rate of success of pure solicitations, and the possible absence of firm intent. We can assume that, once criminal agreements are reached, the substantive crimes agreed upon occur in a substantial percentage of instances and that the agreement is usually critically related to their commission. Neither of these suppositions is warranted for solicitations that do not include an order, an inducement, or a threat. Many solicitations must fall on deaf ears, and, even when the person solicited performs the requested crime, often he would have done so regardless of the solicitation. Probably a relatively small percentage of instances of "pure" solicitation of crime actually produce substantive crimes. Thus, it is at least debatable whether a request or encouragement should be punished if it lacks an inducement or a threat and is not made by a person in authority. Yet, in circumstances when the person soliciting is the more dominant personality, it would be unfair to convict the perpetrator and let the person who effectively controls him go free.

If the infrequent success of pure solicitation is unrelated to free speech concerns, the worry about firm intent slides toward those concerns. In explaining why the law of attempt fixes liability late in the progress toward a crime, I mentioned the problems of determining intent and of gauging firmness of purpose when all one finds are ordinary acts of preparation. These problems have some relevance to "pure" solicitation. Often words are ambiguous, leaving doubt whether the speaker actually urges the commission of criminal acts. When the words are plain on their face, it may still be unclear whether they are intended literally or to make some rhetorical point. The speaker who says, "If the president sends our boys to be shot on foreign soil, someone should shoot him," is probably not seriously suggesting that a member of his audience actually attempt to assassinate the president if the involvement in a foreign war takes place. In some cases the transitory nature of communication may increase the risk of mistaken accusations, and a crime that can be "established" without any external occurrences may be particularly subject to abusive manipulation. Unless the net of criminal liability is cast carefully, persons may be held responsible for communications not actually intended by them to cause criminal behavior.

The point about firmness of purpose is less recognized but perhaps more serious. It concerns the sorts of intentions that often underlie communications. When our emotions are aroused we may express intentions—"I'm going to kill you" or "I want to marry you"—that we are actually not ready to bring to fruition by the acts required. We may fully intend to do what we say at the moment we say it, but it is psychologically easier to intend an act and to express the intention than actually to do as intended. The same analysis applies to many urgings of acts upon others. Suppose Edward finds out from Frank, his brother-in-law, that Edward's sister (Frank's wife) has been raped by a neighbor, and says in deadly earnest to Frank, "You should kill that bastard." Just as people sometimes are freer to express their own intentions than to act, they are sometimes freer to recommend that others do things than they would be to do those things themselves. Consciously or not, they have the sense that final responsibility rests with the person who will perform the acts, and they may give spontaneous verbal encouragements without the hard examination that would precede their own performances. Though it certainly does not follow that their encouragements will be harmless, their less than firm purpose may indicate that they are less to blame and less dangerous than people willing to carry out criminal acts.

On the basis of the concerns so far, a wide variety of legislative positions would be reasonable about "pure" solicitations. First, despite the objections offered, a legislature might find the justifications strong enough to make all criminal solicitations punishable, so long as care is taken to ensure that a definite serious encouragement has been made. After all, someone who urges a crime has a manifested criminal purpose, and prosecutors may be trusted not to go after those whose solicitations are obviously ineffectual. Second, and at the other end of the spectrum, it might be decided not to punish "pure" solicitation directed at actors competent to decide for themselves. Although this would allow the persuasive person with a strong personality occasionally to work criminal purposes through others, that may be deemed an acceptable price for not stretching the criminal law too far. Third, pure solicitation might be punished only if successful;[3] such a rule would permit punishment of many of the really dangerous requests and encouragements, while leaving others unregulated. In that event, the law might require a finding that the crime would not have been committed without the solicitation, but that perhaps is too much to expect the government ever to prove beyond a reasonable doubt. Fourth, criminality might be limited, as it was under the traditional English common law,[4] to solicitation of felonies. Fifth, it might be required that a solicitation be made in circumstances where there is a significant likelihood of success or where the relationship of the persons involved gives the one making the solicitation potential influence. Of course, some of these options might be combined in various ways. Because prosecutions of pure solicitations are very rare, the judgment among these alternatives is not of great practical significance, but it does reflect important conclusions about the use of criminal sanctions. My own view is that, ideally, even putting aside free speech arguments, pure requests or encouragements should be punishable only when they propose serious crimes *and* have a substantial likelihood of being successful, but I am not sure that the drafting refinements necessary to accomplish this limitation are worth the cost, unless one is also troubled by free speech concerns.

Free Speech Perspectives

I now address the relevance of free speech for criminal solicitation. The initial Commentary to the Model Penal Code suggested straightforwardly that the solicitation of crimes has nothing to do with freedom of expression.[5] That position might be defended on various bases.

The most obvious basis is that urgings to action generally lie outside the realm of free expression. Although the statements of fact and value that accompany urgings may warrant protection, the urgings themselves would be seen as efforts to *do* things and not within a principle of free speech. This is essentially the position I have taken about agreements, orders, and other strongly situation-altering utterances; what is involved here is the extension of that position to simple encouragements and requests. The argument for that extension might rely on the situation-altering aspect of requests, which often change the normative situation to a degree by providing a reason to act somewhat stronger than a known but unexpressed wish. Were imperatives considered outside the realm of expression, legislatures would not need to worry about free speech when deciding whether to ban encouragements of even legally permitted actions. If, for example, smoking were regarded as a habit so deeply entrenched that prohibition would be unwise but a habit so harmful that it should be discouraged, there would be no free speech difficulty in forbidding people to urge others to smoke. The idea that all requests and encouragements lie outside a principle of free speech has been rejected in Chapter 3, which notes that these communications are further removed from action than strongly situation-altering utterances and may imply powerful assertions of fact and value, that the line between them and statements of fact and value is often thin, and that requiring people to eschew encouragements while asserting facts and values that come very close to encouragements would be highly constricting.

A more narrow defense of the position that urgings to crime do not fall within a principle of freedom of speech is that such urgings partake more of crime than of expression and thus can properly be punished. Unless it assumes that all urgings are outside free speech (the view just rejected), this position must rest on something special about urgings to crime. On a spectrum of expression to action, urging a crime is no more "action" than urging to permitted behavior; so the claim must be that criminal acts constitute a social harm serious enough so that urgings to commit them may properly be punished even if those urgings implicate considerations underlying free speech to some degree. So understood, the position represents a kind of "balancing" approach. But if what is involved is striking a balance, drawing distinctions in terms of types of crimes and situations may make more sense than generalizing about all encouragements and all crimes. That is the approach explored in depth in the next section.

A final defense of the position that urgings to crime do not come within a principle of free expression calls upon a version of social contract theory. The basic idea is that free speech operates within a society of consent, that among the ground rules of such a society are that people live within the law, that people who urge breaking the law are failing to adhere to the "social contract," and that such urgings therefore are not reached by a principle of free speech relevant for that society.[6] This position does not depend on the social danger of crime; rather it rests on a perspective about basic rights and duties. Citizens have a duty to comply with the ground rules; if in their speech they urge the breaking of the ground rules they have forfeited any right to be free in that speech. In its more extreme form this position would apply to all encouragements of criminal action; in its more moderate form it would reach only urgings of crimes that involve genuine challenges to prevailing political institutions.

The extreme form of the position rests on the supposition that observance of the law all of the time is a basic ground rule of this society. Most people intentionally break laws some of the time—laws against speeding come immediately to mind. If some minor lawbreaking is engaged in by the average citizen, it is more than a bit artificial to say that encouragement to such lawbreaking ("Go a little faster, Jane, I'm in a hurry") violates some fundamental premise of our society. Perhaps more important, some lawbreaking is engaged in in order to contribute to the justice of society, and when people encourage peaceable civil disobedience with submission to punishment, they are rarely trying to subvert the legal order. For both these reasons, not all encouragements to violations of law can be said to breach terms of the "social contract."

The more modest claim that efforts to undermine the legal order, such as serious urgings to commit revolutionary acts, are not covered by free speech can surmount the challenge I have just offered, but both the extreme and the modest versions of the thesis that advocacy of lawbreaking is excluded from free speech are subject to a more pervasive criticism. The whole idea that in a liberal society a principle of freedom of speech should be tailored to the accepted ground rules is misconceived. From the standpoint of the speaker, the degree to which an encouragement expresses emotions or represents an aspect of his autonomy does not depend on whether he is encouraging a crime. Nor do the benefits for an audience depend on that. People learn about severe injustices, government abuses, and intense feelings of discontent within the social system in part because others urge that the legal order be resisted by criminal acts. History is filled with instances in which peaceful reform takes the steam out of revolutionary movements by correcting the worst abuses that have given rise to the movements, and revolutionary rhetoric has undoubtedly contributed to the reform. In other words, many of the justifications for free speech apply with considerable force to urgings of crime and to urgings of criminal revolutionary action.

There is a subsidiary point here that harks back to the thin line between urgings and assertions of fact and value. If only urgings were said to fall outside a principle of free speech, then many ideas favorable to criminal behavior and revolution could be advanced in a different form: "It would be good for people and be morally justifiable to establish a dictatorship of the proletariat by armed force." On the other hand, were such ideas *also* claimed to be wholly unprotected, significant aspects of the range of discourse in social philosophy and political protest would lie outside the range of free speech. That the position excluding criminal or revolutionary encouragements either requires drawing a very thin line between encouragements and claims that crime or revolution is justified or would have radical implications for the status of many assertions of "political" facts and values is itself a reason to reject the position.

At the farthest remove from the claim that encouragements to crime are wholly outside a principle of freedom of speech is the claim that encouragements warrant protection equal to that accorded to most assertions of fact and value. Having already explained that the dominant aim of imperatives to produce action by others renders the justifications for free speech less forceful in application to them, I here reconsider a particular theory for according pure encouragements *absolute* protection. The theory, explored somewhat more fully in Chapter 2, is that the government should treat people as autonomous and that autonomous people would wish to have accessible everything relevant to how they should act, including other people's expressions of desires and their opinions about appropriateness.[7] Since the force of wish and conviction is often best expressed in a direct encouragement, treating people as autonomous means allowing them full exposure to requests and encouragements. If this theory is built on what autonomous people might agree to when settling on social rules, it neglects the likelihood that at this preliminary stage autonomous people might well agree to foreclose some inputs for themselves which they would ideally like to have in some situations. That sacrifice might be an acceptable price for preventing some inputs for other people who are not rational and autonomous when they receive the communications or who, though autonomous, may commit antisocial acts. Were the idea instead that the government must always treat citizens in the audience in a way that maximizes their autonomy at the time they receive the communication, whatever autonomous people would have agreed upon in setting up the rules, the theory must explain why the government must enhance autonomy in this special sense against every other legitimate social objective (such as preventing murders by selfish irresponsible people who are easily subject to persuasion). I am unaware of any reasoned defense of that claim and extremely skeptical that a plausible, much less persuasive, defense could be made.

Considerations of autonomy matter, and the autonomy of speaker and of audience are reasons to permit encouragements to crime, but they are reasons to be considered in relation to other reasons, not absolutely decisive counters in favor of liberty.

Reasonable Legislative Accommodations

When the reasons for nonprohibition based on freedom of speech are added to those based on criminal law policy, a legislature might well decide not to make criminal any "pure" criminal encouragements or any "pure" encouragements that are unsuccessful.[8] Assuming that a judgment has been made that some encouragements do warrant punishment, I shall investigate factors that seem especially relevant, apart from the obvious factors of success or likely success and the seriousness of the crime encouraged. I consider: (1) the publicness of the encouragement, (2) the nature of its appeal, and (3) the mood of the audience.

I comment very briefly on the third factor, the mood of the audience. If the audience is in an emotional state that makes it unlikely that the encouragement will receive deliberate consideration, free speech reasons related to deliberate audience response obviously have diminished force. But because this factor does not fit comfortably into any sensible legislative formulation to punish encouragements to commit crimes, I shall disregard it in the rest of this chapter.

There is more reason to punish private encouragements than public ones and more reason to punish encouragements cast in terms of gain or satisfaction for the listener than those cast in terms of ideological considerations. That the argument for protection is weakest when we focus on private nonideological solicitation can be illustrated by the following example. Cousin Alan, who stands to inherit a great deal of money under his uncle's will, writes a letter urging Cousin Betty, who similarly stands to inherit, to kill their uncle, making an appeal that relies on Betty's dislike of the uncle and her desperate need for money. Although Alan's communication implicitly reflects a good deal about his scale of values and his view of the relationships between himself and Betty and between each of them and their uncle, suppressing the communication poses a minimal danger to free speech. The expressive value of Alan's utterance is slight in comparison with the threat it poses, and most of that expressive value could easily be achieved by other kinds of communication.

The secretive nature of Alan's urging is very important. Since others will not be aware of what he has suggested, any "enlightenment" the message provides will be limited.[9] More important, Betty will probably not be exposed to directly countervailing encouragements, nor will precautionary steps by the uncle or by agencies of law enforcement be taken to prevent the crime Alan has urged. The expressive value of this sort of private encouragement that appeals to self-interest is slight enough so that it may appropriately be punished even if it is not likely to succeed and even if the encouragement is to commit a crime in the nonimmediate future, say when the uncle returns from Europe in two months.

A principle of free speech usually has more to do with public communication encouraging specific crimes. If someone urges illegal action in a street-corner oration or a pamphlet, he will probably make some appeal to notions of right or duty or general welfare or to some broader historical or philosophical understanding within which his particular urging fits. His message, thus, will include what may be labeled, roughly, an ideological appeal. Although the justifications for free speech do apply to appeals to simple self-interest, the expressive value of communications that make claims about public duties or touch other broad themes is much more central for a liberal democratic society. Even those public speeches which include important appeals to self-interest, for example, a union leader's call for workers to improve their working conditions, will typically contain claims of justice and a perspective on history as well. When communication is public, the audience is larger, and, because others are aware of what is said, ample opportunity exists for counterarguments and for precautionary official measures if a serious crime is feared.

Because of the expressive value of public ideological solicitations, protecting them is appropriate unless certain stringent conditions are met that establish their dangerousness. Such solicitations should not be punished unless the speaker urges commission of a specific crime in the very near future and it is reasonably likely that the speech will contribute to the commission of that crime. As many readers are undoubtedly aware, these suggestions fall close to what the Supreme Court has indicated is a constitutional standard,[10] and nuances are explored in Chapter 15 on constitutional interpretation. I reserve for that discussion some additional qualifications that *might* be placed in a carefully constructed statute but probably are too detailed for statutory formulation.

I turn now to the two intermediate categories: public nonideological solicitation and private ideological solicitation. Except for commercial appeals of one kind or another, very few public appeals will lack important ideological components. For this reason, it makes sense to treat all noncommercial public encouragements of crime according to the standards appropriate for ideological encouragements. Less protection is warranted for commercial proposals, which make a limited contribution to understanding of important public issues or personal concerns. Even if a commercial proposal does not amount to an offer and is, thus, not strictly situation-altering,[11] it is much closer to action than is an ordinary encouragement for someone to act in a particular way.[12] Since few enterprises will pay for commercial messages without a substantial likelihood of their being acted upon, a legislature need not concern itself with the precise likelihood that a commercial message proposing illegal behavior, such as a purchase of proscribed drugs, will be acted upon by readers. Whatever ideological message a commercial proposal carries may have less presumptive value because of likely manipulation to serve the enterprise's interests. For all these reasons, public commercial proposals to engage in criminal transactions warrant no more protection than private nonideological solicitation.

Much discussion of serious concerns takes place in private, and ideological solicitation in that context may have substantial expressive value, but it does not follow that the setting is irrelevant to the appropriate level of protection. Except in the context of emotional mass meetings, the influence of a speaker is likely to be much stronger if his audience is small and selected. A personal letter or oral plea to an acquaintance will not enlighten many people, but it will carry much more weight for the addressee's decision than a general circular or public speech, and its influence is more likely to survive a lapse in time. A person with selfish aims may in private and with a selected audience be particularly able to manipulate the ideological predilections of his audience. Since others will not know what has been said, they will lack, as I mentioned with respect to private nonideological solicitation, the opportunity to counteract the speaker's influence. For all these reasons constraint of private ideological solicitation may be warranted when similar public solicitation should be allowed. Because it does have significant expressive value, however, private ideological solicitation should not be punished unless it presents some significant danger of criminal harm.

These various suggestions indicate a difference in appropriate treatment between public and private solicitation; but how is that line to be drawn? The crucial factor for public speech is that the message be communicated so that its content can become known to the public. Speeches made to club groups that have easy access to membership or have criteria of selection that have nothing to do with receptivity to the illegal action that might be urged by the speaker would qualify as public speeches, as would a written message sent to a somewhat selective audience, say, all draft registrants, but which unavoidably would be known to a still wider audience. The troublesome borderline for the public-private dichotomy concerns moderately sized audiences selected because of likely special sympathy for the speaker's encouragement. Important here would be the size of the group, how carefully selected it is, the strictness of its standards of confidentiality, whether or not the basic message of the speaker is also communicated publicly, and whether or not the members of the group are generally known, all factors that bear on public access to the message and the prospect of countervailing communication.

Although omitting many subtleties, I have suggested a number of factors as possibly relevant to legislative choice, but there is a limit to how precise legislation should be. Because of the rarity of prosecutions of pure solicitation, especially unsuccessful pure solicitation, a provision could be rather rough in important ways, leaving untouched some pure solicitation that ideally would be punished or covering some solicitation that ideally would not be punished, or both. Insofar as some solicitation should not be punished because of its speech value, a legislature might leave that to be protected by constitutional interpretation or choose some open-ended statutory terms that courts could interpret in light of free speech.

In the proposal that follows, I assume that the legislature will attend rather closely to the considerations I have advanced. Because the only direct practical significance of the elusive line between ideological and nonideological encouragement would be to demand a significant danger of harm for interdiction of private ideological communication and because that factor is best left to constitutional review, I assume that a general statute would not distinguish ideological from nonideological encouragement. I also assume that the legislature would leave the courts to work out the boundaries of the public-private distinction. A legislature might begin with a basic definition of solicitation like that in the Model Penal Code, and add a special provision along the following lines:

> If an encouragement or request to commit a crime is not accompanied by an inducement or threat, and is not made by a person with authority over the person solicited, it is not punishable unless it presents a significant danger of serious criminal harm; and if it is made in public and is not a commercial advertisement, it is not punishable unless it is designed to produce a crime within the very near future and is reasonably likely to have that effect.

These and other possible qualifications of a general prohibition of solicitation are explored further when constitutional principles are examined.

Variations on Encouragement

In the following discussion, I explore a number of variations on the idea of criminal solicitation. What unites all these instances is that the audience may be influenced to commit a crime that the speaker intends or can predict may happen. I assume that the interests of the law are to prevent the crime that might be committed because of the speaker's utterances and to punish those responsible if the crime occurs. For each of the variations, I say a word about present law, considerations of criminal policy, the relevance of freedom of speech, and appropriate legislative approaches. For most of the variations, the argument for punishment of the speaker is somewhat less powerful than it is for punishing criminal solicitation, because the connection between the communication and the crime to be committed is more remote.

Factual Information

A speaker may communicate facts in order to get his listener to commit a crime. The kind of communication I have in mind here differs from the factual disclosures I have previously treated: the speaker is not already in a criminal agreement with the listener; the speaker is not trying to make it easier for the listener to commit a crime that the listener is already set upon (a form of aid, or attempted aid, even in the absence of agreement between speaker and listener); the speaker is not using a pleasant or unpleasant consequence within his control to induce or threaten the listener. Rather, the speaker conveys independent factual information that he hopes will lead the listener to commit a criminal act. Carla, hoping that Donna will transport a load of drugs, says to her, "I don't see why you are hesitating, the police on the route have been bribed, so there's no chance of getting caught." Or Carla, hoping that David, a leading figure in organized crime, will have Edith killed, says to David, "You know, Edith is a police informant."

In most circumstances in which such factual information is conveyed, the speaker will be overtly encouraging the listener to commit a specific crime, as will be evident either because words of encouragement accompany the statement of fact or because in context the statement of fact—Carla's to Donna is an example—clearly conveys an encouragement itself.[13] The danger from a solicitation is actually increased if the speaker communicates new relevant facts; so the ordinary reasons for punishment are somewhat greater than for weak imperatives unaccompanied by any information except about the speaker's wishes. Free speech reasons do have a slight bearing on the facts disclosed, but the particular facts revealed do not have enough expressive value to alter a conclusion about punishment based on the encouragement itself.

If the speaker does not convey his encouragement of a specific crime, then, as the organized-crime example illustrates, the treatment under present law is less clear. Suppose that Carla lets David know that she supposes he will commit *some* criminal act to take care of Edith, the informer, but does not say anything about various options that both assume are possibilities. The definition of criminal solicitation under the Model Code requires encouraging another "to engage in specific conduct that would constitute such crime (i.e., the crime encouraged)."[14] It is doubtful whether that requisite is met here. I postpone to a later section the discussion of what should be done about encouragement of crimes in general.

The more interesting variation is one in which the speaker and listener understand that the facts "call for" a specific crime, say murder, but the speaker conceals any criminal purpose from the listener. Probably anyone who tells a leader in organized crime that he has an informer in his midst anticipates that trying to murder the informer is a likely response; so we need to make the unrealistic assumption that Carla is a neighbor of David's who has never revealed to David that she knows his true occupation. Over a drink, Carla "lets slip" in passing that her friend Edith, who is an employee of David's, works for the police. Carla wants Edith killed, but she does not let David know that she understands why these facts are so important to him.

Whether Carla is guilty of encouraging David to kill Edith is not certain. Arguably, the word "encourages" in the Model Penal Code is wide enough to include a communication meant to elicit a certain response while concealing the speaker's desire for that response, but the ordinary sense of encouragement is expressed support for a particular action. These doubts about coverage existed under the common law as well. James Fitzjames Stephen thought that Iago's deliberate lies about Desdemona's infidelity would not, without more, have made Iago liable for murder,[15] but Glanville Williams suggests that Iago might very well be guilty as an accessory for intentionally provoking Othello.[16] One South African judge has formulated the test for incitement as "whether the accused reached and sought to influence the mind of the other person towards the commission of a crime,"[17] language broad enough to include both Iago and Carla in the hypothetical. Even if Carla is not liable for encouragement, she is, conceivably, liable for aiding or attempting to aid, on the theory that David has a generalized intention to get rid of informers and Carla is helping him carry this out. And, under the Model Penal Code, because of its particular provisions on causation and attempt, Carla may be liable more directly.[18]

Whatever perplexities this example may present for existing law, only problems of determining intent would present a ground in ordinary penal policy for treating someone who openly encourages commission of a crime differently from someone who intentionally provides information in order to give an incentive for a crime. From the free speech perspective, information has more importance than have simple encouragements or requests, but the expressive value of information designedly revealed to lead to crimes may not seem very great. The worry about speech interests is increased if one considers the problems of proving intent. People might be subject to liability, or at least investigation, for innocently revealing facts that led their listeners to commit crimes. When one considers an example of clear and straightforward manipulation, like Carla's in the hypothetical situation, criminal punishment seems appropriate, but when one takes into account the difficulties of determining unexpressed intentions for apparently innocent remarks and the great infrequency with which cases like this will actually arise, a legislature might decide to so formulate a solicitation provision as not to reach the giving of information with this sort of intent.

Provocation

Essentially similar analysis applies to words that do not convey factual information in the ordinary sense but are uttered for the very purpose of provoking the listener into committing a crime. Frieda, for example, taunts George as a "pathetic chicken" for not responding to Hanna's insult, hoping that George will be aroused to attack Hanna, whom she hates. Or Irving shouts that the police are vicious, brutal crooks, hoping to incite an already angry mob to attack an officer it has surrounded.[19] A preliminary draft of the Model Penal Code section on accomplice liability explicitly made a person liable who intentionally "provokes" a crime,[20] but the dropping of that word from the accomplice section and its absence from the section on solicitation leaves "encourages" as the term in that section that must cover such behavior, if any term does. And if the wish to have members of the audience commit a crime is not evident, the same problems for applying the word "encourages" exist in respect to provocative remarks as in respect to factual statements. Since the difficulties in finding intent are similar in the two situations and since Frieda's and Irving's indicating their views fall within a principle of free speech, the reasons for not including such provocations within criminal solicitation are much like those applicable to factual disclosures. (I leave for a subsequent section possible liability for recklessness concerning a violent response and crimes like harassment and disorderly conduct.)

General Encouragements to Crime

Should persons be liable for communicating general encouragements to criminal action rather than urging the commission of specific crimes? Though A is possibly liable under the common law for incitement if he has recommended burglary to B as a desirable occupation and B has taken his advice,[21] the Model Penal Code limits solicitation to encouragement of "specific conduct" that would constitute a crime—language that apparently precludes any conviction for a sweeping recommendation of a life of burglary and probably even for a recommendation of some vague criminal conduct against a particular person.

General urgings to crime sometimes have effects, but they are usually less likely to produce results than specific encouragements, and when they do lead someone to commit a crime their influence will often be hard to trace. Moreover, the problems of ambiguity and determining seriousness of intention are particularly acute with respect to general encouragements. These problems are sufficient to suggest the wisdom, even from the point of view of narrow penal policy, of not making general encouragements either criminal by themselves or a basis for accomplice liability.

This broad position leaves open the possibility that some general encouragements, say to murder public officials or members of a racial minority or to forcibly overthrow the government, will be extraordinarily dangerous and will warrant a narrow prohibition.

The good sense of not forbidding all general encouragements to crime is confirmed by reflection on the values of speech, and such reflection also suggests the great cost of singling out *some* general encouragements for punishment. General encouragements perhaps more often than specific solicitations convey important ideological messages. They are less likely to be acted upon immediately. Time for reflection and the possibilities of countervailing speech are important when one assesses the "action" aspect of a communication against its expressive quality. The farther off in the distance is the moment for an encouragement to be followed, the more the encouragement may be regarded as expressive. In the section on private solicitation, I did not suggest a temporal restriction; if one suggests a specific murder two months hence, it is reasonable to treat the encouragement as criminal. But the argument for punishing solicitation does weaken somewhat as the time between the communication and the proposed crime extends. That many general encouragements are not meant to be acted on right away is one good reason not to punish them.

Good reasons also exist for not singling out a limited class of general encouragements for punishment. Some of the strongest justifications for free speech concern claims of justice, accommodations of interests, and exposure of abuses of public officials. If the government considers legislating against some kinds of general encouragements to crimes, there is a serious danger that it will overestimate the danger of encouragements that seem threatening to the government itself. Depending on how the prohibited generalized encouragements are categorized, the law may also end up favoring some political positions over others for reasons unrelated to any objective danger arising out of the crimes likely to be committed. The discussion of these points to follow here is brief and abstract, but the chapter on the history of constitutional adjudication provides examples from American legal history.

Of course, any prohibition on encouraging the murder of government officials or violent overthrow of the government would favor peaceful political ideologies over violent ones, but it may be responded that it is a permissible government policy to prefer movements that accept the broad premises of our system and do not seek to overturn it by force. Although even encouragements to depart from the premises of our system have expressive value, I agree that the preference for urging obedience to law over urging violence is not itself the kind of preference that is strongly at odds with a principle of free speech. The worry about preferences for particular political positions becomes serious only if some further preference is involved. Perhaps a rule against urging violence for the remote furture has, in most modern liberal societies, the practical consequence of preferring right-wing over left-wing ideas, especially if the left wing asserts that violence will be required because the right wing will not yield power peaceably. The dangers of preference are increased by the possibility of uneven administration. Further, systematic government violence of certain kinds, say the killing of opposition newspaper editors, may undermine liberal political institutions every bit as much as violence against the government; so a rule against advocating violent revolutionary acts discriminates in favor of advocacy of equally offensive violent measures sponsored by the government.

Whether or not a selective prohibition of general encouragements to crime directed at revolutionary advocacy is "fair" between political positions, it risks both insensitivity to the expressive value of such encouragements and overestimation of their dangers. In sum, legislatures should be extremely hesitant to single out revolutionary kinds of general criminal encouragements for prohibitions, and the farther removed in time the proposed violent actions are from the encouragements, the more hesitant the legislatures should be.

Disinterested Advice

Passive, disinterested advice is on the margin of encouragement. Suppose Adele is asked by her close friend whether he should commit a crime. With no personal stake in the outcome, Adele thinks carefully and then says that the crime would be justified or would serve her friend's interests. Adele has communicated sentiments which she and her friend understand to be in favor of the criminal act, but she has expressed no desire that the act be committed and might consistently hope that it will not. For example, she might say, "I think you'd be morally right to refuse induction, but I hope you don't because I'd hate to see you go to jail."[22]

In most American jurisdictions, criminal solicitation requires a purpose to promote commission of a crime that is lacking in disinterested advice. Though it is questionable whether the earlier common law had as strict an intent requirement for complicity if the substantive crime was committed, at least in the jurisdictions that follow the Model Code the purpose requirement for being an accomplice is the same as for solicitation, and disinterested advice would not create either liability.

Some disinterested advice that approves of specific crimes may seem dangerous enough to warrant criminal penalties, but, even from the standpoint of penal policy, criminalizing advice may be unwise. The person who limits himself to giving disinterested advice, especially when he gives it only upon request, will ordinarily be less dangerous than the person who takes the initiative in urging the same criminal behavior, and, since almost everyone can imagine some circumstances in which he or she believes commission of some crimes is warranted, a rule of liability for advice of this sort would cast the net of liability very wide.

When one reflects on the relevance of a principle of free speech, this position is strongly reinforced. What free speech is mainly about is the honest expression of people's views about facts and values and how they relate to the way we live our lives. That is what disinterested advice amounts to. Such advice falls squarely and most strongly within the justifications for free speech, and it would take extremely powerful reasons to justify its suppression. At least when it is not given by recognized experts or persons in positions of authority, disinterested advice is so slight a threat to the social order that the reasons for suppressing it are far from powerful enough to warrant that course.[23]

Recklessness and Negligence

Criminal codes punish behavior that recklessly or negligently causes injury, and the possibility arises of punishing someone whose remarks risk the commission of a crime by someone else. Were such a ground of liability present, it might reach both some of the communications that have been so far discussed, for example, provocative words and disinterested advice, and other communications outside those categories, such as racial epithets not intended to cause a crime. Although the distinction between recklessness and negligence has not always been clear in criminal cases, I am assuming that recklessness requires subjective consciousness of risk, negligence only a risk of which a reasonable person would have been aware. Under the Model Penal Code, to be liable for recklessness or negligence a person must disregard a "substantial and unjustifiable risk"; for recklessness the disregard must include "a gross deviation from the standard of conduct that a law-abiding person would observe"; for negligence the failure to perceive the risk must involve "a gross deviation from the standard of care that a reasonable person would observe."[24]

The following kind of situation is one in which a speaker might be reckless or negligent about the effect of his words.

> Addressing a group assembled to protest a police shooting of a teenager after some people have become unruly and shoved attending police, Sandra says: "These people are your enemies. They are scum who don't deserve to live. Whoever wipes them out is doing our people a favor." In fact, Sandra wants only to add to the general pressure for change in the police force, but her words risk encouraging others to attack the police.

If the risk of assault or murder is substantial and unjustifiable, and Sandra is aware of it, she would be reckless; if Sandra is unaware of the risk, she would be negligent.

The law's present treatment of situations like this is hard to capsulize. Traditional law has punished reckless and negligent behavior only when harm has actually resulted. And under traditional principles of causation, if Sandra unreasonably risked that a member of the audience would commit a crime, the member's intentional commission of the crime would break the causal chain and relieve Sandra of possible liability for the act. In sum, whether acted upon or not, communications that unreasonably risked leading members of the audience to commit crimes were not subject to liability under general principles.

The Model Penal Code has worked two significant changes that affect this disposition, but one of these changes has not been adopted in many jurisdictions. That change involves somewhat novel principles for what has been referred to in the law as the issue of "proximate cause," roughly, the determination of when actions that constitute a "but for" cause or condition[25] of an event also count as a *proximate cause* to which liability has attached. Under the Model Code,[26] Sandra can be criminally liable if a harm occurs in a manner of which she was or should have been aware. Thus, if the subsequent intentional decision of a listener to shoot a police officer was a predictable risk, the fact of the voluntary intervening act would not preclude her liability, whereas, under traditional "causation" principles, the deliberate and informed act of a responsible third person would relieve Sandra of liability.[27] Under the Model Code, Sandra could be liable for recklessly causing that act if she spoke despite her awareness of the risk; otherwise she could be liable for negligently causing the act. A second innovation in the Model Code, more widely followed, is creation of a crime of *reckless endangerment*. One is guilty of a misdemeanor if one engages in conduct that recklessly places "another person in danger of death or serious bodily injury."[28] Thus, Sandra might be liable for her speech under the Model Code even if no police officer were actually assaulted as a result. What of the jurisdictions that have adopted reckless-endangerment provisions but do not accept the Model Code's approach to causation? Since Sandra would then not be liable for the killing if a listener shoots an officer, she probably also should be relieved of possible liability for reckless endangerment. A reckless-endangerment provision should be interpreted not to reach behavior whose danger inheres in the risk of generating an intentional act for which one would not be responsible. In most jurisdictions, then, Sandra's speech, even if reckless, is not reached by general principles of liability.

Traditionally, however, speakers could be liable for narrower crimes if they engaged in reckless and negligent communications in particular circumstances. Under the common law and many statutory formulations, for example, a person could be convicted for behavior tending to cause a breach of the peace, and Sandra might well be punishable under that catchall offense. The Model Penal Code analogue is disorderly conduct,[29] which has a somewhat more confined definition than the traditional offense of breach of the peace. One is still liable (though only for a violation)[30] who recklessly creates a risk of "public inconvenience, annoyance or alarm" by making "unreasonable noise or offensively coarse utterance, gesture or display, or address[ing] abusive language to any person present." The relevant part of the petty misdemeanor of harassment is narrower still, requiring a purpose to harass and the making of insults, taunts, or challenges likely to provoke a violent or disorderly response.[31] Thus, potential liability is maintained for some communication that is reckless about the possibility that a listener will commit a crime, but the communications reached are categorized, albeit pretty vaguely, imprisonment is eliminated as a penalty when all that can be shown is recklessness, and no liability attaches for mere negligence. In all probability, Sandra's remarks fall outside the relevant sections.[32]

Quite apart from a principle of free speech, there are strong arguments against liability for communication that risks intentional and informed action by others.[33] In contrast to more ordinary examples of recklessness, like someone's aimlessly firing a bullet into a lighted house, the risk that a speech creates is very difficult to assess, and even if the risked crime occurs, the causal connection may be hard to establish. Juries, especially those very unsympathetic to what is said, will be hard put to assess fairly either substantiality of risk or actual consequence. If general speech values are somehow to figure in whether a risk is "substantial" and "unjustifiable," one doubts a jury's capacity to deal sensitively with that evaluation.[34] In contrast to the stray-bullet case where the only wrongdoer is the one who has acted recklessly or negligently, a case of reckless speech involves someone else who intentionally commits a crime after the initial action, and punishment of that latter person probably will be sufficient to satisfy community outrage.

Most communications that risk criminal harm caused by members of the audience are clearly within a principle of free speech. They are likely to fall into the categories I have discussed in previous sections of this chapter or to involve the communication of inflammatory assertions about fact and value. Though it is sometimes claimed that abusive and insulting words are not a part of expression—a subject examined in more detail in Chapter 8—the justifications for free speech do reach many insults. Often, as Sandra's calling the police "scum" shows, insults involve pithy assertions about someone's characteristics and about proper relations to that person, and insults certainly may express the intense emotional feelings of the speakers.

Punishment should never be imposed for communications just because they negligently risk the commission of a crime by a listener, and punishment for reckless communications of this sort should be extremely sparing. If particular classes of communications, for example, epithets or disclosing the names of the country's covert spies,[35] have especially harmful tendencies, an initial legislative decision forbidding that kind of speech may put the speaker on notice as to what speech is beyond bounds. The speaker's blameworthiness, then, lies not in simple indifference to risk, but in intentionally saying things that are proscribed. Because of the value of speech, a legislature worried about the risk of crimes by listeners should be very hesitant to forbid speakers who do not intend crimes from making statements of fact and evaluations they regard as accurate, but a compelling enough case might warrant such a prohibition.

An alternative that is somewhat more protective of speech is to require, as do the Model Code provisions on disorderly conduct and harassment, *both* the utterance of specified kinds of words or thoughts *and* reckless risk creation. The speaker then has some warning[36] of what forms of communication are regarded as dangerous, and the fact-finder determining risk can be guided to some extent by the legislative judgment about the dangers of kinds of communications. Of course, the element of possible warning is reduced if legislative specification of potentially criminal utterances is vague, and terms like "abusive" and "insulting" are certainly somewhat vague.

Solicitation to Solicit, Assist, or Conspire, and Conspiracy to Solicit

Although solicitation to enter a conspiracy could be punished under traditional principles, it is doubtful whether the law reached A's solicitation of B either to get B to assist a crime committed by C or to get B to solicit C to commit a crime. The language of the Model Code makes someone liable for solicitation in all three instances[37] and for the substantive offense if the solicitation produces the result that is aimed for. Of course, if solicitation, assistance, and conspiracy are themselves dangerous, soliciting them also poses some danger, but the wisdom of reaching even farther back from ultimate criminal behavior is questionable.

Whereas solicitation to enter a conspiracy will normally constitute a situation-altering "offer," "pure" solicitation to assist a crime or to solicit a crime is reached by the reasons for free speech to some degree. Although solicitation to assist a crime may not be sensibly distinguishable from solicitation to commit a crime and should, thus, be treated similarly, solicitation to solicit, given the values of speech, is too remote from any final crime to be properly punishable if it is not acted upon. Probably solicitation to solicit should not be punished even if it is successful in getting the person originally solicited to solicit someone else or, more arguably, even if the person solicited by the original listener actually commits the crime.

Another combination of inchoate crimes is a conspiracy to solicit, explicitly made criminal under the Model Penal Code.[38] Here it is enough to say that, in addition to general worries about reaching too far back into preparatory stages of criminal activity, there is a particular free speech problem of holding people liable for agreeing to communicate, unless the content and circumstances of the communication are virtually certain. In the absence of such knowledge, it is difficult to know how forcefully the justifications of free speech will apply to the communication. This point, and the general subject, receive much more extensive elaboration in Chapter 20.

Notes

1. *Model Penal Code* § 2.06(3)(a)(i).

2. Id. § 5.02(1).

3. That is, the independent crime of solicitation would not cover "pure" solicitations, but successful solicitation would render one an accomplice.

4. A very brief sketch of the history and some relevant citations are provided in K. Greenawalt, "Speech and Crime," 1980 *American Bar Foundation Journal* 645, 656–57.

5. *Model Penal Code* § 5.02, Comment 4, at 87–88 (Tentative Draft No. 10, 1960).

6. See generally R. Bork, "Neutral Principles and Some First Amendment Problems," 47 *Indiana Law Journal* 1, 31 (1971); C. Auerbach, "The Communist Control Act of 1954: A Proposed Legal-Political Theory of Free Speech," 23 *University of Chicago Law Review* 173 (1956).

7. See T. Scanlon, "A Theory of Freedom of Expression," 1 *Philosophy & Public Affairs* 204 (1972); B. DuVal, "Free Communication of Ideas and the Quest for Truth: Toward a Teleological Approach to First Amendment Adjudication," 41 *George Washington Law Review* 161, 205–12 (1972). For perceptive criticism, see R. Amdur, "Scanlon on Freedom of Expression," 9 *Philosophy & Public Affairs* 287 (1980).

8. In *On Liberty*, in *Three Essays* 23 (World Classics ed., London, Oxford University Press 1912) (1st ed. of *On Liberty* 1859), John Stuart Mill suggested that instigation to tyrannicide could be punished, but only if an overt act followed and "at least a probable connexion can be established between the act and the instigation."

9. See M. Nimmer, *Nimmer on Freedom of Speech* § 3.02 (New York, Matthew Bender Co. 1984).

10. See *Brandenburg* v. *Ohio*, 395 U.S. 444 (1969).

11. A typical advertisement does not actually commit the advertising company; it invites the viewer or reader to deal with the company by presenting products and their prices in an attractive light.

12. See generally D. Farber, "Commercial Speech and First Amendment Theory," 74 *Northwestern University Law Review* 372 (1979).

13. See generally J. Searle, *Expression and Meaning* 30–48 (Cambridge, Cambridge University Press 1979), on indirect speech acts.

14. *Model Penal Code* § 5.02(1).

15. 3 J. F. Stephen, *A History of the Criminal Law of England* 8 (1st ed., London, MacMillan and Co. 1883).

16. G. Williams, *Criminal Law: The General Part* 364–65 (2d ed., London, Stevens & Sons 1961).

17. *S* v. *Nkosiyana*, 1966 (4) S.A. 655, 658–59.

18. If David commits murder, Carla is liable under Section 2.03 because the result occurs in the way she designed, and she is in any event liable for attempt because she sought to cause Edith's death "without further conduct on [her] part." § 5.01(1)(b). The Model Code's causation section has been little followed, and most jurisdictions probably still accept the traditional principle of responsibility that one is not liable directly when the immediate cause of death is the deliberate and informed intervention of a responsible third person; see H. L. A. Hart and A. Honore, *Causation in the Law* 325–29 (2d ed., Oxford, Clarendon Press 1985).

19. Mill, *On Liberty*, note 8 supra, at 69, said that expression of the opinion that corn dealers are starvers of the poor could be punished "when delivered orally to an excited mob

assembled before the house of a corn-dealer." In this passage, Mill does not explicitly make punishment turn on the actual purpose of the speaker; so perhaps he would allow a criminal sanction for speech that was reckless or negligent as to the danger of attack on the corn dealer. Mill has been interpreted as trying to show that an apparent expression of belief may be something different, that what looks like advocacy can be incitement. D. Munro, "Liberty of Expression: Its Grounds and Limits" (II), 13 *Inquiry* 238, 240 (1970). On this view, the speaker's purpose is critical.

Apparently the modern English law of seditious libel is that speech tending to bring the government under hatred or contempt can be punished only if the speaker intends to cause violence in a matter of State. See E. Barendt, *Freedom of Speech* 152–55 (Oxford, Clarendon Press 1985).

20. *Model Penal Code* § 2.04(3)(a)(i)(Tentative Draft No. 1, 1953).

21. See Williams, note 16 supra, at 365–66.

22. John Searle distinguishes advice from requests in *Speech Acts: An Essay in the Philosophy of Language* 67 (London, Cambridge University Press 1969).

23. I assume that lawyers and doctors, for example, may be penalized for advising clients and patients that committing some crime is the best way to solve their problems. A similar issue was raised by a tort claim in which parents asserted that pastoral advice that suicide was an appropriate way to go "home to God" inflicted extreme emotional distress on their son and increased the likelihood that he would commit suicide, which he did. With one dissent based on the facts, the intermediate appellate court in California held that the allegations were sufficient to require a trial. *Nally* v. *Grace Community Church of the Valley*, 204 Cal. Rptr. 303 (Cal. App. 2d Dist. 1984) (report indicates that California Supreme Court ordered opinion not to be officially published). The California Supreme Court later held that the defendant was without liability, saying ordinary legal duties of care of licensed practitioners do not apply to clergy. 47 Cal. 3d. 278, 253 Cal. Rptr. 97, 763 P. 2d. 948. Under my suggested approach, similar advice by a friend should not be made criminal, and I also believe it should not give rise to civil liability. Such advice by a licensed psychotherapist might be made criminal or tortious. Religious leaders are not licensed for competence by the state, but they do stand in positions of authority. It is debatable whether a pastor's advice about the acceptability of suicide as a way to deal with problems should give rise to liability, but I strongly believe, for reasons having to do with religious liberty, as well as free speech, that it should not.

24. *Model Penal Code* § 2.02(2)(c), (d).

25. Roughly, an action is a "but for" cause if the event would not have happened had the action not occurred.

26. *Model Penal Code* § 2.03(3).

27. See Hart and Honore, note 18 supra.

28. *Model Penal Code* § 211.2.

29. Id. § 250.2(1).

30. The offense is a petty misdemeanor if one has a purpose to cause public inconvenience, etc., or if one persists after a reasonable warning to stop. Id § 250.2(2).

31. Id. § 250.4(2).

32. She lacks the purpose to harass required for that offense. By modern American standards, she has not made an "offensively coarse utterance," and if her language about the police is abusive, it is not really addressed to them; so the disorderly-conduct language does not comfortably apply.

33. What I have said here does not apply to instances where the audience must act before it can inform itself, as when someone shouts "fire" in a crowded theater. This illustration is discussed in the next chapter.

34. I discuss this problem in greater detail in "The Vice of Its Virtues: The Perils of Precision in Criminal Codification, as Illustrated by Retreat, General Justification, and Dangerous Utterances," 19 *Rutgers-Camden Law Journal* 929, 946–48 (1988).

35. See *Snepp* v. *United States*, 444 U.S. 507 (1980).

36. It is a genuine question how important "fair warning" is in a statute governing activities that are likely to occur without the actor's having looked at the law or consulted a lawyer. I do not here defend the proposition, but I suppose that it matters whether criminal behavior is fairly ascertainable in advance even in those sorts of instances.

37. *Model Penal Code* § 5.02(1).

38. Id. § 5.03(1)(a).

7
Fraud and Falsehood

Falsehood and insincerity are the subjects of this chapter, which briefly explores in various contexts the force of arguments to the effect that assertions that are false or insincere or both do not warrant protection under a principle of free speech. Much of this book concerns things people say which they believe[1] and which are not evidently untrue. On the unusual occasions when such assertions may be suppressed, similar false assertions may also be suppressed.[2] This chapter is about the special relevance of falsehood and insincerity: whether false or insincere assertions may be suppressed if similar true and sincere assertions are not suppressed. I begin with some reminders about falsehood and insincerity, before considering crimes whose elements include lying or inaccurate statement and ordinary crimes for which liability might ensue from one's making assertions one thinks or knows are untrue. I close by considering defamation. Since criminal liability for common defamation is no longer a serious option in the United States, this discussion is one of those in the book whose only practical relevance concerns civil liability.

When I talk about "falsehoods" in this chapter, I refer to statements that are demonstrably false or subject to a demonstration of a near certainty of falsenesss. Examples of demonstrably false statements are "Water turns to ice as the temperature rises" and "Fritz Mondale was elected president in 1984." Perhaps no statement about external reality can be known with *absolute* assurance, but these suffice as undeniably untrue for human purposes. On other subjects, fairly persuasive evidence of truth or falsity is available, though the truth of a particular statement may remain somewhat uncertain. Suppose that Joseph claims that Maude, the bank president, has stolen money from the bank on three occasions during the last five years. Since "proving a negative" is hard, one may not be able to establish with practical certainty that Maude did not steal three times. But if no evidence of theft is forthcoming and Joseph positively admits that he lied for malicious reasons, confidence that the statement was false will be very high.

Many assertions of fact and value are either inherently incapable of demonstration as true or false or are not capable at this stage of human history of being demonstrated to be true or false.[3] For most purposes such assertions should be treated legally like true statements. The right and desirability of people's deciding for themselves what is true and what is false and the aptness of distrust of the government's capacity to judge are most obvious when truth is now incapable of demonstration. Among other things, this means that statements of opinion, "she is a marvelous singer," should not be punished unless they clearly imply falsehoods on which punishment could appropriately be based. Except when I indicate to the contrary, I assume that statements whose truth or falsity is not subject to demonstration are assimilated to true statements.

Statements that are actually false can be sincerely made, and statements that turn out to be true can be insincerely made (suppose, contrary to Iago's belief, Desdemona really had been unfaithful to Othello).[4] If free speech relates primarily to honest expression, the question arises whether outright insincerity should be the basis of criminal prohibition, regardless of whether a substantive assertion turns out to be true or false. If A says, "I believe X to be true," when X is true but A believes otherwise, A is lying about his state of mind. If, instead of stating the "I believe," A just says "X is true," he is implicitly claiming that he believes "X" and is effectively lying about his state of mind. Thus, any insincere assertion is in part a lie about one's own beliefs. One can conjure up imaginary cases when the insincerity of a truthful assertion would be clear from the remark and the facts available to the speaker and when criminal liability would be appropriate. One can conceive of a perjury prosecution based on assertions which turn out to be true but which were explicitly claimed as a matter of personal knowledge at a time when the speaker had no way of knowing them. To take a more fanciful example, suppose that the police somehow find out that Sadie plans to tell her blind walking companion to step to the right, where there is a precipice. The police place a net that Sadie cannot see, rendering the step to the right safe. When Sadie tells her companion, "It's safe to step to the right," she is guilty of attempted murder.[5] Putting aside such extraordinary cases, there are two powerful reasons not to criminalize insincere assertions of what actually turns out to be true. The first reason is that true statements do not typically cause the harm that false ones do;[6] the second is that it is too difficult to determine with confidence that the speaker did not believe or at least think possibly true what turns out to be true.

By talking thus far about statements that turn out to be true, I have failed yet to address the troubling problem of insincere assertions about unprovable facts. Suppose, to raise money, a woman claims that she is a messenger of God,[7] and evidence clearly establishes that she has no such belief. Assuming that others have no way of determining who is actually a messenger of God or that the methods for making such determinations are themselves foreclosed to the state, for reasons having to do with freedom and nonestablishment of religion (or free speech), the woman's claim is not demonstrably true or false. The worry that credulous people may be preyed on by insincere religious claims is a serious worry. Whether such insincerity—lying about one's state of mind—should be treated as fraud and made punishable is a hard question, but my view is that the state should not get into the business in fraud prosecutions of determining which religious or political assertions are sincere[8] when the assertions themselves rest on unprovable facts or values.[9] People must be aware that, in this domain, they must protect themselves.[10] For almost all purposes, the law should treat insincere statements that are not false in the same way as other statements that are not false. The statements that require attention here are insincere false assertions, sincere false assertions, and false assertions made by speakers who are unsure about truth or falsity.

Penalizing Falsehoods

As Chapter 1 indicates, the law makes false statements illegal in various contexts. Some of the major instances of criminality involve perjury and other lies told to officials or written on official forms;[11] false statements to obtain property that amount to a form of theft;[12] forgery of documents;[13] impersonating public officials;[14] and misrepresentations about the quality or quantity of products and other deceptive business practices.[15]

From the perspective of penal policy, why many kinds of lying and misrepresentations are made criminal is straightforward. If physically taking property is a crime, then acquiring the same property by a lie that causes someone to hand it over should also be a crime.[16] Trials and official documents depend on the truth's being told; lies pose a serious social danger of mistaken decisions, about guilt or innocence, eligibility or ineligibility. Deceptive business practices cheat consumers and others. Since lying is a common occurrence in the lives of most people and, at least arguably, is a healthy part of self-development and social discourse,[17] the criminal law certainly should not reach all lies. It should not reach even all lies told to public officials or on official documents. But there can be little doubt that many lies are serious enough to warrant criminal punishment. Even apart from free speech concerns, innocent falsehoods should not ordinarily be punished, since people should not often be taken to be guilty of crimes when they are unaware that they are performing criminal or wrongful acts.

When one turns to the application of a principle of free speech to falsehoods, explored briefly in Chapter 3, what the speaker thinks usually matters greatly. If people can be punished for happening to get things wrong, a severe restriction is placed on liberty of speech. People have lapses of memory; their interests or unconscious influences may lead them to believe that events took place in a way different from what actually occurred; they may be misinformed by others. If they make honest assertions of fact at the risk of being punished for mistakes, the constraint on what they say will be considerable. Most of the justifications for free speech strongly favor allowing people to say what they honestly believe to be true in most contexts.

As I suggested in Chapter 3, even false statements made knowingly may have *some* value as expression, perhaps symbolizing what are believed to be deeper truths, or providing an emotional outlet, or serving as an initial gambit in the search for truth, but these possibilities have limited relevance in respect to most falsehoods that are made criminal. Trials and official documents and the labeling of commodities call for literal truth. The expressive importance of self-conscious lies in these contexts is minimal and is far outweighed by the overwhelming social need to reduce falsehood. And one who obtains another's property by claiming it is his own can hardly be let off the hook because his claim is said to represent the deeper truth that the property would be his in a just social order. In sum, brief reflection on the values of free speech confirms the wisdom of the common approach of the criminal law which makes criminal knowing falsehoods that threaten substantial harms and does not punish innocent falsehoods.

In some special instances, when the expressive interest is minimal and the dangers of misinformation great, criminal penalties may appropriately be imposed for falsehoods that are not knowingly communicated, and that may be so even when what is stated cannot be shown to be demonstrably false. Labeling of health products and claims on their behalf afford examples. Those who produce or sell these products need to be very careful about accuracy. Mislabeling can cause serious harm, and the free speech interest in labeling is extremely limited. Whatever the appropriate standards of liability are for making or selling intrinsically defective products, such as adulterated medicines, may also be used for critical labeling mistakes. Thus, liability for negligent labeling is warranted, and, if strict liability is ever appropriate,[18] it may properly be employed for mislabeling.

Unlike labels, many claims on behalf of products are not demonstrably true or demonstrably false; it is not possible to show whether some products really carry some benefits claimed for them. In most areas of life, it is just such questions that are left to individual decision based on competing claims; the propounding of unprovable assertions is plainly within the range of free speech. But people are particularly vulnerable to claims that products will enhance their health, and the dangers of ill-advised use are considerable; moreover, whatever may be true for others, those whose main objective is selling a product usually have a limited expressive interest, and the judgments they communicate to potential buyers are not likely to be very balanced. There is accordingly a substantial argument for forbidding claims that have not been *shown to be true*. If such claims are to be forbidden, however, it makes sense to have some initial form of civil regulation that determines what can be said, reserving criminal sanctions only for companies that knowingly refuse to abide by limitations that have been established.

The exception that I have suggested so far to the principle that one should be free to speak unless one knowingly says what is false can reasonably be extended to the whole range of communications designed to sell ordinary products. I have written briefly in Chapter 6 about encouragements to purchase things; here I am concerned with the informational aspect of advertising, which tells people what sort of product it is that they might buy. Advertising by businesses has little to do with the self-expressive reasons for free speech,[19] and the subjects of communication are rarely of great public significance, but, because advertising does give people information relevant to the choices they make in their own lives, it is reached to a degree by the justifications for free speech.[20] For the great majority of products, consumers lack either the ability or the time to check most informational claims carefully,[21] and those who sell products are certainly not disinterested in what they claim. Furthermore, informational claims in advertising may fairly be viewed as very close to promissory utterances. Although the company may not actually guarantee that the product has the features or will produce the benefits it asserts and although advertising is often published at a stage prior to the definite offers treated in Chapter 4,[22] nevertheless an advertisement is functionally almost like a promise about quality that is part of an agreement to buy and sell.[23] For all these reasons, a free speech principle allows much closer regulation of commercial advertising than of most other communications about facts. Thus, liability may be imposed for negligent claims that are demonstrably untrue, and companies may be required to avoid specific claims[24] that cannot be established, to put claims in a manner that does not mislead, and to include explicit warnings of danger. Again, the main engine of such a regime of regulation should be the civil law or administrative agencies, not direct criminal sanctions for companies that guess wrong about how they may advertise.

Ordinary Crimes

I now turn briefly to how falsehoods can figure in liability when the rule involved does not itself include inaccuracy as an element. Falsehoods can lead listeners to harm themselves or others in a way that makes the speaker criminally or civilly liable. If Sadie tells her blind companion that a step to the right is safe, she is guilty of intentional murder if she has told a lie in order to cause his death and it has that effect. She might similarly be liable for reckless or negligent homicide if, consciously or not, she has made a similar statement despite a substantial and unjustified risk that it was untrue and someone died as a consequence of relying on her statement. A related possibility is that a listener who counts on a statement's truth may cause injury to a third person; for example, a railroad engineer who is told by a dispatcher during a fog that it is safe to proceed may run into the preceding train and injure its passengers. Had the engineer been fully informed, his own actions would have been criminal, but he has acted innocently on the basis of mistaken information from the dispatcher, and the dispatcher may be liable for causing the harm.

The sorts of situations I have posited here are crucially distinguishable from those discussed in the last chapter. There I argued that generally people should not be liable for making true assertions of fact or assertions of value when there was a risk that what they said would cause informed listeners to commit harmful acts. Here, I have posited situations in which the speaker intends his words to be the basis for immediate action by the listener and the listener who reasonably relies on those words ends up being crucially misinformed because the speaker's assertion is false. I have earlier stressed that free speech has relatively little to do with narrow factual statements whose aim is immediate practical action; reasons that relate to truth discovery have almost no place when the actor lacks a basis, or is not supposed to try, to figure out the truth for himself. From the speaker's perspective, these cases are very much like cases in which an intentional, reckless, or negligent noncommunicative act is involved. Sadie's telling her companion to step to the right differs little from her pushing him; the dispatcher's giving false information to an engineer about how to proceed differs little from the dispatcher's mistakenly switching a train onto a wrong track because he has misappraised the facts. When people can be liable for acting on mistaken factual appraisals, it should not matter whether the harm is produced by their own direct actions or by the actions of others who appropriately rely on the accuracy of what they say.

Defamation

What I have said so far in this chapter is not often expressed, but most of it is relatively uncontroversial. I now turn to defamation, a subject that is a source of immense commentary and very considerable disagreement. Although *libel*, written defamation, has been a crime in the past and remains technically a crime in some jurisdictions, in the United States the practical significance of libel and *slander*, oral defamation, now lies in the realm of civil liability. For this reason, because historically the rules of defamation have developed mainly as aspects of common law by courts, and because much of the controversy concerns difficult choices between plausible alternatives, my discussion here is relatively summary, designed to provide a firm grounding for thought about defamation rather than a resolution of the relevant issues. Much of what I say about defamation of persons will also apply to violations of what is called "false light" privacy, which allows recovery for some embarrassing but nondefamatory falsehoods, and to disparagement of commercial products, but I shall not discuss those tort actions separately here.

The spectrum of views over personal defamation runs the gamut from arguments for strict liability to arguments for absolute protection. The position that one could be absolutely liable for falsehoods that damage another's reputation in substantial and specified ways has long represented the common law's treatment of civil liability. The underlying assumptions were that someone who was going to besmirch the reputation of another, say by calling him a thief or a prostitute, should be quite sure of his facts, and that an innocent person who suffered unwarranted damage should have a remedy against the person who uttered the defamation even if the speaker believed what he said. Defamation can cause deep emotional upset, damage personal relationships with friends and acquaintances, and produce serious economic harm.

Although for some time the Supreme Court said that defamation lay outside the First Amendment, the proposition that a principle of free speech has some relevance for defamation is plain. Many statements that injure the reputations of officials and important public figures are of public importance. Accusations that officials have acted dishonestly, to take an obvious example, bear on their fitness for office, and a claim that a famous consumer advocate has been paid by a rival company to criticize the automobiles of General Motors bears both on the credence to give to these particular criticisms and on whether the advocate is someone worthy of future public support. But the relevance of free speech for defamation does not depend entirely on the public significance of the particular damaging remark.

Any defamation conveys information not only about the individual involved but implicitly about people in general. We understand what people are like by knowing what individuals are like. In defense of a position of absolute protection for speech as he defined it, Alexander Meiklejohn managed to arrive at the absurd position that novels, which tell us about human beings, are protected but that defamation falls outside the range of speech.[25] The flaw in this position is evident. We learn not only from fictional accounts of misbehavior; we learn from hearing what friends and acquaintances do. A *true* statement that Vicki, whom we know, has embezzled money and carries on with three men is at least as informative as reading about a character like Vicki in pulp fiction. The only thing that possibly puts the statement outside the realm of speech is its actual falsity, but, if absolute liability were imposed, even those with true information or possibly true information would be hesitant to say what they believe. Perhaps they are pretty sure, but not certain, that what they believe is actually true, but fear that the evidence, say, what they have seen themselves, might not be credited by a judge or jury. Thus, the value of true information about people, combined with the likelihood that absolute liability would discourage speaking the truth, make the truth-discovery justification relevant. And saying what we honestly think about others also is often an important emotional outlet.

The claim is sometimes made that a principle of free speech should guarantee absolute protection for defamation. Such a claim in any plausible version rests on relevant administrative difficulties. But it will clarify the issues to begin by examining the possible assertion that intentional libels should be protected in themselves because of their value as speech. Were this assertion sound, one could embrace a principle of absolute protection without worrying about the unhealthy side effects of any less-than-absolute standard.

It might be said that literally false attacks on character often try to convey some deeper truth about the person attacked. Suppose that Sam thinks that Vicki is inattentive to the interests of her bank and to her husband in hard-to-explain ways. Sam states publicly that Vicki has embezzled money from the bank and is simultaneously involved with three named men, knowing that all these claimed facts are false. If statements like those have some slight value as speech, that is far outweighed by their harm. Most people will have no satisfactory way of determining whether what Sam has said is literally true; both Vicki and her husband, not to mention the three supposed lovers, will be deeply upset; and Vicki is likely to suffer tangible and intangible injury in the way suspicious friends and business acquaintances now deal with her. The unfair consequences of the literal falsehood simply overwhelm the conceivable value of a possible "deeper truth." Protecting the statement would make Sam a largely unreviewable judge of Vicki's fate. If defamation were absolutely protected, Vicki would have no public forum in which to establish that Sam is lying, and it is hard to understand how the ordinary citizen could judge between her story and Sam's. Thus, it is highly doubtful that even the truth-discovery reason for free speech would be served by an absolute protection in this realm.[26]

Moreover, many libels and slanders seek to promote the speaker's advantage, are based on malicious hatred of a victim ungrounded in any perceived flaw relating to the defamation, or pander to the salacious interests of readers and listeners; these libels and slanders do not reflect the speaker's sense of any deeper truth. Barring some radical change in the serious injury defamations can cause, the idea that all intentional defamations should be protected for their own sakes is ludicrous.

A somewhat more colorable argument can be made that all defamations of high public officials and perhaps of leading public figures intrinsically warrant protection. Important officials have more adequate means than ordinary citizens to get their side of a story out. The conceivable "deeper truth" that lies behind a literal falsehood may be of more public importance when leading officials are involved, and the harm to victims may be less because officials have to develop thicker skins. Though these reasons may bolster other arguments for absolute protection of defamations of officials, standing alone they are weak. Officials have access to media, but the unsavory taint of serious accusations is hard to erase, however ill-founded they may be. Whatever "deeper truth" may move the speaker, blatantly false statements will not help anyone else consider in a reasoned way whether the deeper truth in which the speaker believes really has substance. And the "thick skin" argument has a double edge; probably it is not wise to discourage all those with normal sensibilities from seeking office. Even with respect to public officials, any argument for absolute protection of defamation based on the intrinsic value of intentional falsehoods falls far short of being persuasive. Thus, any serious argument for absolute protection based on a political principle of free speech must concentrate on the bad effects of allowing civil damages for intentional falsehoods that do not themselves intrinsically deserve protection.

The claim for absolute protection has to rest on the difficulties of identifying wrongful falsehoods in practice. It begins with the assumption that true statements damaging to reputation should ordinarily be protected, as should statements of opinion not subject to decisive judgments of truth or falsity and hyperbolic uses of language not to be taken literally, for example, "The umpire is a robber." If true statements are to be protected, then incorrect statements should not be the basis for liability if the speaker has acted reasonably, believing that what he says is true and having made appropriate efforts to be sure that it is true. Once this much is conceded, it may be argued that separating genuinely asserted fact from opinion and hyperbole and determining the speaker's state of mind and degree of diligence are too difficult, and, therefore, that publication should be privileged regardless of falsity and regardless of sincerity. So put, the claim rests on fact-finding difficulties and worries about excessive deterrence of those who fear liability even if they publish what they believe is almost certainly true. Serious assessment of this claim requires familiarity with such matters as the effect of applicable legal standards on the results of cases and on people's utterances, litigation costs, and the practices of press and television news organizations.

The law of defamation, within common law systems, has been left largely to courts developing the common law and, in the United States, to constitutional principles. What the Constitution requires is addressed in Part III, but the preceding discussion makes apparent why some balance is desirable between the speech interests of speakers and listeners and the need to protect people against unwarranted damage to reputation caused by falsehoods. Roughly, opinion and hyperbole[27] should not be actionable; at least in noncommercial settings, liability should depend on some culpable wrong done by the speaker; when attacks on reputation have substantial public significance, a standard of liability higher than negligence may be appropriate; falsity, perhaps, should be established to a higher degree of certainty than the ordinary civil law standard of "more probable than not";[28] standards of damages should be set so as not to discourage expression unduly, for example, by limiting punitive damages to flagrant wrongs; in tried cases in which defendant is not liable, the fact-finder might usefully determine whether the statement is true or false; very likely, more emphasis should be put on required retraction rather than on damages as the primary remedy for libel.[29] In many jurisdictions, use of required retraction may require legislative action, because the damage remedy is so typical for common law actions. More generally, drastic alterations in present rules may demand new statutes.

This chapter has surveyed a number of issues about false speech. The general lessons are that intentionally false speech is, by itself, only slightly reached by the justifications for free speech, but a serious concern about deterring true speech and sincere but mistaken speech is raised if criminal or civil liability attaches to lies. And when liability extends to reckless or negligent falsehoods, the worry about deterrence increases. There is no substitute for a careful look at discrete problems, one which assesses both speech value and the need for regulation of falsehoods and which seeks a judicious mix of criminal and civil liability and particular criteria of legal responsibility.

Notes

1. One of the important points of the book, of course, is that, for many utterances, the truth dimension itself is not very important.

2. Some courts have suggested that threats cannot be punished in some circumstances unless they are actually likely to be carried out. On that view, false threats might be unpunished while true threats are punished. My own position, suggested in Chapter 5 and developed more fully in Chapter 18, is that neither from the standpoint of penal policy nor from that of free speech does such a distinction make sense, although it does matter what, from the standpoint of the victim, is the *apparent* intent and ability of a threatener to act on his threat.

3. A statement about God's existence or about life after death may be inherently incapable of convincing demonstration of truth or falsity; some claims about the natural world may be incapable of present demonstration. Of course, we cannot be sure what may be capable of demonstration in the future, and the line between what is capable of demonstration and what is not is not sharp.

As I indicated in Chapter 2, it is debated whether many value judgments can even properly be called true or false; although incompatibilities among value statements can sometimes be shown, demonstrations of falsity are not possible for elements of assertions of value which are not reducible to factual claims.

4. Thus, putting aside for the moment the varying degrees of confidence that people can have in the truth of what they assert, there are four main possibilities: (1) false but sincere statements, (2) false and insincere statements, (3) sincere statements that are not subject to demonstration as false, and (4) insincere statements that are not subject to demonstration as false.

5. Apart from Sadie's inability to see the net, one would never benignly make such a remark to a blind person without warning him to prepare for a net.

6. Against the conceivable argument that even insincere true statements should be punished in order to deter insincere statements that turn out to be false, the answer is that a very high percentage of insincere statements on matters capable of demonstration as true

or false will turn out to be false; letting the statements that turn out to be true, or possibly true, go unpunished will not significantly reduce deterrence.

7. See *United States* v. *Ballard*, 322 U.S. 78 (1944). That case makes clear that courts and juries cannot resolve the *truth* of religious claims, but apparently accepts the appropriateness of making judgments of sincerity.

8. See the dissenting opinion of J. Jackson, in *Ballard*, 322 U.S. at 92 (suggesting that jurors will judge sincerity in light of their own views about what is believable).

It would be comforting but mistaken to suppose that the state should never determine sincerity of religious beliefs. When a legislature affords, or the Constitution requires, an exemption from ordinary responsibilities, such as the conscientious-objector exemption from military service, the person claiming this special treatment must make a threshold showing of sincerity. I treat this in somewhat more detail in K. Greenawalt, "All or Nothing at All: The Defeat of Selective Conscientious Objection," 1971 *Supreme Court Review* 31; K. Greenawalt, "Religion as a Concept in Constitutional Law," 72 *California Law Review* 753 (1984).

9. Probably it is acceptable to prosecute people for fraud when, in the context of raising money on the basis of religious claims, they tell mundane lies, such as that they worked for years with Martin Luther King, Jr., when, in fact, they never met him. A difficult intermediate situation is one in which a person claims to have a vision and, shortly thereafter, tells associates that the claim is "a lot of baloney." Perhaps we can say that, if someone does not believe he is having a vision, he is not having one. A strong danger for prosecutions of such instances is that jurors disbelieving the *truth* of such claims will find insincerity too easily. Even in the case of provably false claims, like the years of working with Dr. King, a jury unsympathetic with a defendant may find too easily that those claims lay at the center of his efforts to raise funds rather than that they were peripheral embellishments.

10. The issue is more complicated when spiritual claims are linked with what appear to be ordinary scientific claims that are untrue, and the point of the claims is to get people to spend money on services or products. Some cases involving the Church of Scientology have presented this problem. See, e.g., *Founding Church of Scientology* v. *United States*, 409 F.2d 1146 (D.C. Cir. 1969), certiorari denied, 396 U.S. 963 (1969).

The statement in the text avoids defining the domain that should be left free, but I am inclined to think it includes the "occult arts," palmistry, astrology, predictions based on tarot cards, and the like. These practices are based on assumptions about the structure of the universe which probably lie outside of scientific evaluation.

11. See *Model Penal Code* §§ 241.1–241.5.

12. See id. § 223.3.

13. See id. § 224.1.

14. See id. § 241.9.

15. See id. § 224.7.

16. For penal liability, it may appropriately matter how easily the lie is discoverable by the listener.

17. See D. Goleman, "Lies Can Point to Mental Disorders or Signals of Normal Growth," *New York Times*, May 17, 1988, Section C, p. 1, col. 1, indicating that, according to one study, adults in the United States admit on the average to lying thirteen times a week, that telling lies is an important aspect of a child's development of independence from parents, and that one psychiatric expert has spoken of the ability to lie as "a human achievement." Much of the *New York Times* story summarizes C. Ford, et al., "Lies and Liars: Psychiatric Aspects of Prevarication," *American Journal of Psychiatry* 145:5, at 554, May 1988. That article refers to many other writings on lying. For a philosophic view, see S. Bok, *Lying: Moral Choice and Private Life* (New York, Pantheon Books 1978).

18. I am skeptical that strict liability, that is, liability without *any* proven fault, is ever a proper basis for significant criminal penalties, but I do not tackle that subject here.

19. See, e.g., E. Baker, "Scope of the First Amendment Freedom of Speech," 25 *University of California in Los Angeles Law Review* 964, 996 (1978).

20. See, e.g., M. Redish, *Freedom of Expression* 60–61 (Charlottesville, Va., The Michie Co. 1984).

21. Of course, they can easily determine whether the price is that which has been advertised.

22. That is, advertisements usually do not allow the prospective purchaser to close a deal with an order. The company must accept the order.

23. D. Faber, "Commercial Speech and First Amendment Theory," 74 *Northwestern University Law Review* 372 (1979).

24. More general and vague claims—"This is the best dishwasher money can buy"— are understood by consumers not to be claims about literal truth.

25. A. Meiklejohn, "The First Amendment Is an Absolute," 1961 *Supreme Court Review* 245, 259.

26. M. Nimmer, *Nimmer on Freedom of Speech* 2–48 (New York, Matthew Bender Co. 1984).

27. If a proposition about literal truth can clearly be distilled from an opinion or from the hyperbolic use of language, then the claim of literal truth might be the subject of a defamation action.

28. In an ordinary civil law case, a plaintiff need only produce a balance of proof in his favor. In defamation cases the burden of proving truth has often been put on the defendant, but, even if the plaintiff bears the ordinary civil law burden of showing falsity, that may not be enough. Possibly, he should establish falsity by "convincing proof" or some other standard more rigorous than the standard civil law test.

29. Retraction before suit can now serve to mitigate damages, but its significance could be made much greater, perhaps *precluding* any damages but provable financial loss (e.g., canceled engagements). Were retraction to become the centerpiece of defamation remedies, the injured party would not need to establish culpable behavior in order to get a retraction; proof that the libelous utterance was definitely false would be enough; and a failure to publish a retraction upon clear proof of falsity might itself be made actionable.

8

Offensiveness and Diffuse Harms

The communications and reasons for prohibition which I consider in this chapter move in some ways beyond those I have thus far examined. I have concentrated on situations where an utterance leads directly to a harmful act performed by a listener, or threatens the listener in order to obtain property or restrict liberty, or falsely asserts some fact that causes damage. Here, I focus on communications whose harm may not lie primarily in falsity or threat or the risk that a listener will cause a direct injury. The examples I examine briefly are insults, epithets and slurs, pornography, and disclosures of embarrassing private truths. With respect to each, I inquire about the need for legal control, the manner in which language is being used, the expressive value of the utterances, and sensible boundaries of criminal or tort liability.

Although the main emphasis is different, the discussion here links in important ways to what has preceded it. For insults, epithets and slurs, and pornography, two critical questions are: how language is being dominantly used, and whether that use should be made of legal relevance. The threatened harms also overlap with those we have already looked at. Insults and epithets often risk a violent response; the possibility of punishing provocative words that are intended to trigger a violent reaction or are fairly likely to do so has been treated in Chapter 6. Here attention is on the psychological hurt that insults and epithets can cause to listeners, a reason for prohibition that has figured prominently in Chapter 5's discussion of "pure," unconditional threats, which make no demands but let the listener know that his life or well-being is highly vulnerable. The strongest argument for punishing such threats is that they can seriously disturb the persons subject to them.[1] Indeed, although falsity is a distinguishing feature of recovery for defamation and damage to reputation can lead to tangible financial loss, an important aspect of why recovery for libel and slander has seemed warranted is the psychic hurt of being subject to accusations of serious misbehavior or perceived defects which one's acquaintances may believe. The embarrassment caused by the revelation of very private truths is similar.

Because of its tie to defamation and because its analysis is most straightforward, I begin by discussing the tort right of privacy, and then consider in turn communications that are abusive and insulting and communications that are pornographic. In each instance, I examine arguments for and against prohibition or liability in light of the principle of freedom of speech. Since, in the United States at least, no one seriously proposes criminal liability for disclosures of embarrassing truths, the practical importance of arguments about them concerns civil liability. In respect to pornography, outright prohibition is what mainly is at stake, although forms of civil recovery arguably have a role. For insults and epithets both criminal and civil liability remain significant options.

Because of the chapter's diversity in subject matter, one cannot discern useful general guidelines applicable to all three areas, but scrutiny of each yields some understanding of alternative and sensible approaches.

Privacy and Truthful Disclosures

The disclosure of true but embarrassing facts is, in the United States, the subject of civil recovery under one of the three branches of the tort right of privacy which involve liability for communication.[2] In order to highlight what is special about that branch, it helps to contrast it with the other two: misappropriation of one's name or character for commercial purposes, and what is called "false light." The use of an individual's name or picture for commercial purposes may have some slight communicative value, but regarding a name or image as a kind of property that can be used only with someone's consent does not significantly touch the justifications for free speech.[3] The false-light aspect of the law of privacy is an extension of the law of libel, covering mistaken reports of facts that cause some embarrassment but are not actually defamatory. What is distinctive about "true privacy" cases is the notion that one can actually be liable for publishing accurate but highly embarrassing information, say that a woman has terrible sores over the clothed part of her body or was once a prostitute.

Viewed by itself, the distress over having secret facts about oneself disclosed and the worry about how others will react to such disclosure are serious enough to warrant a civil remedy, but substantial reasons of free speech stand in the way. Some "secret" facts about some people are of genuine public importance, and disclosures of these must be protected; so any restrictive standard has to include line drawing for difficult borderline cases. Even secret facts that are of no public importance in the ordinary sense can have the sort of value for listeners traced in the last chapter. More specifically, knowing that other individuals have embarrassing secrets and are able to live with them without presenting some fatal flaw in their social interactions tells us something of importance. If we ourselves have secrets about which we feel guilty or embarrassed—and perhaps few among us do not—concrete awareness that others have such secrets may provide a degree of reassurance about our own worth. If secrets involve famous people, revelation may suggest their vulnerability and dampen our envy. These reassurances might be offset if disclosure of another's secrets led us to fear the disclosure of our own, but people who are not famous and have "ordinary" secrets need not fear wide disclosures. Finally, whatever the expressive value of disclosure of embarrassing secrets, they are a subject of abiding interest for many people, a staple of ordinary gossip. Were these disclosures to be penalized when they occur among private persons, the crimp on spontaneous conversation would be very considerable.

Concluding that the accurate disclosure of facts should be wholly free of general legal restraint is certainly a reasonable position, but, given the genuine value of protecting the private aspects of people's lives[4] and the fact that "further speech" is no remedy for breach of the private sphere, I believe that liability is sometimes warranted. Although private gossip among individuals should be protected if what is said is true, broad disclosure, or disclosure as part of a profit-making endeavor, of facts that are highly embarrassing and of no genuine public importance, should give rise to a civil remedy.[5]

Personal Insults and Group Epithets and Slurs

I now address one of the most troublesome problems about free speech in a liberal democracy: what should be done about strong personal insults, like "You fucking bastard," group epithets, like "Let's get those dumb niggers[6] out of our neighborhood," and more elaborate slurs, like "Puerto Ricans are lazy and dishonest." I consider these kinds of utterances together both because group epithets are often used to insult in face-to-face encounters and because, even when epithets or slurs lack the quality of immediate personal insult, they threaten some of the same social harms.

Describing the present law is not simple because many of these utterances tend to be criminal, if at all, under vague disorderly-conduct or breach-of-the-peace provisions, and the main source of civil recovery in the United States may be the relatively novel tort of "intentional infliction of mental or emotional distress."[7] The Model Penal Code is slightly more precise than is common among governing criminal standards. For *disorderly conduct*, one must purposely or recklessly create a risk of "public inconvenience, annoyance or alarm" by making "offensively coarse utterance, gesture or display" or by addressing "abusive language to any person present."[8] For *harassment*, one must have a purpose to harass and insult, taunt, or challenge another in a manner likely to provoke a violent or disorderly response.[9] A few states, and many other countries, have specific provisions against derogatory remarks directed against racial or ethnic groups,[10] but the Model Code does not.

An analysis of how the law should treat gross insults and group epithets calls for examination of the reasons for possible restriction and of the extent to which these uses of language have expressive value. Four concerns about insults and epithets might justify making them criminal. One is that their use will provoke responsive violence. Another is that they deeply wound those at whom they are directed. The third concern is that the language of insult and epithet offends those who hear it. The last concern, especially relevant to group epithets and slurs regarding members of underprivileged minorities, is that denigrating remarks will have an insidious effect on social relations, reinforcing prejudice and contributing to unjust discrimination, generating resentment and undermining self-esteem among members of the groups about whom the remarks are made, and lowering the quality of public dialogue. In the absence of any expressive value, these concerns could warrant criminal prohibition, although drawing the line between rough but acceptable common discourse and what is beyond acceptability is extraordinarily difficult.

Any supposition that personal insults and group epithets and slurs never have expressive value would be both wrong and oversimplified. To think seriously about the speech value of those sorts of utterances, it helps initially to distinguish between situations in which the personally insulting language is directed at listeners (or persons the listeners care deeply about) and situations in which all or most of those listening are not subjects of the abusive terms. It is one thing to say to someone who is Jewish, "You kike"; it is another to say at a meeting of a club that has so far admitted only Christians, "We don't want any kikes in here." Quite possibly the latter statement is the more harmful socially, but it undoubtedly asserts facts and values. A speaker who consciously chooses a denigrating term and uses it seriously means to attribute some vague but negative characteristics to the group in question and to suggest that the members of the group are degraded, falling below some standard of what is good, right, or acceptable. Similarly, when a speaker employs an insulting phrase about a third person who is not present, for example, "That prick," he conveys the message that the person is personally bad or extremely inconsiderate. While it cannot be said that most insults and epithets convey messages that are very precise, there is a message, and it invokes a highly negative appraisal.

When one considers personal insults and group epithets and slurs directed toward the listener in a face-to-face encounter, analysis is more complicated because the point of such remarks is more varied. In that setting, abusive remarks often approach closer to action and may even amount to situation-altering utterances.[11] I shall attempt a rough classification that moves from circumstances in which assertion of fact and value seems minimal to those in which it is an important element.

At the extreme we can imagine social convention establishing that certain insults "call for" set responses; in that event uttering the insult could be essentially a situation-altering utterance. The words "I challenge you to a duel" would clearly constitute a situation-altering offer according to the analysis of Chapter 3; a slap on the cheek or the words "You are a cad" could have exactly the same import if all understood them in that way.[12] It is true that "You are a cad" seems to have some fact-and-value content, but if people understand that this just happens to be the language by which you challenge to a duel, the utterance of the language would indicate little more than the explicit challenge;[13] in any event, the situation-altering aspect would dominate any message about the qualities of the person challenged. I strongly doubt that any insults function generally with this kind of precision in modern societies, but among various subgroups conventions may approximate this kind of clarity. In such settings, if a person who wants to start a fight utters abusive language that indicates his wish to fight and clearly invites his listener to respond, the utterance is dominantly situation-altering.

A subtly different situation[14] is one in which the speaker hopes to provoke such anger in the listener that a fight will ensue. If the speaker is seeking deliberately to manipulate the listener into fighting, his own expressive interests have not significantly increased, but the import of the utterance on the listener is different now. Instead of understanding that he has been "offered" a fight, the listener is angered because very bad things have been said about him or about a group to which he belongs. *His* reaction now is, at least in part, to the message of fact and value and its intensity.[15]

A variant of the last situation is one in which the speaker deliberately sets out to humiliate or wound the listener. His aim is simply to make the listener feel degraded and hated; he chooses words to achieve that effect.[16] In that event, the speaker will usually feel, at least temporarily, that the listener has the characteristics whose expression in the insult is what humiliates and wounds, but that need not be so. A person might pick words to impose the maximum wound, though not personally carrying the attitudes that the words imply.[17] The less the words convey what the speaker actually feels the less they are expressive for him, but even when the speaker "believes in" the abuse he deliberately heaps on the listener, his aim diminishes the expressive importance of what he says. He does not use words to inform anyone, since he is not really trying to enlighten the listener; nor is he really attempting to indicate his feelings, since he is aiming to wound and the congruence of what he says with his actual feelings is almost coincidental.[18] In what they do, utterances of this sort are not very different from physical assaults, like slaps or pinches, that do not cause real physical hurt. Insults and epithets are often a deliberate form of psychic assault.[19]

A not infrequent situation is one in which elements of the last two situations I have noted merge. The speaker wants to humiliate and wound and would also welcome a fight. But it is important to recognize that, in many of the harshest instances of abusive words, no fight is contemplated: white adults shout epithets at black children walking to an integrated school; strong men insult much smaller women.[20]

For many people, including, I hope and suppose, most readers of this book, serious use of group epithets is regarded as reprehensible and is quite rare, and the serious use of gravely insulting and abusive words in face-to-face encounters occurs only during moments of great emotion when one has less than full control of oneself. Out of frustration and anger one hurls words that express this intensity of feeling and are also meant to wound; one does not expect physical force in response, but one is not very cautious about preventing it. Abusive words in these situations are a rough barometer of one's feelings at the moment and, as such, have substantial importance as expression. We might think of a scale of escalation of personal quarrels as going from discussion to argument to raised voices to abusive words to minor physical force (pushing, slapping, breaking plates) to serious physical force. Some well-controlled people rarely raise their voices and never use abusive words; more people manage to stop short of physical force. But, regardless of whether an angry person ever goes beyond abusive words to physical force, the words as used fall somewhere between attempts to express ideas and feelings and frustrated striking out to wound.

Deciding how the law should treat abusive words in light of the values of speech is immensely difficult. As I have indicated, there are radically different sorts of situations and values of speech; without getting into the mind of the speaker, there are also tremendous problems in distinguishing among them. In deciding what should be punished or subjected to civil liability and what should be left free, we need to relate the value of speech to the harm that may be produced in various situations. It is time now to review the four main bases for suppressing abusive speech: (1) the danger of immediate violence; (2) offense that such language is used; (3) psychological hurt that one is the subject of abusive remarks; (4) the insidious long-term effects of the attitudes reinforced by such language. I shall say a few words about the first two kinds of harm before proceeding to the latter two.

The prevention of violence is of obvious and great social importance. If one intentionally provokes a violent response, then criminal punishment is appropriate; I have suggested in Chapter 6 that if one is reckless about that possibility, punishment is appropriate only if one also has fair warning about the kinds of words deemed dangerous, something attempted in the Model Penal Code provision on disorderly conduct. For situations in which the main concern is a violent response by the person subjected to an insult, the interest in preventing violence is not in itself a basis for tort recovery. If the only harm to be prevented were a violent act by the listener against the speaker, it would not make sense to have the listener recover damages for the abusive words.[21] Emphasizing violence prevention to the exclusion of other reasons for suppression also has a highly troublesome implication which follows from a faithful application of the Model Penal Code provisions and on which I shall comment at greater length in Chapter 17: an insult directed to a strong young male who might fight back can be punished; the same insult directed at an isolated small child or a woman in a wheelchair could not, since those instances present no immediate propensity for physical violence.

The second kind of harm, which I shall call "general offensiveness," is the disquiet that is caused by the use of certain words and expressions, no matter at whom they are directed. Words like "fuck" and "nigger" have a shock effect; they disturb many people quite apart from whatever message they convey in context. But what words are appropriate depends a great deal on social group, and in the last few decades conventional restraints on language have loosened considerably. At least in the United States, there are no words or expressions that should be prohibited generally or made the subject of civil liability simply because they offend members of audiences.[22] On the other hand, in certain more formal settings, constraints on use of language may be appropriate. Lawyers in a courtroom may be held in contempt if they call opposing counsel a "fucking bastard" or a "stupid wop," not mainly because of hurt to the subject of the insult but because that language is destructive of the level of civility at which court proceedings aim. A more debatable situation is a public meeting at which citizens are free to speak. It may be argued that people there should have the freedom of more informal settings, but, if other citizens need to attend the meeting, flagrantly abusive language will be directed toward a kind of captive audience and may undermine the attempt to maintain reasoned discourse.

The sharpest problems for a principle of free speech concern the hurt and long-term social harm that abusive insults, epithets, and slurs can cause. As I have suggested, when the speaker's dominant aim is to injure or provoke a fight, words have less expressive significance than otherwise, and we can imagine situations, taken in isolation, when the emotional hurt to the listener is great enough to warrant civil recovery and perhaps even criminal penalties (although the evident availability of an individual plaintiff is one reason to rely on civil damages rather than a criminal sanction for face-to-face encounters). One thinks especially of situations in which adults who are strangers scream insults and epithets at children.

Sometimes language that hurts can also be intimidating;[23] an insult implies a readiness to proceed to physical force if the insulted person does not stop what he has been doing. The harm to the listener is increased if he feels intimidated as well as insulted.

Major problems, however, involve mixed motives, line drawing, and accurate determinations. As I have said, words intended to wound also often express strong feelings; this is, indeed, the typical use of abusive language in personal quarrels. A recent Supreme Court case illustrates mixed motives in a different context.[24] Having published in *Hustler Magazine* a scathing and highly offensive parody about Rev. Jerry Falwell, who was portrayed as having sexual relations with his mother in an outhouse while drunk, Larry Flynt acknowledged that he wanted to humiliate Falwell, but obviously he was also trying to convey some (negative) message about Falwell to his readers. Even if one could be certain of the facts of particular cases, it would be hard to say at what point the limits of rough language that one needs to learn to cope with are passed and the truly outrageous wounding that should be unprivileged begins. It is also hard to say how much "hurt" ordinary people should have to tolerate and how tough their skins should be. As the Supreme Court held, parodies about public figures with political significance, like that published about Falwell, should not be actionable at all. If we somehow arrive at a sense of which uses of abusive language should be actionable, we then face the difficulties of determining the facts, given the impossibility of recapturing subtle inflections of voice and conversational contexts and of assessing just what the speaker had in mind and what hurt the listener felt.

In light of all these problems, tort law's present general treatment of abusive language is probably about right: only truly outrageous behavior is subject to recovery. When an evident intent to intimidate is present, that should be viewed as contributing to the outrageousness of abusive communication.[25] As far as the criminal law is concerned, insulting or abusive words that would cause a substantial number of addressees to fight is a reasonable standard of what should be punished. But it is unfair to make an inability or obvious disinclination to fight back on the part of the addressee the test of whether a speaker can actually be punished. The tendency to provoke physical violence should be taken partly as a standard of outrageousness and unacceptability. And even to the extent that the aim is to prevent violence, that aim should be implemented in a way that preserves equality among addressees—a subject I deal with in more detail in Chapter 17.

Are there any abusive expressions that are so generally hurtful when directed at listeners in face-to-face conversations that they should be singled out as commonly illegal? The most obvious candidates are racial, ethnic, and religious epithets and slurs.[26] Perhaps in a decent society people should not have to acclimatize themselves to being the victims of such remarks. A point that I will stress in connection with long-term harms is the absence of equality in potential victimization. "Honkey" hurts a lot less than "nigger," and "WASP" hurts a lot less than "kike."[27] Those who rest secure in a majority and favored status can accept the denigrating terms and appraisals that apply to their privileged position with much more equanimity than those who feel that the terms reflect a widespread distaste for the group to which they belong. Despite all the line-drawing difficulties, there is a substantial argument for making criminal or actionable the serious use of racial and ethnic insults designed to injure and demean.[28]

I now turn to the fourth interest, avoidance of long-term harms. Personal insults, "You fat slob," can wound, and, if repeated often enough by enough people, they may have a detrimental effect on one's self-esteem. But the effect of most such insults is contained and dissipates fairly quickly; so worry about long-term consequences would not be an appropriate basis for legal regulation. In contrast, epithets and slurs that reflect stereotypes about race, ethnic group, religion, and gender[29] may reinforce prejudices and feelings of inferiority in seriously harmful ways and reduce the level of reason in public discourse. These harms do not depend on whether the audience is mainly composed of persons who are the subject of the epithets. For men to use denigrating expressions about women in conversations with each other may be just as bad in the long run as for them to talk to women in these ways. All-male conversations can certainly support male prejudices. And feelings of inferiority in the insulted group may come from knowing how one is talked about as well as from reacting to how one is talked to. So, if one focuses on long-run harms alone, there is no strong reason to concentrate too much on the particular audience; in fact, in other countries most laws directed against racial, ethnic, and religious epithets and slurs do not distinguish on that basis. But it must be recognized that these long-term harms flow largely from the message the speaker wants to convey. Trying to prevent the harms is regulating speech because of its dangerous content. It is just such regulation that is in strongest tension with a principle of free speech. To forbid racial slurs *in general* is not to nibble at the edges of expression, as recovery for intentional wounding with words might be;[30] it is consciously to attack communications because the ideas that they powerfully express in unconsidered form are so abhorrent. No doubt whatever ideas are involved could be put in less unpalatable language, but the force of feeling might be less well conveyed. An important aspect of free speech is letting people express themselves in their own way, and circumscribing forms of speech is particularly troublesome for spontaneous remarks. Also, knowing that some people have the irrational hostile feelings that epithets and slurs reflect does amount to important, if unwelcome, information about social attitudes.[31] Faced only with a political principle of free speech, a legislature might decide nevertheless to go ahead and regulate, believing that the messages conveyed by such epithets are messages about whose destructiveness we can be sure and believing further that the critical goals of dignity and social equality warrant this restriction on expression.

The accommodation of values these inquiries suggest is not easy, and we should not suppose that one set of answers is good for all time, even for one time in all societies. Tensions among racial, ethnic, and religious groups vary among societies and over time. Where racial and religious conflicts are not serious and gross inequalities along racial and religious lines do not exist, even the literature of racial and religious hate should be allowed, but what should be tolerated in one country and one time may be too dangerous in another country or another time.

Pornography

All the states and the federal government, as well as most other countries, have laws making criminal the distribution and sale of obscene literature and photographs. Although the word "obscene" in its origins referred to that which is repugnant or disgusting generally, the term now connotes mainly offensive pornographic material, highly explicit material about sex that is erotically stimulating.[32] Among the multiple reasons for prohibition, explored in extensive commentary, are fears that such material: will lead viewers to commit sexual crimes or to develop unwholesome attitudes toward sex, members of the opposite gender, and family responsibilities; will displace better literature and photographic art; will be used in connection with unhealthy sexual activities; will offend many people who are exposed to the material against their wishes or are disturbed by knowing that others are using the material.

Are these reasons sufficient to warrant any prohibition, and, if so, of what material? That depends on the appropriateness of forbidding behavior that does not directly injure anyone else and on how far the material involved is reached by a principle of free speech. It is with respect to obscenity that free speech claims connect most closely to claims about liberty of "self-regarding" acts. If one puts aside the conceivable argument that the government may suppress obscenity simply because some people are offended by its availability to others, the critical issues about pornography resemble those about abusive language, especially abusive language that is not designed to wound in a face-to-face encounter. These issues concern the speech value of the communications and their long-term effect on healthy social attitudes and acceptable behavior. I shall first examine arguments to the effect that most pornography does not qualify as full-fledged speech, and then consider what feared harms might justify prohibition.

The question whether pornographic literature, photographs, and moving pictures are the kinds of communication to which a principle of free speech applies, combines concerns about communication as action and concerns about the place of aesthetic expression. I concentrate first on speech as involving assertions of fact and value and then consider the significance of aesthetic expression. Only after analysis in terms of relatively clear categories do I comment on problems of line drawing and legal determination.

Imagine a ten-minute moving picture, without artistic aspiration, focused only on the sexual organs of a man and woman having intercourse. Frederick Schauer argues that obscenity is not really speech at all, because what it does is simply to stimulate sexual desire without having ideational content, much in the manner of an actual physical device used to stimulate the sex organs.[33] If this view were accurate, then, as long as the material could be adequately defined, consideration of prohibition of pornography could proceed without worry about free speech.

Can it be said that pornography has no ideational content? Much pornography at least conveys the notion that involvement in the kind of sex portrayed is highly pleasurable.[34] Of course, that idea is portrayed rather than stated, but much fiction and photography involves showing how people feel in situations, not giving some abstract account of what causes pleasure or pain. Much pornography may also have a broader implicit message of rejection of conventional attitudes toward sex.[35] Both these messages matter for people deciding how to conduct their personal lives.

Moreover, given the suggestion in Chapter 3 that aesthetic expression, which creates "forms symbolic of human feeling,"[36] warrants some protection as speech even when it conveys no statement of fact and value, an absence of ideational content would not necessarily disqualify pornography. Pornographic pictures are importantly different from the physical devices to which Schauer compares them. Pictures initially affect one's mental states and emotions, and whatever physical stimulation occurs is a product of those mental states and emotions;[37] sexual stimulation by physical devices is also accompanied by changed mental and emotional states, but their role is less primary.[38] Nevertheless, a distinction might be drawn between pornography and genuine aesthetic expression. Aesthetic expression may require distance between the observer and the work of art; physical distance to grasp the symbolic representation has been called the intellectual component in the aesthetic attitude. The effect of pornography may be to destroy distance between the viewer and the material.[39] If the effect of representations is only to involve the viewer in immediate experience, whether a principle of free speech applies at all remains a question, but it is arguable that if pornography has neither ideational content *nor* aesthetic merit it does not qualify as expression.

My discussion thus far has attended to the material itself, but a closely related inquiry involves the aims and interests of producers and consumers. Most pornography may differ from literature and genuine art in that neither its authors and publishers nor those who consume it care about a communicative message or aesthetic experience. The latter seek stimulation; the former want only to make money. Of course, most authors, photographers, and publishers also want to make money, but most writers and photographers also have *some* message or aesthetic aim, and many publishers also count those as of some intrinsic importance. If ideational and aesthetic aims and interests are slight for producers and consumers of pornography, that fact bears on expressive value. The fact that *some* purveyors of pornography may have serious ideological objectives is also important, but a legislature could reasonably consider how high this percentage is, and conclude that it is very low.

In summary, there is no easy path by which all pornography can be treated as nonspeech, but its dominant aim and effect of causing immediate physical stimulation, rather than consideration of ideas or aesthetic experience, substantially reduce its expressive significance. In this respect at least, pornography that aims to stimulate resembles abusive words that aim to wound. I shall not here go into line-drawing problems in any detail, but the history of suppression of obscenity amply shows that categorizing what materials have little expressive value is not easy. Since it is highly doubtful that any effective legal test for pornography can depend directly on the aims and interests of particular producers and consumers of specific material, the possibility of emphasizing subjective intent offers no real escape from the problem of categorization.

I now consider how far interests that may be served by a suppression of pornographic materials should figure in a legislative judgment whether to suppress. I shall dispose of the wish to avoid offense and the wish to preserve good literature and art fairly quickly. Without developing the position here, I assume that some people's displeasure at knowing what others are reading and looking at is not itself an appropriate reason in a liberal society for suppression. A wish not to have oneself exposed to materials one finds offensive, however, is relevant, but if that were the only legitimate reason for government interference, a more circumscribed form of regulation would be called for, for example, carefully limiting posters in public view.[40] The worry about displacement of better literature and photographs is itself disquieting. First, there is the question of the likely validity of its factual premises. To put that crudely, is it plausible that those who buy and peruse obscenity might otherwise use that time to read good books, rather than cutting their toenails or watching wrestling on television? Second, however confident most of us may be that we can distinguish good literature from absolute junk, there is something troubling under a regime of free speech about the government's deciding that some literature and photographs are so bad *and* so powerfully attractive that they should actually be forbidden. Embarking on such a course would seem warranted only if one were deeply worried about the extended effect of viewing pornography instead of reading good literature. The claim of justification would then lie close to those now to be examined: that the government should suppress pornography in order to reduce criminal violence, unhealthy sexual acts, and harmful attitudes.

If it could be shown that viewing pornography, or pornography of a certain kind, made it more likely that some people would commit crimes, and the correlation between viewing and committing the crimes was rather high, that would be a very solid ground for prohibition, one identical with the main reason why criminal solicitations are punished. If thirty percent of the men exposed to movies graphically portraying rape ended up committing rape and if only a very slight proportion of them would otherwise have done so, any sensible legislature would decide to forbid showing such movies to men, despite minimal costs to free speech.[41] Of course, no correlation of anything like this magnitude exists. Indeed, the social science literature does not establish that pornography generally causes criminal acts. Evidence does suggest, however, that graphic portrayals of violent sex which explicitly or implicitly convey the view that engaging in such sex is appropriate do contribute to attitudes of acceptance of such behavior on the part of a proportion of viewers,[42] and perhaps one can infer that these attitudes will lead to the actual commission of violent sexual crimes by a much smaller proportion. A crime-prevention rationale plausibly applies to such portrayals of violent sexual acts and, perhaps, to portrayals of nonviolent sexual acts in which women are degraded; for those categories, it can reasonably be debated whether the concern is great enough to warrant suppression.

The "unhealthy sex activities" worry is a bit more complex. I shall deal first with activities that are an aspect of production and then with activities in which consumers engage. It is often said that the pornography business causes severe harm to those who are photographed and filmed. The concerns about children encouraged to perform sexual acts before a camera and about adults, almost always women, who are actually coerced to participate are undeniable, but these concerns could be adequately met without banning all pornography. A more subtle point is that women who participate are often dominated in some way short of what the law would count as illegal coercion, and that, in any event, having one's participation in sexual acts photographed and published in some form is degrading. There is much to this worry, but I assume that, in a liberal society in which the viewing of pornography were otherwise deemed acceptable, potential adult actors should be permitted the choice whether to participate in producing pornographic materials.

A justification for prohibition cast in terms of sexual activities of consumers presumes a basis for saying that some voluntary sexual activities are better than others, since, if one believed that no basis existed or that no such basis should fall within the judgment of the state, this justification for restriction would collapse. Many people are willing to assume that, whether forbidden or not, some sexual activities, such as adultery and masturbation, are socially less desirable or psychologically less healthy, or both, than sex as an aspect of the marriage relationship. A large part of the concern about adultery is, of course, its tendency to undermine stable marriages important for children. Many people also think that sexual relationships of rough equality are psychologically and socially better than relationships in which one partner dominates the other.

If one focuses on sexual activities like masturbation and adultery, it is uncertain whether pornography increases their incidence; that pornography is often used as an aid to masturbation, for example, does not establish that masturbation is more frequent because pornography is available. Supposing that the empirical data were supportive of a connection or that an intuitive judgment to that effect were deemed adequate, a further question would arise: Why is prohibiting pornography all right if the state does not also prohibit the activities, for example, adultery, that it really wants to curb? As earlier chapters have suggested, proceeding by such indirection is not illogical. A law directly against adultery might be too hard to enforce or it might mistakenly interfere with very strongly motivated choices. Reducing instances of adultery might still be an appropriate aim, as reducing the legally permitted behavior of smoking might be the aim of a ban on cigarette advertising. However, much of the basis for free speech is that people should have available to them communications that affect choice; suppression on just the ground that communications in some indirect way encourage the wrong choices is disturbing.[43] And since many of those who view pornography will not increase their incidence of undesirable sexual acts as a result, the indirect approach of forbidding pornography fits much less well the behavior to be discouraged than would a direct ban on the activities themselves.

There is, of course, no sharp break between equal sexual relationships and ones of domination, and the law could not set out to forbid all sexual activities in which one partner dominates another. The worry about sexual relationships of domination falls very close to concern about more pervasive attitudes toward sex and gender, an aspect of the larger concern that pornography may have a destructive effect on social attitudes.

To oversimplify considerably, it is claimed that pornography generates undesirable attitudes toward sexual partners and toward women. Among conservative proponents of restriction the emphasis is on debasement of family and related institutions and corruption of the ideal of disciplined life.[44] Feminist proponents stress the way pornography reinforces male domination of women.[45] Pornography treats sex as a means to pleasure and sexual partners as objects of pleasure, disregarding emotional ties and commitments. Since most pornography is for men, women are the ones usually portrayed as the objects of desire and the means of satisfaction. Forbidding pornography may be a way to reduce these unhealthy, unjust, and socially undesirable attitudes and to promote freer and more equal relationships between the sexes. From this perspective, the danger of pornography in relation to women is quite close to the danger of racial epithets in relation to members of minorities. The particular worry about the domination of women that serves as a justification for suppression also reaches much that is not pornographic but portrays women in a degraded or subservient way; it probably reaches violent pornography with women victims more strongly than "ordinary" pornography; and it may not cover some pornography at all, that which treats women and men as equals or women as dominant and men as submissive.

A powerful objection may be raised to reliance on any of the arguments for prohibition that concentrate on the behavior and attitudes of consumers of pornography. The arguments seem to strike at the fundamental reasons for a principle of free speech. After all, they make the very messages that the materials most strongly convey the basis for stopping them; is not prohibition straight suppression because of disfavored content? A partial answer to this objection is that the *ideas* of approval of exploitation of sexual partners and male domination can still be otherwise expressed and that an aspect of what is so objectionable about pornography is that the "ideas" can affect viewers even when they consciously reject them. Unlike the object of subliminal advertising, the person who views pornography is at least aware of the nature of the material, but if the more enduring messages of pornography operate largely at nonconscious levels and alter attitudes without any considered judgment by the viewer, that surely is a reason for counting them as of lesser value.[46] Thus, on examination, the contention that at least some forms of pornography should be suppressed most plausibly relies on a combination of factors: the dominant aim to stimulate rather than communicate; the largely unconscious quality of the messages communicated; and the harmfulness of those messages.[47]

If one believes that, on balance, some degree of suppression is apt, defining the categories is by no means easy. One must first decide which, if any, arguments are strong enough to support suppression of some materials. As we have seen, the arguments themselves reach somewhat variant categories of materials, and the strength of each argument must be considered not only in terms of its persuasiveness about social harm but in terms of how it fits with a principle of freedom of speech. Once one has a sense of what materials warrant suppression, one must address the statutory phraseology, trying to draw lines that will track one's objectives and be effectively administrable.

Because, in the United States, the question of sensible statutory formulation is so closely linked to constitutional limitation, I shall save both those problems for Chapter 17. My own judgment is that a legislature might reasonably either not prohibit pornography at all or prohibit only hard-core or violent hard-core pornography, that is, highly explicit material meant primarily to excite. Probably any restriction should be limited to pictorial materials. Insofar as the feminist arguments for suppression extend to materials that do not qualify as "hard core," I do not think they are finally persuasive. My reasons have much to do with the difficulties of definition, and these connect closely to standards of constitutional adjudication. Chapter 17 offers a somewhat fuller, though still brief, account of this issue.

Notes

1. More specific crimes, such as those forbidding harassing telephone calls, are similarly grounded; see *Model Penal Code* § 250.4(1).

2. W. Keeton et al., *Prosser and Keeton on Torts* 856–63 (5th ed., St. Paul, Minn., West Publishing Co. 1984). The fourth branch of the tort involves intrusions into privacy like electronic eavesdropping.

3. Other schemes of regulation limit expression in a much more serious way, by circumscribing copying of books, etc., in an aim to safeguard some property-like right of the original author or publisher. Except for passing mention, I do not comment on these in this book.

4. See, e.g., E. Barendt, *Freedom of Speech* 190 (Oxford, Clarendon Press 1985); F. Schauer, *Free Speech: A Philosophical Enquiry* 176–77 (Cambridge, Cambridge University Press 1982); K. Greenawalt, "New York's Right of Privacy—The Need for Change," 42 *Brooklyn Law Review* 159, 177–82 (1975). For a poignant case, see the publication of the fact that a college student-body president had undergone a sex-change operation. *Diaz v. Oakland Tribune, Inc.* 139 Cal. App.3d 118, 188 Cal. Rptr. 762 (1983).

5. In the interests of completeness, I should mention that various professional rules of confidentiality, sometimes backed by legal sanctions, also preclude the disclosure of embarrassing facts. Since the willingness of people to reveal highly embarrassing matters to doctors, lawyers, and ministers is vitally important for their work, the appropriateness of such rules of confidentiality is evident; the special way in which professionals acquire information about those they serve renders it appropriate to curb their freedom to disclose.

6. To readers who may be offended by seeing such words in print, I apologize. My sense is that one can come to grips with the issues best if one has to come to terms with use of the words.

7. See *Prosser and Keeton on Torts*, note 2 supra, at 57–65. According to traditional tort law, words themselves do not amount to an assault, but such words could give color to gestures that might be threatening.

8. *Model Penal Code* § 250.2(1)(b).

9. Id. § 250.4(2).

10. See E. Barendt, note 4 supra, at 163–65; L. Bollinger, *The Tolerant Society*, 38–39 (New York, Oxford University Press 1986); H. Arkes, "Civility and the Restriction of Speech: Rediscovering the Defamation of Groups," 1974 *Supreme Court Review* 281, 283–84; Note, "A Communitarian Defense of Group Libel Laws," 101 *Harvard Law Review* 682, 689–94 (1988). In a Public Order Act of 1986, the British Parliament amended previous enactments to provide that "A person who uses threatening, abusive or insulting words or behaviour, or displays any written material which is threatening, abusive or insulting is guilty . . . if (a) he intends thereby to stir up racial hatred, or (b) having regard to all the circumstances racial hatred is likely to be stirred up thereby." See Public Order Act 1986, § 18, in *Public General Acts and Measures of 1986* (Part IV, Ch. 64) (London, Her Majesty's Stationery Office 1987). A similar standard governs publication or distribution of material, public performance or recording of plays, and radio and television

broadcasts, id. §§ 19–22. For the Federal Republic of Germany, relevant statutes and interpretations, as well as recent legislative reform, are carefully described in E. Stein, "History against Free Speech: The New German Law against the 'Auschwitz'—and Other—'Lies'" 85 *Michigan Law Review* 277 (1986). Although some foreign legislation seems very broad to American eyes, Lee Bollinger has observed about distinguishing racist rhetoric from other speech, "It seems a significant piece of corroborating evidence that virtually every other western democracy does draw such a distinction in their law; the United States stands virtually alone in the degree to which it has decided legally to tolerate racist rhetoric." See Bollinger, supra, at 38.

11. Austin, interestingly, treated insults as an unusual kind of performative utterance. See J. L. Austin, *How to Do Things with Words* 68 (2d ed., J. Urmson and M. Sbisa, eds., Cambridge, Mass., Harvard University Press 1975).

12. See J. Feinberg, *Offense to Others* 226–32 (New York, Oxford University Press 1985); Bollinger, note 10 supra, at 183.

13. The comment in the text oversimplifies a good deal. We can imagine that, if you challenge a person whom you regard as honorable but who has regrettably done something that "requires" a duel, you might say neutrally "I challenge you, etc."; but if you regard your prospective opponent as dishonorable, you begin with the standard insult. In that event, the uttering of the insult would convey something significant beyond the obvious idea that you think the person is someone who should be dueled.

14. For purposes of clarity, I am describing a sharp distinction which is clearly drawn and perceptively analyzed in Feinberg, note 12 supra. Often the two aspects, conventional challenge and anger provocation, will be mixed in such a way that even a thoughtful speaker aware of his own state of mind might have a hard time saying which he is mainly doing.

15. It has been suggested that "fighting words" trigger an automatic reaction. See J. Nowak et al., *Constitutional Law* 942–43 (3d ed., St. Paul, Minn., West Publishing Co. 1986); M. Rutzick, "Offensive Language and the Evolution of First Amendment Protection," 9 *Harvard Civil Rights–Civil Liberties Law Review* 1, 8 (1974). No doubt these words can trigger intense responses that reduce control, but many listeners must still be able to use some judgment about their chances in a physical conflict and are not likely to attack an abuser who is also pointing a gun at them.

16. See generally R. Delgado, "Words that Wound: A Tort Action for Racial Insults, Epithets, and Name-calling," 17 *Harvard Civil Rights–Civil Liberties Law Review* 133 (1982); D. Downs, "Skokie Revisited: Hate Group Speech and the First Amendment," 60 *Notre Dame Lawyer* 629 (1985). See also Feinberg, note 12 supra, at 30, 89–91.

17. For example, a woman with no prejudice against Italian-Americans who wished to wound a particular Italian-American man who annoyed her might say "You wop," hoping that expression would be wounding to him.

18. On this point, Donald Downs writes, note 16 supra, at 651, "[W]hen the *primary* purpose of speech is not communication, but rather the infliction of harm, the law can no longer construe any resulting harm as a secondary result."

19. See, e.g., Bollinger, note 10 supra, at 198; Delgado, note 16 supra.

20. See generally A. Montagu, *The Anatomy of Swearing* (New York, Macmillan Co. 1967).

21. However, the initial use of abusive words might foreclose the speaker's recovering against the listener for a physical assault or might at least mitigate damages.

22. See, e.g., M. Nimmer, *Nimmer on Freedom of Speech* 2–30 (New York, Matthew Bender Co. 1984); Rutzick, note 15 supra, at 27. For an elaborate and sophisticated account of varieties of offensiveness and the circumstances in which offensive behavior may properly be punished in a liberal society, see Feinberg, note 12 supra, at 1–96.

23. See Downs, note 18 supra, at 647–48, citing cases.

24. *Hustler Magazine* v. *Falwell*, 108 S. Ct. 876 (1988).

25. If intimidation is sufficiently clear in its purpose and is designed to restrict liberty, it can constitute criminal coercion, which is discussed in Chapter 5.

26. Perhaps one should also add epithets aimed at sexual preferences and epithets related to one's gender.

27. See Delgado, note 16 supra, at 180.

28. See id. It seems likely that, at this stage in the United States, epithets about religious affiliation are not disturbing enough to warrant special regulation.

29. I include gender here, although not in the text of the immediately preceding discussion. Words and phrases men use to depict women as sex objects may reinforce strongly undesirable attitudes, but I unconfidently suppose that these words and phrases do not "wound" most individual women to the degree that serious racial and ethnic slurs typically wound. Whether that assumption is accurate is obviously an important question if a statute directed at wounding epithets is considered.

30. See, e.g., Downs, note 18 supra.

31. See D. Farber, "Civilizing Public Discourse: An Essay on Professor Bickel, Justice Harlan, and the Enduring Significance of *Cohen* v. *California*," 1980 *Duke Law Journal* 283, 301.

32. See Schauer, note 4 supra, at 179. For a thorough and illuminating exploration of the idea of the obscene and how it relates to pornography, see Feinberg, note 12 supra, at 97–164.

33. Schauer, note 4 supra, at 181–84. See also Feinberg, note 12 supra, at 169.

34. It might be said that Schauer's illustration is not of this sort, because the faces of the actors are not shown. I am assuming that even a film limited to movements of the body will convey, in light of the past experiences of viewers, that a pleasurable experience is happening.

35. See, e.g., D. Richards, "Free Speech and Obscenity Law: Toward a Moral Theory of the First Amendment," 123 *University of Pennsylvania Law Review* 45, 81 (1974).

36. See, e.g., J. Finnis, "'Reason and Passion': The Constitutional Dialectic of Free Speech and Obscenity," 116 *University of Pennsylvania Law Review* 222, 232 (1967).

37. See M. Redish, *Freedom of Expression* 75 (Charlottesville, Va., The Michie Co. 1984).

38. I shall not attempt to say just what the role of the changed mental and emotional states is. They are an effect of the use of the physical device, but sexual stimulation does not occur separate from the mental states. A physical device may not have its "ordinary effect" on a person who is depressed or preoccupied. So the mental states are both an effect of use of the physical device and at least a partial cause of the sexual excitement that follows.

39. Finnis, note 36 supra, at 235–36. Joel Feinberg quotes a number of views and provides his own thoughtful analysis of whether pornography can be art. He concludes, interestingly, that the two are more likely to be combined in still pictures than in either movies or writing. See Feinberg, note 12 supra, at 130–38.

40. See T. Scanlon, "Freedom of Expression and Categories of Expression," 40 *University of Pittsburgh Law Review* 519, 542 (1979). Scanlon goes on to suggest, id. at 543–50, that those who disseminate pornography may have a legitimate interest in reaching those who would prefer no exposure.

41. I assume that the thirty percent who become rapists are not identifiable in advance, so that showing the movies only to the other seventy percent is not feasible.

42. N. Malamuth and V. Billings, "Why Pornography? Models of Functions and Effects," 34 *Journal of Communication* (2) 117, 128 (1984); See also Feinberg, note 12

supra, at 147–57, on the complicated causal relationship between violent pornography and violent acts.

43. The aim of cigarette advertising is to get people to buy and smoke cigarettes. The aim of pornography is not to get people to commit adultery.

44. See, e.g., H. Clor, *Obscenity and Public Morality: Censorship in a Liberal Society* 168–88 (Chicago, Chicago University Press 1969).

45. See A. Dworkin, *Pornography: Men Possessing Women* (New York, Putnam 1981); C. MacKinnon, "Not a Moral Issue," 2 *Yale Law & Policy Review* 321 (1984); P. Brest and A. Vandenberg, "Politics, Feminism, and the Constitution: The Anti-Pornography Movement in Minneapolis," 39 *Stanford Law Review* 607 (1987). For a helpful account of how the more traditional bases for opposing obscenity relate to modern feminist ideas, see Comment, "Feminism, Pornography, and the First Amendment: An Obscenity-based Analysis of Proposed Antipornography Laws," 34 *University of California in Los Angeles Law Review* 1265, 1286–94 (1987).

46. See Scanlon, note 40 supra, at 547–48, drawing the comparison to subliminal advertising, but suggesting that those who believe in the implicit messages of pornography may say that they have a right to present them in an exciting way that will enable the viewer to understand their attraction.

47. See generally C. Sunstein, "Pornography and the First Amendment," 1986 *Duke Law Journal* 589.

9

Regulation of Expressive Activities for Reasons Unrelated to Content and Regulation of Activities That Are Not Inherently Expressive

This chapter deals with prohibitions that differ importantly from suppression of particular sorts of oral or written communications discussed in earlier chapters. I now treat two situations: those in which a prohibition is in a sense directed against communicative acts, but for reasons that have nothing to do with the content of the communications; and those in which a prohibition is apparently not directed at communicative acts at all, but has a substantial impact on those who wish to communicate. The line between these two sorts of situations is blurred, but that does not matter greatly for our purposes, since in both settings legislatures should give considerable weight to the interests in free speech and should be especially careful not to end up suppressing particular sorts of messages.

Constraint of Expressive Activities for Reasons Other Than Content

Expressive activities can have harmful effects that have nothing to do with what is communicated. Parades and picketing can interfere with traffic; sound trucks can make disturbing noise; leaflets that are passed out can lead to littering.

If the government genuinely acts only to protect some interest that has nothing to do with what is communicated, at least it is not picking the messages it wants people to hear as opposed to contrary messages, but extreme measures to protect other interests obviously can curtail opportunities for communication, and almost certainly the curtailment will work unequally among groups of citizens and points of view. Suppose that, in the interests of clean streets and parks and quiet neighborhoods, all street demonstrations, all public use of sound-amplifying equipment, and all distribution of leaflets were prohibited. This would constitute a serious impairment of speech, which would especially affect groups without resources and power to get their positions heard over television and in the newspapers.

Whenever a legislature considers regulations that directly interfere with ex-pressive activity, it should give great weight to the need to keep open a variety of communicative outlets. Often a reasonable compromise is some regulation of time, place, and manner which leaves outlets open but in a way that minimizes inconvenience and annoyance.

Regulation of Nonspeech Activities

Legislation can significantly inhibit communication even though it does not ostensibly treat expressive activity at all. Of course if, without some extraordinary justification, the legislature aims at the suppression of unpopular messages by adopting a law that formally deals with something else, it wrongly contravenes a principle of free speech. When a statute has a genuine justification different from suppressing speech, the proper legislative treatment of expressive acts is more complicated. I shall treat these two sorts of instances with three examples: destruction of flags, destruction of draft cards, and public nudity.

Aiming at the Message: Desecrating Flags and Burning Draft Cards

In the United States, many laws prohibit defiling, mutilating, or defacing of American flags.[1] Since the only reason to prevent flags from being defiled or defaced is that the flag has symbolic importance for citizens, these laws on their face come extremely close to being directed at expression. It might be said that the laws are partly designed to prevent careless treatment of the country's sacred symbol and that simply being irresponsible in one's treatment of the flag is not an expressive act in any sense that matters for free speech, but the answer is that the criminal provisions are not plausibly aimed at people who are negligent, and one strongly doubts that such people are ever prosecuted.[2] Rather, the laws are aimed at those who burn or deface their flags as a sign of disrespect of the government or country.[3] If so, the laws aim clearly at communicative acts, acts that happen to be offensive to many fellow citizens.

Ideas underlying the disrespect could be otherwise expressed, but a speaker should ordinarily be allowed to choose a preferred form of speech, and defacing the flag may express feelings more intensely[4] and attract the attention of an audience better than any other manner of expression. Some hurt and offense may be involved for members of an immediate audience,[5] but, because that is in their capacity as citizens, rather than as abused individuals or members of a hated minority, they need less protection than persons subjected to individual insults or group epithets.[6] Conceivably, the reaction of the immediate audience will be so severe that violence is likely to break out. But it is doubtful that, at this stage of American history, defacing or destroying flags will often produce that effect unless it is done in circumstances highly likely to produce retaliation, e.g., at a Memorial Day ceremony. Defacing the flag might be regarded as one kind of coarse display to which the Model Code's disorderly-conduct provision would apply if there was also recklessness about public annoyance or alarm,[7] but protection against audience reaction is an insufficient reason for a general ban on flag desecration.

Once it is acknowledged that forbidding flag desecration is directed at expression, and, more, is directed at the content of the messages likely to be communicated, that does not necessarily end the inquiry about regulation. A legislature faced only with a political principle of free speech might take the position that preserving a sacred national symbol from disturbing and disruptive political discourse could warrant imposing this limited interference with liberty of expression. But, so long as the flag is used extensively at public and publicized ceremonies that support government policies, any ideal of "neutrality" for the national symbol is elusive,[8] and a ban on desecration obliquely supports the status quo.

I shall say a word about legislative purpose and draft-card burning. When the Supreme Court passed on a federal statute that prohibits knowing destruction of one's draft card, the Court declined to go beneath the surface and discern that the aim of Congress was to clamp down on antiwar protests.[9] But what the Supreme Court does or does not discern as a matter of constitutional law does not settle what legislators properly do under a principle of free speech. Given what I have said so far, an aim to inhibit antiwar protests is not a legitimate legislative aim. If that aim did lie behind the action of Congress, as it almost certainly did, given the prior law and the legislative history, Congress infringed a political principle of free speech.

Destroying Draft Cards and Public Nudity

I now address circumstances in which the legislative aim is not to curb expression, but in which some predominantly expressive behavior is foreclosed. Prior to the explicit congressional law forbidding destruction of draft cards, there existed a more general law prohibiting violation of selective-service regulations, which in turn required keeping one's registration and classification cards.[10] To burn one's card intentionally constituted a willful violation of the regulations and could be punished with a five-year prison term (the same maximum penalty as for the subsequently enacted prohibition of draft-card destruction).

Let us suppose that the government had a substantial enough interest in young men's keeping their draft cards to warrant such serious penalties for ordinary violations and that expressive acts constituted only a small proportion of all violations of the relevant regulations. Presented with such a situation, a legislature concerned with expression has three alternatives. If it thinks a significant number of violations would be expressive, it might refrain from otherwise desirable legislation; it might create an explicit exemption for the expressive acts;[11] or it might go ahead and adopt the prohibition without exemption, simply treating the expressive acts like all other acts. Certainly a substantial incidence of expressive acts could constitute a reason not to legislate if the question is already close. Although an exemption for expressive acts might seem unfair to those whose willful violation has some other basis, such an exemption is a reasonable accommodation to interests in free speech *if* the expressive acts are easily identifiable. Burning of draft cards in public almost inevitably represents expression of a powerfully felt point of view.[12] I have not done the hard job of surveying all the relevant violations of selective-service regulations and figuring out how an exemption might be drafted, but if one considers only destruction of draft cards, an exemption for acts that are on their surface expressive might be warranted.

An illustration that presents more intractable problems for any exemption is a prohibition on public nudity. Some people who appear nude in public do so mainly because they want to communicate a message, for example, that wearing clothing unnecessary for warmth reflects a harsh and harmful puritanical attitude toward the human body; some people have no communicative message, for example, a college student "streaks" (runs nude) across campus on a dare; and some people have a mix of noncommunicative and communicative motives, for example, a bather lies nude on the beach mainly because he likes the sensation but partly because he wishes to express his rejection of conventional puritanism. The fact that public nudity fairly often expresses a communicative message is a reason to allow it, but the offensiveness of public nudity to most of the population is sufficient reason to prohibit it in places where other people cannot easily avoid exposure. Once a legislature decides that some general prohibition is warranted, it cannot sensibly exempt particular acts whose significance is apparent only after an interview with the actor. It would be foolish and unadministrable to make appearing nude on a public beach a crime if a person's only, or dominant, motives were physical pleasure and an even suntan, but to allow such nudity for those whose dominant motive is to communicate a "liberated" view of nudity and sex.

These comments complete my discussion of a purely political principle of free speech that might constrain legislative action. I have assumed that, even when it is not subject to binding constitutional limits, a legislature in a liberal society should give considerable weight to the values of free speech in deciding what laws to adopt, and I have tried by examples to show what serious attention to a principle of free speech entails. The particularistic nature of the comments reflects my view that conflicts between free speech and other values yield no easy resolution and that broad abstract principles do not produce decisive solutions of difficult social issues concerning speech. People who are sensitive to the values of speech can disagree about what justifies overriding these values, and what is a good resolution may depend on time and place.

Notes

1. See, e.g., *Street* v. *New York*, 394 U.S. 576 (1969); *Spence* v. *Washington*, 418 U.S. 405, 406–7 (1974); Uniform Flag Act, 9B *Uniform Laws Ann.* 48 (1966). In addition to provisions on flag desecration, there are laws about improper use of the flag. The relevance of free speech for laws largely designed to prevent trivialization of the flag for commercial or other purposes is not nearly so plain. I discuss that relevance briefly in Chapter 19.

2. It is highly likely that courts would not interpret these laws to reach instances of negligent or reckless defacement. See J. Ely, "Flag Desecration: A Case Study in the Roles of Categorization and Balancing in First Amendment Analysis," 88 *Harvard Law Review* 1482, 1502 (1975).

3. See, e.g., V. Blasi, "The Checking Value in First Amendment Theory," 1977 *American Bar Foundation Research Journal* 521, 640; A. Loewy, "Punishing Flag Desecrators: The Ultimate in Flag Desecration," 49 *North Carolina Law Review* 48, 64 (1970).

4. The person defacing the flag may feel that the act expresses his emotions better, *and* the audience may better understand the intensity of these emotions.

5. See generally J. Feinberg, *Offense to Others* 1–96 (New York, Oxford University Press 1985), for a thorough exploration of notions of offense. Flag desecration is discussed and compared with mistreatment of dead bodies, id. at 53–56.

6. See Loewy, note 3 supra, at 83–84.

7. See *Model Penal Code* § 250.2(1)(b).

8. A dissenting group may, of course, use the flag in a respectful way at its own meetings, but there are enough public ceremonies, especially military ceremonies, at which the flag is associated with the government, that it is hard to dissolve the idea that the flag is partly a symbol of those who *now* represent citizens in some formal way, i.e., the present government.

9. *United States* v. *O'Brien*, 391 U.S. 367, 382–86 (1968).

10. See id.

11. In that case, a predominantly expressive aim would excuse what would otherwise count as a violation.

12. Of course, the illegality of such acts is both a reason why they are not engaged in frivolously and a reason why their communicative impact is as great as it is. *That* expressive aim cannot be accommodated by an exemption. See Ely, note 2 supra, at 1489–90. Further, some may want to express their protest by choosing an act *because* it is illegal and perhaps even because punishment will be imposed. Those aims cannot be accommodated by creating a legal privilege to engage in the act. I am assuming that some young men would feel draft-card burning an important symbolic expression even if it was privileged and that relatively few people would burn cards without a serious expressive purpose.

III
CONSTITUTIONAL LIMITS ON PROHIBITING SPEECH

10

The First Amendment and Its Interpretation

In this third part of the book, I explore constitutional principles for freedom of speech and press. What has been said up to now has relevance for any modern government, or at least any liberal democratic government. The remainder of the study directly concerns the law in the United States of America, though it has powerful implications for other constitutional regimes. This chapter outlines factors that are relevant when the First Amendment is interpreted and explores briefly the understanding of freedom of speech held at the time the amendment was adopted. The next chapter is a longer but still fairly summary account of the development of First Amendment law. These chapters are background for the analysis that follows, first of competing general approaches to First Amendment adjudication, and then of particular problems that have been the subject of discussion in Part II.

Constitutional Construction and Legislative Responsibility

Constitutional interpretation by courts involves judicial construction of a written constitution which takes precedence over legislative and executive choices that conflict with it. Accordingly, interpretation of a constitutional provision dealing with freedom of speech will not be precisely the same as legislative responsiveness to a political principle of freedom of speech. Exactly how great the difference is between the criteria for sound judicial interpretation and legislative wisdom will depend on what the former criteria are—a subject summarily sketched in this chapter. Some points are obvious.

Courts deal with specific constitutional language. The reach of language governing freedom of speech might be broader or narrower than that of a sound political principle. If, as I shall contend, the language leaves courts free to develop constitutional standards in light of sound principles, judicial construction of the Constitution and ideal legislative judgment may still not coalesce, since important differences exist between the functions of constitutional interpretation and of legislative choice.

Constitutional standards to be used by courts must be based on criteria that courts are capable of applying. Courts, for example, cannot easily investigate the secret motives of individual legislators.[1] Thus, what may be an unacceptable legislative motive from the perspective of political theory, what may even be in some sense a constitutionally unacceptable motive, may be irrelevant to what a court says about constitutionality. It is generally supposed that courts interpreting the Constitution should employ fairly broad principles. Courts may need to draw sharper, more distinct lines than would a legislature considering only a political principle of free speech.[2] Legislatures can be attentive to matters of degree and balances of considerations that shift slightly from one circumstance to the next; responsiveness to such shifts may be difficult or inappropriate for courts developing constitutional doctrines.

Related to this last point is the possibility that in regard to some matters the Constitution may establish only minimal standards for protecting expression; part of legislative wisdom may consist in giving more protection than the constitutional minimum. It is also possible that, because of the need for broad categorization, constitutional law may rightly protect some communications that would not be protected by a finely tuned assessment of the values of speech against competing considerations.

Constitutional principles, of course, are not just a matter for the courts; they partly determine what is a proper legislative choice. In the absence of a written constitution, legislators responsive to a political principle of free speech would carefully consider the impact of proposed laws on expression, exercising considerable self-constraint. In light of the recognition that people deciding at a particular moment are likely to overrate the dangers of particular communications and underestimate the costs of interfering with speech, legislators would hesitate to interfere with speech, even if that seemed immediately the best course to follow. Nonetheless, assuming that the subject under discussion did not fall under some "absolute principle" that should be adopted by legislators as a matter of political wisdom, the legislature would properly engage in suppression if the reasons for doing so seemed *strong enough*.

Since a written constitution is a charter of government, which legislators are bound to uphold, it adds a new dimension to legislative deliberations. Legislators should not pass laws that are unconstitutional, even if such laws can escape judicial review. So, in our system, conscientious legislators must ask themselves both what they are constitutionally authorized to do and what will conform with a political principle of free speech.[3] In deciding about constitutional authorization, the legislature should not, except in highly exceptional circumstances, adopt rules that fly in the face of Supreme Court decisions about what is allowable, since our political system can function well only if the political branches ordinarily accord practical deference to such decisions.[4]

Though legislatures should not pass laws that are unconstitutional, it does not follow that they should never pass laws that, foreseeably, will have some unconstitutional applications. For some matters, not all the complex factors that determine the constitutionality of applications will be susceptible to sensible legislative formulation. A desirable and well-drafted law may prohibit a relatively few actions that are constitutionally protected. Since legislatures cannot worry about and try to meet every possible unconstitutional application, even appropriate legislative standards will leave room for some judicial declarations that a statute is unconstitutional as applied.

Standards of Constitutional Interpretation

What are the proper standards of constitutional interpretation for courts is a heated issue of constitutional theory in the United States. Rejecting the idea that any single criterion of interpretation counts for everything, I sketch here a pluralistic theory of interpretation and indicate its elements.

This chapter is much too brief to constitute a genuine defense of that theory, or even to establish how the theory fits with a coherent conception of the responsibilities of courts, but the treatment is sufficient to show roughly how the theory stands against more single-minded "reductionist" competitors and to supply the foundation for subsequent claims about what the First Amendment protects. The reader should not suppose, however, that all of this last part of the book rests precariously on acceptance of just the general interpretive approach I explicate. Although I do not trace all the potential bases of support as I proceed, much that I say in later chapters could be defended under one or more alternative approaches to interpretation.

In the discussion that follows I concentrate on the Supreme Court, the highest interpreter of the federal Constitution. The authority of that court renders the interpretive task of other courts somewhat different, since they have less scope than the Supreme Court itself has to disregard Supreme Court precedents that are deemed to have been misguided but have not yet been challenged by anything the Supreme Court has said. Of course, state supreme courts have, with respect to state constitutions, an authority and task similar to that of the federal Supreme Court for the federal document, and as long as what they do does not conflict with federally guaranteed rights, state supreme courts have room to develop their own theories and principles regarding constitutional rights like free speech. Thus, while I mainly discuss federal constitutional law, what I say has relevance for state constitutional law as well.

Judges in constitutional cases are properly guided by a number of criteria: constitutional language, historical background and contemporaneous documents shedding light on "original intent," the relationship of the particular issue to the structure of constitutional government, precedents and other relevant law at the time the court decides, deference to other organs of government, considerations of justice and social welfare, and what one's fellow judges are willing to say and do. Each of these criteria is somewhat complex, and the overlap among them is considerable; yet, with the possible exception of deference, for judges making practical choices none of the criteria is wholly collapsible into one or more of the others. It is in this respect that I disagree with more reductionist accounts of constitutional interpretation.[5]

The Constitutional Language
The Relevance of the Language

By "language" I mean the words in which constitutional provisions are framed. The language itself is, of course, a crucial indicator of what the drafters and adopters of the language had in their minds to do. But it also has independent significance; for it is the vehicle by which the drafters communicated to officials who must make and apply the law and to the public affected by the law. There is some reason to adhere to the understanding that the language conveys, even if this departs in certain respects from one's appraisal of what those who wrote and adopted the language subjectively intended or what would be suggested by other criteria of interpretation. Legal language is not wholly indeterminate. Perhaps interpretations that it forecloses absolutely[6] will never be urged, but, even among conceivable interpretations, the language can render some more plausible than others.

What is the understanding of the language that matters? If the language is to count as an independent standard, the guide must be what a reasonable person, or a reasonable lawyer, would understand it to mean, taking into account the extent to which some language may have a special technical legal meaning.[7] Of course, a modern person cannot put himself in the shoes of someone two hundred years ago, but it remains an important question whether the aim is to discern what a reasonable person *then* would have taken the language to mean or what a reasonable person *now* would take it to mean.[8] Were the modern meaning of a word or phrase *wholly different* from the original, the original meaning should control, but if the ordinary meaning of words has shifted subtly over time from adoption to the present, it is arguable what should be determinative. If one stresses what was actually adopted, the guide should be usage at the time of adoption; if one emphasizes what the words convey to those presently subject to the Constitution, a reasonable contemporary understanding is important. The claims of original and present understanding are briefly examined in the section on original intent; I shall here say only that each understanding of the language should carry some weight for a court whose perception is refined enough to ascertain any difference.

The language that is mainly relevant for our purposes is the language of the First and Fourteenth Amendments. The latter matters because it is clear that the First Amendment originally had no application against the actions of individual states, and it is commonly supposed that either the "due process clause" or the "privileges and immunities clause" of the Fourteenth Amendment is the vehicle by which most free speech protections of the federal Constitution constrain state and local governments as well.

The language of the free speech and free press clauses standing by itself provides only the most general guidance for interpretation. The provision that Congress shall not abridge "the freedom of speech, or of the press" does not settle whether all verbal or written communication counts as speech. It does not settle whether everything classifiable as speech is necessarily beyond government prohibition, though the phrase "*the* freedom of speech" may be taken to suggest reference to existing principles rather than to a more absolute standard. The language neither indicates why speech warrants protection nor how far development of the clause should be responsive to changing social conditions and social values. Less obviously open-ended than a phrase like "cruel and unusual punishments," the relatively broad language still does not preclude the view that what constitutes freedom of speech and the permissible infringements of speech may vary over time.

I shall say relatively little about the Fourteenth Amendment here and elsewhere, because the application of the First Amendment to the states is now so firmly established by precedent. Certainly the words of the Fourteenth Amendment do not compel that result. Given the due-process language of the Fifth Amendment, which accompanied the many explicit protections of the rest of the Bill of Rights, it is something of a strain to find in the Fourteenth Amendment's due-process clause the source of many substantive protections against the states. Present doctrine would be more easily defensible if it were rooted in the vaguer wording of the privileges-and-immunities clause.

The Language in Historical Context

Given the generality of the language of the free speech and free press clauses and of the first section of the Fourteenth Amendment, one who seeks to ascertain what that language would have conveyed at the time of adoption would need to delve into the legal and political history of the preceding periods and especially into the known problems to which the amendments were meant to respond and through which their purposes would have been understood.[9] It turns out that for the free speech and free press guarantees this method is largely the same method that would have to be used to decipher the subjective intent of the framers and adopters, since they left us relatively little distinctive material on that subject. I undertake that inquiry in the next section, but it has application to the reasonable meaning of the language as well.

The Original Intent of the "Framers"

The Relevance of Intent

Whether correct interpretation involves discerning the original intent of the Framers has during the last decade been the most sharply argued question about the Supreme Court's authority. Opinions range from the idea that original subjective intent is *the* standard of proper interpretation, the view suggested by high officials of the Reagan administration, to the idea that subjective intent counts for nothing. I take the intermediate position that it counts for something but certainly not for everything.

The claim that original intent is the key to interpretation rests on the notion that, since the people who adopted the Constitution were those who made the relevant law, later interpreters should be trying to figure out what they meant to do.[10] If there are extensive sources of "legislative history" chronicling views about what particular language was supposed to do or explaining why originally proposed language was dropped for something else, a "Framers' intent" approach may differ in its practical import from a view that assigns central importance to the text as understood by a reasonable citizen or lawyer at the time of adoption. Thus, whether the text or the subjective intent of the drafters is given emphasis may matter for the Fourteenth Amendment, about which there is substantial history in congressional debates and elsewhere. But, since the congressional history of the Bill of Rights is so sketchy and the history in the ratifying states slighter still, the version of originalism that one chooses does not matter much for the First Amendment itself. Nevertheless, because the claims of both reasonable original understanding of the language and of the Framers' intent must be evaluated against other criteria of interpretation, the question about Framers' intent matters even for the First Amendment.

I shall first examine what the most plausible version of a Framers'-intent theory might look like. The "intents" that would count would need to include those of the persons who ratified the amendment, as well as those of the members of Congress who drafted and proposed the language, since both groups were necessary to make law.[11] I shall call these groups together the *approvers*. Intent could not be limited to a single level.[12] One kind of intent concerns the particular practices that those who proposed and ratified a provision wanted to allow or prohibit; a second kind of intent concerns their broad aims in adopting particular language; a third, overlapping kind of intent concerns their views about interpretive practice and the capacity of the language they used to adapt to changing conditions. If the Framers' main intent was to adopt language whose application would change with society and if they expected that the main focus of interpretation would be on the constitutional language itself,[13] attempting to be faithful to their subjective views about particular practices would not be really faithful to their dominant intent. And even if dominant intent is deemed mainly to concern particular practices, in respect to some practices intent will be impossible to discern, say, because the practice was unforeseen by the Framers or because any evidence about whether they wanted to protect it or not is evenly divided. In those cases in which specific intent is no guide to resolution, courts would have to rely on general intent, though a version of general intent might focus on how the challenged practice relates to practices about which the Framers did have a view. The overall objective of a plausible theory that emphasizes original subjective intent would be to remain as faithful as possible to the dominant and subsidiary intents of those who enacted relevant constitutional provisions.[14]

Any serious defense of *exclusive* reliance on the narrow intent of the Framers (or, indeed, the original reasonable understanding of the language as it applied to particular practices) faces grave difficulties. Much existing constitutional law is hard to square with the original intent understood in light of intent about particular practices. Constitutional doctrine is largely built on earlier cases, and a rigorous original-intent approach might have to abandon a great deal of constitutional doctrine, perhaps including much of the law against racial and gender discrimination and a good bit of what has been done under the free speech and free press clauses. Most observers concede that the Supreme Court should not simply overthrow huge chunks of constitutional doctrine; they acknowledge that original intent must yield to precedent in some cases. But it is hard to know how to contain this qualification. If well-established precedents are not to be directly overturned, what is to be done about cases not exactly alike but rather similar to what the precedents deal with, if original intent would require deciding contrary to the import of the precedents? A related point stresses the importance of continuity of doctrine; it would be destabilizing if the right result in many kinds of cases could change quickly with changes in the present balance of historical evidence and interpretation. Another problem with an original-intent approach concerns practices that are genuinely novel, like television and radio broadcasting; for them, it is impossible to conceive original intent except in a very general sense, and it is hard to think that what modern judges are really doing, or should be doing, is to ascertain the slightest glimmers of original intent as they might apply to those practices.

Some objections to original-intent theory go much deeper, however, challenging the ascertainability or relevance of original intent. Of course, if original intent is never ascertainable, it cannot ever be, despite rhetorical smoke screens, a genuine guide to decision. Critics point out that the interpretive act involves the contemporary interpreter as well as the ancient document, that the interpreter can never completely shed his modern understanding. No doubt this is true, but perhaps the interpreter should try as best he can to discern the subjective understanding of the approvers (or the reasonable understanding of the language), just as a person attempting to act morally should perhaps try to disregard his own selfish perspective, though doing so completely is not humanly possible.[15]

This response to the impossibility of interpreting intent is tenable only if the idea of original intent is itself coherent, but even that may be doubted, at least for multimember bodies. Those voting may have disagreed. Many may have had no distinct idea what a particular provision accomplished, and others may have had hopes about what the language would accomplish that did not conform with their expectations. Any systematic theory of subjective intent would somehow have to decide what sort of wish or expectation counts, determine whether the understandings of those who voted against the measure matter,[16] and decide what is to be done about those who voted for the measure without any definite intention. Where I believe these difficulties and the efforts needed to resolve them lead is neither to the conclusion that original subjective intent is never more than a fiction nor to the conclusion that that intent is wholly beyond ascertaining, but that what *constitutes* original intent is hard to say and highly debatable, that any plausible version of that intent will often be extremely hard to ascertain and will become harder as the years from adoption increase,[17] and that in many instances a vague general intent will be easier to ascertain than an intent about any specific practice that is now debated.[18]

A different challenge concerning original intent goes not to its existence and ascertainability but to its authority. At its broadest the question is: Why should the intent of people in times past control the decisions of the present? The short answer to this challenge, which also attacks emphasis on the original reasonable understanding of the language, is that it is part of our system of government that people at one point in time make law that controls at later points in time. That, after all, is what both statutory law and the doctrine of precedent are about. It may be questionable whether altering the law should be as difficult as the formal process of constitutional amendment makes it, and skepticism on this score may be turned into an argument against heavy reliance on original intent, but there is no doubt that our present system of government—and perhaps any viable system of government—includes some dictation of present decisions by past determinations.

If that much is conceded, it still may be argued that the only power those who wrote and approved the Constitution had was to adopt authoritative language, not to bind by any subjective intent that goes beyond the language, and perhaps not to constrain by how reasonable people would have understood the language.

On these questions, the intent of the approvers would not necessarily be critical.[19] Even if it were acknowledged that they meant to bind by their original subjective intent or by some reasonable original understanding of the language, we might *decide now* that their only legitimate power was to bind by authoritative language in some more open-ended way. Though perhaps an understanding about legislative power shared at the time and continued would be entitled to great weight,[20] arguments of political theory would need to be advanced about why either subjective intent or original understanding of the language should matter. I shall not undertake that task here, but I shall report my view that when the intent of those who adopted a provision is ascertainable, there is *some* reason to follow it, just as there is some reason to follow the originally understood implications of the language (which probably deserve more weight).

If these judgments are correct, we need to examine the history leading up to the First and Fourteenth Amendments to determine both the reasonable import of the language and the views of the Framers, and we need to have in mind both particular practices and any broader theory of free speech that may be discernible. Although then unpublished deliberations of the approvers would be relevant only in respect to the subjective intent of the groups involved, all the prior legal and social history bears both on that and on what a reasonable person would then have understood by the language. Given the relative absence of revealing legislative history for the First Amendment,[21] it does not matter a great deal, as I have said, whether one's focus is on what a reasonable person would then have understood about the language or on the original subjective intent of the approvers.

The Scope of the Speech and Press Clauses

Apart from the Ninth Amendment's reservation of unnamed rights and the Fifth Amendment's due-process clause, perhaps no clause of the Bill of Rights has evoked such disagreement over original intent as the clauses guaranteeing freedom of speech and of the press. Since the press clause was regarded at the time as covering all printed matter, primary attention was directed at it. I shall continue the pattern in the book of not drawing a distinction between the two clauses,[22] although the Framers may have had no clear view that published and spoken utterances would be treated similarly.

As for what the Framers meant to accomplish, the divergence of views is substantial. At one extreme is the view that Congress and the ratifying state conventions accepted William Blackstone's idea of liberty of expression and meant only to preclude prior restraints,[23] censorship in the traditional and narrow sense, leaving it open for Congress to use subsequent punishment for expression, so long as it did not infringe the powers of states. As late as 1907, the Supreme Court in an opinion authored by Justice Holmes spoke in almost those terms.[24] At the other end of the spectrum is the position, especially associated with Justice Hugo Black, that the amendment was meant to protect speech absolutely, reaching everything properly defined as speech rather than action and affording that speech complete protection against prohibitions.[25] Though Justice Black never worked out in detail how speech and action were to be distinguished, he did say he would countenance no restriction on obscenity and libel.[26] Black's position lacks solid historical support, and even the amendment's language, cast in terms of *"the* freedom of speech," suggests reference to existing principles of law rather than a sweeping new doctrine of liberty of expression. There is, however, an argument in favor of Justice Black: that the federal government was thought to have no business regulating speech and press anyway, that such regulation was to be left to the states. If so, the approvers might have intended an absolute prohibition against the federal government, leaving it to the states to punish speech that should be punished. If one takes this view of the First Amendment, it is hard to explain why the Fourteenth Amendment should be construed to carry that absolute protection forward against the states. The reason is this. If the approvers of the First Amendment assumed that desirable and necessary restrictions on speech would continue to be undertaken by the states, there is little basis for supposing that the approvers of the Fourteenth Amendment thought these restrictions should be eliminated altogether.[27]

Much of the historical dispute concerning the First Amendment has been over the status of seditious libel: Was the language meant to abolish that crime, to require that truth be a defense and that the jury be permitted to return a general verdict, or to leave the entire crime to legislative and judicial choice?[28]

Under the English common law of seditious libel, as summarized by J. F. Stephen, a person was criminally responsible for "the intentional publication, without lawful excuse or justification, of written blame of any public man, or of the law, or of any institution established by law."[29] Sporadic and ineffective enforcement reduced the practical significance of this rule, but those who launched vigorous attacks on established authority may have taken some risk.[30] Under the common law of the seventeenth and eighteenth centuries, truth was not a defense, the notion being that true criticisms could be as damaging to public authority as false ones; the judge decided whether material was seditious, and the jury determined only whether the defendant had published it. Most explicit objections to the law in England and in the American colonies were aimed at establishing truth as a defense and at permitting the jury to return a general verdict of guilt or innocence.[31]

The failure of most critics in the colonies to challenge the entire concept of seditious libel is some evidence of its acceptance, although the greatly declining significance of seditious libel during the eighteenth century can be used to argue that it was already rejected in practice.[32]

In 1798 Congress passed the only federal statute in our history labeled a Sedition Act.[33] It made it criminal to write or publish:

> . . . any false, scandalous and malicious writing or writings against the government of the United States, or either house of the Congress . . . , or the President . . . , with intent to defame [them] . . . , or to bring them . . . into contempt or disrepute; or to excite against them . . . the hatred of the good people . . . , or to stir up sedition.[34]

Manned by Federalist judges, lower federal courts held the statute constitutional, but, when Jefferson became president, he pardoned those convicted, and Congress repaid fines on the ground that the act was unconstitutional. According to the 1964 Supreme Court, the attack upon the statute's validity "has carried the day in the court of history."[35]

Even if it is granted that the First Amendment was meant to abolish seditious libel, it does not, of course, follow that it was meant to affect more ordinary crimes involving communication. For example, as far as I am aware, no one seriously disputed the appropriateness of punishment for successful incitement of criminal behavior, treated in passages of Coke, Hale, and Blackstone.[36] Occasional writings on religious conscience or seditious libel intimated that the state should interfere only with overt acts, but the relevant passages reflect no attention to the problem of speech explicitly directed toward the commission of a crime and, in any event, mainly represented the voices of a radical minority.[37]

It is possible that many of those in Congress and the states who voted on the First Amendment did not consider its relation to the law of seditious libel; it is certain that few or none paid any attention to its application to ordinary crimes involving communication. If they accepted the idea that complicity could be based on successful incitement or other communicative acts, it is highly doubtful that they would have considered unsuccessful communications of the same kind to be within the umbrella of First Amendment protection.

Rationales for Freedom of Speech: The Late-Eighteenth-Century View

In terms of the general objectives of those who approved the First Amendment, it is important how far they shared what now appear to be the strongest justifications for freedom of speech. No systematic defense of a regime of open discussion had yet been developed, but, from writings concentrating on liberty of religious conscience and those urging changes in the law of seditious libel, we can construct a theory of free speech that contains many of the crucial elements of a modern theory. That is not to say that libertarians in the late eighteenth century would have understood and endorsed all the claims and practical implications of a modern theory, but what we perceive as the dominant justifications for free speech are in continuity with those which appeared compelling two hundred years ago.

A fundamental tenet of American political thought in the late eighteenth century was the limited authority of government, an idea expounded most influentially by John Locke and transmitted to the colonies by generations of English Radical Whigs.[38] In *A Letter Concerning Toleration*, Locke had urged that the commonwealth is constituted only to protect civil interests—life, liberty, health, and possessions.[39] Claiming that the care of a person's soul belongs to him, Locke argued for religious liberty. The impact of his argument is much broader, since the category of opinions that do not significantly touch the protection of civil interests is obviously much wider than religion. As John Plamenatz suggested, "Religion was in those days held so important that to allow people to hold what religious beliefs they wanted was virtually to concede full intellectual freedom."[40]

The idea that open discussion promotes discovery of truth is found in Locke as well as in the earlier *Areopagitica* of John Milton. In his *Letter Concerning Toleration*, Locke said, "truth certainly would do well enough, if she were once left to shift for herself."[41] An important theme of critics of the law of seditious libel was that accurate criticism of government was an essential safeguard against tyranny. "Father of Candor" wrote, for example, that without speeches and writings prosecuted as libels the Glorious Revolution would not have occurred "nor should we [in England] now enjoy . . . one jot of civil liberty."[42]

That the founding fathers considered free speech important both for responsible government and for nongovernmental aspects of social life is suggested by the statement of the Continental Congress to the inhabitants of Quebec:

> The importance of [freedom of the press] consists, besides the advancement of truth, science, morality and arts in general, in its diffusion of liberal sentiments on the administration of Government, its ready communication of thoughts between subjects, and its consequential promotion of union among them, whereby oppressive officers are shamed or intimidated, into more honourable and just modes of conducting affairs.[43]

Writings around the constitutional period did not urge that speech contributes to autonomy and development of personality,[44] but different language and concepts hinted at similar justifications. In an 1823 letter, for example, Thomas Jefferson wrote that freedom of expression "is also the best instrument for enlightening the mind of man and improving him as a rational, moral and social being."[45] Less explicitly, the statement of the Continental Congress contains the germ of the same idea. Some arguments for liberty of speech that focused on the speaker were based on Locke's theory that ideas are involuntary, the inevitable consequences of one's particular life experiences.[46] The claim was made that, if beliefs are involuntary, "men should be allowed to express [their] thoughts, with the same freedom that they arise."[47] As put, this claim is not very persuasive, since society rightly expects people to refrain from acting on dangerous desires that may have arisen involuntarily. But the deeper implicit point may be that the psychological link between thought and speech is closer than the link between desires and other actions, and that, as J. B. Bury wrote much later, it "is unsatisfactory and even painful to the thinker himself if he is not permitted to communicate his thoughts to others."[48] From this perspective, the theory can be viewed as a precursor of assertions that speech is a crucial emotional outlet and an integral aspect of the development of personality.

To summarize, prior history and commentary at the time of the amendment are inconclusive about what the free speech and free press clauses were meant to accomplish and how flexible or inflexible their interpretation was meant to be. Although the perceived justifications for free speech were not articulated in a systematic way, an assessment based on writings that were then highly respected suggests that the Framers' reasons for valuing speech were connected to those which dominate modern adjudication.

If a justification for speech has been conceived as relevant throughout the history of the country, that is a reason for judges to give it some weight in modern adjudication, unless the justification is now demonstrably fallacious or generally rejected. Thus, for example, the "truth discovery" claims for free speech should not be lightly rejected by judges, even if the judges entertain more qualms about those claims than I do. The conclusion that the Framers embraced more than one justification for free speech should also make us extremely wary of any proposal that a single justification should now be taken as undergirding the First Amendment and employed as a central guide for resolving legal issues of speech.

The Framers' Views of Constitutional Interpretation

Another piece of the puzzle of original subjective intent is what the approvers thought about legal and, more narrowly, constitutional interpretation. In a careful treatment, Jefferson Powell emphasizes that they did not subscribe to the view that legislation should be interpreted according to the subjective intent of its adopters.[49] One of the dominant preconstitutional perspectives was that legal language should not be construed at all but should be taken for what it plainly means—a position influenced both by Protestant views that people did not need anyone to interpret Scripture for them and by the Enlightenment view, represented by Cesare Beccaria, that the law should be made clear and easily comprehensible. The other dominant perspective was derived from the common law; this view emphasized language and objective reasonable understandings rather than subjective intent. The latter was the prevailing view among those Framers who wrote on how the constitution should be interpreted. If Powell is correct, genuine faithfulness to the subjective intent of the approvers of the First Amendment probably means rejecting subjective intent as a guide to interpretation of specific constitutional provisions. An emphasis on the document's language does not, by itself, settle how far prior history is to count in its reasonable understanding or how flexibly the words may be interpreted over time. But when the language has a generality as great as that of the free speech and the free press clauses, one is drawn to more general accounts of what it encompasses rather than to lists of understandings about specific practices. Moreover, according to Powell, "the framers did not endorse strict literalism as the proper stance of future interpreters. The framers were aware that unforeseen situations would arise, and they accepted the inevitability and propriety of construction."[50]

The Fourteenth Amendment

Interpretive conclusions are complicated by the fact that one thing that is clear about the original First Amendment is that it applied only against the federal government[51] and that, if the federal Constitution restricts state action concerning expression, it does so mainly[52] through the Fourteenth Amendment.[53] Roughly, the three conceptual possibilities are: that the Fourteenth Amendment provides no protection of liberty of speech; that it provides protection that corresponds, at least in virtually all details, with that against the federal government; and that it provides some protection of the most fundamental values of free speech, but protection not nearly so broad as that afforded by the First Amendment. Passages from the extensive debates in Congress can be used to support each of the three positions. I shall not rehearse the fully developed competing positions here, but I do report on my own sense that the historical claim that the approvers of the Fourteenth Amendment actually intended the First Amendment to apply in full force against the states is not finally convincing.

Many writers on original intent and the First Amendment do recognize that full application against the states is something of an embarrassment for those who urge exclusive reliance on Framers' intent, but what is not so often seen is that, if one accepts "incorporation" of the First Amendment by the Fourteenth and adopts an approach to interpretation of the First Amendment that emphasizes

Framers' intent, it follows that the view of free speech and free press and of interpretation held by the approvers of the Fourteenth Amendment matters. After all, when the free speech and free press clauses are to be applied against state governments, the view of their scope taken by the people who adopted language that produces this effect should count at least as much as—and probably more than—the view of those who adopted the original clauses.

Matters become even more complicated when one considers perspectives on interpretation. If it is true, as Powell suggests,[54] that, by the time of the Civil War, it was believed that subjective intention was highly important for constitutional adjudication *and* if one supposes that judges should be constrained by the adopters' concepts of interpretation, then it might follow that First Amendment adjudication involving restrictions by states should emphasize subjective intent about free speech more than such adjudication involving federal restrictions. Despite the logical attractions of this approach, we can reject it out of hand as requiring too much subtlety of judges dealing with similar cases.

At a minimum, a thorough historical evaluation would need to trace the sense of free speech that developed in the nineteenth century up to 1865. I am unaware of any systematic effort of this sort, and I do not undertake it here. Since virtually all states had their own clauses protecting freedom of speech and press, we can probably assume that the approvers of the Fourteenth Amendment did not suppose that forms of criminal liability then common were unconstitutional. Almost certainly, the Romantic movement and the American phenomenon of Transcendentalism contributed to a sense that expression promotes individual fulfillment as well as political justice.

Relationship of the First Amendment to the Rest of the Constitutional Structure

In interpreting any particular provision, courts should, as Charles Black has emphasized,[55] consider how a decision either way would fit with the values implicit in the structure of our government and with the proper allocation of responsibilities among political authorities.

Since the Constitution establishes a representative democracy and since liberty of political expression is a prerequisite to the independent formation of opinion and to the public political participation on which that system of government is grounded, the rest of the Constitution provides strong support for the protection of political expression. The Court has on occasion suggested that discussion of public affairs is at the core of the free speech and free press clauses,[56] and the whole Constitution does implicitly suggest the centrality of free discussion of public affairs. Yet the Court has usually not distinguished between political speech and other speech, and nothing in the speech and press clauses indicates that the constitutional freedom they protect is limited to public affairs. Not only can that conclusion not be drawn out of the rest of the Constitution; it is virtually inconsistent with the free-exercise clause of the First Amendment.

The position of some academic critics, notably Alexander Meiklejohn[57] and Robert Bork,[58] that only speech about public affairs is protected under the speech and press clauses, is untenable, however broadly or narrowly discussion of public affairs is construed. The line between protected and unprotected speech that this position requires is much too elusive, given its proposed singular importance, and, more fundamentally, insufficient reason exists for declaring other sorts of assertions of fact and value outside the boundaries of the First Amendment. In both respects, the free-exercise clause plays a role in the analysis.

No one denies that the free-exercise clause protects not only acts of worship but the expression of religious ideas. Thus, the only plausible minimalist position about First Amendment coverage is that speech about public affairs *and* about religion is protected. This minimalist position is not illogical but has little sense. Once freedom of religious ideas is acknowledged, distinguishing protected speech from unprotected speech, say about science or personal morality, becomes almost absurd. Imagine an article about the physical and psychological benefits of running. Should a sentence like "Some runners experience a religious sense of oneness" or a conclusion that "City governments should facilitate running" alter the status of the article? Even without such sentences, the reader may be influenced to reach conclusions that are religious ("If running makes one feel so good, maybe I don't need to go to church") or political ("If running is so great, maybe Central Park should be closed to cars"). To take another example, articles about the personal morality of having an abortion may implicitly make or reject religious claims and have obvious political relevance. If constitutional protection were afforded only to *explicitly* political and religious speech, the inclusion of a sentence here and there in a long article could be determinative. If protection were limited to speech that is "explicitly and predominantly"[59] on these subjects, many explicit claims made in passing would be unprotected. Under either approach, much speech that is implicitly on these subjects or has powerful significance for them could be suppressed. If the unfeasibility and ill-wisdom of these line-drawing exercises were squarely faced, one might protect all speech that has some bearing on religion or public affairs. As Meiklejohn, limiting himself to speech concerning public affairs, recognized in one of his later writings, such speech would include virtually all communication about facts and values, including fictional portrayals, since these together inform the judgment of voters and develop their capacities.[60]

Even if the line between protected and unprotected speech could be drawn satisfactorily, there would be no sufficient basis for limiting the speech and press clauses to expression that bears on public affairs. The reasons are essentially the same as those already explored in Chapter 3. In terms of what matters to people, questions like whether abortion is morally acceptable or running is a useful antidote to anxiety loom as important as many public issues. People's desires to express their own feelings and to learn from others are as great for nonpolitical subjects as for political ones. And the need for a countermajoritarian check is not restricted to political matters. Governments are often inclined to suppress positions on moral questions that offend dominant public views. As Zechariah Chafee wrote, the Framers used the phrase "freedom of speech" to "embrace the whole realm of thought."[61] Neither their own lack of clarity about freedom of speech nor the importance of political speech for representative government supports the argument that only expression vital to the political process should be treated as beyond legislative regulation. And that argument largely founders on the undoubted protection of speech about religion, certainly regarded in 1789 as the most important nonpolitical subject, intertwined closely with many ideas about morality, philosophy, history, and even science. If such speech clearly had and has protection that does not derive from its implicitly political import, accepting protection for remaining speech of vital human concern is not a large step.

There may be room in some particular contexts, for example, with respect to libel, for affording special protection to a relatively clearly defined class of speech that relates directly to public affairs. The Supreme Court, however, has rightly resisted any notion that, because the general structure of our Constitution establishes freedom of speech about public affairs as central to governance, it somehow follows that that is all the speech and press clauses are about.

Precedent and Other Relevant Law

By "precedent and other relevant law" I mean not only decisions that are more or less on point, but the whole corpus of related law, constitutional and nonconstitutional.[62] Prior decisions are significant for their treatments of particular situations, their formulations of relevant constitutional standards, and their assumptions about underlying values.

The next chapter contains a summary account of the development of First Amendment law. What that account shows is the Supreme Court's growing appreciation of the value of speech and a broad and open-ended view of the speech and press clauses. The application of the clauses to new subject matters reflects an approach to interpretation more closely tied to the perceived values of speech than to the historical boundaries of protection, a development that corresponds to a similarly open-ended approach to most other guarantees of individual rights.

Deference

A dominant issue for all constitutional interpretation is how far the courts should defer to the judgments of political organs of government about what is constitutionally permissible. The degree of deference courts should show to other bodies with legal authority is indeed one crucial question about constitutional structure; it is singled out for independent treatment because of its pervasive importance.

Among the guarantees of the Bill of Rights, freedom of speech is one of the most significantly countermajoritarian. The speech and press clauses are directed not mainly at excessive acts by inferior executive officials but at decisions that might be made by Congress itself. If the clauses go beyond the prohibition of prior restraints, they are designed to prevent ruling groups from suppressing antagonistic points of view and to protect unpopular dissidents from outraged community sentiment. Reason may exist for considerable deference to legislative and executive judgments on specific questions regarding regulations that affect expression, but the force of the amendment would be largely undercut if the Court's general posture were one of great deference. Such deference is inappropriate, as the Court has more or less consistently recognized for the last fifty years, both because the political branches are less to be trusted on these questions than on some others and because freedom of speech is itself the groundwork for an acceptable political process.[63]

Justice and Social Welfare

By the phrase "justice and social welfare" I mean to include considerations of moral and political philosophy as well as narrow questions about social welfare. Though I do not defend my position here, I reject any claim that other criteria of interpretation exhaust what the courts may do in respect to considerations of morality and community welfare. In the United States in constitutional cases courts are not supposed to make value judgments that are wholly detached from what the Constitution authorizes, but, when particular textual provisions, previous decisions, and basic constitutional structures leave matters in doubt, courts may properly be influenced by judgments about what is right and good that cannot fairly be said to be drawn from the preexisting legal materials.

What judges should look to in making such judgments is complex. Usually judges will not perceive a difference between what they think is morally right and socially desirable and what the community thinks, but should a case arise in which such a difference is perceivable I think each view should count for something. That is, I do not think that a judge's sense of what is correct has weight only as an indicator of broader social judgments, nor do I think that community sentiment is relevant only as an indicator of what is really the "correct" position.

How a judge assesses the community's sense of free speech raises a special problem. Since the guarantee of free speech is so pointedly countermajoritarian, its reaches cannot be defined in terms of a transient majority's view of whether particular speech is dangerous enough to control. Something more subtle is required: a perception of people's sense of the liberty they should have if their own beliefs diverge from popular opinion and of the liberty of speech necessary to promote the choices people think they should be able to make; an assessment of the place accorded to free speech within public and private institutions; and an evaluation of social morality that gives more weight to the views of people who think seriously about issues of personal and social choice than to the views of people who blindly follow dominant opinion. Such a reconstruction would be quite different from the kind of opinion-poll approach that arguably might be used to determine whether people think that capital punishment is cruel.[64]

Certainly, since the end of the period of Joseph McCarthy's anticommunist crusades, the expression of diverse viewpoints has been increasingly accepted, a result produced by disquiet over the Vietnam War, distrust of public officials, and fear of expanding government power, as well as by various forms of "liberation" which have asserted freedom from social constraints and liberty to choose one's pattern of life. Among political organs, increasingly tolerant attitudes have been reflected in the relative dearth of prosecutions of speech during World War II, the Korean War, and the Vietnam War.[65] In a broad sense, then, social morality now supports a libertarian approach to freedom of speech, which protects speech even when its value appears to be in conflict with other values and which embraces all subject matters of importance to individuals.

What Other Judges Are Willing to Say and Do

As members of panels, judges on appellate courts are properly influenced to a degree by what their fellows are willing to do. Achieving a less than ideal majority opinion may be better than writing an ideal concurring opinion that leaves the Supreme Court with a much weaker majority opinion or no majority opinion. And very occasionally, considerations of sound collegial results might properly lead a judge to vote in a case differently from how he would vote if he were sitting alone. Thus, though I do not defend the position here, I think that what will "fly" with other members of the court is a legitimate factor to consider for a judge who is writing an opinion and, rarely, for a judge deciding how to vote.

Since any recommendations I offer in succeeding chapters concern how the Supreme Court as a whole might act, I do not discuss how an individual justice should act if others are unwilling to do what would be best. Thus, I have no further occasion to mention this basis for decision.

Notes

1. One can conceive of a practice of legislators' being questioned at trials about why they legislated, but, for many reasons, including impropriety and time, such a practice is beyond the pale of serious thought.

2. It is generally supposed by academic commentators that the court's development of principled categories in free speech cases will help over time to promote open debate and tolerance. For a highly skeptical view of the systemic benefits of adjudication of free speech cases, see R. Nagel, "How Useful Is Judicial Review in Free Speech Cases?" 69 *Cornell Law Review* 302 (1984).

3. It is, however, a debatable question how well equipped to deal with constitutional issues the legislative process actually is. Martin Shapiro has argued forcefully that, given the complex and fractionalized manner in which legislation is produced, legislators would find it hard to make responsible judgments of constitutionality. M. Shapiro, *Freedom of Speech: The Supreme Court and Judicial Review* 29–31 (Englewood Cliffs, N.J., Prentice-Hall 1966). If that view is sound, perhaps legislators should not attempt highly refined judgments of constitutionality, but they certainly should not adopt laws that are blatantly unconstitutional.

4. I discuss this problem in K. Greenawalt, "Constitutional Decisions and the Supreme Law," 58 *University of Colorado Law Review* 145 (1987). The "practical deference" I refer to pertains to the immediate activities of government; I do not foreclose criticism of what the Court has said or efforts to get judges appointed who will say different things.

5. See generally R. Clinton, "Original Understanding, Legal Realism, and the Interpretation of 'This Constitution'," 72 *Iowa Law Review* 1177 (1987).

6. Some astonishing things have been said in recent years about the indeterminacy of legal language. When I say that the language "absolutely forecloses" some interpretations, I assume that the language must be set in some social context, since the "meaning" of words and phrases cannot be divorced from the way people use the words and phrases. An example of an interpretation that I think is absolutely foreclosed is the following: "Permitting a right of self-defense to the victim of actual deadly force violates a right of free speech of the original assailant."

7. Any simple dichotomy between ordinary and technical legal meaning would be misleading. Although a few words and phrases may make sense only to lawyers, not many

such are found in our Constitution. Much more common is language that reflects ordinary usage to some extent, but is also colored by special legal understandings; the principle that no one in a criminal case need be a "witness against himself" would be an example. The meaning connects to ordinary understanding, but it also represents the peculiarly legal development of the privilege against self-incrimination. One might talk more precisely about *the degree to which* particular language reflects technical legal meaning. As to some provisions, it may be very important whether one takes a lay person's or a lawyer's perspective for deciding how much technical meaning will be infused into the reasonable reading of the language.

8. Of course, if one is talking about a reasonable lawyer and if the ultimate guide is understanding two hundred years ago, a reasonable and competent modern lawyer would take as his present understanding his best assessment of a past understanding.

9. As the Supreme Court said in *Maxwell* v. *Dow*, 176 U.S. 581, 602 (1900), a court should read language "in connection with the known condition of affairs out of which the occasion for its adoption may have arisen, and then to construe it, if there be therein any doubtful expressions, in a way so far as is reasonably possible, to forward the known purpose or object for which the amendment was adopted."

10. See generally R. Berger, *Government by Judiciary: The Transformation of the Fourteenth Amendment* (Cambridge, Mass., Harvard University Press 1977).

11. David Anderson, "The Origins of the Press Clause," 30 *University of California in Los Angeles Law Review* 455, 485 (1983), suggests that because Congress merely "proposes" and the state legislatures hold "the ultimate power," "logically, the controlling intent should be that of the ratifying legislatures." Whatever the persuasiveness of this view in respect to the original Constitution, amendments, according to Article V of the Constitution, are made by a prescribed process or, more strictly, by alternative processes, which require both congressional and state approval. (Even in the extraordinary instance when Congress responds to a state initiative to call a convention, the requirement that it vote by two-thirds in each House makes clear that federal approval is a critical part of the process.) If intent counts, it is the intent of both Congress and the state legislatures or conventions.

12. See generally R. Dworkin, *A Matter of Principle* 33–71 (Cambridge, Mass., Harvard University Press 1985); P. Brest, "The Misconceived Quest for the Original Understanding," 60 *Boston University Law Review* 204 (1980), for illuminating comment on the complexities of "original intent" theory. See also D. Richards, *Toleration and the Constitution* 22–40 (New York, Oxford University Press 1986).

13. Jefferson Powell suggests forcefully that, at the time of the Bill of Rights, it was assumed that interpretation should concentrate on the text, though understandings had altered by the time of adoption of the Fourteenth Amendment. See J. Powell, "The Original Understanding of Original Intent," 98 *Harvard Law Review* 885 (1985). If one focuses on the language, there remains a question how far outside the text one should go to try to determine how the language would then have been understood.

14. If the dominant intent did not push one way or the other in respect to decision, it would make sense to give weight to a subsidiary intent. I use the plural "provisions" in the text because, even when interpretation is under one provision, other provisions may well be relevant.

15. More precisely, an individual attempting to act morally should perhaps count his own selfish wishes as of no more weight than the selfish interests of others affected by his action. I do not question that in some instances people manage to give their own selfish interests appropriate or less than appropriate weight, especially if they are feeling guilty. What I deny is that they can make a choice while being wholly detached about their selfish interests.

16. The common assumption is that only the views of those voting in favor of a measure count, but I am inclined to think that, when a law is adopted by a deliberative

body after discussion, the opinions of those who voted negatively should also count, though very likely they should count less than the opinions of those who voted affirmatively.

17. It becomes more and more difficult to recapture the environment of the time. On the other hand, in regard to some matters, newly available historical sources may enhance ability to gauge intent.

18. I think intent about specific practices is ascertainable and significant on many matters, e.g., whether a criminal defendant can be declared guilty or held in contempt for failing to testify, but these matters are not those which tend to be litigated. It is also possible that in all or virtually all instances in which subjective intent is clear, the same result would be derivable from the language as understood by reasonable lawyers at the time in light of historical practices and problems.

19. Of course, if the Framers thought they had authority only to bind by language, then the implications of a dominant-intent approach and the implications of the view that lawmakers generally can bind only by authoritative language would coalesce.

20. If virtually all relevant people then assumed that lawmakers could bind by subjective intent, that practice arguably would have been a subject of implicit consent. It might then have been the continuing basis for government as the population changed, and, even now, those who approve of the approach could claim that change would violate the terms of the "social contract."

21. The language of the First Amendment did go through five versions, and the final version represented a compromise. These changes are not very illuminating about what Congress was trying to do, partly because it is hard to know why a particular change was made. See Anderson, note 11 supra, at 476–80.

22. For a summary of modern issues for which a distinctive treatment of the institutionalized press may be important, see W. Van Alstyne, "The First Amendment and the Free Press: A Comment on Some New Trends and Some Old Theories," 9 *Hofstra Law Review* 1 (1980).

23. 4 W. Blackstone, *Commentaries on the Laws of England* *151–52. It has never been supposed that the protection of religious speech under the free-exercise clause was limited to prior restraints. As William Mayton has pointed out in "Seditious Libel and the Lost Guarantee of a Freedom of Expression," 84 *Columbia Law Review* 91, 120 (1984), the breadth of the free-exercise clause is some reason not to read the free press clause so narrowly.

24. *Patterson* v. *Colorado*, 205 U.S. 454, 462 (1907).

25. See H. L. Black, *A Constitutional Faith* 43–63 (New York, Alfred A. Knopf 1968).

26. H. L. Black and E. Cahn, "Justice Black and First Amendment Absolutes: A Public Interview," 37 *New York University Law Review* 549, 557–59 (1962).

27. It is logically conceivable that the approvers of the Fourteenth Amendment really embraced a much more absolutist view of what speech *any* government could restrict than did the approvers of the First Amendment, but there is no basis for supposing this to be true.

28. Compare Z. Chafee, *Free Speech in the United States* 3–35, 497–516 (Cambridge, Mass., Harvard University Press 1942), with L. Levy, *Legacy of Suppression: Freedom of Speech and Press in Early American History* (Cambridge, Mass., Belknap, Harvard University Press 1960). In his substantially revised and enlarged account, *The Emergence of a Free Press* (New York, Oxford University Press 1985), Leonard Levy softens some of the judgments of his original book, but he remains convinced that the Framers did not mean to abolish the crime of seditious libel.

David Rabban has suggested that the Framers might have wished to provide significant protection for political expression without entirely eliminating the law of seditious libel.

D. Rabban, "The Ahistorical Historian: Leonard Levy on Freedom of Expression in Early American History," 37 *Stanford Law Review* 795, 800 (1985).

29. 2 J. F. Stephen, *A History of the Criminal Law of England* 353 (London, Macmillan & Co. 1883). See generally P. Hamburger, "The Development of the Law of Seditious Libel and the Control of the Press," 37 *Stanford Law Review* 661 (1985).

30. See Levy, *Emergence of a Free Press*, note 28 supra, at 11–15.

31. Fox's Libel Act of 1792 in England and the Sedition Act of 1798 in America provided both safeguards.

32. For the view that at least some Americans rejected seditious libel and that Levy now accepts this position, see Rabban, note 28 supra, at 816. And Anderson, note 11 supra, at 514, points out that most of the Framers were seditious libelers, having sharply attacked not only the pre-Revolutionary British government but also the Articles of Confederation.

33. Against the argument that this act shows that the Framers accepted seditious libel, Anderson notes the big changes in the personnel of Congress in the intervening nine years and a corresponding shift in ideas. See Anderson, note 11 supra, at 515–19. It is also possible, of course, that, under stress, legislators departed from ideals they had accepted.

34. An Act in addition to the act, entitled "An Act for the Punishment of Certain Crimes against the United States," Ch. 74, § 2, 1 Stat. 596 (1798).

35. *New York Times* v. *Sullivan*, 376 U.S. 254, 276 (1964).

36. See E. Coke, Second Part of the *Institutes of the Laws of England* 182 (London, E.D. et al. 1642); M. Hale, *Pleas of the Crown* 177–80 (London, R. Tonson 1678); Blackstone, note 23 supra, at *36.

37. William Mayton takes a drastically different view on this point. Relying substantially on the overt-act requirement of the treason clause, on writings of Spinoza, Montesquieu, and Furneaux, and on Jefferson's preamble to the Virginia Statute for Establishing Religious Freedom, he concludes that an overt-act requirement was made part of the Constitution. Mayton, note 23 supra, at 109–14.

38. See Rabban, note 28 supra, at 823–30. See also Richards, note 12 supra, at 29–32, 55–56. For a thoughtful account of this and other influences on the Framers' ideas about free speech, see D. Bogen, "The Origins of Freedom of Speech and Press," 42 *Maryland Law Review* 429 (1983).

39. J. Locke, [Second] *Treatise of Civil Government* and *A Letter Concerning Toleration* 172, ed. Charles L. Sherman (New York, D. Appleton-Century Co. 1937) (1st eds. London 1690 and 1689, respectively).

40. 1 J. P. Plamenatz, *Man and Society: Political and Social Theory* 67 (London, Longmans, Green & Co. 1963).

41. Locke, note 39 supra, at 205.

42. Father of Candor [pseud.], *An Enquiry into the Doctrine Lately Propagated Concerning Libels, Warrants, and the Seizure of Papers* 33 (New York, Da Capo Press 1970) (reprint of 1st ed., London, J. Almon 1764).

43. 1 W. C. Ford, ed., *Journal of the Continental Congress, 1774–1789*, at 108 (1774) (Washington, D.C., Government Printing Office 1904). How much significance should be given to this statement is unclear. See Anderson, note 11 supra, at 464, 523–24.

44. Anderson, id. at 488–93, 534, concludes that the press clause was seen as a bulwark of political liberty, not personal autonomy, but that the speech clause may have had more to do with an incipient notion of individual autonomy underlying the religion clauses.

45. See L. Levy, ed., *Freedom of the Press from Zenger to Jefferson: Early American Libertarian Theories* 376 (Indianapolis, Bobbs-Merrill Co. 1966).

46. Levy, *Legacy of Suppression*, note 28 supra, at 313–20.

47. J. Thompson, *An Enquiry Concerning the Liberty and Licentiousness of the Press* 11–12 (1801) (reprint ed., New York, Da Capo Press 1970).

48. J. Bury, *A History of Freedom of Thought* 1 (2d ed., London, Oxford University Press 1952).

49. See Powell, note 13 supra.

50. Id. at 904.

51. Not only does the amendment start with the word "Congress"; an amendment aimed explicitly at the states had been defeated in the Senate. See Anderson, note 11 supra, at 483.

52. I say "mainly" because state infringements interfering with citizens' relations to the federal government and perhaps some other infringements would be independently unconstitutional. The Fifth and Ninth Amendments may also be relevant.

53. As I indicated above, the due-process clause is now considered the main vehicle of incorporation; the privileges-and-immunities clause is a possible alternative, or both could work together. Another possible ground is the provision conferring national citizenship.

54. Powell, note 13 supra, at 947.

55. C. Black, *Structure and Relationship in Constitutional Law* (Baton Rouge, Louisiana State University Press 1969). See also J. Ely, *Democracy and Distrust* (Cambridge, Mass., Harvard University Press 1980); L. Lusky, *By What Right? A Commentary on the Supreme Court's Power to Revise the Constitution* (Charlottesville, Va., The Michie Co. 1975); Richards, note 12 supra, at 282–88. Powell indicates that this was an important approach to constitutional interpretation at the time of the Framers; see Powell, note 13 supra, at 888. As Vincent Blasi suggests, emphasis on structural relations leaves considerable room for activist decisions. Review, "Creativity and Legitimacy in Constitutional Law," 80 *Yale Law Journal* 176 (1970).

56. See, e.g., *Garrison* v. *Louisiana*, 379 U.S. 64, 74–75 (1964); *New York Times* v. *Sullivan*, 376 U.S. 254, 270 (1964).

57. See A. Meiklejohn, *Political Freedom: The Constitutional Powers of the People* (New York, Harper & Bros. 1960).

58. R. Bork, "Neutral Principles and Some First Amendment Problems," 47 *Indiana Law Journal* 1, 20–35 (1971). Bork's position on this point had moderated to a degree, even before his acknowledgment in the hearings on his Supreme Court nomination that he took as settled judicial doctrine a much more expansive interpretation of the scope of the First Amendment.

59. See id. at 26.

60. A. Meiklejohn, "The First Amendment Is an Absolute," 1961 *Supreme Court Review* 245, 256–62.

61. Z. Chafee, Book Review, 62 *Harvard Law Review* 891, 898 (1949).

62. See generally R. Dworkin, *Taking Rights Seriously* 81–130 (Cambridge, Mass., Harvard University Press 1978).

63. For a forceful contrary argument about the comparative wisdom of judges and legislators regarding free speech issues and about the systemic effects of active judicial involvement, see Nagel, note 2 supra.

64. I do not mean to suggest that such an approach is actually correct for capital punishment; I believe it is not.

65. As Harry Kalven, "Ernest Freund and the First Amendment Tradition," 40 *University of Chicago Law Review* 235, 237 (1973), said, drawing a comparison with convictions for speech during World War I of a sort sustained by the Supreme Court: "During the Vietnam War thousands of utterances strictly comparable in bitterness and sharpness of criticism, if not in literacy, were made; it was pretty much taken for granted they were beyond the reach of government."

11

The Developing Law of the Free Speech and Free Press Clauses

In this chapter I explore what the courts have said about freedom of speech. I concentrate mainly on the Supreme Court, whose cases provide the context against which the First Amendment is now interpreted and whose views are also heavily influential as state courts deal with state constitutional documents. I concentrate also on those areas of First Amendment law which are particularly important for this study, paying only slight attention to effects on expression of government actions that do not render forms of communication or other behavior illegal. Some cases and doctrines that have peripheral relevance for the book receive more intensive scrutiny in subsequent chapters than they are given here.

The discussion in this chapter serves related purposes. It charts in a summary fashion what the Supreme Court has done up to now. Whatever one's view about standards of constitutional interpretation, sensible thought about proper approaches to freedom of speech requires understanding of approaches that have actually been taken. Because the Supreme Court has struggled with so many free speech problems for so long a time, many of the problems it has dealt with and many of the alternative resolutions it has proposed illuminate both interpretive and legislative possibilities; accordingly, the treatment here will enrich earlier chapters, illustrating with examples some of the more abstract generalizations offered there. One who offers political or constitutional guidelines for speech needs to have such examples in mind as ways of testing possibilities. Moreover, given the Court's present and past approach to constitutional interpretation, which I have argued in the last chapter is sound in this respect, the decisions themselves count for a good deal. The Court rightly tries to preserve continuity with past decisions and is hesitant to abandon firmly established doctrine. Thus, it matters whether a proposed approach to interpretation of the First Amendment fits reasonably well with existing doctrine. The background provided here is thus essential for evaluating the suggestions in subsequent chapters about sound constitutional approaches.

Before World War I

From the time of Jefferson until World War I, it was not clear whether the First Amendment provided any protection at all against subsequent punishment of publications. In his Commentaries, Justice Joseph Story accepted the restricted Blackstonean position that liberty of the press concerns only protection against prior restraints.[1] But later in the nineteenth century Thomas Cooley, in his well-known *Constitutional Limitations*, took the more expansive view that liberty of speech and of the press

> implies a right to freely utter and publish whatever the citizen may please, and to be protected against any responsibility for so doing, except so far as such publications, from their blasphemy, obscenity, or scandalous character, may be a public offense, or as by their falsehood and malice they may injuriously affect the standing, reputation, or pecuniary interests of individuals.[2]

Some interpretations of state provisions supported Cooley's view that limitations on speech could be unconstitutional even though they did not involve prior restraint. Other state cases and a number of cases that reached the Supreme Court declared certain expressions punishable, but without resolving the question of what expressions might be constitutionally immune from sanction,[3] and said that the Constitution did not protect license or abuse.

Among the state cases, *People* v. *Most*,[4] decided by the New York Court of Appeals in 1902, is of special interest for our purposes. John Joseph Most, who had the misfortune to publish an article urging the murder of government officials on the day President McKinley was assassinated, claimed that his conviction for seriously endangering the public peace violated New York's constitutional protection of liberty of speech and press. The article, which argued that all government is based on murder and that citizens should, therefore, murder their rulers, said:

> Let murder be our study,—murder in every form. . . .
> . . . Yes crime directed against them is not only right, but it is the duty of every one who has an opportunity to commit it, and it would be a glory to him if it was successful.
> . . . We say, murder the murderers, save humanity, through blood and iron, poison and dynamite.

According to the court, the article, although "it did not urge the murder of any particular individual, . . . advocated the murder of all rulers" and called "for action on the part of his readers without delay." Such urging endangered the public peace, the court said, and would have made Most guilty of murder had his advice been taken. The court decided that publications promoting murder are clearly outside the range of constitutional protection, saying, "The punishment of those who publish articles which tend to corrupt morals, induce crime, or destroy organized society is essential to the security of freedom and the stability of the state."[5]

Although some scholars took a significantly protective view of free speech,[6] one might sum up the law before World War I as being that any expressions considered harmful or dangerous or offensive could be punished.

The World War I Cases and the Clear-and-Present-Danger Test

Substantial Supreme Court development of First Amendment doctrine began with review of convictions under the 1917 Espionage Act, which made it criminal "willfully [to] cause or attempt to cause insubordination, disloyalty, mutiny, or refusal of duty in the military or naval forces" or "willfully [to] obstruct the recruiting or enlistment service of the United States."[7] It was in the course of that review that opinions written by Justice Holmes first elaborated the *clear-and-present-danger test*, which in subsequent years became a significant protection of speech, which for a period served to dominate Supreme Court treatment of free speech cases, and which has very heavily influenced the approaches that are now prevailing for prohibitions of speech.

In 1919 the Court decided three cases under the Espionage Act. I shall concentrate on *Schenck* v. *United States*,[8] which contained the most expansive discussion of the First Amendment, but the other two cases, decided a week later, shed substantial light on how the justices understood the language of *Schenck*.

Schenck was charged with being involved in a conspiracy to cause insubordination and obstruct recruiting and enlistment, by agreeing to help print an antiwar tract and to circulate it to men called and accepted for military service. The leaflet, which asserted that conscription violated the Thirteenth Amendment, talked of "your right to assert your opposition to the draft." It said, "If you do not assert and support your rights, you are helping to deny or disparage rights which it is the solemn duty of all citizens . . . to retain," and "You must do your share to maintain, support, and uphold the rights of the people of this country."

Justice Holmes's opinion for the Court assumed that the statute required an illegal purpose, but had no trouble concluding that such a purpose could be found on the basis of the content of the pamphlet and Schenck's involvement with it. That such a purpose could be discerned from advocacy that falls considerably short of explicit encouragement is illustrated strongly by the other two cases, *Frohwerk* v. *United States*[9] and *Debs* v. *United States*.[10] Frohwerk had helped publish twelve articles favorable to Germany which called those who resisted the draft "technically . . . wrong" though more "sinned against than sinning." Debs's speech blamed the war on the ruling classes and included praise of particular draft resisters; it exhorted the audience, "Don't worry about the charge of treason to your masters; but be concerned about the treason that involves yourselves." Many convictions that never reached the Supreme Court demonstrated, even more strongly than the facts of *Frohwerk* and *Debs*, that a requirement of illegal purpose did not prove a very sturdy safeguard for unpopular speakers.

In his discussion of Schenck's claim that his actions were protected by the First Amendment, Justice Holmes first acknowledged: "It well may be that the prohibition of laws abridging the freedom of speech is not confined to previous restraints." Then he said:

We admit that in many places and in ordinary times the defendants in saying all that was said in the circular would have been within their constitutional rights. But the character of every act depends on the circumstances in which it is done. . . . The question in every case is whether the words used are used in such circumstances and are of such a nature as to create a clear and present danger that they will bring about the substantive evils that Congress has a right to prevent. It is a question of proximity and degree. When a nation is at war many things that might be said in time of peace are such a hindrance to its effort that their utterance will not be endured so long as men fight and that no Court could regard them as protected by any constitutional right. It seems to be admitted that if an actual obstruction of the recruiting service were proved, liability for words that produced that effect might be enforced. . . . If the act (speaking, or circulating a paper) its tendency and the intent with which it is done are the same, we perceive no ground for saying that success alone warrants making the act a crime.

This initial formulation of the clear-and-present-danger test leaves much unclear. The story of the following decade includes abandonment of the test by the Court's majority and amplification and refinement of the test in separate opinions by Holmes and Brandeis. It is the composite of the Holmes and Brandeis opinions that came to represent the classic formulation of the standard. Those opinions have been highly influential, and many of the questions with which they deal still represent perplexing legal problems. The opinions repay careful examination, though one must be cautious not to place more weight on isolated passages than they were intended to bear.

During the period when Holmes and Brandeis were developing the clear-and-present-danger standard, the Court's majority rejected it in major cases and evidenced a willingness to defer almost completely to legislative judgments that speech should be suppressed. In *Gitlow* v. *New York*,[11] the first case to declare that the federal Constitution guarantees liberty of speech against state as well as federal interference, the Court affirmed a conviction under the state's criminal-anarchy statute. The statute covered one who "advocates, advises or teaches the duty, necessity or propriety of overthrowing . . . organized government by force or violence . . . or by any unlawful means." Declaring that legislatures have broad power to punish "utterances inimical to the public welfare," the Court rejected any test of clear and present danger for statutes that directly proscribe forms of speech, since in such instances "the legislative body itself has previously determined the danger of substantive evil arising from utterances of a specified character." Instead, the appropriate standard was whether the statute was "arbitrary or unreasonable," a standard met by New York which had protected its right of self-preservation by reaching "the threatened danger in its incipiency." So long as the statute itself was valid, an instance of speech covered by it could be punished, without examination of the particular dangers of that expression. Two years after *Gitlow*, in *Whitney* v. *California*,[12] the Court took a similar approach in affirming a conviction under the California Criminal Syndicalism Act, for helping to organize a group whose purpose was to engage in forbidden advocacy.

Gitlow and *Whitney*, especially *Whitney*, mark important steps in the transformation of the clear-and-present-danger test from a standard that could win a unanimous Court and did little to safeguard speech to one that gave expression substantial constitutional protection. Though to modern ears, "clear and present danger" sounds like a fairly stringent constitutional standard, demanding a serious evil, a substantial likelihood that speech will cause the evil, and a close temporal nexus between speech and evil, that was not its original import.[13] The affirmance of the convictions in *Schenck*, *Frohwerk*, and *Debs* shows plainly that the Court did not consider the formula to be highly speech-protective. Whether Holmes already had a more protective view, cleverly writing the opinions to paper over substantial divisions, or, as is more probable, subsequently shifted his position, it is only in separate opinions in later cases that the clear-and-present-danger test emerged as a genuine safeguard of speech. That evolution began in 1919 and culminated in Brandeis's *Whitney* opinion in 1927.

In the discussion that follows, I focus on a number of critical questions about the test: whether presentness is an independent criterion; how great the evil must be; the relation of actual and intended danger; the expression to which the test applies; and the respective roles of judge and jury. The analysis provides both a sense of what the test has come to stand for and which matters Holmes and Brandeis failed to resolve.

The *Schenck* opinion does not settle whether "presentness" is simply highly relevant to the likelihood that an evil will occur or constitutes an independent requirement of temporal proximity between speech and evil. In *Abrams* v. *United States*,[14] dissenting from the affirmance of convictions under the 1918 Espionage Act, Holmes largely resolved that doubt. Defendants, who had distributed a circular calling for a general strike to discourage the government's intervention against the revolutionary government in Russia, had been convicted for conspiring to incite resistance to the war effort against Germany and to urge curtailment of production with an intent to hinder the prosecution of that war. Having first disagreed with the Court that the defendants "intended" consequences that were highly likely if their more proximate goal was achieved but were not their actual aim, Holmes went on to urge that the First Amendment barred conviction, because no one could suppose that the five thousand leaflets created "any immediate danger that its opinions would hinder the success of the government arms." He talked of a need for a "clear and imminent danger" of substantive evils, and his reference to emergencies that make it immediately dangerous to leave the correction of evil counsel to time suggests that, when evils do not quickly follow expression, competing speech can correct the effects of inflammatory rhetoric. In a famous passage, Holmes asserted that the commitment of our society is to "free trade in ideas."[15]

The theme that a close temporal nexus must exist between speech and evil is developed in Holmes's dissent in *Gitlow*[16] and in Brandeis's concurrence, joined by Holmes, in *Whitney*.[17] The latter opinion, which contains some of the most eloquent passages in the language about the value of speech for the development of human faculties and for political freedom, said that suppression can be justified only if there is a reasonable ground to believe that the danger apprehended is imminent: "If there be time to expose through discussion the falsehood and fallacies, to avert the evil by the processes of education, the remedy to be applied is more speech, not enforced silence. Only an emergency can justify repression."[18]

The *Schenck* formulation leaves murky whether the magnitude of the harm that speech threatens is important. Taken literally, the statement that speech can be punished if it creates a clear and present danger of "substantive evils that Congress has a right to prevent" does not distinguish between serious preventable evils and slight ones, but the comment about speech being permitted in peacetime that is not permitted in wartime may imply that the magnitude of the evil does matter. The question is explicitly addressed in the Brandeis opinion in *Whitney*. It says that clear and present danger depends on a finding that "immediate serious violence was to be expected or was advocated" and indicates that advocacy of a moral right to trespass would be constitutionally protected "even if there was imminent danger that advocacy would lead to a trespass."[19] The view of Holmes and Brandeis, then, is that, in circumstances where the test applies, only a clear and present danger of a relatively serious evil will suffice.

A highly important question for our purposes is the significance of subjective and objective elements. Is the clear-and-present-danger test exclusively about actual likelihood of the evil occurring, or can it be satisfied by a subjective wish to bring the evil about? The formulation in *Schenck* is cast in objective terms, but in *Frohwerk* Holmes commented, "we venture to believe that neither Hamilton nor Madison, nor any other competent person then or later, ever supposed that to make criminal the counselling of a murder within the jurisdiction of Congress would be an unconstitutional interference with free speech."[20] More explicitly, he wrote in *Abrams* that "by the same reasoning that would justify punishing persuasion to murder, the United States constitutionally may punish speech that produces *or* is intended to produce a clear and imminent danger" of substantive evils.[21] And, in *Whitney*, Brandeis indicated that the constitutional test could be satisfied if the immediate serious violence "was to be expected or was advocated."[22] Thus, Holmes and Brandeis assumed that at least in some circumstances expression with an *intent* to create a clear and present danger could be deprived of constitutional protection.

One of the most important and troubling questions about the clear-and-present-danger test is the kinds of communications to which it applies. Must the test be met whenever society's concern is that some substantive evil will be generated by a reaction to speech, or are some kinds of speech either protected despite a clear and present danger or unprotected in the absence of such a danger?

Since the Holmes-Brandeis opinions were written in settings in which illegal purpose was a statutory requisite and had been found by jurors, it might be thought that the clear-and-present-danger test permits punishment only when such a purpose exists, but the formulations of the test from *Schenck* onward imply that speech that creates a grave enough danger can constitutionally be punished even in the absence of an illegal purpose. This, of course, does not mean that a person can actually suffer criminal punishment *whenever* his communication generates a clear and present danger. In the United States one can be guilty of an ordinary crime only if one violates some statute; so one's speech must also be within the ambit of what a legislature has proscribed. What the broad coverage of the test does mean is that a legislature may make criminal some communications that are highly dangerous but are not made with a criminal purpose; courts developing common law civil liability without statutory direction may also premise recovery on such communications.

Schenck and the other Espionage Act cases do not make plain whether the clear-and-present-danger test must always be satisfied if speech is to be punished. For speech uttered with a purpose to lead others to commit a crime, this general question arises in at least three contexts: when the substantive evil occurs as a result of the speech, but the probability of its occurring was slight; when a nonserious substantive evil occurs as a result of the speech; and when a person explicitly urges the commission of a serious crime that neither occurs nor was likely to occur.

The first context is of little practical interest, since it will be a rare actual case in which an evil that occurred as a result of speech seemed very improbable. But we can imagine urging which seems highly unlikely to succeed from the objective point of view that is contemplated by the test but which, fortuitously, strikes an unpredictably responsive chord and leads to a crime. Of course, if the clear-and-present-danger test can always be satisfied by an "intent" to create such a danger, then it will be satisfied in such a case, but if the test requires a high objective probability and that is lacking, the speech could not be punished if it was not acted upon. Some of Holmes's language in *Schenck* implies that speech in such cases should be governed by the same constitutional principles whether it is acted upon or not, but other language suggests that liability could undoubtedly follow if the speech in fact produced the evil.

A more significant practical question concerns situations where speech predictably causes an evil that is not grave enough to make the speaker liable under the Holmes-Brandeis test. Given his view in *Whitney* that advocacy of a moral right to trespass would be protected even if there was an imminent danger of trespass following the advocacy, Brandeis presumably believed that such advocacy would be protected if trespass actually occurred, in which event some speech actually causing crime would be constitutionally protected.

The most important problem about the applicability of the clear-and-present-danger test is whether the standard must be met if a defendant's expression explicitly urges the commission of a specific crime. We have already seen that Holmes apparently thought that a person who counsels the immediate commission of a serious crime and, thereby, intends to create a clear and present danger, can be punished regardless of actual danger. We now want to ask what the relevance of the test is if a person explicitly urges the commission of a serious crime some time in the future or urges a less than serious crime imminently. Holmes's suggestion in *Frohwerk* that no one would suppose that counseling of a murder is protected speech may be taken to mean that the Constitution imposes no constraint on explicit counseling, but in *Abrams* Holmes equated persuasion to murder with an intent to produce a clear and imminent danger. Possibly Holmes believed that the common law standard of counseling or the constitutional standard of clear and present danger rendered a person immune from punishment if his urging to criminal action was directed to a nonimminent future, but one cannot reach that conclusion confidently from these passages.

Whether one can be punished for urging a nonserious crime is addressed more directly. In his *Whitney* concurrence, as a prelude to his assertion that advocacy of a moral right to trespass would be protected despite imminent danger, Brandeis said that a state might "punish an attempt, a conspiracy, or an incitement to commit the trespass."[23] Since the reason why advocacy of a moral right to trespass is not punishable is that the evil of which there is a danger is not serious enough, it follows that the person who incites the trespass does not even intend to create a clear and present danger of the sort contemplated by the test. Thus, according to Brandeis, someone who explicitly urges a specific crime may be punished though he does not intend and does not create a danger of a crime serious enough to satisfy the clear-and-present-danger test.

A final problem about the clear-and-present-danger test concerns the respective roles of judge and jury. Since in *Schenck*, *Frohwerk*, and *Debs*, the juries had not been instructed about any need to find a clear and present danger, the Supreme Court's affirmance of the convictions would suggest that the test is for judicial application, but, in a dissent joined by Holmes in *Schaefer* v. *United States*,[24] Brandeis indicated that the jury should ordinarily apply the test unless a judge determined that people "judging in calmness" could not reasonably find such a danger.

Though later cases have resolved some of the questions left unsettled by Holmes and Brandeis, many of the perplexities continue, including the precise relationship between the crime of criminal solicitation and the constitutional test for speech advocating crime. One thing that is clear is that, in cases of public advocacy of illegal action, the modern approach, which I shall consider in a subsequent section, combines objective and subjective elements.

Some of the roots of the modern approach are found in an opinion of Learned Hand, writing as a district court judge, two years prior to *Schenck*. On its face, Hand's opinion in *Masses Publishing Co.* v. *Patten*[25] represented only an exercise in statutory interpretation, one rejected by the court of appeals, but subsequent correspondence reveals that Hand regarded his analysis as a sound constitutional approach as well.[26]

The case involved review of the decision of the Postmaster of the City of New York to treat a revolutionary journal called *The Masses* as nonmailable material under a section of the Espionage Act of 1917. The issue contained some anticapitalist, antiwar cartoons, as well as praise, in prose and poetry, for conscientious objectors and for Emma Goldman and Alexander Berkman, who had been convicted for urging draft resistance. Hand assumed, as the government had argued, that publications violating other provisions of the Espionage Act were nonmailable. According to Hand, even intemperate criticism and abuse of government policies was not enough to violate the act. He continued:

> Yet there has always been a recognized limit to such expressions, incident indeed to the existence of any compulsive power of the state itself. One may not counsel or advise others to violate the law as it stands. Words are not only the keys of persuasion, but the triggers of action, and those which have no purport but to counsel the violation of law cannot by any latitude of interpretation be a part of that public opinion which is the final source of government in a democratic state.[27]

Although he acknowledged that the *Masses* issue might arouse discontent among the troops, Hand denied that the magazine counseled disobedience of law:

To counsel or advise a man to an act is to urge upon him either that it is his interest or his duty to do it. While, of course, this may be accomplished as well by indirection as expressly, since words carry the meaning that they impart, the definition is exhaustive. . . . If one stops short of urging upon others that it is their duty or their interest to resist the law, it seems to me one should not be held to have attempted to cause its violation.[28]

Hand's approach is more speech-protective than the clear-and-present-danger test insofar as it demands unambiguous encouragement of criminal acts.[29] Although the words need not always be taken literally, "the literal meaning is the starting point for interpretation." Undoubtedly Hand would have allowed reference to obvious uses of metaphor, irony, and similar devices, and to tone of voice and context, in attempts to discern a speaker's meaning, but he would not have permitted punishment on the basis of a finding by a judge or jury that a speaker meant to encourage a crime, when such encouragement would not have been apparent to members of the audience.

That Hand saw important distinctions between his own approach and that adopted by the Supreme Court in *Schenck* is evidenced by his objections in correspondence to the latter approach. He worried that a jury having only to find an intent to violate the law would end up convicting unpopular opinion, and he could not "see any escape from construing the privilege as absolute, so long as the utterance, objectively regarded, can by any fair construction be held to fall short of counselling violence."[30]

The 1930s and 1940s: Clear and Present Danger Broadly Applied and the Development of Ancillary Speech-Protective Doctrines

In the two decades after *Whitney*, the Supreme Court moved toward a much more expansive interpretation of the First Amendment, and the clear-and-present-danger test emerged not only as the critical test for subversive advocacy, but also as a standard for a wide range of free speech and free press problems. If the Court was not always lucid about the relevance of that formula to those different problems, its use of the test and its employment of ancillary doctrines did evince a growing disposition to protect expression.

This summary examination of what the Court did in that period not only serves to sketch a historical progression; it highlights the Court's treatment of some of the dilemmas regarding subjective purpose and objective danger and sheds light on the variety of free speech issues and their unsusceptibility to any single formula.

Subversive Advocacy

Two 1930s cases that marked the beginning of a more protective attitude toward speech did not involve the Court in laying down any general substantive standard for when speech may be suppressed. In 1931 in *Stromberg* v. *California*[31] the Court invalidated a conviction under California's "red flag" law, on the ground that, given its instructions, the jury might have found defendant guilty for using the flag to express perfectly legal opposition to the existing government or to government generally. Six years later in *DeJonge* v. *Oregon*[32] a criminal-syndical-ism conviction was reversed on a similar basis, the Court holding that a man could not permissibly be convicted (as the state court's construal of the indictment made possible) for simply participating at a political meeting organized by a group (Communists) whose members had urged illegal action on other occasions.

Herndon v. *Lowry*,[33] decided by a one-vote margin, represented a more patent doctrinal shift in favor of speech. Herndon, a Communist party organizer among blacks in Georgia, was convicted of attempting to incite insurrection by inducing "others to join in any combined resistance to the lawful authority of the state." In the absence of evidence that Herndon had urged revolutionary violence upon those he solicited for membership or had distributed revolutionary literature found in his possession, the majority held that, as applied to him, the statute unreasonably limited freedom of expression. In the course of its discussion, the majority treated with approval the clear-and-present-danger test of *Schenck*.

That the Supreme Court had only two occasions during World War II to discuss the troubling constitutional issues raised by the Espionage Act cases illustrated not only the altered judicial attitude toward expression but also the relatively permissive attitude of the executive branch toward dissent.

In *Taylor* v. *Mississippi*,[34] the Court unanimously reversed convictions under a state sedition law. Defendants, Jehovah's Witnesses, had made such statements as "[I]t was wrong for our President to send our boys across in uniform to fight our enemies." The Court said that "criminal sanctions cannot be imposed for such communication of beliefs and opinions concerning domestic measures and trends in national and world affairs."[35]

The second case, *Hartzel* v. *United States*,[36] was more difficult, and the Court's response more complex, with the plurality and the dissent stating conflicting positions on the relationship between intent and clear and present danger.

Hartzel, a well-educated and mature man, wrote and had mimeographed short articles that denounced the English and the Jews, called the war a gross betrayal of America, and urged conversion of the war into a racial conflict, suggesting "occupation [of America] by foreign troops until we are able to stand alone." He mailed about six hundred copies to community leaders, including commanders of the American Legion, and to important government officials, including the Commanding General of the United States Army Air Forces. The five-member majority considered the evidence insufficient for a jury to find the "specific intent" required for Espionage Act violations, but only a plurality of four explicated its reasoning. The four dissenters, citing Holmes's language in *Schenck* and faithful to the import of earlier Espionage Act cases, concluded that a jury could easily have found that Hartzel possessed the evil purpose, and they saw no constitutional barrier to conviction: "the necessity of finding beyond a reasonable doubt the intent to produce the prohibited result affords abundant protection to those whose criticism is directed to legitimate ends."[37] The plurality agreed with the dissenters that the required intent to cause the proscribed harms need not be obvious from the face of the published writings, but that reference may be made to "circumstances surrounding their preparation and dissemination." But the plurality insisted that more definite proof was needed before a finding of intent could be drawn beyond a reasonable doubt. Although the plurality did not say that its treatment of the intent point was directly influenced by First Amendment considerations, it might well have taken a less stringent position on the permissible inferences a jury could draw had speech not been involved.

Though its reversal on the intent point relieved the plurality of having to think very hard about other problems, the opinion did comment at an early point that "two major elements" are necessary for conviction under the Espionage Act: "a subjective one, consisting of a specific intent" and an "objective one, consisting of a clear and present danger that the activities in question will bring about the substantive evils which Congress has a right to prevent."[38] If the plurality meant what it said—that an actual clear and present danger is always a required element for conviction—its position was significantly more protective in this respect than anything it drew from Holmes or Brandeis, or could have drawn from Hand.

A decision not long after *Hartzel*, *Keegan* v. *United States*,[39] casts some doubt that all members of the *Hartzel* plurality did accept this implication of the opinion. A majority of the Court overturned convictions of leaders of the German-American Bund for conspiracy to counsel "evasion" of service in the armed forces, some justices on the ground that defendants' urging of open refusal was not urging of evasion, some justices on the ground that defendants had not even urged open refusal unconditionally. Chief Justice Stone's dissent claimed that defendants had urged refusal and that evasion encompassed refusal. The opinion intimated no constitutional doubt about punishment, although the principles of the *Hartzel* plurality, joined by Stone, appeared to demand a showing of clear and present danger.[40]

Public Order

A number of cases during the 1930s and 1940s in which the Supreme Court used clear-and-present-danger language can be loosely categorized as involving public order. Cases in that broad area also established other important First Amendment principles whose relevance continues.

Without using clear-and-present-danger language, *Lovell* v. *City of Griffin*[41] and *Schneider* v. *State* (*Town of Irvington*)[42] gave content to the notion that the state cannot prohibit speech in order to eradicate minor evils, particularly if alternative means exist for dealing with the problem. In *Schneider* Justice Roberts wrote for the majority, "The purpose to keep the streets clean and of good appearance is insufficient to justify an ordinance which prohibits a person rightfully on a public street from handing literature to one willing to receive it."[43]

Cantwell v. *Connecticut*,[44] decided in 1940, represented the importation of clear and present danger to public-order problems. In that case the Court overturned a conviction for breach of the peace of a Jehovah's Witness who on a public street played a phonograph record attacking the Roman Catholic Church which incensed his two Catholic listeners. Writing for the Court, Justice Roberts acknowledged the state's power to prevent or punish speech when "clear and present danger of riot, disorder, interference with traffic upon the public streets, or other immediate threat to public safety, peace, or order, appears."[45] He noted that someone may be guilty of breach of the peace "if he commit acts or make statements likely to provoke violence and disturbance of good order, even though no such eventuality be intended." Such statements have almost always consisted of "profane, indecent, or abusive remarks directed to the person of the hearer. Resort to epithets or personal abuse is not in any proper sense communication of information or opinion safeguarded by the Constitution."[46] But Cantwell was not personally abusive; he was merely expressing a highly controversial religious belief. The Court concluded that "in the absence of a statute narrowly drawn to define and punish specific conduct as constituting a clear and present danger to a substantial interest of the state," Cantwell's communication "raised no such clear and present menace to public peace and order as to render him liable to conviction of the common law offense in question."[47]

The *Cantwell* opinion apparently requires a clear and present danger of some sort, whether a statute is narrowly addressed to particular problems or forms of speech or is, like breach-of-the-peace provisions, very broad. However, the test is more rigorous in the absence of a legislative judgment about the dangers of particular speech. The threat must be to a *substantial* interest of the state, but in this context that obviously means less than a threat to government survival, embracing such matters as traffic control. Speech may be punished, even under an open-ended standard like "breach of the peace," for threatening evils that the speaker does not intend, but the Court brushes aside the instances in which such punishment has been typical as not involving communication of information or opinion safeguarded by the Constitution.

In *Chaplinsky* v. *New Hampshire*,[48] the Court confirmed the *Cantwell* dictum about abusive words by upholding defendant's conviction for calling a police officer a "God-damned racketeer" and a "damned Fascist." The conviction was under a statute that forbade calling someone any "offensive" name in a public place, offensive name having been construed by the state court to include only expressions that "men of common intelligence would understand would be likely to cause an average addressee to fight." The Supreme Court wrote,

> There are certain well-defined and narrowly limited classes of speech, the prevention and punishment of which have never been thought to raise any Constitutional problem. These include the lewd and obscene, the profane, the libelous, and the insulting or "fighting" words—those which by their very utterance inflict injury or tend to incite an immediate breach of the peace. It has been well observed that such utterances are no essential part of any exposition of ideas, and are of such slight social value as a step to truth that any benefit that may be derived from them is clearly outweighed by the social interest in order and morality.[49]

Feiner v. *New York*,[50] decided in 1951, involved another encounter with provocative speech. Feiner had made a street-corner speech in which he called various politicians "bums" and urged that Negroes "should rise up in arms and fight for their rights." When the crowd became restive, police officers, in order to prevent a fight, asked Feiner to get off the box and stop speaking. Feiner was convicted of disorderly conduct for refusing to comply with the police order. The Supreme Court majority said Feiner had "passe[d] the bounds of argument or persuasion and undertake[n] incitement to riot." But what was crucial to its affirmance of the conviction was its view that the police have the power to intervene when there is a "clear and present danger of riot, disorder, interference with traffic upon the public streets, or other immediate threat to public safety, peace or order."[51] The dissenters objected that Feiner had been engaged in protected speech, that no persuasive evidence of imminent disorder had been adduced, and that the police should have protected Feiner from possible assailants, not stopped him from speaking.[52] They argued that the rule of the majority would permit officials effectively to suppress unpopular views on the basis that suppression is necessary to prevent an outbreak of violence.

If the basis for the police order was that Feiner's controversial message might cause antagonists to attack him or his supporters, then his speech was stopped because it created the same kind of danger of violent retaliation as do fighting words. Since not all speech likely to have such an effect can comfortably be categorized as personally offensive and without social value, *Feiner* contemplates restriction of speakers who are making remarks that, at least initially and taken by themselves, warrant constitutional protection. Perhaps it follows that police officers should be able to silence such speakers only if police manpower is insufficient to preserve the peace in some other way, and perhaps it also follows that, when the perceived reactions of an actual audience are the basis for silencing a speaker, he must first be asked to stop, and be prosecuted only, as Feiner was, for disobeying an order found to be reasonable.[53]

Some of the troublesome dimensions of the problem of potential mob violence are illustrated by the facts of a case decided two years before *Feiner*, *Terminiello* v. *Chicago*.[54] Terminiello, a suspended Catholic priest of right-wing sympathies, had delivered a highly provocative address, attacking Jews and "Communists" like Eleanor Roosevelt. The hall was filled, mostly with supporters, and an angry crowd, mostly antagonistic, was assembled outside. After the speech a riot broke out. The majority overturned Terminiello's conviction on the *Stromberg*-like basis that the jury instructions permitted a finding of guilt for controversial but protected speech. It is Justice Jackson's dissenting account of the underlying facts that gives rise to disquiet about the workability of constitutional standards for such situations. Jackson, influenced by his tenure as chief American prosecutor at the Nuremberg trials, wrote that Terminiello's speech "followed, with fidelity that is more than coincidental, the pattern of European fascist leaders." Though Terminiello's words actually were opposed to the use of violence against opponents, Jackson was willing to accept a jury finding that the speech "was a provocation to immediate breach of the peace." He relied to some extent on Terminiello's use of epithets such as "scum," "snakes," and "bedbugs," which Jackson considered fighting words, but his major point was that Terminiello had intentionally incited the mob without appearing to do so. He said:

> The ways in which mob violence may be worked up are subtle and various. Rarely will a speaker directly urge a crowd to lay hands on a victim or a class of victims. An effective and safer way is to incite mob action while pretending to deplore it, after the classic example of Antony, and this was not lost on Terminiello. And whether one may be the cause of mob violence by his own personification or advocacy of ideas which a crowd already fears and hates, is not solved merely by going through a transcript of the speech to pick out fighting words.[55]

Jackson, who thought mob violence almost always started in speechmaking, feared that, unless speeches like Terminiello's could be punished, local authorities would be powerless to prevent fighting from breaking out in a mob, but his own approach leaves little constraint on unsympathetic juries who determine that unpopular speeches are meant to incite mob violence.

In *Beauharnais* v. *Illinois*,[56] in 1952, a slender majority of the Court upheld a conviction under a state statute punishing vilification of racial and religious groups. Though the majority's emphasis on the likely contribution of extreme racial propaganda to racial violence reflected its attention to the public-order dimension of the statute, its characterization of defendant's segregationist hate literature as a form of group libel allowed it to place that literature outside the embrace of the First Amendment and relieved it of having to apply the clear-and-present-danger test. Justice Black complained about the expansion of libel to cover discussion of matters of public concern, and Justice Douglas objected to the failure to employ the clear-and-present-danger standard.

Contempt for Out-of-Court Comments

Another area in which the Court employed clear-and-present-danger language was criminal contempt based on out-of-court publications that might affect deliberations of judges or grand juries. The relevant cases raise the troubling relation of objective to subjective standards and strain the plausibility of an objective standard for this context.

In *Bridges* v. *California*,[57] Justice Black's majority opinion brushed aside the argument that the power of courts to punish out-of-court publications by contempt was a recognized common law exception, instead accepting the view that "one of the objects of the Revolution was to get rid of the English common law on liberty of speech and of the press." The *Bridges* opinion and subsequent majority opinions assumed that a state has a substantial interest in keeping decisions of particular cases free from the influence of external appeals,[58] but found insufficient the threat that the publications in question would actually interfere with the impartial administration of justice or create disrespect for the judiciary. Rejecting the California Supreme Court's view that publications could constitute contempt if they have "a reasonable tendency to interfere with the orderly administration of justice," the Court in *Bridges* said that the proper test was clear and present danger, "a working principle that the substantive evil must be extremely serious and the degree of imminence extremely high before utterances can be punished."[59] Taking it for granted that application of the test demands estimation of the actual likelihood that the evils of influence will occur, the majority opinions in that and subsequent cases did not address the possibility suggested by Holmes that it may be enough in some circumstances to act with an intent to create a clear and present danger, nor did the opinions explain why, if such an intent underlies communications designed to bring about the substantive evil, that should not be an acceptable basis for punishment.

The cases raise doubt about the significance of "clear and present danger" in this context. If it is assumed that judges, at least, are relatively hardy,[60] and if communications about the case involve sharp criticism but not personal threats or bribes, how would one court decide that communications to other judges create clear and present danger of actual influence or disrespect? It is, in fact, hard to imagine how application of the clear-and-present-danger standard in this context would differ from an absolute constitutional privilege.

Labor Relations

Because of special features about the labor relationship and picketing, the First Amendment law of labor relations has never fit comfortably into the ordinary categories of free speech analysis, as is evidenced both by how the Court has treated labor picketing and by the regime of regulation of employer speech under labor relations law, treated briefly in a subsequent section.

In 1940, in *Thornhill* v. *Alabama*,[61] the Court treated peaceful labor picketing as just another form of expressive activity. It rejected an absolute ban on peaceful picketing because "no clear and present danger of destruction of life or property, or invasion of the right of privacy, or breach of the peace can be thought to be inherent in the activities of every person who approaches the premises of an employer and publicizes the facts of a labor dispute involving the latter."[62] In subsequent cases, the Court came to treat picketing as something more than speech and allowed more pervasive regulation.[63] After initially allowing prohibitions on picketing when the picketing was designed to achieve the illegal objective of "racial hiring" or was intertwined with coercive violence, it then upheld limits on peaceful secondary picketing (away from the location of the dispute) and on picketing at the primary site that was deemed unfair, results that were much harder to support if labor picketing is like any other sort of peaceful demonstration.

If the special problem of labor picketing is that it is "a signal for the application of immediate and enormous economic leverage"[64] or, to put the point somewhat differently, that many persons respond to the fact that it is taking place without respect to the substance of the message the picketers convey, then the same difficulty could arise with more pure forms of speech.[65]

I shall here discuss a little more thoroughly a labor case which did not involve picketing and which contains the most negative comments in a Supreme Court opinion about any line between outright solicitation and lesser encouragements. In 1945, in *Thomas* v. *Collins*,[66] a narrow majority relied on clear-and-present-danger analysis to rule that Texas could not limit solicitation of union membership to persons who had registered as union organizers.

Justice Rutledge's opinion for the Court spoke of the "priority" of the freedoms secured by the First Amendment. Rejecting the state's proposal of a "rational-basis test" and finding the state's interests in stopping solicitation of union funds to be inadequate to support the challenged restriction, the opinion said that "any attempt to restrict those liberties must be justified by clear public interest, threatened not doubtfully or remotely but by clear and present danger. . . . Only the gravest abuses, endangering paramount interests, give occasion for permissible limitation" on orderly discussion and persuasion.[67]

In answer to the state's argument that the statute left Thomas free to speak about union matters as long as he did not solicit membership, the Court said:

[T]he statute forbids any language which conveys, or reasonably could be found to convey, the meaning of invitation. . . . General words create different and often particular impressions on different minds. No speaker, however careful, can convey exactly his meaning, or the same meaning, to the different members of an audience. How one might "laud unionism" . . . yet in these circumstances not imply an invitation, is hard to conceive. . . .

. . . In short, the supposedly clear-cut distinction between general discussion, laudation, general advocacy, and solicitation puts the speaker in these circumstances wholly at the mercy of the varied understanding of his hearers and consequently of whatever inference may be drawn as to his intent and meaning.

Such a distinction offers no security for free discussion.[68]

Although the Court's distaste for the distinction between general discussion and solicitation is in the special context of the lawful activity of joining a union, nevertheless its reasoning can be used to challenge the importance under the First Amendment of any line between soliciting criminal acts and more general advocacy that may lead to criminal acts.

Dennis v. United States and Its Successors: Watered-down Clear and Present Danger, Advocacy of Action, and Ad Hoc Balancing

If the 1930s and 1940s represented a broad expansion of First Amendment protection, the 1951 case of *Dennis* v. *United States*[69] halted that trend. In *Dennis* the Supreme Court considered again the sort of revolutionary rhetoric involved in *Gitlow* and *Whitney*, and, during a period of growing international Communist power and virulent domestic anticommunism, it responded by substantially diluting the clear-and-present-danger test. The case involved the prosecution of eleven leading Communists under the Smith Act, federal antisubversive legislation closely resembling the New York Criminal Anarchy statute under which Gitlow had been convicted. The Smith Act makes it illegal "to knowingly or willfully advocate, abet, advise, or teach the duty, necessity, desirability, or propriety of overthrowing or destroying any government in the United States by force or violence."[70] Other sections make it criminal to help organize any group that advocates violent overthrow of the government or to conspire to advocate or organize. Although the domestic Communist party was hardly a new organizaion, Dennis and his companions were actually prosecuted under one count for conspiring to organize a group that would advocate overthrow, a theory of liability that moved the locus of proscribed activity yet a step farther back than even *Whitney* from the ultimately feared illegal behavior.

Judge Medina in the United States District Court had charged the jury that the statute denounces not the abstract doctrine of violent overthrow but "advocacy of action . . . with the intent to cause the overthrow . . . of the Government . . . by force and violence as speedily as circumstances would permit." The jury, having sat through a complex nine-month trial, convicted upon these instructions. Believing that the clear-and-present-danger test was a question of law for the judge, Judge Medina did not put that issue to the jury, instead deciding himself that its conditions were satisfied.

The Supreme Court accepted Judge Medina's narrowing construction of the language of the statute and affirmed the convictions. Four of the eight sitting judges joined a plurality opinion authored by Chief Justice Vinson that followed closely the opinion of Learned Hand for the court of appeals. Without quite overruling *Gitlow* and *Whitney*, the plurality acknowledged that later opinions had followed the Holmes-Brandeis rationale and proceeded as if that were the relevant approach. But, considering all concepts relative, it declined to treat the "shorthand phrase" of clear and present danger as a "rigid rule." Instead it adopted Hand's formulation: that, in each case, the court (not the jury) should "ask whether the gravity of the 'evil', discounted by its improbability, justifies such invasion of free speech as is necessary to avoid the danger."[71] Given the highly disciplined, secretive nature of the domestic Communist party and the worldwide position of communism, the advocacy of violent overthrow in the party context was determined to be sufficiently dangerous to warrant prohibition.

One respect in which the plurality transformed the traditional test was in abandoning a more or less uniform standard of likelihood, signaled by the word "clear." Under the Hand-Vinson test, if the evil is very great, speech may be proscribed even though the danger of its causing the evil is comparatively slight. At an abstract level this revision makes sense. If speech S, which creates a 60 percent chance of evil X, may be suppressed, should it not be possible also to suppress speech T, which creates a 30 percent chance of a much more momentous evil Y? Of course, the matter is more complicated, because few cases will be limited to a single evil. Among the possible substantive evils in *Dennis*, for example, are successful overthrow of the government (very great evil—very small likelihood), substantial unsuccessful revolution (great evil—small likelihood), violent acts preparatory to revolution (less evil—greater likelihood). Presumably the test requires that each evil be discounted by its improbability and the sum of the products assessed against the constitutional requirement.

In eliminating the word "present" from the test and dropping imminency as an independent requirement, the plurality implied that all that matters about imminency is the likelihood that an evil will occur, apparently accepting Hand's assumption that the crucial relevance of time for countervailing speech is the possibility that such speech will prevent the evil. This view implicitly rejects the possibility that imminence has independent significance, that, whether or not discussion reduces the likelihood of an evil occurring, opportunity for discussion may be important to ensure considered action.

Justices Frankfurter and Jackson, the two other Justices voting to affirm the conviction, strongly objected to the unworkability of the plurality's standard. Justice Frankfurter wrote, "To make validity of legislation depend on judicial reading of events still in the womb of time—a forecast, that is, of the outcome of forces at best appreciated only with knowledge of the topmost secrets of nations—is to charge the judiciary with duties beyond its equipment."[72] And Justice Jackson agreed that "the judicial process simply is not adequate to a trial of such far-flung issues."[73]

Neither Jackson nor Frankfurter regarded clear and present danger as an adequate standard for the case, though Jackson thought it should be "unmodified, for application as a 'rule of reason' in the kind of case for which it was devised."[74] Jackson made the conspiratorial and secretive nature of the Communist party central. Without quite facing up to the issue in these terms, Jackson apparently determined that Congress could punish as a crime an agreement to engage in advocacy with an illegal purpose that would be constitutionally protected if actually engaged in by separate individuals. While pointing out that conspiracies to engage in direct incitement may be punished and that "Congress may make it a crime to conspire with others to do what an individual may lawfully do on his own,"[75] Jackson never really explained the basis on which Congress may make criminal an agreement to do what is not only lawful by itself but constitutionally protected. He may have supposed that the presence of conspiracy adequately established illegal purpose and strikingly augmented the danger that actors would persevere until bringing about the substantive evil; or perhaps he regarded the basic conspiracy as one actually to overthrow the government rather than merely to advocate.

Justice Frankfurter's abandonment of the clear-and-present-danger test was more complete. He adopted the ad hoc balancing approach as a general principle for First Amendment interpretation, applicable to cases of direct suppression, like *Dennis*, as well as cases of indirect interference. Under such an approach the government's interest in suppression is weighed against the interest in liberty on a case-by-case basis. Frankfurter stated: "The demands of free speech in a democratic society as well as the interest in national security are better served by candid and informed weighing of the competing interests, within the confines of the judicial process, than by announcing dogmas too inflexible for the non-Euclidian problems to be solved." But "primary responsibility for adjusting the interests . . . belongs to the Congress," and its judgment should be set aside "only if there is no reasonable basis for it."[76] Although Justice Frankfurter did indicate that he would have disagreed with the majority in *Gitlow* on the facts of that case, nevertheless his use of an ad hoc balancing test combined with explicit and substantial deference to legislative judgment produced weak protection for interests of speech, and it was not surprising that he, though penning eloquent phrases in favor of liberty of expression, ended up voting with the majority.

Justices Black and Douglas each dissented, arguing that the convictions could not stand against application of the clear-and-present-danger test. According to Douglas, the teaching of methods of terror would be unprotected by the First Amendment, but the defendants had been charged with advocating violent overthrow of the government, not with "teaching the techniques of sabotage, the assassination of the President, the filching of documents from public files, the planting of bombs, the art of street warfare, and the like."[77]

Six years after *Dennis*, the Court reversed the convictions of a second group of leading Communists in *Yates* v. *United States*,[78] on the ground that the trial judge had declined to instruct the jury that defendants' advocacy had to be of illegal action rather than simply doctrine. Justice Harlan's majority opinion acknowledged that the Court's interpretation of the statute in this respect was influenced by the First Amendment interest in speech. The Court's standard can best be understood in light of its review of the evidence, which showed that the instances of general revolutionary teaching far outweighed instances of advocacy of action and which led the justices to worry that "in the absence of more precise instructions" the jury might have given too much weight to "vague references to 'revolutionary' or 'militant' action of an unspecified character."

Dissenting on the ground that acquittal should have been directed, Justice Black suggested the absolutist position about freedom of speech that he later developed at more length: "I believe that the First Amendment forbids Congress to punish people for talking about public affairs, whether or not such discussion incites to action, legal or illegal."[79]

Justice Harlan wrote again for the majority four years later when the Court sustained one conviction under the membership clause of the Smith Act, in *Scales*, v. *United States*,[80] and reversed another for insufficient evidence, in *Noto* v. *United States*.[81] The membership clause was interpreted as reaching only "active" members who shared the illegal purposes of the Communist party. In rejecting Scales's claim that the evidence was insufficient for a conviction, Justice Harlan clarified the approach of *Yates*, saying that "Smith Act offenses, involving as they do subtler elements than are present in most other crimes, call for strict standards in assessing the adequacy of the proof needed to make out a case of illegal advocacy." As for the kind of evidence needed for a conviction under the Smith Act, he said that *Yates* indicates

> at least two patterns of evidence sufficient to show illegal advocacy: (a) the teaching of forceful overthrow, accompanied by directions as to the type of illegal action which must be taken when the time for revolution is reached; and (b) the teaching of forceful overthrow, accompanied by a contemporary, though legal, course of conduct clearly undertaken for the specific purpose of rendering effective the later illegal activity which is advocated.[82]

This passage leaves uncertain, as did *Yates* itself, whether unambiguous but general urging to illegal action would alone be sufficient.

The Warren Court's "Liberal" Period: Expansive Protection for Freedom of Expression and the *Brandenburg* Test

When Arthur Goldberg became a justice in 1962, he joined Chief Justice Warren and Justices Black, Douglas, and Brennan to make up a "liberal" majority for many constitutional issues, including most of those involving speech. With some change in personnel, this majority continued until the end of Earl Warren's tenure as chief justice. Surprisingly, this Court did not directly face the sort of issue posed by the Espionage Act cases or *Dennis* until 1969, though it had already altered the face of First Amendment law.

Its major analytical techniques were doctrines of vagueness and overbreadth and the compelling-interest test. The Court often spoke interchangeably about vagueness and overbreadth, though an important distinction exists between the two sorts of statutory defect. A *vague* statute does not give fair warning about what behavior is prohibited. An *overly broad* statute reaches instances of constitutionally protected behavior. Overbroad statutes are often vague on their face as well, but, even when they are not, they may generate a vagueness difficulty. So long as part of the statutory coverage is impermissible, a citizen unsure how courts will draw the line between permissible and impermissible coverage will be uncertain as to what he can safely do. For this reason and because many people will hesitate to disobey laws despite a plain constitutional right to do so, the Court concluded that overly broad statutes would chill protected expression, and it proceeded to invalidate such statutes on their face even when the constitutional issues were raised by defendants or plaintiffs for whom the application of the statutes may have been constitutional.[83]

In form, invalidation on vagueness and overbreadth grounds left the legislature free to redraw a prohibition or regulation (although, for such endeavors as the framing of loyalty oaths, few efforts could succeed).[84] Thus these grounds did not appear to present so sharp a conflict with legislative judgment as would a direct holding that what the legislature had attempted to do violated the First Amendment.

In cases involving indirect restrictions on speech, such as questioning people about their opinions and political activities, the Court substituted for the ad hoc balancing test the principle that interferences with speech must be based on a compelling state interest and must be necessitated by the absence of less restrictive alternatives.[85] This approach shifted the balance heavily in favor of expression and eliminated the strong element of deference to legislative judgment.

Another aspect of the Warren Court's extended protection for expression was its application of the First Amendment to areas previously assumed to be outside its ambit. The most notable stroke was its application of constitutional limits to the law of libel, precluding recovery for defamatory criticism of public officials and public figures unless the defamation was made with knowledge or reckless disregard of its falsity and requiring that plaintiff's case be established with convincing clarity. The landmark decision, *New York Times Co.* v. *Sullivan*, contributed importantly to general First Amendment doctrine in its explicit statement that the Sedition Act was unconstitutional and in its more general assertion of a "profound national commitment to the principle that debate on public issues should be uninhibited, robust, and wide-open, and that it may well include vehement, caustic, and sometimes unpleasantly sharp attacks on government and public officials."[86]

Before Justice Goldberg joined the Court, a majority in *Roth* v. *United States*[87] had held that obscene materials, materials that predominantly appeal to the prurient interest, lack constitutional protection. The Court reasoned that such materials are without redeeming social value. In succeeding cases a critical plurality developed a threefold test of what was obscene: material could not be suppressed unless: (a) the dominant theme of the material taken as a whole appeals to a prurient interest in sex; (b) the material is patently offensive in affronting community standards about the portrayal of sexual matters; and (c) the material is utterly without redeeming social value.[88] What is evidently referred to by the last criterion is value *as expression*, since it might be argued that any commodity that gives pleasure or plays a part in satisfying sexual feelings has *some* value. In cases of borderline materials, it could matter whether they had been advertised and distributed in a manner pandering to a prurient interest in sex.[89] With the plurality applying these standards, the Court struck down a great many attempts to suppress materials as obscene.

Prior to establishing a new standard for when a legislature may permissibly prohibit speech deemed to be dangerous, the Court indicated in *Bond* v. *Floyd*[90] that it would not construe ambiguous words as intended to encourage illegal action, an attitude far different from that found in the early Espionage Act cases. Julian Bond had been excluded from membership in the Georgia state legislature on the ground that, given statements he had made or to which he had subscribed, he could not conscientiously take the oath of office. Among these statements was one issued by the Student Nonviolent Coordinating Committee which said, "We are in sympathy with, and support, the men in this country who are unwilling to respond to a military draft which would compel them to contribute their lives to United States aggression in Viet Nam in the name of the 'freedom' we find so false in this country." Asserting that Bond could not be excluded from a seat in the legislature for constitutionally protected remarks, the Court inquired whether he had violated the part of the "Selective Service laws" that makes it criminal to counsel another "to refuse or evade registration." It decided that the SNCC statement "alone cannot be interpreted as a call to unlawful refusal to be drafted" and, upon canvassing Bond's other comments, concluded that they tended to resolve any opaqueness in favor of legal alternatives to the draft.

The Court reached a similar result in *Watts* v. *United States*,[91] acting per curiam and without a hearing to reverse a conviction for making a "knowing and willful threat against the President." At a small, informal political gathering Watts had said, "If they ever make me carry a rifle the first man I want to get in my sights is L.B.J." The majority, without resolving whether a person who did not intend to carry out a threat could violate the statute, said that there must at least be a true threat, and that in context Watts' statement could not be interpreted as a true threat.

Shortly after *Watts*, the Court decided *Brandenburg* v. *Ohio*,[92] the case that established the modern general formulation for constitutional protection of subversive advocacy. Given the Court's recent decisions, its unanimous determination that the state's criminal-syndicalism statute was invalid and that *Gitlow* and *Whitney* were no longer authoritative was not startling. Nor, in the absence of a showing that defendant had urged the commission of any crimes, was its conclusion that his speech at a Ku Klux Klan meeting was constitutionally protected. But the per curiam opinion, citing *Dennis* v. *United States* in its support, sprang the astonishing statement that

> later decisions have fashioned the principle that the constitutional guarantees of free speech and free press do not permit a State to forbid or proscribe advocacy of the use of force or of law violation except where such advocacy is directed to inciting or producing imminent lawless action and is likely to incite or produce such action.[93]

If *Dennis* stands for anything, it is that the lawless action need not be imminent, so the Court's citation of that case as a basis for the announced principle must be disingenuous, unless it represents some equivocal reservation that the *Brandenburg* standard does not apply to secret political conspiracies aiming at overthrow of the government. As the preceding survey has established, the Court had never before indicated that a significant actual danger of unlawful action is a condition of punishment when the speaker unambiguously urges the commission of a specific crime. The Court in *Brandenburg* did not make any serious effort either to sort out the implications of earlier cases or to relate its own approach to general principles governing criminal solicitation. It remains a puzzle why, in light of all this and the complete absence of necessity to lay down such a principle to resolve the case before it, the Court chose to take such an apparently bold step.

Justice Douglas's concurring opinion treated the *Brandenburg* test as a clear-and-present-danger formulation and rejected that test as insufficiently protective of speech. Justice Douglas urged that the proper constitutional line is between ideas and overt acts; speech cannot be punished unless it is "brigaded with action." He gave as an example the person who falsely shouts "fire" in a crowded theater, and can be punished for "the overt acts actually caused."[94]

Because the *Brandenburg* test remains the prevailing approach for prohibition of advocacy and because it attempts to combine objective and subjective elements in a way that provides significant protection for speech, it is important to understand what it clearly settles and what it does not.

The Court tells us that advocacy of law violation is punishable only upon two conditions: the advocacy must be (1) "directed to inciting or producing imminent lawless action" and (2) "likely to incite or produce such action." Since no narrower definition was suggested, "advocacy" as used by the Court apparently includes all urging of the appropriateness of illegal action, of which remarks directed to inciting or to producing imminent lawless action are a subcategory. One who unambiguously urges specific criminal action is protected so long as he does not urge *imminent* lawless action.

Under the Court's test, advocacy is protected unless it is actually likely to produce illegal action. Suppose a radical speaker in a university setting is inveighing against authority and says to his emotionally aroused audience, "I want you to show me right now how you spit on the lackeys of imperialism by beating that university guard, the one standing right there, to death." Even if the speaker fully intends that his words be carried out to the letter, his comments are protected if it is "not likely" that the audience will act upon his counsel.

The Court's standard requires that the words be *directed* toward inciting or producing illegal action. To say that someone's words are directed toward producing a result implies that the purpose of the speaker is to produce that result and, perhaps more, that this purpose is evident in the words he uses. So long as the speaker does not actually intend to produce imminent lawless action, the Court's standard bars punishment even though the speaker is fully aware that his words may provoke illegal action and that such action is virtually certain to follow. And perhaps it protects the speaker who, like Marc Antony in Shakespeare's *Julius Caesar*, cleverly avoids conveying to the audience his approval of illegal action, but speaks for the very purpose of producing it.

A pervasive concern about the *Brandenburg* test is its failure to qualify its reference to "advocacy" of law violation. Criminal acts are urged upon various people in settings that have never been assumed to raise First Amendment problems. To draw from an example in Chapter 6, Alan urges Betty, in a private letter, to kill their rich uncle upon the uncle's return from Europe so that both can share in the proceeds of the uncle's will. Can the Court have meant that this sort of communication is protected speech if the uncle's return is not imminent or if

Betty is unlikely to act upon Alan's suggestion? It may be responded, probably accurately, that the Court was not thinking of ordinary private solicitations to commit crimes. Conceivably the Court's use of the term "advocacy" was meant to imply some principled, ideological basis for illegal action in contrast to the usual grounds of private gain or revenge. But the fate of solicitations that are private or nonideological or both is left uncertain after *Brandenburg*.

Although the Warren Court itself never had to determine directly what behavior constitutes "counseling" under the Selective Service Act and might permissibly be punished under the First Amendment, the First Circuit Court of Appeals faced these questions in *United States* v. *Spock*,[95] the most highly publicized case arising out of the Vietnam conflict. In a judgment weeks after the *Brandenburg* decision, the court overturned the convictions because the trial judge had erroneously put special questions to the jury; it also reviewed the evidence to see whether that could support findings of guilt.

Benjamin Spock, the famous pediatrician, and William Sloane Coffin, then chaplain at Yale University, and two other defendants were convicted for conspiring to "counsel, aid and abet" Selective Service registrants to refuse service in the armed forces and to fail to perform other duties required of registrants. Three of the four had signed "A Call to Resist Illegitimate Authority," which labeled the Vietnam War immoral, illegal, and unconstitutional, and continued:

5. [We] believe . . . that every free man has a legal right and a moral duty to exert every effort to end this war, to avoid collusion with it, and to encourage others to do the same. . . .
6. We believe that each of these forms of resistance against illegitimate authority [refusing to obey specific illegal and immoral orders, educating fellow servicemen, applying for status as conscientious objectors, refusing induction] is courageous and justified. Many of us believe that open resistance to the war and the draft is the course of action most likely to strengthen the moral resolve with which all of us can oppose the war and most likely to bring an end to the war.
7. We will continue to lend our support to those who undertake resistance to this war. We will raise funds to organize draft resistance unions, to supply legal defense and bail, to support families and otherwise aid resistance to the war in whatever ways seem appropriate.

Coffin and Goodman (another defendant) subsequently joined in a statement that characterized the Call as a way of aiding, abetting, and counseling against conscription, and Coffin said at an occasion when draft cards were turned in to the Attorney General, "We hereby publicly counsel these young men to continue in their refusal to serve in the armed forces as long as the war in Vietnam continues."

Chief Judge Aldrich's majority opinion concluded that, given the importance of maintaining an army, "If a registrant may be convicted for violation of the draft laws, surely '[a] man may be punished for encouraging the commission of [the] crime." In contrast to the cases involving Communist defendants, here the call was for "immediate action to thwart the [war] at hand." Relying on *Scales* and *Noto*, however, the court characterized the alleged agreement as bifarious, including both legal and illegal objectives, and said that when agreement is both bifarious and political within the shadow of the First Amendment, we hold that an individual's specific intent to adhere to the illegal portions may be shown in one of three ways: by the individual defendant's prior or subsequent unambiguous statements; by the individual defendant's subsequent commission of the very illegal act contemplated by the agreement; or by the individual defendant's subsequent legal act if that act is "clearly undertaken for the specific purpose of rendering effective the later illegal activity which is advocated."[96]

The court believed that a jury could properly conclude that the Call upon its face encouraged unlawful resistance to the draft, but that, in view of the legal action also encouraged by the Call, the illegal aspect would not by itself be enough to make each signer liable. Coffin and Goodman by their subsequent statements and behavior had evidenced plainly their support of this encouragement to illegality. Spock, on the other hand, had to be acquitted under the *Scales-Noto* principle of *strictissimi juris*, since the evidence did not establish with the requisite clarity his acceptance of the illegal aspects of the Call.

The Burger Court: Reaffirmation of the *Brandenburg* Test and Continued Protection for Speech

As far as freedom of speech and press are concerned, the major pattern of the Burger Court was continuity with its predecessor, with curtailments of liberty of expression in some areas and novel expansion in others.[97] I shall begin with the reaffirmation of the *Brandenburg* formulation, briefly mention some areas of trimming, and then discuss protective doctrines and qualifications that bear significantly on our subject.

In *Hess* v. *Indiana*,[98] the Court in 1973 applied the formulation from *Brandenburg* v. *Ohio* in review of a disorderly-conduct conviction of a demonstrator who had remarked to his fellows, "We'll take the fucking street later." According to the Court, even if Hess's words could be taken to urge illegal action at a later time, his conviction had to be overturned in the absence of evidence that he intended to produce "imminent disorder." Like *Brandenburg*, *Hess* was a per curiam opinion largely devoid of analysis, and the implausibility of interpreting Hess's words as a serious urging to crime may have affected the result. Nonetheless, the case represents an explicit reaffirmation of the *Brandenburg* standard and an interpretation of imminence that is very restrictive. The Court said that "at worst" the statement "amounted to nothing more than advocacy of illegal action at some indefinite future time." Now, if Hess really did mean to urge illegal action, common sense tells us that "later" must have meant later during the day of the demonstration; so the opinion seems to mean that, in that setting at least, illegal action some hours hence is not imminent. Even if "imminent" contains some degree of flexibility, the term connotes and is used by the Court to suggest a very short time span between an incitement and the hoped-for action. If imminence in other contexts would constitute a longer period than in *Hess*, the Court failed to explicate the factors in the street-demonstration setting—for example, the short attention span of the audience, distractions, the presence of the police—which led to the conclusion that activity proposed to be carried out later in the day would not be "imminent."

Some of the Burger Court's trimming involved overbreadth doctrine, obscenity, and libel. The Court declined to strike down statutes as overbroad unless it discerned substantial overbreadth.[99] It redefined obscenity in a manner marginally more favorable for suppression, stating that when state law specifically defines the kinds of depictions of sexual conduct that are forbidden, prohibition is permitted of "works which, taken as a whole, appeal to the prurient interest in sex, which portray sexual conduct in a patently offensive way, and which, taken as a whole, do not have serious literary, artistic, political or scientific value."[100] In respect to libel, the Court decided that the protective formulation of *New York Times* v. *Sullivan* did not apply to matters of public interest generally, but it said that some fault in publishing a defamation must be proved and that damages must be limited to actual injury unless publication was with "actual malice," that is, with knowledge or reckless disregard of falsity.[101]

Among the Burger Court's decisions protecting speech, one of the most important for our purposes established narrow boundaries for the "fighting words" doctrine. In *Cohen* v. *California*,[102] the Court overturned the breach-of-the-peace conviction of a man who in a courthouse had worn a jacket bearing the words "Fuck the draft." The state court had affirmed the conviction on the ground that it was foreseeable that Cohen's conduct might provoke a violent response. Justice Harlan's majority opinion noted that the words on Cohen's jacket were not addressed to anyone as a personal insult, the typical context of "fighting words." No evidence had been produced that Cohen's jacket was likely to provoke violence. Nor could the state purge "offensive" words from political discourse, because no principled basis exists for making distinctions, and Cohen's language could not be said to be without value:

> [M]uch linguistic expression serves a dual communicative function: it conveys not only ideas capable of relatively precise, detached explication, but otherwise inexpressible emotions as well. In fact, words are often chosen as much for their emotive as their cognitive force. We cannot sanction the view that the Constitution, while solicitous of the cognitive content of individual speech, has little or no regard for that emotive function which, practically speaking, may often be the more important element of the overall message sought to be communicated.[103]

In subsequent cases involving offensive language, the Court has typically relied mainly on vagueness and overbreadth grounds, finding that relevant provisions confer on state officials too much latitude to treat language as forbidden,[104] but the opinions taken together cast serious doubt on whether words may be punished as offensive unless they create a substantial risk of responsive violence. When the Village of Skokie adopted an ordinance against display of markings that promote racial hatred, attempting to forestall a Nazi march in the village, the Seventh Circuit Court of Appeals indicated that intervening cases had eroded the authority of *Beauharnais* v. *Illinois* and that the "fighting words" doctrine applied only to speech with a direct tendency to cause violence.[105] The Supreme Court has accepted restrictions on certain offensive words in one special context, daytime broadcasting.[106]

The Burger Court's extension of First Amendment protection to commercial advertising is significant both for what it accomplished directly and for its implications about justifications for free speech and levels of protection of speech.

Most advertising, insofar as it is helpful at all, aids people to decide how best to pursue goals they have already chosen for themselves—how to save money, be comfortable, be healthy, etc. The coverage of advertising by the First Amendment bars any argument that messages that appeal explicitly to the perceived self-interest of listeners do not warrant constitutional protection. In its trailblazing decision on drug advertising, the Court stressed both the consumer's direct interest in commercial information and the importance of such information for evaluation of the economic system.[107] The Court assumed, however, that advertising is subject to a degree of permissible regulation that would be forbidden for most other kinds of communication. As Justice Powell put it for the majority in upholding a prohibition of personal solicitation of ordinary legal business:

> We have not discarded the "common-sense" distinction between speech proposing a commercial transaction, which occurs in an area traditionally subject to government regulation, and other varieties of speech. . . . To require a parity of constitutional protection for commercial and noncommercial speech alike could invite dilution, simply by a leveling process, of the force of the Amendment's guarantee with respect to the latter kind of speech. Rather than subject the First Amendment to such a devitalization, we instead have afforded commercial speech a limited measure of protection, commensurate with its subordinate position in the scale of First Amendment values, while allowing modes of regulation that might be impermissible in the realm of noncommercial expression.[108]

In a subsequent case, writing for the Court, Justice Powell indicated that nondeceptive commercial speech could be restricted if the government has a substantial interest, if the regulation advances the interest, and if it is no more extensive than necessary to serve the interest.[109] In the commercial-speech context, therefore, certain forms of communication may be within the coverage of the First Amendment but enjoy less full protection than other forms of communication.

Whether such an approach has broader applicability has sharply divided the Court. In a plurality opinion, upholding Detroit's attempt to regulate the locations of "adult" movie theaters, Justice Stevens remarked that society's interest in material that "is on the borderline between pornography and artistic expression" is less than "the interest in untrammeled political debate"[110] and used that distinction to sustain the city's ordinance. In another plurality opinion approving FCC limitations on the broadcast of offensive speech, Stevens indicated that "patently offensive references to excretory and sexual organs and activities . . . lie at the periphery of First Amendment concern."[111] In both cases, other justices objected to the idea of affording differential levels of protection to different kinds of speech, and such objections were actually subscribed to by a majority of the justices in the Detroit case, in which Justice Stewart's dissent urged that one of the "cardinal principles of First Amendment law" is "that time, place and manner regulations that affect protected expression [must] be content neutral except in the limited context of a captive or juvenile audience."[112]

Neither the Warren Court nor the Burger Court had occasion to deal with "coercive" speech except in special contexts. The two most relevant Supreme Court decisions during the past two decades concern civil rights activity and labor regulation. In *NAACP* v. *Claiborne Hardware Co.*,[113] the Supreme Court held that even though most group boycotts may be made illegal by states, those which are engaged in for political protest are protected under a First Amendment right of association. If pressure by group boycott is itself constitutionally protected, then, in those circumstances, informing a store owner that the store will be boycotted unless corrective steps are taken must also be protected.

The principles governing what employers and union officials may say prior to voting by employees whether to join a union constitutes a fairly extensive, if somewhat confusing, body of law which is closely analogous analytically to the issue of criminal coercion.[114] The general rules are that: the National Labor Relations Act protects the expression of views, but speech that coerces employees or interferes with their exercise of rights constitutes an unfair labor practice. Construing the Act and the applicability of the First Amendment, the Supreme Court said in 1969 in *NLRB* v. *Gissel Packing Co.*[115] that employers may warn of likely economic consequences outside their control or about a fixed decision to close a plant upon unionization, but may not make threats of economic reprisal to be taken of their own volition. The development of that distinction by the National Labor Relations Board and the courts of appeals makes clear that virtually anything that fits into the category of what I have called "manipulative threats" would be unprotected. Many warning threats about (legally permissible) responses an employer might make to unionization and even some warnings about what third parties, such as crucial customers, might do have also been held to be unprotected, the view being that loose talk by employers will be taken by employees as more threatening than its literal import might suggest. In many instances, apparent predictions of likely consequences have been held to be threats because they lack a convincing objective basis. The cases reveal a purpose to protect plain statements of fact and unvarnished opinions about unionization and to leave unprotected intimations of future behavior that employees will consider threatening.

A more general prohibition on coercive speech was addressed in 1982 by the Oregon Supreme Court, which struck down the state's criminal-coercion provision under the free speech guarantee of the state constitution.[116] The court's opinion, written by Hans A. Linde, who is also a leading First Amendment scholar, concentrates on the broad language chosen by the Oregon legislature, but the reasoning casts doubt on the validity of provisions in many other states. The case is important not only because it is the most thorough constitutional examination of coercive communications, but also because it employs a theoretical approach to free speech adjudication that stands in significant respects as an alternative to the approaches that have dominated the Supreme Court.

The state court, adopting a position that Justice Linde earlier proposed in his academic writings,[117] had previously held that the state constitutional guarantee of free expression precludes legislative prohibitions of expression itself. As the opinion in *Robertson* puts the point, no law is valid that is:

written in terms directed to the substance of any "opinion" or any "subject" of communication, unless the scope of the restraint is wholly confined within some historical exception that was well established when the first American guarantees of freedom of expression were adopted and that the guarantees then or in 1859 [the year the state constitution took effect] demonstrably were not intended to reach.[118]

Because the coercion statute was aimed at forbidden effects and not at "speech as such," the court concluded that its enactment was not wholly withdrawn from legislative authority. But the relation between the statute and speech was much more than incidental because "speech often would be the offender's only act in committing this crime"; "because speech is a statutory element in the definition of the offense, the statute is susceptible to attack for possible overbreadth."

The court in *Robertson* started with the vital premise that communications of threats are speech within the understanding of constitutional protection of speech. The court noted that, under the statute, neither the threatened action nor the conduct demanded of the victim need itself be wrongful and that included among the kinds of threatened action are exercises of constitutional privilege and of legal duty. According to the court, the statutory language reached many threats that obviously enjoy constitutional protection, threats such as "If you don't quit making love to my wife, I'm going to tell your wife"; and "Change your opinion, or I shall dissent and expose your complete ignorance of this area of the law." The central issue was whether the statute could be given "a principled interpretation that excludes its application to these and other instances of free expression."

Assuming that Oregon's extortion statute, which concerns compulsion to obtain property, is valid, even though it covers exactly the same threatened consequences as the coercion provision, the court determined that by adopting blanket coverage of demands of any conduct or failures to engage in conduct that are within the legal rights of the victim, the legislature had extended the reach of the coercion provision very broadly. The court regarded the failure of the legislature to limit the statute to private communications as a further problem, given United States Supreme Court cases establishing rights for demonstrators whose aim is to induce action.

The Oregon court at one point suggested a variety of possible relevant elements for determinations about constitutional protection: (1) the lawfulness of the demanded conduct, (2) the nature of the threatened conduct, (3) the aim and the motive of the person making the threat, (4) the relationship of the parties to the demand or the threatened consequences, (5) the relationship between the demand and the threatened consequences, (6) the means of expression employed in the demand or threat, (7) the likelihood and imminence of the threatened acts, and (8) other distinctions in the social setting or function of the demand.[119] With its generous view of the scope of constitutional privilege, the court did not have to achieve more precise constitutional delineation to conclude that the broad statutory language did reach many threats that are protected against criminal penalties. Given the narrow situations in which the Oregon drafters had privileged threats that would otherwise be within the statute, the court concluded that it should not attempt to rewrite the provision to eliminate its unconstitutional features and, therefore, held the statute invalid on its face.

Summary

This survey has been highly selective, omitting many important areas of First Amendment adjudication and giving uneven attention to the areas that have been covered. The principal concentration has been on general themes and particular cases which are especially relevant to speech that encourages crime or that risks a criminal response and to speech that is coercive in some sense. Certain other cases that have significant implications for problems discussed in subsequent chapters are addressed there. These cases include some decided since William Rehnquist became chief justice.

The next chapter seeks to draw some general lessons about First Amendment approaches that may be partly derived from the history of adjudication this chapter has traced. Much of what has been described here is also the foundation for the more specific doctrinal analyses and proposals found in the rest of the book.

Notes

1. 2 J. Story, *Commentaries on the Constitution of the United States*, ed. M. Bigelow, § 1880 (5th ed., Boston, Little, Brown & Co. 1891).

2. 2 T. Cooley, *Constitutional Limitations which Rest upon the Legislative Power of the States of the American Union*, ed. W. Carrington, 886 (8th ed., Boston, Little, Brown & Co. 1927).

3. The state cases are summarized and the Supreme Court opinions analyzed in D. Rabban, "The First Amendment in Its Forgotten Years," 90 *Yale Law Journal* 514, 522–55 (1981).

4. 171 N.Y. 423, 64 N.E. 175 (1902).

5. Id. at 431, 64 N.E. at 178.

6. See Rabban, note 3 supra, at 559–78.

7. See Z. Chafee, *Free Speech in the United States* 39, 51–52 (Cambridge, Mass., Harvard University Press 1941). There were roughly 2000 prosecutions under the act.

8. 249 U.S. 47 (1919).

9. 249 U.S. 204 (1919).

10. 249 U.S. 211 (1919).

11. 268 U.S. 652 (1925).

12. 274 U.S. 357 (1927).

13. Rabban argues persuasively that, when originally formulated, the clear-and-present-danger test was not seen as a sharp departure from the older principle that speech could be punished because of its "bad tendency." Rabban, note 3, at 580–86. See also E. Freund, "The Debs Case and Freedom of Speech," 40 *University of Chicago Law Review* 240–42 (1973); Y. Rogat and J. O'Fallon, "Mr. Justice Holmes: A Dissenting Opinion—The Speech Cases," 36 *Stanford Law Review* 1349 (1984).

14. 250 U.S. 616, 624 (1919).

15. Id. at 630. This passage is often cited as the classic statement of the "marketplace of ideas" concept discussed in Chapter 2.

16. 268 U.S. at 672 (1925).

17. 274 U.S. at 372 (1927).

18. Id. at 377. As Robert Cover emphasized, the main significance of an emergency for Brandeis concerned "disruption of the natural deliberative political process." R. Cover, "The Left, the Right, and the First Amendment: 1918–1928," 40 *Maryland Law Review*, 349, 380 (1981). The apparent addition of such broad and eloquent language about an issue not properly raised before the lower courts in the case is explained by Brandeis's having written much of the opinion for a dissent in a highly important case involving a leader of the Communist party, whose death made that case moot. Id. at 384–85.

19. 274 U.S. at 376–78.

20. 249 U.S. at 206.

21. 250 U.S. at 627 (emphasis added). Holmes's view here is more debatable than the text intimates, because he had a distinctly objective view of intent for purposes of criminal law.

22. 274 U.S. at 376.

23. Id. at 378.

24. 251 U.S. 466 (1920).

25. 244 F. 535 (S.D.N.Y. 1917), reversed 246 F. 24 (2d Cir. 1917).

26. See G. Gunther, "Learned Hand and the Origins of Modern First Amendment Doctrine: Some Fragments of History," 27 *Stanford Law Review* 719, 725–32 (1975).

27. 244 F. at 540.

28. Id.

29. Hand says that to counsel is to urge someone that it is his interest or duty to perform an act. I take this to mean that abstract approval of actions does not count as counseling, but I do not think Hand means to suggest that an explicit encouragement, "Kill him now, Jack," should be immune from punishment because it includes no reference to interest or duty.

Since Hand does not make likely harm an aspect of his test, that test is less speech-protective than "clear and present danger" in that respect.

30. G. Gunther, note 26 supra, at 749.

31. 283 U.S. 359 (1931).

32. 299 U.S. 353 (1937).

33. 301 U.S. 242 (1937).

34. 319 U.S. 583 (1943).

35. Id. at 590.

36. 322 U.S. 680 (1944).

37. Id. at 694.

38. Id. at 686–87.

39. 325 U.S. 478 (1945).

40. The First Amendment issue was not treated by the litigants, and this might explain Stone's failure to mention it, but one would have expected him to note that reservation if that was what was involved.

41. 303 U.S. 444 (1938).

42. 308 U.S. 147 (1939).

43. Id. at 162.

44. 310 U.S. 296 (1940).

45. Id. at 308.

46. Id. at 309–10.

47. Id. at 311.

48. 315 U.S. 568 (1942).

49. Id. at 571–72.

50. 340 U.S. 315 (1951).

51. Id. at 320.

52. Dissenting opinions of Justices Black and Douglas. Id. at 321, 329.

53. See *Gregory* v. *City of Chicago*, 394 U.S. 111 (1969).

54. 337 U.S. 1 (1949).

55. Id. at 35.

56. 343 U.S. 250 (1952).

57. 314 U.S. 252 (1941).

58. See *Pennekamp* v. *Florida*, 328 U.S. 331 (1946); *Craig* v. *Harney*, 331 U.S. 367 (1947); *Wood* v. *Georgia*, 370 U.S. 375 (1962). In the *Wood* case, however, some of Chief Justice Warren's majority opinion, id. at 390, reads as if the attempt to influence a grand jury investigating possible political abuse may actually have been beneficial.

59. 314 U.S. at 263.

60. In *Craig* v. *Harney*, 331 U.S. at 376, the Court said that "Judges are supposed to be men of fortitude, able to thrive in a hardy climate."

61. 310 U.S. 88 (1940).

62. Id. at 105.

63. See, e.g., *International Brotherhood of Teamsters* v. *Vogt*, 354 U.S. 284 (1957).

64. T. Emerson, *The System of Freedom of Expression* 445 (New York, Random House 1970).

65. See *Gompers* v. *Bucks Stove & Range Co.*, 221 U.S. 418, 439 (1911) (boycotts based on union lists of employers as "Unfair" and "We don't patronize"; id. at 420).

66. 323 U.S. 516 (1945).

67. Id. at 530.

68. Id. at 534–35.

69. 341 U.S. 494 (1951).

70. Id. at 496.

71. Id. at 510.

72. Id. at 551.

73. Id. at 570.

74. Id. at 568.

75. Id. at 573.

76. Id. at 524–25.

77. Id. at 581.

78. 354 U.S. 298 (1957). One author has reported that all Smith Act convictions appealed between the Supreme Court's decisions in *Dennis* and *Yates* were affirmed at the intermediate appellate level. R. Mollan, "Smith Act Prosecutions: The Effect of the *Dennis* and *Yates* Decisions," 26 *University of Pittsburgh Law Review* 705, 723 (1965).

79. 354 U.S. at 340.

80. 367 U.S. 203 (1961).

81. 367 U.S. 290 (1961).

82. 367 U.S. at 234.

83. For example, *Aptheker* v. *Secretary of State*, 378 U.S. 500 (1964); *United States* v. *Robel*, 389 U.S. 258 (1967). See generally H. Monaghan, "Overbreadth," 1981 *Supreme Court Review* 1.

84. Compare *Elfbrandt* v. *Russell*, 384 U.S. 111 (1966), and *Keyishian* v. *Board of Regents*, 385 U.S. 589 (1967), with *Cole* v. *Richardson*, 405 U.S. 676 (1972).

85. See, e.g., *NAACP* v. *Button*, 371 U.S. 415 (1963); *Gibson* v. *Florida Investigation Committee*, 372 U.S. 539 (1963).

86. 376 U.S. 254, 270 (1964). For the view that this case put the theory of the speech clause "right side up," see H. Kalven, "The New York Times Case: A Note on 'The Central Meaning of the First Amendment,'" 1964 *Supreme Court Review* 191.

87. 354 U.S. 476 (1957).

88. *Memoirs* v. *Massachusetts*, 383 U.S. 413 (1966).

89. *Ginzburg* v. *United States*, 383 U.S. 463 (1966).

90. 385 U.S. 116 (1966).

91. 394 U.S. 705 (1969).

92. 395 U.S. 444 (1969).

93. Id. at 447.

94. Id. at 456–57.

95. 416 F.2d 165 (1st Cir. 1969).

96. Id. at 173.

97. For an appraisal that concludes that free speech was faring badly under the Burger Court, see T. Emerson, "First Amendment Doctrine and the Burger Court," 68 *California Law Review* 422 (1980).

98. 414 U.S. 105 (1973).

99. For example, *Broadrick* v. *Oklahoma*, 413 U.S. 601, 618 (1973); *Brockett* v. *Spokane Arcades, Inc.*, 472 U.S. 491 (1985). A critical view of the Burger Court's approach to overbreadth is found in M. Redish, "The Warren Court, the Burger Court and the First Amendment Overbreadth Doctrine," 78 *Northwestern University Law Review* 1031 (1983).

100. *Miller* v. *California*, 413 U.S. 15, 24 (1973).

101. See, e.g., *Gertz* v. *Robert Welch, Inc.*, 418 U.S. 323 (1974). In *Dun & Bradstreet* v. *Greenmoss Builders, Inc.*, 472 U.S. 749 (1985), the Court held that, when communication is to a limited business audience, punitive damages may be imposed without a showing of actual malice. In *Time, Inc.* v. *Firestone*, 424 U.S. 448 (1976), the Court indicated that someone is not a public figure unless he is especially prominent or has thrust himself into the forefront of particular public controversies.

102. 403 U.S. 15 (1971).

103. Id. at 26.

104. For example, *Gooding* v. *Wilson*, 405 U.S. 518 (1972); *Lewis* v. *City of New Orleans*, 415 U.S. 130 (1974). See also *Rosenfeld* v. *New Jersey*, 408 U.S. 901 (1972). See also *Spence* v. *Washington*, 418 U.S. 405 (1974), in which the Court indicated that affixing a peace symbol to a flag is constitutionally protected despite possible offense to the sensibilities of observers.

105. *Collin* v. *Smith*, 578 F.2d 1197 (7th Cir. 1978), certiorari denied, 439 U.S. 916 (1978). See also *State* v. *Harrington*, 67 Or. App. 608, 680 P.2d 666 (1984), holding that under the state constitution abusive language cannot be punished in order to protect listeners.

106. *FCC* v. *Pacifica Foundation*, 438 U.S. 726 (1978).

107. *Virginia Board of Pharmacy* v. *Virginia Citizens Consumer Council*, 425 U.S. 748 (1976).

108. *Ohralik* v. *Ohio State Bar Ass'n*, 436 U.S. 447, 455–56 (1978).

109. See *Central Hudson Gas & Elec. Corp.* v. *Public Service Comm'n*, 447 U.S. 557 (1980).

110. *Young* v. *American Mini Theatres*, 427 U.S. 50, 61, 70 (1976).

111. 438 U.S. at 743.

112. 427 U.S. at 85–86.

113. 458 U.S. 886 (1982).

114. See generally S. Williams, "Distinguishing Protected from Unprotected Campaign Speech," 33 *Labor Law Journal* 265 (1982).

115. 395 U.S. 575 (1969).

116. *State* v. *Robertson*, 293 Or. 402, 649 P.2d 569 (1982).

117. See H. Linde, "'Clear and Present Danger' Reexamined: Dissonance in the Brandenburg Concerto," 22 *Stanford Law Review* 1163, 1183–86 (1970).

118. 293 Or. at 412, 649 P.2d at 576.

119. 293 Or. at 420, 649 P.2d at 581.

12

General Approaches to
First Amendment Interpretation

This chapter, a bridge between the two preceding chapters and those to follow, draws from my general observations about constitutional interpretation and the summary of First Amendment adjudication and discusses some general matters involving interpretation of the free speech and free press clauses. After some introductory words about a broadly libertarian approach toward the constitutional protection of speech and about the core of constitutional protection, I consider the edges of what counts as speech under the Constitution and the appropriate tests for determining whether suppression is permissible for communication that does count as speech. These questions are interrelated, because what is to be protected at all will depend on how strong the protection is, and vice versa. The chapters in Part II have already reflected this close nexus, as I have proceeded from the outer boundaries of what falls within a political principle of free speech to what communications should actually be unrestricted. The course of most of the chapters following this one is similar. Here I reverse the order, considering tests for suppression first. This reversal helps strongly to emphasize that what reasonably counts as speech rests in no small part on how absolute the protections of speech are. The chapter's order also suggests another point: that some standards that are practically identical in import might be viewed either as tests for suppression of what counts as speech or as principles for what qualifies as speech in the first instance. A principle that communication causing immediate harm may be punished, for example, may be treated as a test for prohibiting otherwise protected speech or as a standard for what amounts to action rather than speech and falls outside the First Amendment for that reason.[1]

As throughout the book, I focus on possible criminal penalties and to a much lesser extent on direct civil liability for communication. Much of the modern development of First Amendment law has concerned time, place, and manner restrictions and indirect interferences with expression: Can distribution of materials for religious or other causes be restricted at state fairs?[2] Must public buses carry ideological messages if they carry commercial messages?[3] May candidates and their supporters be restricted in their campaign expenses?[4] Any full account of First Amendment law would have to give close attention to these sorts of cases. Although some of them come in for occasional mention in the pages that follow and although much of what I say has implications for their successors, my treatment of free speech tests pertains to the issue of suppression.

The rest of the chapters in Part III suggest rather specific doctrinal principles for initial inclusion in what is to count as speech and for permissible prohibition of what is initially included. As a consequence, much of this chapter has a negative tone. I say comparatively little about the three broad approaches derivable from Supreme Court opinions which I believe are most highly relevant to criminal suppression of speech: clear and present danger, incitement, and the distinction between speech and action. I focus instead on a number of other approaches and explain why each of these is unsound or incomplete, needing to be employed in conjunction with other sorts of approaches rather than taken as *the key* to First Amendment analysis. These explanations clear the ground for the more particular treatment of concrete problems and specific doctrinal principles that occupy the rest of the book.

I have suggested that the historical direction of First Amendment adjudication has been toward broader protection of speech and press. The present decisional law definitely represents a libertarian approach to free speech, and I have argued that social morality, sensitively interpreted, supports that approach. Although this libertarian position may not fairly be *derivable* from the open and general language of the First Amendment[5] and preconstitutional history, it is not in conflict with those criteria of interpretation.

The libertarian position is characterized by these central features: (a) a strong preference for speech when it is in competition with other values; (b) an interpretation of significant expression that is not limited to narrowly political concerns but embraces all subject matters of importance to individuals;[6] (c) a view that speech is valuable not only because of the rational content of communication but also because individuals should be able to transmit to others and give vent to their feelings. This approach, or important features of it, need not necessarily be right for all times and all societies with a commitment to liberal democracy. If, for example, the United States were subjected to the kind of religious and political violence that now characterizes Northern Ireland or Lebanon or if social conditions resembled those in Germany in the 1920s, perhaps legislatures would properly refuse to tolerate many forms of communication that may exacerbate hatreds among groups, and perhaps the First Amendment would properly be interpreted flexibly enough to permit suppressions not now properly allowable in the United States. I do believe that a strongly libertarian approach captures an ideal and is appropriate for our era in this country, and I assume that doctrinal standards should continue to embody it.[7]

What follows in this chapter and succeeding chapters rests on the assumption that the free speech and free press clauses, like a political principle of liberty of speech, centrally concern expressions of belief about values and facts, including expressions of feeling. Assertions of values and of general facts should, with very limited exceptions, be beyond government suppression. This safeguard embraces, as has been clear since *Schenck*, expressions of belief in what are commonly thought to be abhorrent practices, for example, revolutionary violence, racial genocide, polygamy. So long as the speaker merely states in a theoretical way that such practices are desirable or justified and does not urge action upon his listeners, he is protected by the First Amendment.

If the expression of ideas about what is good, right, or desirable can ever be suppressed, the basis must be a great risk of substantial harm that does not derive from considered acceptance of the ideas in question. General factual assertions, claims about the truths of science and social science, are similarly protected. Perhaps the dissemination of *some* general facts, for example, how to make an atomic weapon, is so very dangerous that suppression is acceptable, but such cases, discussed later, are highly exceptional. Expressions about more particular matters—who killed whom, where troops are stationed, how one feels about events or people, what is the nature and availability of specific commercial products—are also generally protected, though here the claims that government may suppress in order to protect national security, emotional tranquility or reputation, or consumer interests are more frequently strong. Nevertheless, the general principle remains that assertions of fact and feeling and abstract statements of value enjoy First Amendment protection, unless contrary treatment is warranted by some specifically justified exception.

Constitutional Tests for Suppression of What Qualifies Initially as Speech: Categorical and Protective Tests

I turn now to standards that might be used to decide whether forms of expression enjoying some preliminary protection under the First Amendment may nevertheless be forbidden, subjected either to criminal penalties or to civil liability.

I assume generally that the same standards are appropriate for state and for federal action. The principle that the Fourteenth Amendment makes federal guarantees of free speech and free press applicable against the states and the underlying ideas that for something as important as expression the states should be subject to constraints like those which apply to the federal government, are both so widely accepted now that "incorporation" of the free speech and free press clauses can be taken as a settled part of our law. Even if the federal constitution were to provide no protection against state restrictions on speech, courts interpreting state constitutions would appropriately protect speech. Since state constitutional language usually differs from that of the First Amendment, some outcomes would rightly vary depending on the jurisdiction involved, and that can happen even under the regime of incorporation when state texts arguably give greater protection to speech than does the federal document.

When one considers particular standards for adjudication of First Amendment cases of the sort studied here, some standards are plainly unacceptable. I begin with those.

Reasonableness and Dangerous Tendency

The reasonableness test used by the Court in *Gitlow* v. *New York* is most obviously misguided. Even when a legislature has focused upon and forbidden particular classes of speech, the Supreme Court would be giving insufficient effect to the value of expression if it upheld a statutory prohibition whenever it could find a "reasonable" basis for its enactment. In part, the problem is that the legislature's judgment in an earlier period of time about the harmful potentiality of classes of speech can hardly be taken as conclusive at a later time. The danger of, say, anarchist doctrine may have decreased radically since passage of a criminal-anarchism statute; yet legislatures do not remain continually attentive to the degree of present need and often do not repeal statutes when the need for them has diminished beyond the level of justification. But, quite apart from this temporal point, legislation unsupported by *any* reasonable argument is very rare; to allow a legislature to prohibit speech subject only to that very relaxed test would be virtually to write out the First Amendment as a significant protection of speech.

The *Gitlow* majority indicated that a court must inquire about the dangerous tendency of speech only when the legislature has not made a judgment about its harmfulness. It would be possible to stiffen the *Gitlow* approach slightly by demanding in each case a judicial determination that particular speech has a dangerous tendency. But allowing speech to be punished because of a finding that its natural or probable effect would be to cause harm would still fall woefully short of appropriate constitutional protection. Conceivably, a "dangerous tendency" approach radically more protective than the traditional version might be developed, one that demanded substantial dangers of great harms. I shall not discuss such a possibility, both because it is so far from the historical understanding of "dangerous tendency" and because a very strict "dangerous tendency" approach would approximate "clear and present danger."

Ad Hoc Balancing

Despite the superficial attractiveness of a standard that allows all relevant considerations to be taken into account, the "ad hoc balancing test," proposed as a general standard in Justice Frankfurter's opinion in *Dennis* v. *United States*, is also inapt. Under an *ad hoc balancing test*, a court balances "the competing private and public interests at stake in the particular circumstances shown."[8] Whatever the merits of such an approach for a variety of situations in which regulation indirectly inhibits speech, it is not satisfactory for the problem of criminal prohibitions on expression.[9] Examination of why this approach is unsatisfactory affords a brief exploration of "categorical balancing" and other possible alternatives.

When ad hoc balancing includes substantial deference to the legislature, as did the version elaborated by Justice Frankfurter in *Dennis*, it is subject to the fatal objection that its practical bite is almost as slight as that of the rational-basis test. If the ultimate criterion is whether the legislature might reasonably have balanced the factors as it did, only rarely will a court give a negative answer. That objection to ad hoc balancing might be overcome by balancing in a way that does not give legislative judgments such deference, but a nondeferential approach may be easier to state than to put into practice. Once the Court announces that its standard is simply an open-ended examination of all relevant considerations to determine whether the weight in favor of suppression is greater than the weight against it, a conclusion that the legislature's attempt to weigh all relevant considerations has been inadequate may be too impolitic to swallow. Because there is no single correct way to decide what interests are to be thrown into the balance, no standard to determine the level of abstraction at which they are stated, and no evidently detached method for weighing relevant factors once they are formulated, a judicial decision to invalidate is bound to look like the judges' imposing their subjective judgments in preference to the judgments of the legislature. Since judges will not want to appear frequently in that position, a simple ad hoc balancing test is inherently likely to introduce considerable deference.

Even if deference could be avoided, the test would be inadequate. If the justices simply engaged in a candid weighing of all relevant factors without a predisposition to decide one way or another, the standard would be insufficiently protective of speech; for speech should be proscribed only for very strong reasons. Theoretically, a court could use an ad hoc balancing approach with a strong predisposition in favor of speech, and a "compelling interest" standard could be employed in this way. Unfortunately, unless the courts undertake to define what kinds of statutes are permissible and what classes of speech are protected, a test of constitutionality gives insufficient guidance to legislative bodies and to those who wish to engage in legislatively proscribed speech. No matter how speech-protective its flavor, a genuinely ad hoc or highly particularistic approach is defective for the basic First Amendment problems discussed in this study, whether or not it is the best that can be done for various indirect interferences with speech.[10] Although alternative techniques cannot eliminate judicial choice among values, they can constrain and focus the range of choice, afford more predictability about many situations,[11] and give judges a basis for invalidation other than a determination that the political branches have not wisely balanced competing interests on a particular occasion.

This conclusion raises the question whether the Court can do without balancing, a question relevant for tests applied both to presumptively protected speech and to the criteria for what is presumptively protected speech. Put generally, the alternative to ad hoc balancing is *categorical adjudication*: cases are determined by whether situations fall inside or outside particular categories. Now, we can perhaps imagine categorization that is virtually blind to evaluation, trying only to give effect to the ordinary significance of constitutional language. But a consistent theme of this book has been that free speech must be understood in terms of the justifications for it; if there are to be critical categories of First Amendment adjudication they should be sensitive to the values of speech. Does it follow that the only practical alternative to ad hoc balancing is categorical balancing? That depends on how narrowly or loosely categorical balancing is conceived.[12]

Explicit and full categorical balancing would involve a balancing of relevant considerations on each side to settle what the determinative categories are to be. Thus, one might look at all the reasons to protect and suppress encouragements to crime in order to arrive at classifications of protected encouragements. After the basic categories are set, adjudication would consist mainly of deciding how particular facts relate to those categories, but a second stage of balancing might also occur: in deciding how to deal with borderline instances, the courts might balance the considerations bearing on these instances to determine on which side to place them.

Once categorical balancing is understood in this way, we can see that not all principles of categorization that involve evaluation *necessarily* involve balancing.

A court might focus on a single central value, say expressive value, in deciding how to categorize, not taking competing considerations into account at all. Or a court might admit as relevant one competing value, say the danger of violence, without undertaking a comprehensive weighing of considerations. Either at the stage of initial characterization or at the stage of application to borderline instances, or at both stages, the court might proceed by some methodology other than explicit balancing.

Showing, as the last paragraph does, that categorization other than categorical balancing is a conceptual possibility does not establish that it is a practical alternative and, if it is, that it is a methodology preferable to categorical balancing. On the first question, there can be no doubt that an implicit evaluation of competing interests often influences exercises in categorization that do not refer to a balancing of factors. Nonetheless, judges and lawyers often engage in categorizations to give effect to central concepts in a manner that does not represent a conscious attempt to weigh interests on each side.[13] There is no reason to suppose that in practice all evaluative categorization inevitably involves full categorical balancing.

The question of a preferred methodology is troublesome. A strength of balancing is that it takes everything relevant into account. The corresponding weaknesses are that lawyers and judges may not be well suited to weigh all relevant factors and that the absence of objective standards for weighing makes judgment seem rather arbitrary. These worries are diminished somewhat when balancing is categorical rather than ad hoc, but they are not eliminated. On behalf of conceptual elaboration, it may be said that this lies more within the lawyer's competence, but such elaboration risks arid conceptualism and unpalatable results in extreme cases, where competing, disregarded interests are very strong.

I believe that no set of abstract comments can establish a single best methodology. Close attention has to be given to kinds of constitutional problems and different levels of legal relevance. Perhaps, for example, the different treatments of encouragement and advice should be based on some sort of categorical balancing, but the line between encouragement and advice should depend exclusively on an elaboration of what those concepts mean that does not involve explicit balancing. The rest of the book may be understood as an implicit demonstration that First Amendment categories need to be based on some combination of explicit balancing and evaluative conceptualization that does not involve explicit balancing.[14] Exactly where evaluative conceptualization leaves off and explicit balancing begins is not transparent; for many legal standards, people can argue whether they are a form of categorical balancing or not. In what follows, I do not attempt to label each established or proposed standard as involving ad hoc or categorical balancing or some other approach to classification; nevertheless, my defense of various standards and the distinctions they draw will indicate to what extent an explicit or implicit balance of competing factors is involved.

Evil Discounted by Improbability

The revision of the clear-and-present-danger test endorsed by the plurality in *Dennis* is, like reasonableness, dangerous tendency, and ad hoc balancing, an unacceptable approach. Under *Dennis*, what controls is the magnitude of the evil discounted by its improbability. By requiring guesses about the remote likelihood of serious evils, the test makes impossible demands on judges or juries. And its abandonment of any requirement of imminency reflects inadequate attention to the significance of countervailing speech. Not only do the uncertain effects of countervailing speech make prediction extremely difficult; such speech creates the possibility of considered decision, which is important in its own right. As the decision in the case shows, the *Dennis* test is not likely to yield significant protection of speech.

Content Regulation

The standard I now discuss is undoubtedly an important part of First Amendment jurisprudence which certainly has relevance for criminal prohibitions of speech. Here I try briefly to clarify its significance for the main subject matter of this study and to indicate its limited usefulness for our purposes.

A distinction between constitutional treatment of content-based and content-neutral regulations has been said by Geoffrey Stone to be "the Burger Court's foremost contribution to first amendment analysis, and . . . the most pervasively employed doctrine in the jurisprudence of free expression."[15] When the government prefers some messages over others, its action will be subjected to a more stringent standard than when it treats all messages equally, say by banning all billboards.[16] The underlying principle is that popular messages should not be favored over unpopular ones. In a thorough treatment of the topic, Dean Stone suggests that safeguarding equality,[17] limiting prohibitions aimed at communicative impact, preventing distortion of public debate, and curtailing prohibitions based on disapproval of ideas justify the Court's more protective treatment of content-based restrictions.[18] The category of content-based restrictions overlaps to a high degree with the category of restrictions aimed at communicative impact,[19] which important commentators have regarded as the category to which courts should afford greater protection by applying a more stringent standard of review.[20] What I say in this section largely applies to the distinction between restrictions which are aimed at communicative impact and those which are not, as well as to the distinction between content-based and content-neutral restrictions.

Exactly what counts as a content-based restriction is a bit slippery. The obvious examples are regulations that plainly prefer one viewpoint over another, but the Supreme Court has talked sometimes about distinctions concerning subject matter, say politics as compared with sex, as content regulation as well.[21] And what is one to say of restrictions of profanity or of speech that threatens independently defined social harms such as crimes? Is the basis for content regulation the face of a statute or apparent legislative motivation or a combination of these? If the reason for subjecting content restrictions to more stringent standards of review lies in free speech values, one needs to ask, within the confines of appropriate judicial inquiry, how far the particular distinction explicitly or implicitly drawn by the legislature threatens those values.[22]

How the distinction between content-based and content-neutral restrictions relates to the main subjects of this study is complicated. I should note at the outset that the distinction can be relevant not only to regulation of what obviously counts as speech within the First Amendment; it also touches what is reached by a free speech principle and by the First Amendment. Let us suppose that a city can and does forbid sleeping in the public parts of its railway and bus terminals. On its face such a regulation does not implicate free speech. But if the city forbids only those sleepers who sleep in order to convey criticism of the government, it has engaged in content regulation,[23] and such a regulation is presumptively invalid under the First Amendment.

A central theme of this book is the different ways in which language is used. How does this theme relate to content regulation? I have urged that certain uses of language, such as words of agreement, do not raise free speech issues. If that is correct, the legislature's distinction between words of agreement (conspiracies to steal are punished) and words of advocacy (claims about the justice of theft by the poor from the rich are unpunished) cannot be a content regulation calling for stringent review. The distinction is based on the content of the communications, but the relevant content determines whether a principle of free speech applies at all. What of distinctions within the treatment of agreements (agreements to steal are punished, agreements to play chess are not)? These are certainly content distinctions; criminal prohibitions turn on the substance of the agreements. But, again, no free speech issue is involved. If words of agreement are really a form of "action" rather than "speech," it is all right to forbid forms of action that are dangerous or harmful, just as one might forbid shooting a gun at a person as distinct from shooting a gun at a paper target. We may conclude that, although excluding a form of communication from a free speech principle and from the First Amendment does involve attention to content, neither that exclusion nor most differences of treatment within the excluded category involves content regulation in the sense that calls for careful scrutiny under the First Amendment.

Although my ultimate conclusions are the same, matters become more complicated when we turn to "weak imperatives," requests and simple encouragements, which I have claimed are covered by a free speech principle, but covered less powerfully than are expressions of fact and value. Is a legislative distinction between solicitation (of a particular theft) and advocacy (of theft by the poor) content regulation? Here we have two forms of communication to which the First Amendment applies, but, if I am right that requests and encouragements are more "action" and less "speech" than advocacy of ideas, their less favored treatment should not, of itself, count as the kind of content regulation that generates concern. That leaves distinctions within the form of communication (urgings to specific crimes are punished, urgings to read an article carefully are not). It might be argued that this distinction does turn on how the comparative messages are viewed, that the legislature favors approval of careful reading and not approval of crime. But the point of punishing solicitations is their close relation to action; for the legislature to punish communications that are close to harmful actions and not to punish communications that are close to desirable actions does not involve viewpoint or subject-matter discrimination of the worrisome kind.

In short, for many communications likely to cause crimes, the idea of content-neutrality is not a quick fix for most statutes and situations. Unless the idea that content regulations are subject to stringent review is very carefully understood, it can become a hindrance rather than an aid to thoughtful analysis. In the chapters that follow, analysis proceeds more directly in terms of the values of free speech; with limited exceptions, the distinction between content-based and content-neutral regulations fails to illuminate what is at stake.

Review of Legislation

The standard addressed here, which does not fit neatly the dichotomy between tests for suppression of presumptively protected speech and criteria of original exclusion and inclusion, suggests that the main job of courts is to review what legislatures have done, not to pass on whether individuals are protected in particular situations. Taken alone, this standard leaves open what criteria courts will employ in deciding whether legislation is acceptable, and thus crosscuts many of the other standards examined in this chapter.

There is much that is sound in the proposal defended by Hans Linde in his writings on and off the bench: that the First Amendment is basically directed at legislatures—"Congress shall make no law"—and that the main force of the amendment is to forbid legislation that is directed at speech.[24] Legislators considering statutes need to be guided by constitutional standards, and these standards should be comprehensible to them. Undoubtedly a substantial part of judicial implementation of the First Amendment is to review the adequacy of legislative formulations. And one of the clearest directions that can be given legislators is that they are not to suppress ideas that they disfavor.

One should not suppose, however, either that the whole of the judicial function can be reduced to assessing the permissibility of legislative formulations or that every piece of legislation explicitly directed at speech is presumptively invalid. Since even the best drafted legislation may have some applications that raise serious free speech problems, courts have room to decide whether particular activity is constitutionally protected and whether particular applications of statutes are unconstitutional. The idea that it is legislation *directed at speech* that is presumptively invalid is treated in the section on "speech" and "action."

Clear and Present Danger and Incitement

Once inadequate tests are set aside and the ideas of "no content regulation" and attention to legislative formulation are understood to be of significant but limited help for analyzing criminal speech, we are left with two standards of review in Supreme Court opinions that reflect a libertarian approach to speech: clear and present danger, and incitement. Our survey of the cases has revealed some of the difficulties with each of these standards standing alone and with the requirement of *Brandenburg* v. *Ohio* that incitement and clear and present danger coalesce. Rather than review the strengths and drawbacks of each test in general, I indicate in the following chapters what are sound principles for dealing with the problems that the tests address, explaining how far these principles coincide with what the Supreme Court has said and done and attempting to show why the principles are preferable to alternative answers that might be derived from exclusive reliance on one of these two standards.

The Range of Coverage

With at least some rough sense of the sorts of constitutional tests that might be applied to speech that the First Amendment preliminarily reaches, we are ready to address the threshold question of coverage: Are there some communications or other activities with expressive significance that are simply outside the boundaries of the free speech and free press clauses, at least in the absence of some legislative aim that itself is impermissible under those clauses?

In Chapter 2, I indicated that a principle of free speech claims that expression is deserving of protection to a degree that exceeds what is afforded by a general principle of liberty. The First Amendment plays the same role in constitutional adjudication. In theory at least, any legislative restriction of liberty is subject to some judicial test of reasonableness under the due-process clauses of the Fifth and Fourteenth Amendments. The reason why it matters whether or not something falls within the First Amendment is that if it does then some more stringent test applies. Under a libertarian approach to free speech, a substantially more stringent test applies, at least in many instances.

These general observations form the background for this initial consideration of constitutional coverage. In the ensuing chapters, I deal with a number of more specific questions. Here I offer some broad comments which build on the ideas of previous chapters.

Expression versus Action

In various contexts, the Supreme Court has considered whether behavior amounts to protected speech or unprotected action, and some commentators, most notably Thomas Emerson, have suggested that the distinction between expression and action is the key to First Amendment adjudication,[25] rendering unnecessary and inapt standards of review like clear and present danger.

Speech, of course, is itself a form of action, but the ground for the dividing line is that some behavior is distinctly expression and other behavior is not. Under the *expression-action approach*, status under the First Amendment depends on the category into which the behavior falls. In reality, the purported distinction is really a combination of distinctions, and the divisions required are often less a matter of separating apples from oranges than deciding where along a continuum to fix a demarcation. Among the reasons why something expressive may be considered action are: (1) the speech is mixed with nonspeech conduct, such as blocking traffic; (2) the speech is part of an integrated course of action whose aim is to cause a reaction by a listener that has little to do with the values of expression, as in committing blackmail; (3) the speech is an intimate part of a nonexpressive project, such as the giving of instructions on how to rob a bank; (4) the speech may cause a listener to commit an immediate harm; (5) the audience must react without making an assessment of its own, as when the speaker falsely shouts "fire" in a crowded theater; (6) the speaker aims for a reaction, fear or pleasure, that has nothing to do with the listener's considered response to what the speaker has said; (7) the speaker aims to do something directly by his words, such as make an agreement. If someone thought that any or all of these divisions were important constitutionally, he might think either that what mattered was the basis for the legislature's prohibitions—that is, what the legislation was aiming at—or that what mattered was the character of individual actions, or both.[26] He might think, with Emerson, that all that properly qualifies as speech is absolutely protected against suppression or direct civil liability or that speech is protected less than absolutely; he might think that the expression-action distinction, properly understood and applied, resolves all First Amendment problems or instead that supplementary standards are needed.

My strenuous reiteration of the different uses of language and my claim that much language does something rather than says something may be understood as developing distinctions between speech and action. A great deal of what I have said in Parts I and II and will say about particular constitutional problems in Part III is an elaboration of some divisions between speech and action. This book, then, reflects in many respects the inclination to divide speech from action.

Nevertheless, I do not believe that the expression-action distinction is *the* central key to First Amendment adjudication. For some problems, it is not particularly helpful for understanding what is at stake; for some others, it is positively misleading, either not taking into account initially relevant variables or doing so only at the expense of distortion of its own significance. That is true about copyright restrictions, which preclude speech by the person who breaches the copyright.[27] It is also true, I shall contend, about encouragements to crime, a category of usage that I have suggested floats uncomfortably between expression and action, combining elements of each. Much of what I argue in the remaining chapters could comfortably be translated in terms of distinctions between speech and action, though I shall not usually speak in just those terms. Other claims do not fit the distinction so well, and in Chapter 15 I explain why the line between expression and action is not well suited to making some of the appropriate demarcations for encouragements.

In this chapter, I shall address one particular variant of the line between speech and something more: the view that, when a penal provision is directed at speech, it is subject to more severe scrutiny than when the provision contains other elements. The Oregon Supreme Court has employed this view in resolving a number of cases under the free speech clause in the Oregon Constitution.[28]

Some ambiguity exists in the notion of legislation directed at speech, and courts should resist understanding that notion in a manner that would place undue weight on a formal distinction. An illustration makes the point. Suppose that state legislature *A* makes criminal the acquisition of money through use of a coercive threat to destroy property. On one interpretation, that is not legislation directed at speech, because the crime requires an element other than speech, the giving of money by the person threatened. Suppose that state *A* also has a general attempt statute, making criminal unsuccessful attempts to commit crimes, and that within the state it has always been supposed that threats can constitute a kind of attempt. In that event, a person making an unsuccessful threat can be punished. Suppose that the legislature of state *B* adopts as a basic substantive crime the making of a coercive threat to destroy property with the intent to acquire money. The practical result of the legislation is the same. But now it might be said that the legislation is directed at speech, generating a more serious First Amendment problem, since making the threat is the only element of the crime.[29] Such a formalistic approach would be implausible; the legislature should certainly be able to do directly what it can do indirectly by a combination of substantive-crime plus attempt doctrine. Another possible approach is to say that, when the legislature aims at certain kinds of harms, such as physical fear or coercive influence, its action is not directed at speech, even if communication is the only actual element of the crime.[30] But on this view, the basic notion that legislation directed at speech is subject to special scrutiny may no longer provide much help in the analysis, since one is reduced to drawing distinctions based on the effects speech is intended to cause.

The Possible Inclusion of Everything Communicative or with Expressive Value

One possible approach to the question of what counts as speech is that *some* First Amendment test is appropriate whenever behavior the legislature prohibits has expressive value or is communicative.

The broadest formulation would be that whenever it is proposed to prohibit anyone from engaging in any activity that has any expressive value, a serious First Amendment question would be presented. Virtually every human endeavor has some expressive value; so the result of this approach would be effectively to eliminate the relaxed "rational basis" test. Every prohibition on liberty would call for some more stringent test under the First Amendment. More might be said about this approach, but it is enough to notice its absurdity. Whatever they were meant to do and might reasonably be interpreted to do, the free speech and free press clauses were not meant as a general protection of liberty and should not be so interpreted.

A second, narrower formulation would be that whenever it is proposed to prohibit anyone from engaging in oral or written communication or other *distinctly* expressive activity, a serious First Amendment problem would be presented. What I have in mind by "other distinctly expressive activity" is something, like flag burning, that is intended or is taken by its audience as mainly expressive. Not every claim of liberty would be reached by the First Amendment, but some things other than verbal and written communication would be. The reason for including all verbal and written communications would be that these are easily classifiable and that each communication has some expressive value. Under this approach, room might be left to distinguish among kinds of communications for the application of various constitutional tests, but all communications would come within the broad ambit of coverage.

In this chapter, I shall concentrate on the claim that all verbal and written communications fall within the reach of the First Amendment. Since the language of federal and state provisions and their history yield little support for the position that all communications are reached by the First Amendment, the argument for the position might be that only such broad coverage will give adequate protection of speech over the long run and will provide a workable approach for legislative drafting and judicial review.

To be tenable at all, the claim cannot be that every situation involving an utterance would trigger a *highly stringent* constitutional test. If the legislature can forbid restraints of trade without establishing a highly compelling need to do so, presumably it can forbid explicit agreements to restrain trade without establishing a highly compelling need to do so. If the First Amendment is to cover every utterance, the tests of constitutionality will have to be shaded in terms of expressive value or other criteria. This is the alternative I compare with my contention that some utterances do not raise First Amendment problems at all (beyond calling for an initial determination that they fall outside the range of constitutional protection).

On behalf of this alternative, one might urge that it is more sensitive to all relevant considerations, permitting an assessment of degrees of expressive value and a weighing that takes into account those degrees of value, as well perhaps as degrees in the social costs engendered by different types of utterances.

There are decisive objections to this claim. The expressive value of some kinds of utterance, including many words of agreement and other situation-altering utterances, is no different in quality or amount from the expressive value of many "ordinary" actions that do not involve utterance at all. Such expressive value is not sufficient to trigger a free speech balancing process for all these ordinary actions; nor should it be sufficient, simply because the action in question happens to be a kind of utterance. Moreover, a scheme that requires a judicial balance of expressive value against social harm for all kinds of utterances with *any* expressive value either becomes a kind of charade or else places excessive demands on courts. It becomes a charade if courts say that slight expressive value is enough to trigger a test marginally more stringent than "rational basis," but end up sustaining virtually any government reason for suppression. It places excessive demands on courts if they seriously try to compare the strength of the state's need with the expressive value of a broad range of classes of utterance. A critical practical defect of this approach is that it envisions a great number of claims of free speech protection which would be treated as initially valid but which would then be outweighed by fairly pale government showings of need. Such "weak" free speech tests might well start to spill over to cases in which the expressive value of utterances is genuinely significant and in which stringent protection has always been required. Thus, we can see that excluding some utterances from the ambit of the First Amendment may actually help to safeguard protection of utterances that are squarely within that ambit.[31]

Once one comes to understand how complicated the constitutional tests would need to be if all utterances were regarded as within the scope of the First Amendment, it becomes clear that such an approach, far from rendering legislative and judicial life relatively simple, would call for intricate distinctions and subtle differences of weight. The succeeding chapters provide a standard of comparison by offering approaches that exclude some communications from First Amendment coverage. They proceed on the assumption that a proper analysis looks mainly to the justifications for free speech to determine what utterances and other activities fall within or outside the First Amendment.

History as the Ground for Exclusion and Inclusion

One possible basis for deciding what is protected by the First Amendment is to ask which utterances were regarded as protected at the time the First and Fourteenth Amendments were adopted and which were obviously then thought to be unprotected since they had traditionally been made criminal. Obviously, it would matter exactly how the question about history was put, since there may have been no ascertainable view about some kinds of utterances. And the historical question might be treated as affecting the stringency of constitutional tests rather than possible exclusion. That is, instead of receiving no protection, communications historically regarded as not covered by the Constitution might receive some constitutional protection, but much less than communications historically envisioned as protected by the First and Fourteenth Amendments. I shall here consider this position in a relatively simplified form: if a type of communication was criminal at the time and if the approvers evidently accepted its having that status, it would receive no constitutional protection; other communications would be protected unless the government met some very high burden of justification.[32]

Taking the boundaries of crime at the time of adoption of the First and Fourteenth Amendments as settling the question whether something is within or without the free speech and free press clauses would be mistaken. Crimes once accepted without much examination may now be understood as seriously implicating the values of speech, and room should be left for expanding the ambit of constitutional protection to reach them, especially since those adopting free speech guarantees certainly did not survey the whole catalogue of crimes to see whether any ran afoul of liberty of expression. On the other hand, the creation of new crimes involving communication should not necessarily be suspect. Suppose that at the time of adoption certain threats to obtain money were treated as criminal, but that employing the same threats to obtain sexual favors was not criminal. That distinction hardly reflected some judgment about the boundaries of free expression; it reflected only a view, perhaps benighted, about what needed to be made criminal. If the scope of the original crime is constitutionally permissible, an extension of the crime to reach sexual favors should not be subject to a much more stringent constitutional test. The history matters, in terms of views about specific communications and in terms of general principles, and as a deposit of human experience, but historical intent as evidenced by the contemporaneous law of crime is not *the* critical First Amendment standard for what counts as speech or for degrees of protection.

The Possible Exclusion of Private Communications

I now address and reject three conceivable bases for exclusion. As I indicated in Chapter 3, a great deal of communication takes place in private; private communication, even self-communication, is a source of learning, of emotional expression, and of testing one's thoughts. There is no basis for supposing that communications in private are simply outside the reach of the First Amendment. As the Supreme Court has held when it actually addressed the problem, the free speech guarantee covers private communication.[33] That is not to say that it will never matter whether communication is in public or private; but the First Amendment applies to both.

The idea that the First Amendment protects only speech about general concerns—history, politics, morality, aesthetics, and so forth—is more plausible; but there are two powerful reasons for protecting speech about personal subjects. The first is that narrow personal subjects, say whether Jones is a trustworthy person or whether Rural Living, Inc. is a wise investment, matter a great deal to people, and discussion with others can illuminate judgment. The second reason is the manner in which general and personal concerns are intermingled. We learn about "human nature" or "liberal capitalist human nature" by understanding our acquaintances; our sense of business and economics in general is educated by evaluation of the prospects of a single firm. Both because the intrinsic reasons for free speech are relevant and because the appropriate line would be impossible to draw, the First Amendment reaches speech about personal as well as public concerns, though, again, some such distinction may make sense for the level of protection of some kinds of speech.

The Possible Exclusion of Nonpolitical Speech

Discussions in Chapter 3 and Chapter 10 have suggested that distinguishing political speech from other kinds of speech is extremely difficult, that much nonpolitical speech has obvious political relevance, and that most of the justifications for free speech are not limited to public affairs. The reasons why nonpolitical speech falls within a principle of free speech are ample to bring it within the coverage of the speech and press clauses, especially given the absence of any indication in language or historical intent that the clauses were meant to be limited to political speech. This conclusion is strengthened by the coverage of the free-exercise clause of religious speech, a clause that aimed to place outside state control what would then have been regarded and is still regarded by many as the most important domain of human understanding. As I have argued at more length in Chapter 10, if the free-exercise clause protects nonpolitical discourse about religious affairs and related matters of morality and history, it would be senseless to consider the free speech and press clauses as restricted to political affairs.

The Possible Exclusion of All Communications Designed to Promote Crimes or Designed to Promote Revolutionary Activity

Occasionally, writers have claimed that speech encouraging criminal action or revolutionary action simply falls outside the scope of the First Amendment.[34] That constitutional claim rests on the idea, explored in Chapter 6, that a commitment to free speech takes place within the context of a commitment to orderly ways of resolving issues and that speech encouraging illegal action or revolutionary action falls outside the boundaries of the "social contract" and thus does not warrant protection. My rejection of this idea in relation to a political principle of free speech indicates why the idea in either form is unsound for constitutional interpretation.

To address the constitutional question, we must first clarify the proposal. If it were said that any speech designed mainly to induce any action is outside the First Amendment, we would have not a thesis about criminal or revolutionary speech but a general thesis about action-inducing communication. The proposal here must be understood more narrowly as excluding speech that encourages crime or revolution, even if speech that encourages legally permitted acts is covered by the First Amendment; the exclusion is based on the nature of the actions urged.

One problem with the proposal is that it makes too much depend on the state of mind of the speaker. As we have seen, much of the justification for free speech lies in its effect on the audience, and much speech proves valuable for those who do not follow the recommendations of the speaker. Speech of considerable social importance cannot reasonably be placed wholly outside the First Amendment because of the impure intent of the speaker.

A second problem is that the proposal seems to assume the erroneous approach to the free speech and free press clauses that limits coverage to political speech. Speech about what persons are morally justified in doing is an important branch of expression. Among important moral choices is decision when it is acceptable to disobey the law or to engage in revolutionary activity. In the domain of practical morality, discussion of possible illegality cannot be ruled out, even if what is suggested transgresses our common political morality.

The third significant problem with the proposal is that not all encouragements of crime—or even of revolutionary activity—reject the ground rules of our society. I have already made the obvious point that many crimes, like speeding, have little political significance, and the more subtle point that occasional illegal civil disobedience to protest injustice occupies a legitimate place in our political system. Expressed approval for specific acts of disobedience cannot, without extensive analysis, be labeled as a rejection of shared political premises.

Further, in the American political tradition, even recommendations of revolutionary activity need not breach our shared understandings. Although it might be argued that any support of nonpeaceful overthrow of government is outside shared premises, a more accurate rendering of the ethos of this country founded by a revolution in which many approvers of the First Amendment participated is that revolutions are sometimes warranted and that a government must be justified in terms of what it actually does. Thus, the argument that our government has done, or might within its present constitutional form do, something so pernicious that violent overthrow would be warranted seems to me within the boundaries of our "social contract." And, even if I am wrong about that, revolutionary speech is covered by the First Amendment because it represents an important view in practical morality and because of its many effects on listeners not inclined to perform the recommended revolutionary acts.

Constitutional Standards and Levels of Generality

Before embarking in the next chapter on more particularistic analysis, I offer a few general comments about the development of First Amendment standards that are to influence legislators and to be applied by courts of law. I begin with a general point about all constitutional principles and then briefly address the relation between the First Amendment and a political principle of free speech.

Every decision about what legal norms, including constitutional norms, should be presents a choice between simplicity and complexity. A constitutional rule complex enough to reflect the multiple variables that seem intrinsically relevant to a proper outcome may bog courts down in drawing subtle and endless distinctions and be virtually incomprehensible to legislatures and to those whose behavior is to be affected by the rule. A rule that is simple is likely either to exclude from consideration factors that should be relevant or to be cast in such an open-ended form that it gives insufficient guidance about outcomes to judges and affected citizens. Although any simple test with one or two variables must be rejected for freedom of speech, avoidance of inordinate complexity necessitates disregard of some subtle distinctions.

Some readers may conclude that in what follows I have disregarded too many relevant distinctions; others—rather more, I strongly suspect—will believe that I have accepted a degree of complexity that is ill-advised for constitutional principles governing criminal prohibitions of communication.[35] In any event, the initial test of these matters lies in the plausibility of the distinctions suggested in the following chapters.

These chapters involve delineation of working principles for interpretation of the free speech and free press clauses as they affect communications a legislature might choose to prohibit. In the main, what I say is faithful to the outlines of the treatment of these matters by the Supreme Court and other courts. In some respects, I undertake to suggest a detail about relevant principles that exceeds what is yet to be found in judicial opinions. I am aware that this is a risky, perhaps even foolhardy enterprise, particularly since I am incapable of guessing all the rich variety of circumstances that human relations will throw up, but I believe that proposing relatively concrete principles is the best test of the soundness of the more abstract analysis. I also believe that, as patterns of law develop over time, they almost always increase in complexity. In many respects my analysis may seem complex in relation to what courts have said mainly because courts have yet to sort out critical variables in multiple cases. Frequently, principled alternatives to those I propose could also be supported consonant with my broad analysis, and I sometimes indicate what these may be.

The aim of the book initially to present a political principle of free speech applicable to liberal democracies generally and freed from the complexities and controversies of American constitutional law leaves me with something of a dilemma concerning presentation in the remaining chapters. I have suggested that interpretation of the First Amendment has been proceeding and should continue to proceed in light of the same basic justifications that support a political principle of free speech. If I am right, what matters for political theory overlaps substantially with what matters for constitutional law. That creates a problem: How much of Part II's analysis of how free speech values should constrain the definition of crimes should be repeated? Rather than either re-present the analysis or talk only about distinctive concerns of constitutional law, I have chosen the intermediate course of briefly reminding the reader of basic conclusions in the earlier chapters and then proceeding to deal with the special aspects of constitutional interpretation.

Notes

1. See, e.g., A. Fuchs, "Further Steps Toward a General Theory of Freedom of Expression," 18 *William and Mary Law Review* 347 (1976), arguing that Thomas Emerson's distinction between speech and action, a distinction between speech and nonspeech, is substantially identical with the Supreme Court's clear-and-present-danger test, which has been taken to be a test for suppression of communications that initially qualify as speech.

2. *Heffron* v. *International Society for Krishna Consciousness*, 452 U.S. 640 (1981).

3. *Lehman* v. *City of Shaker Heights*, 418 U.S. 298 (1974).

4. *Buckley* v. *Valeo*, 424 U.S. 1 (1976).

5. As Eric Barendt, *Freedom of Speech* 4–5, 35–36 (Oxford, Clarendon Press 1985) notes, constitutions of other countries and important international documents have more detailed provisions on freedom of expression, thereby leaving somewhat less room for the use of abstract moral and political theories in interpretation.

6. As the Supreme Court said in *Abood* v. *Detroit Board of Education*, 431 U.S. 209, 231 (1977), "[O]ur cases have never suggested that expression about philosophical, social, artistic, economic, literary, or ethical matters—to take a nonexhaustive list of labels—is not entitled to full First Amendment protection."

7. For a sharp attack on the idea that expansive judicial protection of speech makes a significant contribution to the openness and quality of public debate, see R. Nagel, "How Useful Is Judicial Review in Free Speech Cases?" 69 *Cornell Law Review* 302 (1984).

8. *Barenblatt* v. *United States*, 360 U.S. 109, 126 (1959).

9. On the merits of ad hoc balancing, compare the critical remarks of L. Frantz, "The First Amendment in the Balance," 71 *Yale Law Journal* 1424 (1962); L. Frantz, "Is the First Amendment Law?—A Reply to Professor Mendelson" 51 *California Law Review* 729 (1963), with the defense of W. Mendelson, "On the Meaning of the First Amendment: Absolutes in the Balance," 50 *California Law Review* 821 (1962); W. Mendelson, "The First Amendment and the Judicial Process: A Reply to Mr. Frantz," 17 *Vanderbilt Law Review* 479 (1964).

10. On indirect interference, see, e.g., Note, "Politics and the Non-Civil Service Public Employee: A Categorical Approach to First Amendment Protection," 85 *Columbia Law Review* 558 (1985).

11. There remains a question of *how much* predictability is attainable and desirable. No legal principles can yield complete predictability across the range of relevant situations. For an author who emphasizes the desirability of flexibility, see L. Bollinger, *The Tolerant Society* 192–93, 222 (New York, Oxford University Press 1986) (abstract or conscientiously ambiguous doctrine desirable). For stress on the benefits of categorization, see F. Schauer, "Categories and the First Amendment: A Play in Three Acts," 34 *Vanderbilt Law Review* 265 (1981).

12. My colleague Louis Henkin probingly analyzes various ways in which the Court may balance in constitutional cases. "Infallibility under Law: Constitutional Balancing," 78 *Columbia Law Review* 1022 (1978). See also C. Fried, "Two Concepts of Interests: Some Reflections on the Supreme Court's Balancing Test," 76 *Harvard Law Review* 755 (1963). The Court's increasing use of explicit balancing and the values of alternative approaches are illuminatingly explored by Alexander Aleinikoff, "Constitutional Law in the Age of Balancing," 96 *Yale Law Journal* 943 (1987). Schauer, note 11 supra, perceptively examines the need for categorization in First Amendment analysis and stresses that categorization is not an alternative to balancing.

13. For example, in many cases involving the edges of the privilege against self-incrimination, courts do not undertake to weigh public and private interests to develop discrete categories.

14. Compare J. Ely, "Flag Desecration: A Case Study in the Roles of Categorization and Balancing in First Amendment Analysis," 88 *Harvard Law Review* 1482 (1975); S. Shiffrin, "The First Amendment and Economic Regulation: Away from a General Theory of the First Amendment," 78 *Northwestern University Law Review* 1212, 1251–53 (1983).

15. G. Stone, "Content Regulation and the First Amendment," 25 *William and Mary Law Review* 189 (1983). See, e.g., *Schacht* v. *United States*, 398 U.S. 58 (1970); *Regan* v. *Time, Inc.*, 468 U.S. 641 (1984).

16. Precluding altogether particular outlets of expression may have a differential effect on those with various sorts of messages, but in most instances the Supreme Court has not been much affected by arguments based on differential effect.

17. See especially K. Karst, "Equality as a Central Principle in the First Amendment," 43 *University of Chicago Law Review* 20 (1975); M. Redish, *Freedom of Expression* 102–16 (Charlottesville, Va., The Michie Co. 1984).

18. Stone, note 15 supra, carefully analyzes which justifications are relevant to which instances of content regulation. Martin Redish expresses skepticism about how much a distinction between content-based and content-neutral restrictions should matter. See Redish, note 17 supra.

19. Stone, note 15 supra, at 208, 234–39, comments briefly on the lack of perfect coincidence and its significance.

20. See L. Tribe, *American Constitutional Law* 789–92 (2d ed., Mineola, N.Y., Foundation Press 1988); J. Ely, note 12 supra. Tribe suggests that a "track one" of stringent constitutional review exists for abridgments aimed at communicative impact and a "track two" of more relaxed balancing for abridgments aimed at noncommunicative impact.

21. See, e.g., *Police Department of Chicago* v. *Mosley*, 408 U.S. 92 (1972); G. Stone, "Restrictions of Speech because of Its Content: The Peculiar Case of Subject-matter Restrictions," 46 *University of Chicago Law Review* 81 (1978); D. Farber, "Content Regulation and the First Amendment: A Revisionist View," 68 *Georgetown Law Journal* 727 (1980).

22. But, as Stone, note 15 supra, at 251–52, perceptively observes, in this area, as in many others, is posed the "central jurisprudential conflict between precision of analysis and clarity of doctrine."

23. For further treatment of this sort of problem, see Chapter 19.

24. See, e.g., *State* v. *Robertson*, 293 Or. 402, 649 P.2d 569 (1982); H. Linde, "'Clear and Present Danger' Reexamined: Dissonance in the Brandenburg Concerto," 22 *Stanford Law Review* 1163 (1970).

25. See, e.g., T. Emerson, *The System of Freedom of Expression* 9–17 (New York, Random House 1970).

26. In that event, an actor might receive constitutional protection either because a statute was directed at speech or because his behavior amounted to speech.

27. See M. Nimmer, *Nimmer on Free Speech* 2–55 to 2–84 (New York, Matthew Bender Co. 1984).

28. See, e.g., *State* v. *Robertson*, note 24 supra; *State* v. *Garcias*, 296 Or. 688, 679 P.2d 1354 (1984).

29. I understand the court in the *Robertson* case, note 24 supra, to take this position. K. Greenawalt, "Criminal Coercion and Freedom of Speech," 78 *Northwestern University Law Review* 1081, 1118–19 (1983).

30. That appears to be the court's approach in *State* v. *Garcias*, note 28 supra.

31. See V. Blasi, "The Pathological Perspective and the First Amendment," 85 *Columbia Law Review* 449 (1985).

32. See *State* v. *Robertson*, note 24 supra.

33. *Givhan* v. *Western Line Consolidated School District*, 439 U.S. 410 (1979).

34. See R. Bork, "Neutral Principles and Some First Amendment Problems," 47 *Indiana Law Journal* 1, 31 (1971); L. BeVier, "The First Amendment and Political Speech: An Inquiry into the Substance and Limits of Principle," 30 *Stanford Law Review* 299, 309–10 (1978); C. Auerbach, "The Communist Control Act of 1954: A Proposed Legal-Political Theory of Free Speech," 23 *University of Chicago Law Review* 173 (1956).

35. On the virtues of simplicity, see W. Van Alstyne, "A Graphic Review of the Free Speech Clause," 70 *California Law Review* 107, 109 (1982).

13

Agreements, Offers, Orders, Implementation, and Training

This chapter mainly concerns communications that I claim fall outside the coverage of the First Amendment because they are too far removed from ordinary statements of fact and value to deserve even moderately stringent constitutional protection. Utterances that aim for agreement to commit crimes, that order crimes, or that constitute part of an ordinary criminal effort, are outside the range of the free speech and free press clauses. I begin with kinds of communications that are strongly situation-altering, in the sense of that term developed in Chapters 3 and 4, and then turn to words that are used to implement criminal aims. As an adjunct to the last discusson, I also inquire whether actions that are concededly constitutionally protected, standing alone, may be used to count as overt acts in conspiracies or as evidence of a criminal purpose.

Agreements to Commit Crimes

Chapter 3 urges that, when people use words to agree, they change the normative environment in which they live, and Chapter 4 suggests that a political principle of free speech is no barrier to criminalizing serious agreements to engage in socially harmful activity. Words of agreement are dominantly used to *do* something by binding the participants, not to *say* something; in the constitutional dichotomy between "conduct" and "speech," they are conduct. Words of agreement that alter a situation in this way should not be considered to be speech protected by the First Amendment. As the Iowa Supreme Court said, when defendants convicted of conspiring to fix prices urged that their conviction was improper under *Brandenburg*, "entering into an *agreement* to fix prices may hardly be said to be speech, symbolic speech, or expression under the ambit of Amendment 1."[1]

As Chapter 4 explains, the law of criminal conspiracy rests on assumptions that agreement is a surer indication of firm intent to commit a crime than early preparatory steps by an individual and that the mutual commitment of two or more persons enhances the likelihood that the crime will be committed. Whether or not the criminal law is wise to draw such a sharp distinction between individual preparatory acts and agreement, making criminal an agreement to commit a crime that itself has nothing to do with speech does not violate the First Amendment, even if liability is imposed for the agreement alone without further conduct by the parties.

This principle requires some elaboration and limitation, in light of problems raised in Chapters 3 and 4 about ambiguous words of agreement and what I have called "weak agreements." A speaker may utter the words "I agree" as assent to an assertion of fact or value or to the desirability of a proposed course of action, without intending to undertake any new normative commitment and without being understood to have done so. These expressions are not words of agreement in the sense I have been discussing. For First Amendment purposes, words should not be treated as constituting an agreement unless new commitments have unambiguously been undertaken.

The proper treatment of weak agreements, involving a genuine commitment but no substantial mutual dependence or reliance, is more complicated. In Chapters 3 and 4, to illustrate "agreements" in which a sense of commitment is present but highly attenuated, I used the example of some young men attending a meeting who "agree" not to submit to the draft at some later date. It is certainly a defensible position that, whatever concerns there may be about punishing weak agreements, they do not rise to constitutional status and may be left to legislative choice and prosecutorial discretion. But I believe that such weak commitments should be treated differently from ordinary agreements under the First Amendment because the "commitment" is so unimportant. If this view is sound, the question arises whether a weak agreement should be treated like a statement of intention or like an encouragement. Since the aim of the agreement is largely to induce people, including the others who have agreed, to act similarly, I believe that weak agreements should be viewed as encouragements.[2] This would bring them within the umbrella of the First Amendment, but would permit punishment in accord with the principles discussed in Chapter 15.[3]

The proposed distinction between weak and strong commitments can work only if the two can be distinguished in practice. One possibility would be some open-ended test put to a jury, which would then determine the weight of the commitment undertaken by the speaker. But this is hardly an appropriate approach to an important constitutional demarcation. Instead, the search should be for a more objective indication of strong agreement. If two people have unambiguously agreed to perform specific acts, one of three further conditions, none present in the draft-refusal example, should have to be met for the agreement to be considered strong. The acts of one or both would have to be dependent on the acts of the other; one or both would have to enjoy a significant advantage from the acts of the other; or the two would have to have been engaged in actual joint planning of their crimes. Any of these conditions shows that those who have agreed are really participating together or counting on each other in a serious way. If one of the three conditions is met, the fact-finder should infer the presence of a strong agreement.

The bearing of the First Amendment on agreements, therefore, mainly concerns how easily agreements may be found. If a claim that a strong agreement has occurred is disputed and that claim is critical, something like the "strict proof" approach of the *Spock* case is called for. That is, there must be clear evidence that strong agreement and not something else is involved. Now, the reader may wonder what a requirement of "clear evidence" can add to a requirement of proof "beyond a reasonable doubt," the standard in any criminal case. The answer is that, given only the reasonable-doubt standard, a jury might draw an inference about a person's intent from verbal or written comments whose significance was arguable. The "clear evidence" standard would require some evidence that, if believed, would render the presence of a strong agreement unmistakable. Such a standard permits review by appellate courts as to whether the constitutional requisite has been satisfied.

Despite this modest qualification, the general lesson for legislators is the following. If there is authority to make behavior criminal, there is also authority to make real agreement to engage in the behavior criminal. No First Amendment problem is posed by penalizing the agreement.

The special questions arising from agreements to commit crimes involving communication are postponed for Chapter 20, which follows discussion of the constitutional principles for the communications themselves.

Offers to Agree or Participate in or Submit to Criminal Acts

In this section, I treat offers of agreement and other utterances that look toward agreement or joint criminal participation, as well as "offers" that waive constraints on the commission of criminal acts. The "offer" of tangible inducements to the listener to engage in criminal behavior is reserved for the next chapter.

Offers to Enter Agreements and Preliminary Remarks

As Chapter 3 shows, when Alice offers to make an agreement with Bruce, she has already significantly altered their normative relations by giving Bruce the power to complete an agreement with his communication. An offer to enter into an agreement partakes as much of action as the utterance that completes an agreement. Thus, it appears that the offer to make a strong agreement to commit a crime should not be considered protected by the First Amendment.

This conclusion alone is of profound practical importance for the law of criminal solicitation. The great preponderance of private solicitations may, in the words of the Model Code Commentary, "be thought of as . . . attempt[s] to conspire."[4] A solicitation *need not* be an attempt to conspire; Alice can encourage Bruce to commit a crime without offering to join his enterprise. But most successful private solicitations eventuate in agreement. If the analysis here is correct, solicitations to crime that do offer the listener the opportunity to make a strong agreement do not warrant constitutional immunity. Since such solicitations warrant no constitutional immunity, a legislature should be on safe constitutional ground in not introducing into its criminal-solicitation provision a general requirement of likelihood or imminency of the sort that may be called for in respect to some or all "pure" encouragements or requests, a subject addressed in Chapter 15. Although not always clear or consistent about the rationale, courts have regularly held that offers to perform criminal acts together do not enjoy constitutional protection.[5]

A worry might be raised about the practicality of leaving offers of agreement unprotected. Perhaps the courts or juries will find it too difficult to ascertain when, short of actual agreement, an offer is genuine and proposes a strong agreement; if that were the case, offers not actually eventuating in strong agreement might best be treated for First Amendment purposes like simple encouragements to crime. No doubt the relevant facts may sometimes be hard to determine, but in other circumstances written or spoken comments in context will clearly constitute an offer of a strong agreement. Concern about administrability should not put all unsuccessful offers within the range of constitutional protection. Instead, when the character of an utterance prior to agreement is critical, the constitutional requirement should be that the utterance may be treated as an offer of a strong agreement only upon clear evidence that the utterance is unambiguously an actual offer and unmistakably proposes a strong agreement.

I shall say a word about offers that look toward concerted activity but may not call for any verbal agreement. The law of criminal conspiracy covers some situations in which explicit agreement is lacking but each person's behavior is based on his expectation of the other person's behavior. If Alice says, "Let's push this car over the cliff," begins to push without effect, and is then joined by Bruce, Alice and Bruce have conspired to move the car. Alice's initial comment is situation-altering, since her expressed invitation makes Bruce's cooperative effort to push the car appropriate as far as she is concerned.[6] Alice's comment should be treated as an offer of strong agreement, as should offers to engage in illegal sexual activities which may be responded to directly by beginning the activities proposed rather than by a verbal response.

On the other hand, when a person is addressing a large crowd, an expressed willingness to participate is itself likely to be of only minor significance and should not alter the status of the speech. Thus, if Alice is addressing hundreds of student demonstrators and says, "Let's break into that building," instead of "Break into that building," her unsuccessful utterance should be treated like an encouragement rather than as an offer of agreement.[7]

Does it matter for free speech purposes whether the activities in which a person offers to engage are themselves criminal? Ordinarily, solicitations to lawful activities are not forbidden, but, as Chapter 5 suggests, a legislature might rationally decide to permit acts regarded as undesirable while trying to reduce their incidence by prohibiting agreements or offers made in public to perform the acts. According to my analysis—and contrary to what some courts have supposed[8]—such prohibitions of situation-altering offers are not reached by a free speech principle or by the First Amendment.

I turn now to communications that precede an offer, which present somewhat troublesome problems. Suppose Alice says, "What would you think of robbing this bank together?" or "I am suffering terrible pain from my illness; how would you feel about putting poison in my injection?" In the first example, Bruce cannot now close the deal by his response; he must make an offer to Alice or communicate to her his own attitude of receptivity, in which event she may then make an offer he will accept. In the example of the painful illness, Bruce is not yet authorized by Alice to perform any actions that he would initially assume she would regard as harmful. The main thrust of both original communications is, thus, not strictly situation-changing; they imply certain attitudes on Alice's part and make an inquiry of Bruce.

Plainly, not every communication that might lead to criminal agreement should be outside the ambit of First Amendment protection. Alice's inquiry about Bruce's attitude toward poisoning her may initiate an exploration of facts and values that will lead Alice to reject that possibility. Of course, sometimes language that is not explicitly an offer clearly in the setting amounts to an offer: "I'd like to make love with you; how would you feel about making love?" But utterances that are genuinely preliminary to an offer are precisely different from offers in that they partake less of action. Inquiries about possible criminal acts are not beyond the range of constitutional protection.

More debatable is the status of such preliminary remarks when the speaker's intention to proceed with the ultimate criminal action is quite plain; "I've got heroin to sell; have you any interest in it?" or "I'm going to rob a bank; should I consider making it a joint effort?" The suggestion that such remarks be treated as offers is plausible, but it is mistaken. Both the Supreme Court's advertising cases and the general theory we have considered indicate that publication about the availability of particular goods or services at particular prices constitutes significant information on which personal decisions may be made, information that is embraced within the rationales for protecting speech. If this is so, then information that an individual or firm stands ready to perform criminal acts is also speech. That does not necessarily mean that one has a constitutional right to provide such information (a subject addressed in Chapter 15), but it does mean that such information cannot easily be put altogether outside the First Amendment.

Offers of Opportunities to Commit Criminal Acts

A close variation of offers to agree occurs when a speaker offers the listener an opportunity to commit a criminal act without agreement or concert. Suppose Alice asks her doctor to put poison in her daily injection and to do so without letting her know. Alice's invitation of a crime that involves no victim besides herself is situation-altering, since it grants a permission and assures the doctor that Alice can be regarded, at least from her own point of view, as a potential beneficiary of the act rather than as someone harmed by it. If the crime were to be carried out in a manner of which Alice was aware and were such that she would survive the crime, she would by implication commit herself not to resist the doctor[9] or complain to the authorities if the doctor did what she asked. Such invitations to criminal action, if unambiguous, are, like invitations to strong criminal agreement, unprotected by the First Amendment.

Orders

Because orders issued by persons in authority create new normative responsibilities and implicitly bring to bear forms of social pressure, they are situation-altering and fall outside the coverage of the First Amendment.[10] What counts as a relevant order or command is an instruction, however it happens to be couched, by someone in authority, concerning acts as to which his authority generally extends. Thus, a grocery store owner's instruction to an employee to place a false label on packaged meat and a police captain's instruction to an officer to beat up a suspect would be orders. A person who is an authority in one limited domain cannot "command" a subordinate in that domain to act in an entirely different domain. Though what she says might well be punished as an impermissible encouragement, discussed in Chapter 15, a store owner cannot "command" an employee to assault someone who has abused the store owner's parents, since both owner and employee recognize that that is not an area within which the employee has a duty to obey the owner's instructions.[11]

Implementation, Training, Overt Act, and Evidence

In this section I first consider statements of fact that are closely connected to criminal activities, because they either implement a criminal plan in some straightforward way or help train people to commit crimes. My thesis is that these communicative acts may be treated as outside the reach of the First Amendment because their "action element" heavily dominates any expressive value. I then examine whether statements can be treated as overt acts in conspiracy cases and used as evidence of intent.

Implementation

Alice and Bruce have agreed to burglarize an office. While Bruce enters the office, Alice stands outside to warn Bruce when someone is approaching. Although Alice's only participation in the crime may be to tell Bruce particular facts, that involvement is clearly sufficient to ground substantive liability.[12] Neither Alice nor Bruce is interested in the particular facts except in order to accomplish the criminal objective. The expressive value of the communication is extremely slight, and pinning criminal liability on Alice should not be understood as raising any First Amendment issue. What would raise a First Amendment question is grounding liability on statements that Alice makes which she does not *intend* to be put to criminal use but which she is aware may be put to that use. The constitutional problems of knowing facilitation and reckless statements are discussed in Chapter 16.

Training

When one uses one's communicative capacities actually to train someone to perform particular actions, the combination of one's utterances should be considered a form of action. Writing an article about how to dance is one thing; training particular dancers by planning detailed activities for them and commenting minutely on their movements is another. Typically, training someone involves physical demonstration of how actions are to be performed, but the basic nature of training is not altered even if the trainer limits himself to verbal supervision and even if he talks only in factual terms about how to accomplish a given objective, e.g., breaking into a safe. So long as it is plain that the training *is* for criminal activities, punishing people for training others to commit crimes, as Justice Douglas's dissent in *Dennis* indicates,[13] raises no First Amendment problem, whether or not precisely which crimes will be committed has been decided at the time of training.

Overt Acts and Evidence of Intent

I turn now to use of communications in the criminal process not as the basic ground of liability, but instead as overt acts or evidences of intent. Since an individual opinion of one Supreme Court justice expressed doubt about use of constitutionally protected speech to constitute an overt act for purposes of a conspiracy prosecution,[14] it is worth pausing to inquire briefly about that and about the even more common use of communications to establish intent. Because an overt act can be viewed as a kind of element in the crime of conspiracy, considering a communication as an overt act lies closer to other subjects of this chapter than using a communication as evidence of intent, but I begin with the latter more straightforward use, whose discussion helps clarify the question about overt acts.

Even constitutionally protected communications can help establish intent. If Alice has shot Claude on a hunting expedition, Alice's earlier comment to Bruce that she intended to kill Claude at the first convenient opportunity is pretty powerful evidence that Alice did not accidentally hit Claude while shooting at a deer. Even if all Alice has said is that she passionately hates Claude and would like to see him dead, what Alice has said bears on her probable intent. Either of those communications of Alice to Bruce is reached by the First Amendment, since both are statements about Alice's thoughts and emotions. The second statement, and probably the first,[15] are constitutionally protected; that is, they could not themselves be made criminal. But freedom to say what one feels and believes and hopes to do does not constitute freedom from use of one's statements as evidence. Almost certainly the same conclusion obtains if Alice has revealed her hatred of Claude in a public speech, despite a conceivable argument that some special constitutional protection should be accorded remarks in that context. Possibly expression would be more unconstrained if what we said could never be used to our detriment, but this slight increment to free speech would be overwhelmed by the social cost of forgoing such a helpful source of information about what people intend. For this reason, we can simply regard the First Amendment as not ordinarily precluding evidentiary use of what people say.

The problem of overt acts in a conspiracy prosecution is a bit more complex. The overt-act requirement may be viewed partly as an assurance that a conspiracy does really exist and partly as a concern that a genuine agreement has moved to the stage of action, even if that action falls far short of an attempt to commit a crime. I have previously suggested that communications that merely help implement a criminal plan are not themselves within the First Amendment. Thus, if Alice sends to Bruce a detailed account of the bank's security measures so that Bruce may steal money from the bank, Alice's communication is not protected. Using such communications as overt acts presents no problem.

The difficulty arises when the communication itself is protected, say if it is a speech by Alice about injustice of the bank to its employees which Alice and Bruce hope will lead to a strike that will lower the quality of bank security, so that Bruce can proceed with the burglary. In *United States* v. *Johnson*,[16] the Supreme Court held that overt acts in a conspiracy could not include speech protected for legislators under the speech-and-debate clause. Though that clause may be unique in the absolute protection it provides, the more general point of the case concerns the danger of calling into question motives underlying protected communications. If prosecutors are able to ascribe evil purposes to speech innocent on its face, like the claims about bank injustice, and treat such speech as a critical element in criminal conduct, people might be discouraged from speaking freely. Perhaps communication itself protected by the First Amendment should not constitutionally be usable to constitute an overt act[17] unless it reveals on its face a criminal intent or is indisputably a step in a criminal plan.[18]

Notes

1. *State* v. *Blyth*, 226 N.W.2d 250, 263 (1975). In *Brown* v. *Hartlage*, 456 U.S. 45, 55 (1982), the Supreme Court said that agreements to engage in illegal conduct are unprotected, "that such an agreement necessarily takes the form of words does not confer upon it, or upon the underlying conduct, the constitutional immunities that the First Amendment extends to speech."

2. This represents a modest shift in position from K. Greenawalt, "Speech and Crime," 1980 *American Bar Foundation Research Journal* 645, 744, where I suggested that weak agreements should be regarded like statements of individual intention. On reflection I find that that view is mistaken; one willing to undertake a weak commitment should not be treated as more protected than one who simply encourages. A practical consequence of this shift is indicated just below in note 3.

3. Thus a secret "weak agreement" to commit murders could be punished; an open public weak agreement not to submit to the draft could not be punished.

4. Section 5.02, Comment, at 365–66.

5. See, e.g., *District of Columbia* v. *Garcia*, 335 A.2d 217, 224 (D.C. App. 1975), certiorari denied, 423 U.S. 894 (1975) (solicitation "implies no ideological motivation but rather is the act of enticing or importuning on a personal basis for personal benefit or gain"); *United States* v. *Moses*, 339 A.2d 46, 52 (D.C. App. 1975), certiorari denied, 426 U.S. 920 (1976) (communication with the sole purpose of arranging a purely commercial transaction "is in no sense an attempt to express social concerns or grievances publicly"). *Cherry* v. *State*, 18 Md. App. 252, 306 A.2d 634, 639 (Ct. Spec. Apps. 1973) (solicitation to prostitution is an act, not mere words); *Pedersen* v. *City of Richmond*, 219 Va. 1061, 1066, 254 S.E.2d 95, 98 (1979) ("First Amendment protection is not afforded statement made in solicitation of criminal acts. . . . Laws prohibiting solicitation are not directed against words but against acts. A solicitation is in itself, an act"). See also *Pryor* v. *Municipal Court*, 25 Cal.3d 238, 158 Cal. Rptr. 330, 599 P.2d 636 (1979); *State* v. *Huie*, 52 Or. App. 975, 630 P.2d 382 (1981).

6. Interestingly, in this example, even a silent effort by Alice to push the car might generate the same assumption, since usually people welcome help in pushing cars. But one can imagine other crimes, such as assaulting a spouse, in which a bystander would not assume, without an invitation, that help was wanted.

7. Suppose the utterance is successful in that, while Alice remains at the podium, some students move toward the building with an intent to break in, but the police stop them from committing the substantive crime. I conclude that at most Alice is involved in a weak agreement to commit the crime, both because the element of concert is so tenuous and because her urging of the act does not amount to joint planning of the crime in the sense relevant for strong agreement. (The alternative conditions of mutual dependence or reciprocal advantage are also missing.)

8. See *Pedersen* v. *City of Richmond*, 219 Va. 1061, 1065, 254 S.E.2d 95, 98 (1979) ("It would be illogical and untenable to make solicitation of a noncriminal act a criminal offense"); *State* v. *Tusek*, 52 Or. App. 997, 630 P.2d 892 (1981) (quoting the language of Pedersen); *Pryor* v. *Municipal Court*, 25 Cal.3d 238, 254, 158 Cal. Rptr. 330, 339, 599 P.2d 636, 666 (1979) (First Amendment issues would "attend a statute which prohibits solicitation of lawful acts"). There are two important clarifications of what I have said in the text. If an activity is not only legally permitted but constitutionally protected, I assume that, generally, offers to engage in the activity are also protected, though under the part of the Constitution that protects the activity rather than under free speech provisions. If the legislature's demonstrable *reason* for prohibiting solicitations is *their offensiveness* rather than a wish to curb the underlying activities that are solicited, the prohibition is rightly judged by constitutional standards relating to offensive communications. See *State* v. *Tusek*, supra. In such instances the reason for a prohibition triggers an examination under free speech guarantees.

9. The invitation to "Try and hit me" is a little different in this respect. It gives permission to commit an assault, but leaves the listener on notice that the attempt to strike will be resisted by some means.

10. In his dissenting opinion in *Parker* v. *Levy*, 417 U.S. 733, 768 (1974), Justice Douglas said, "A command is speech brigaded with action."

11. Underlying this sentence is a complicated question about domains of authority. In some families and in some very close-knit religious communities an authority without limitation of domain may be recognized. A superior may be thought to have authority to direct in any area of life. Sometimes the dimensions of a domain of authority will be unclear. The controlling perspectives would be the understandings of one or both of the people involved. Since what matters mainly in the relegation of orders beyond the range of the First Amendment is the speaker's sense that he is *doing* something, the critical understanding is probably the speaker's.

12. See, e.g., *Giboney* v. *Empire Storage & Ice Co.*, 336 U.S. 490, 502 (1949) ("it has never been deemed an abridgment of freedom of speech or press to make a course of conduct illegal merely because the conduct was in part initiated, evidenced, or carried out by means of language, either spoken, written, or printed"); *United States* v. *Jeter*, 775 F.2d 670, 678 (6th Cir. 1985), certiorari denied, 475 U.S. 1142 (1986) ("His conduct would seem to constitute merely another type of ordinary criminal communication in a conspiracy that has been traditionally found undeserving of any First Amendment protection").

13. 341 U.S. 494 (1951), at 581. Justice Douglas had in mind terrorist or violent revolutionary acts. In dictum, the Ninth Circuit Court of Appeals has suggested that if one gave seminars on blatantly illegal tax shelters for which one charged substantial amounts of money, one could be punished only if commission of the lawless acts was imminent. *United States* v. *Dahlstrom*, 713 F.2d 1423, 1428 (9th Cir. 1983), certiorari denied, 466 U.S. 980 (1984). That suggestion seems mistaken, assuming that the seminars provided detailed instructions about how to break the law. Compare *United States* v. *Daly*, 756 F.2d 1076 (5th Cir. 1985), certiorari denied, 474 U.S. 1022 (1985). In *The System of Freedom of Expression* 73-75 (New York, Random House 1970), Thomas Emerson addresses the constitutional line between protected advice and persuasion and unprotected instructions

and preparations, which count as conduct for him. He says, "The essential task would be to distinguish between simply conveying an idea to another person, which idea he may later act upon, and actually participating with him in the performance of an illegal act." This formulation alone leaves a bit unclear exactly how under certain circumstances to treat some of Emerson's own illustrations, "advice or instruction in various illegal methods of evading the draft—for example, how to feign insanity, drug addiction, homosexuality, chronic illness or the like." If what is involved is more than the comment that feigning insanity is a good approach and includes highly detailed instructions about how to feign insanity for this purpose, the speaker is doing more than conveying an idea, but less than "actually participating with [the listener] in the performance of an illegal act." Since Emerson, however, talks of "thorough training in the preferred technique of deception" as at one end of the spectrum between advice and instruction, I understand him to believe that such training is unprotected. That, in any event, is my position.

14. See Justice Douglas dissenting from a denial of certiorari in *Epton* v. *New York*, 390 U.S. 29, 30 (1968). See also Note, "Conspiracy and the First Amendment," 79 *Yale Law Journal* 872, 894 (1970).

15. I assume here that Alice is not aiming to threaten Claude indirectly, but confiding in Bruce.

16. 383 U.S. 169 (1966).

17. This conclusion may have implications for when communicative acts could be held to be sufficient to satisfy the requirements of attempt liability.

18. If correspondence between Alice and Bruce indicated that a part of their plan was for Alice to make the speech about bank injustices, the speech could be indisputably a step in a criminal plan, though innocent on its face.

14

Conditional Threats and Offered Inducements

This chapter considers threats and offers that are designed to lead the listener to do what the person making the threat or offer wants. The threats considered are conditional; the constitutional status of "pure," unconditional, threats is reserved for Chapter 19. The offers I am concerned with here are not offers to agree or to waive normative restraints, which are treated in the last chapter, but offers to reward someone for doing what is desired. If Tammy wants Victor to give a job or a kidney to her cousin, she might offer him $1000 for doing that or threaten to hurt him badly if he fails to do it. How the First Amendment relates to this sort of utterance is the topic of this chapter.

The discussion proceeds on the basis of what I claimed in Chapters 3 and 4 and supported in more analytical detail in Chapter 5, namely that, for purposes of a political principle of free speech, manipulative inducements and manipulative threats are fundamentally similar: they propose consequences which are within the speaker's control[1] and which would not occur but for the opportunity to offer or threaten and the possible advantage to the speaker that opportunity confers.

To recapitulate briefly, my basic position is that such utterances are genuinely situation-altering. They do not inform the listener about the environment he or she inhabits; they change that environment by generating options which did not previously exist and which would never have existed had it not been for the offer or threat. Because they *do* something rather than *say* something, they fall outside a principle of free speech. My thesis in this chapter is that, subject to certain qualifications and problems of line drawing, manipulative inducements and manipulative threats also fall outside the reach of the First Amendment. This conclusion is one manifestation of my more general claims that the coverage of the First Amendment should be sensitive to the justifications for free speech and that the application of those justifications depends largely on the particular uses to which language is put. Also, in accord with those claims, I assert that what I call warning threats and advisory inducements are reached by a free speech principle and at least provisionally by the First Amendment. These utterances tell the listener what would happen in any event, "I'll quit unless you stop harassing me"; they are statements of facts, of one's future intentions formed without regard to the opportunity to communicate to the listener. Although I conclude that some warning threats and advisory inducements may constitutionally be punished, I argue that such punishment must pass a First Amendment test.

Before proceeding to a more detailed analysis, I contrast my approach with two possible alternatives. The first alternative is the view that all offers and threats are essentially like other uses of language, their possible punishment depending on whether some general First Amendment test—such as that speech may be punished only if it is likely to lead to some imminent and serious harm—is satisfied. A sobering example is provided by a California case[2] involving a national director of the Jewish Defense League, Irving Rubin, who said at a press conference:

> We are offering five hundred dollars, that I have in my hand, to any member of the community, be he Gentile or Jewish, who kills, maims, or seriously injures a member of the American Nazi Party. . . . The fact of the matter is that we're deadly serious. This is not said in jest, we are deadly serious.

The trial court had set aside the prosecution prior to trial on the theory that only political hyperbole was involved. Rejecting this view and concluding that the statement invited political assassination, the appellate court moved on to consider the First Amendment. Referring to cases of ordinary criminal solicitation and advocacy (cases of the sort dealt with in the next chapter), it said that imminence was the critical consideration and that for such a serious crime the requirement of imminence was met here. Although it was debatable, despite Mr. Rubin's explicit reassurances, whether the statement represented a serious offer, the court failed to see the distinctive situation-altering character of serious offers and ended up applying concepts that are not suited for such offers, rather than saying that they simply are outside the First Amendment.

A possible variation on the approach of treating offers and threats like other utterances is to say that their situation-altering character goes only to the First Amendment balance, not to whether the amendment applies at all. Melville Nimmer proposed this resolution for all performative utterances, partly on the ground that they were too hard to distinguish from other communications.[3] If the distinction is too hard to draw, whether a situation-altering character should even figure in a balance is arguable, but, in any event, a defense of my own position does require an explication of how the relevant distinction would figure in constitutional adjudication.

Another alternative to my approach, discussed at some length in Chapter 5, is that proposed by Edwin Baker.[4] What counts for him is whether a threat or offer imposes improper pressure, is coercive. I shall not repeat the theoretical analysis of the earlier chapter, but I will remind the reader that the practical conclusions to be drawn from Baker's approach are not significantly different from my own. My essential challenge to Baker is that the distinction I draw has more to do with *free speech* values than his. Attention to constitutional adjudication shows most strikingly a serious weakness of Baker's position as a practical standard. Remember that for him improper pressure depends on what activities would be treated as matters of autonomous choice in a good society; often to determine improper pressure judges would need to evaluate the underlying activity that the speaker encourages or demands. Contrary to the import of Baker's approach, a court faced with a free speech problem, say involving an offer of money to become a prostitute or a threat to fire someone unless he stops smoking marijuana, cannot be expected to engage in a systematic analysis of what activities would be free in a good society; it must start with what the law (including other branches of constitutional law) and perhaps social morality now take as the range of liberty.

In developing the constitutional implications of my earlier discussion, I concentrate on threats. Since offers are frequently not regarded as socially harmful even when threats would be, since offered inducements less often express strong emotional feelings or indicate responses that might occur in any event, their analysis is somewhat less important and less complex, and it largely follows in relevant aspects what I say about threats.[5]

Like the other significantly situation-altering utterances treated in the last chapter, manipulative threats made in a calculated manner simply do not involve speech in the relevant sense. When a person threatens consequences that are not a natural response to the activities of the subject of the threat or intimates a willingness that is not natural to forgo a natural response in return for some advantage, his utterance is outside the reach of the First Amendment. What counts as a warning threat for which the amendment is relevant is a threat of behavior which would constitute a natural response to a failure to act by the person threatened and which suggests a willingness to forgo that action that represents a natural reaction to the changed behavior of the person threatened ("If you don't stop the affair, I'll have to tell your wife"). Although warning threats provide information about what will occur in the ordinary course of events and, therefore, fall broadly within the range of the First Amendment, not all warning threats are actually constitutionally protected. Rather, their proper treatment calls for categorization that strikes a rough balance between expressive value and social harm.

The practical significance of developing sensible constitutional approaches for threats is shown by judicial invalidations of provisions on criminal coercion and intimidation on the ground that they are overly broad in their prohibition of constitutionally protected communications[6] and by concerns expressed in other opinions about the coverage of threats that might be too extensive.[7] The distinction between manipulative and warning threats might actually be employed in constitutional adjudication or it might inform in some more general way what threats warrant protection. The latter relevance is what I finally recommended for statutory drafting. If the distinction is actually to be employed directly by courts interpreting the First Amendment, it is critical that it be capable of application in the review of statutory provisions and particular factual situations and that it fit within an overall set of principles that makes good sense.

I now embark on the inquiry whether these requisites can be met. I begin with some elaborations of and qualifications to the general claim that manipulative threats lie outside constitutional protection. I next comment on the permissibility of prohibiting substantial numbers of warning threats. Then I address aspects of the line-drawing question, which ends by posing less of a practical difficulty than might initially be supposed, both because in many cases there will be no doubt that a threat is manipulative and because, for most sorts of threats that will actually be prosecuted, even a warning threat could be punished.

Manipulative Threats That Convey a Firm Determination

An important clarification is that what counts as a threat does not depend entirely on the language used. On some occasions, one person may effectively threaten another without using threatening language. Suppose an employee is aware that a store owner has more than once told employees to commit assaults against persons with whom she is angry. Each employee who has failed to carry out an assault has been immediately fired, and the employer has told the remaining employees that the failure was the reason for the firing. When the store owner tells George, "I want you to beat up Henry," both she and George understand that she is threatening to fire him, though no words to that effect have been spoken. In clear enough circumstances, a manipulative threat may be found in the absence of threatening language, but, given the values of speech, an utterance should not count as involving a threat unless both the speaker and the listener would clearly understand it in that way.[8]

Whether a threat is manipulative does not depend on whether the speaker actually intends to carry out the threat; it is sufficient that he intentionally lead the listener to think that he will carry out the threat if his demand is not met. Against this conclusion, it might be argued that an insincere threat changes the listener's perception of his environment only as does a false statement of fact. But this argument misses the point. What the listener perceives is not an increased understanding about an environment that already exists; the listener perceives that the speaker has altered the environment in an undesired way, and this is exactly the perception the speaker has tried to create. That accomplishment of the speaker's objective makes the threat manipulative, and it means that an absence of intent to carry out the threat does not make the First Amendment relevant.[9]

Suppose a threat is unsuccessful in the sense that the listener assumes, rightly or wrongly, that the speaker will not carry it out, despite the speaker's aim to create the contrary perception. That also is not relevant.[10] The critical reason for treating manipulative threats as unprotected is the manner in which the speaker uses language. The speaker is using language to *do* something, whether or not success crowns his efforts even in the limited sense of convincing the listener of serious determination to act on the threat.

I suggested in earlier chapters that some apparent manipulative threats are rhetorical, not seriously intended, and that others, hurled verbally in highly charged interchanges, have a force that will obviously lapse quickly as tempers cool. These expressions of strong feeling are among those communications reached by the justifications that underlie a political principle of free speech and should be regarded as covered by the First Amendment. Since a passing intent to manipulate by threatening an unnatural response does not pose a serious social danger, any ostensible threat should be regarded as constitutionally protected, whatever its content, if it does not convey a firm (i.e., stable) determination to carry out the threatened harm. Apparent firmness of purpose should be regarded as a constitutional requisite for treating any conditional threat as criminal. This requirement would also put within the range of constitutional protection vague threats to take action under amorphous circumstances in a distant future, threats such as "Unless Chicagoans renounce their sinful ways it may become necessary to poison the city's water supply."[11]

Some specific manipulative threats are both emotionally expressive and made in a manner that conveys a firm determination. Though such threats are not devoid of speech value and though an argument can be made that they should enjoy greater protection than calculated manipulative threats, once a person has fixed seriously on the course of manipulating another by threatening an unnatural response, the strongly situation-altering character of the combined demand and threat should be viewed as sufficient to make constitutional protection inapposite.[12]

The Treatment of Various Warning Threats

The proper constitutional treatment of warning threats is more complex. Although there may be expressive significance in telling a potentially affected person what one plans (naturally) to do, the kind of pressure that such threats can put on people may be harmful enough so that forbidding them is permissible despite their speech value. In respect to warning threats, the conclusion that the First Amendment reaches them in some sense does not inevitably yield protection.

To think more precisely about the limits of legal constraint for warning threats, we need to attend to the action that is threatened and the action that is demanded. If the demanded action is itself criminal, the demand constitutes a form of solicitation of criminal behavior, solicitation that goes beyond simple urging and provides the person threatened with an incentive to avoid unpleasant consequences by performing the act. Even though the threat conveys some "natural" response that will follow failure to commit the crime, the demand should certainly enjoy no more protection than ordinary solicitation of a crime, which itself often includes significant assertions of fact. In the absence of separate grounds for treating a demand and warning threat *less favorably*, they should be regarded constitutionally like simple requests or encouragements; that is, like criminal solicitations that are unaccompanied by manipulative threats or offers of money or other benefits. The proper treatment of such solicitations is the central topic of the next chapter.

Another possible basis for punishing warning threats is that they constitute some kind of independent wrong. In Chapter 5, I sketched examples where a warning threat could amount to an abuse of authority (the police officer tells a motorist she will write a ticket if he does not contribute to the P.B.A.)[13] or would itself violate a substantive right (a person in a cooperative apartment building tells a black potential applicant that she will not be admitted). The gender specifications in want ads held to be unprotected by the Supreme Court in *Pittsburgh Press Co.* v. *Human Relations Commission*[14] provide a close analogue of the second example. When a threat already constitutes a wrong in either of these senses, the First Amendment permits its punishment even though the threatened response is "natural."

Still another basis for punishing a warning threat is the wrongfulness of the harm threatened. If the threatened harm is imminent and could itself achieve the threatener's objective, as when immediate physical force is threatened, the threat should be viewed like the harm itself, even if the particular threatener is inclined naturally to use force to get his way.

The relevance of the wrongfulness of the threatened harm is more troublesome if the harm is not imminent. Here we may distinguish serious criminal harm, minor criminal harm, and permitted behavior. If a person backs a demand with a warning threat that he will commit a criminal act if his wishes are not satisfied— "If you touch my sister, I will kill you"—the demand and threat together should enjoy no more protection than would a simple threat that is not coupled with any demand for behavior by which the threat may be avoided. That subject is discussed in Chapter 17, where I contend that serious threats of personal violence are not constitutionally protected.

A thornier problem is presented when the warning threat is of a nonimminent minor criminal act, such as trespass, that is not likely to create serious emotional disturbance, and when the threat itself is neither a denial of rights nor an abuse of authority. One might take the view that any threat to do a legal wrong can itself be punished, but that resolution would plainly be unacceptable for simple threats. Suppose Thelma tells a neighbor whose children have played on her property that she will ruin the neighbor's lawn, or she is so incensed at her treatment by the Internal Revenue Service that she writes a letter to the district director saying that in future years she will fail to file a return. These statements should be regarded as constitutionally protected speech enjoying immunity from criminal punishment. The same conclusion should apply if the threats are warning threats: "Stop your children or I'll ruin your lawn," "Give me my refund or I'll refuse to file." In such instances, the threats themselves do little or no direct harm, and criminal enforcement must constitutionally be left for the occasion when an actual attempt is made to commit the wrongful act.

If neither the demanded act nor the threatened act is seriously wrong in any of the senses yet indicated, the reasons for freedom of speech are sufficient to warrant constitutional protection. If the threatener demands something that is not wrongful and the threatener can lawfully react in the way that he says he will react, he should be able to inform the affected person of that prospect, whether or not the pressure this puts on the listener is regarded as entirely appropriate or somewhat undesirable. The giving of such information should be treated as privileged, and it is reassuring that the examples the Oregon Supreme Court gives in *State* v. *Robertson* of threats that are obviously protected by a free speech guarantee, discussed below, fall into this category.[15]

Drawing the Line between Manipulative and Warning Threats

My analysis suggests that in some situations it should matter for a free speech principle whether a conditional threat is manipulative or warning. But that distinction can play a direct role in constitutional adjudication only if it can somehow be drawn in actual cases. Thus, translating the distinction into constitutional standards is important not only in order to determine *how* the distinction is to be drawn but also for determining whether it *should* be drawn. The draft statute near the end of Chapter 5 represents an effort in the direction of line drawing. Here I deal with two particular problems: in light of fact-finding difficulties, how can manipulative and warning threats be distinguished? and how should threats uttered within broadly manipulative courses of action be regarded?

In my theoretical analysis, the question whether a threat is manipulative or warning depends on the state of mind or ordinary behavior of the person making the threat. If he normally reacts to behavior in a particular way or has made up his mind to do so, independent of his ability to tell the person whose behavior disturbs him, then his response is natural and he makes a warning threat. If his reaction is made up in order to manipulate, then the response is unnatural and the threat is manipulative.[16] Outsiders are not in a position to draw this line with confidence in every case, since they will not always be sure how the threatener would have responded to a rejected request or demand if he had not made the threat. Indeed, as I mentioned in Chapter 5, even the person who threatens in emotionally intense situations may not always be certain how he would have responded to a failure to satisfy the demand if he had not also made the threat.

If constitutional law is to give any significance to the distinction between warning and manipulative threats, it must rely largely on objective standards. What the law can reasonably ask is whether the threatened response is of the kind that would commonly be a natural response if someone made a simple request or demand, unaccompanied by any threat, and were refused. Interestingly, in almost every case hypothesized by the Oregon Supreme Court in the case that held the state's criminal coercion provision to be overbroad, the responses would clearly be natural in this sense. The court referred, for example, to "situations in which one man tells another: 'If you don't quit making love to my wife, I'm going to tell your wife,' or someone proposes to disclose an airline pilot's secret illness if he does not get medical attention, or a politician's embarrassing past if he does not withdraw his candidacy from office."[17] In each instance the threatened act would represent a "natural" next step if a request or demand were not satisfied. Other threats, such as, "Pay me $500 or I will put a bomb in your store," are obviously not warnings of natural responses; planting bombs is not how most people react to being refused $500. If a response would be natural for many people or for many people within a discrete subgroup to which a person belongs (such as devout Muslims), it should be considered natural; the availability of the constitutional defense should not depend on guesses by juries or judges about how a particular person might have acted had he or she not made the threat.

The ultimate determination of what would count as a manipulative threat is a bit more debatable. Plainly the state should not have to offer evidence to prove that a threat is manipulative for a particular individual. If the threatened response is not behavior in which people or some identifiable subset of people would commonly engage, the initial assumption should be that the threat is manipulative. Although a good argument can be made for a test that is exclusively objective in this sense,[18] I am inclined to think that if someone really can convince a jury or judge that the threatened behavior is the way he or she ordinarily acts, then the threat should count as natural in that case. This position could be realized by allowing the person who has made a threat to show that an unusual response really is natural for him, for example, by producing evidence that he has responded in such a way when no threat was involved.[19]

One elusive question about the line between manipulative and warning threats involves the possible application of repeated unpleasant consequences to achieve a particular result. Imagine that Tim has decided that he will harass Vicki by playing his stereo loud every night until she stops selling drugs in her apartment. This in itself would not be a natural response to Vicki's actions; Tim would have no interest in playing his stereo loud unless he saw that as a means for altering Vicki's behavior.

Imagine that Tim first plays the stereo very loud one evening and then tells Vicki, "You see, that is my response to your selling drugs." This message in form is a statement of a past or present motivation for action rather than a threat; but it implicitly conveys an indication that future loud playing will depend on whether the sale of drugs continues. If that implication is clear, the message should be regarded as a manipulative threat, since Tim would not continue this course of action if he were unable to communicate its significance to Vicki.

Suppose that, instead of first playing the stereo, Tim tells Vicki that he has decided to play the stereo loud in order to discourage her from selling drugs. Given Tim's reason for playing the stereo, this message implicitly lets Vicki know that she can prevent that consequence by agreeing to stop the sale of drugs. However phrased, this is a threat coupled with a demand; but is the threat warning or manipulative? The argument that it is only a warning threat goes as follows. Tim has already decided to play the stereo loud at least one evening. He would do that even if he were unable to communicate with Vicki beforehand; so his initial threat is not situation-altering; it merely warns Vicki of what will happen anyway. The argument that the threat is manipulative rests on the manipulative nature of the overall course of conduct and the necessity that Tim communicate at some stage the significance of his conduct if that conduct is to have any point at all. Trying to decide at what stage Tim would feel a need to communicate if he were to continue the conduct would be highly artificial. For that reason and because of the close linkage between the initial communication and Tim's manipulative plans, the threat should be treated like manipulative threats.[20]

This determination, however, does not settle all questions of constitutional protection concerning repeated acts of pressure. In the ordinary situation in which a single harm, say disclosure of embarrassing information, is threatened, a judgment may reasonably be made that the harm itself is socially acceptable, or even desirable, but that a threat to engage in it coupled with a demand puts socially unacceptable pressure on the victim to comply with the demand. When the threatened behavior is itself an attempt to pressure the victim, the analysis is different. A judgment is needed about the status of exerting pressure in this way. If that pressuring course of conduct is itself deemed constitutionally protected, as are some boycotts under the First Amendment freedom of association,[21] then the communication that precedes the first practical steps should also be deemed constitutionally protected, since it would be senseless to encourage persons to proceed to apply pressure without their being initially able to inform the prospective subjects of that pressure about what is going to happen. The constitutional protection of the threat then derives not from its being a warning threat, but from the constitutional privilege afforded to the course of action of which it is a part.[22]

Lest some of the distinctions drawn in this chapter be thought too elusive or complicated to be profitably employed in constitutional interpretation, putting them in a realistic context may prove helpful. Criminal coercion is not a frequently prosecuted crime, and its content overlaps considerably with the crimes of extortion and blackmail. Most of the threats that will be prosecuted under these offenses will be obviously manipulative. And most actual cases in which any doubt is raised on this score may be cases in which the threatened harm is serious enough so that even warning threats are punishable. Thus, troublesome individual borderline cases are rarely going to perplex the courts. The justifications for free speech provide powerful reasons for distinguishing manipulative from warning threats in some, limited, circumstances, and the line is appropriately drawn in constitutional adjudication if not directly in statutory drafting.

Perhaps the main importance of the lines I have drawn would lie in review of legislation of the kind involved in *State* v. *Robertson.* If a statutory provision covers a great many warning threats of natural consequences that do not fall into the prohibitable categories, then the statute is vulnerable on its face. It will matter in this respect not only what behavior is initially covered under the statute, but also how broad a set of exemptions is provided.[23] As I mentioned in Chapter 5, a legislature can proceed directly by excluding many warning threats or it can develop classes of prohibited and permitted threats which are cast in other terms but which end up covering few, if any, protected warning threats.

A final word is appropriate in respect to labor law. I have spoken in this chapter about the treatment of conditional threats generally. Although I have concentrated on criminal sanctions, an implication of what I have said is that warning threats that do not suffer any of the defects I have noted should be regarded as constitutionally privileged, even against civil remedies. My general conclusions are not in accord with existing labor law in certain respects. I have not set out to describe under what conditions organizational boycotts should themselves be constitutionally protected, but criticism has been directed at the Supreme Court's assumption that consumers pursuing political objectives have more latitude than workers seeking justice in the workplace.[24] The point of severe tension with what I have written, however, concerns what employers may say prior to votes by union members or potential members of unions. On the theory that workers need to be shielded from fears employers may engender, the Supreme Court has held that employer comments like, "If you join the union, labor disputes may make it likely the company will move from this location," constitute an unfair labor practice which can invalidate the results of elections.[25] That the Court's conception of workplace democracy fits uncomfortably with the general law of the First Amendment has been noticed.[26] The claim I have made in this chapter that ordinary warning threats are privileged is consonant with that general law and out of line with labor law's treatment of employer speech.

No one has yet suggested that the circumscribed limits of speech for participants in labor controversies are appropriate general guidelines for regulation for speech; so either there is a serious problem with labor law or labor law is a special domain warranting extraordinary principles. Whatever may once have been true, it seems doubtful that employees are as vulnerable to fears generated by open employer speech as the present legal regime supposes;[27] but I am not nearly knowledgeable enough about labor relations to have an informed judgment about the principles appropriate in that domain. What is clear is that existing principles need to be rigorously reviewed in light of general First Amendment standards to determine whether the marked discrepancies have powerful enough justifications.

Notes

1. It is also sufficient if the speaker is acting as the agent of someone who controls the consequences.

2. *People* v. *Rubin*, 96 Cal. App.3d 968, 158 Cal. Rptr. 488 (1979), certiorari denied, 449 U.S. 821 (1980).

3. M. Nimmer, *Nimmer on Freedom of Speech* § 3.05 (New York, Matthew Bender Co. 1984).

4. See Chapter 5, discussion accompanying notes 37–56.

5. For this reason, the elusive line *between* offers and threats, while it may matter for application of statutory provisions, is rarely if ever relevant for First Amendment purposes. On the distinction generally, see R. Nozick, "Coercion," in P. Laslett, W. Runciman, and Q. Skinner, eds., *Philosophy, Politics and Society* (fourth series) 101, 112–20, 127–35 (Oxford, Basil Blackwell 1972); R. Pennock and J. Chapman, eds., *Coercion* (Nomos XIV) (Chicago, Aldine Atherton 1972); P. Westen, "'Freedom' and 'Coercion'—Virtue Words and Vice Words," 1985 *Duke Law Journal* 541.

6. See, e.g., *Wurtz* v. *Risley*, 719 F.2d 1438 (9th Cir. 1983); *State* v. *Robertson*, 293 Or. 402, 629 P.2d 569 (1982).

7. See, e.g., *Landry* v. *Daley*, 280 F. Supp. 938 (N.D. Ill. 1968), rev'd sub nom *Boyle* v. *Landry*, 401 U.S. 77 (1971); *State* v. *Moyle*, 299 Or. 691, 705 P.2d 740 (1985).

8. In *United States* v. *Quinn*, 514 F.2d 1250 (5th Cir. 1975), the court concluded that a conversation overall could be understood to threaten, although at no one point was the language of direct and explicit threat used.

9. Compare *State* v. *Moyle*, note 7 supra, which interprets a harassment statute very narrowly on the apparent assumption that if insincere threats were covered, the statute would (or might) be unconstitutional.

If my own analysis is rejected and an insincere threat is not regarded as manipulative, it could still be constitutionally punished under principles that permit the punishment of harmful falsehoods. Perhaps this approach might be necessary to justify punishing insincere warning threats (that is, threats that lie about one's natural responses) that would not otherwise be punishable. Since I believe insincere threats are punishable whether manipulative or warning, clear proof that an intent to carry out a conditional threat was missing might make it unnecessary to decide whether a threat was manipulative or warning.

10. Compare *State* v. *Moyle*, note 7 supra.

11. The example is used by Judge Richard Posner in *Alliance to End Repression* v. *City of Chicago*, 742 F.2d 1007, 1014 (7th Cir. en banc 1984). Compare *Brown* v. *Hartlage*, 456 U.S. 45 (1982), involving a promise by a candidate to lower his salary. Here the promise might be regarded as a kind of offer, whose satisfaction depended on getting enough votes. The promise was specific, but the ability and firm intention to carry it out were questionable. (It turned out that such a step would have been illegal.) In any event, special First Amendment protections may apply to discourse in the electoral process. The

Supreme Court held the promise to be constitutionally protected in the absence of reckless disregard of falsity.

12. This view fits with the basic understanding of courts that have made comments like "It may categorically be stated that extortionate speech has no more constitutional protection than that uttered by a robber while ordering his victim to hand over the money, which is no protection at all." *United States* v. *Quinn*, note 8 supra, at 1268.

13. As far as analogous offers are concerned, if someone says to an official, "I'll give you $100 if you decide in my favor," the offer is wrong in itself because of the inappropriate influence it may exercise on the official, even if the person making the offer would in any event give a gift of $100 to any official deciding the matter favorably.

14. 413 U.S. 376 (1973).

15. See text accompanying note 17 infra.

16. I pass over here the extra complexity of a threat that *purports* to be a warning but is actually manipulative.

17. 293 Or. 402, at 418, 649 P.2d 569, at 580.

18. Since I have assumed that a defendant could argue that he is a member of a class, such as devout Muslims, for which a response is natural, the test would not be fully objective in the sense of looking only at the "reasonable person" in the society in general.

19. This issue is not of enough practical significance to warrant the creation of a special affirmative defense; so what I say here would be fitted into standard ways of presenting constitutionally relevant facts.

20. Threats to those who inform about organized criminal activity may be similarly viewed. See, e.g., *United States* v. *Velasquez*, 772 F.2d 1348 (7th Cir. 1985), certiorari denied, 475 U.S. 1021 (1986).

21. See, e.g., *NAACP* v. *Claiborne Hardware Co.*, 458 U.S. 886 (1982).

22. Suppose the form of pressure is permitted but not *constitutionally* privileged. It would be senseless for the legislature to forbid informing someone that pressure of this sort was to be applied, and a court would interpret a generally worded criminal-coercion statute not to cover it; but is the verbal threat constitutionally protected? So long as the threatened behavior is natural, the bounds of protection would be like those sketched for encouragements in the next-to-last section of the next chapter, on Encouragements to Harmful Actions that Are Not Criminal.

23. The Oregon Supreme Court in *Robertson* was influenced by the narrowness of the privileges provided and compared the state provision unfavorably with the Model Penal Code in this respect.

24. See generally J. Getman, "Labor Law and Free Speech: The Curious Policy of Limited Expression," 43 *Maryland Law Review* 4 (1984); L. Tribe, *Constitutional Choices* 201 (Cambridge, Mass., Harvard University Press 1985); M. Harper, "The Consumer's Emerging Right to Boycott: *NAACP* v. *Claiborne Hardware* and Its Implications for American Labor Law," 93 *Yale Law Journal* 409 (1984); J. Pope, "The Three-systems Ladder of First Amendment Values: Two Rungs and a Black Hole," 11 *Hastings Constitutional Law Quarterly* 189 (1984).

25. See *N.L.R.B.* v. *Gissel Packing Co.*, 395 U.S. 575 (1969). The hypothetical quote in my text is a rough paraphrase of the employer speech in that case.

26. See, e.g., Getman, note 24 supra.

27. Id. at 8–12, 19–20.

15

Encouragements of Crime

This chapter considers constitutional principles for encouragements to others that do not involve threats, orders, offers of agreement, or offers of benefits the speaker will confer. I have suggested in Chapters 3 and 6 that requests and other encouragements to action that are not strongly situation-altering fall to a greater degree within the justifications for freedom of speech than do situation-altering utterances like orders, offers, and manipulative threats. Some expressions of encouragement are virtually indistinguishable from evaluations, and many others are accompanied by explicit evaluations or statements of fact. In respect to influence on future action, distinguishing expressions of opinion from encouragements is much harder than distinguishing expressions of opinion from orders, offers, and threats. And requiring speakers to reformulate their thoughts and feelings in a manner that would purge explicit elements of encouragement would inhibit spontaneity and intensity of expression. Nevertheless, what I have called weak imperatives are not as fully within the ambit of liberty of speech as evaluations and statements of fact. A simple imperative, like "Kill him," is certainly not the sort of utterance that a principle of free speech obviously embraces. The purpose of an imperative is to induce another to action and to do so in a much more direct way than by ordinary expressions of fact and value. If requests and encouragements are, as a class, less "action" than are orders and agreements, they are more "action" than are statements of fact and opinion.

My fundamental claim in this chapter is that weak imperatives should be accorded *some* protection under the First Amendment, but that they may be subject to punishment in some circumstances when factual assertions or evaluations that lack the element of explicit urging may not be made criminal. The effort here involves the elaboration of guidelines sensitive to a political principle of free speech and responsive to the general standards of constitutional interpretation I have suggested.

Because, as Chapter 6 has made clear, the values and dangers of encouragements to criminal behavior depend greatly on the context in which they are uttered and on the reasons given to support them, the precise level of constitutional protection should vary. Following are some proposals regarding the elements that should be regarded as central and the appropriate degree of protection for the classes thus marked. Most importantly and in line with legislative possibilities suggested in Chapter 6, private, nonideological solicitations to crime should enjoy much weaker constitutional protection than that accorded to public ideological solicitations.[1]

Private Nonideological Solicitation

The reasons for protecting solicitations are least strong for situations in which one person privately urges another to commit a crime without any ideological motive or appeal, that is, without serious reference to duty, right, overall welfare, or some historical, philosophical, political, or religious view that would make the crime appropriate. In Chapter 6 I used the example of cousin Alan, who stands to inherit under his uncle's will, urging cousin Betty to kill the uncle, appealing to her dislike of the uncle and her need for money. The expressive value of such utterances is slight in comparison with their dangerous tendencies, and most of that expressive value could be easily realized by other kinds of communication. The secretive nature of Alan's urging reduces the import of countervailing communication which is an important assumption underlying First Amendment protection; no one is likely to argue directly to Betty that she should not murder her uncle. In such a setting, the conclusion expressed in the Commentary to the Model Code is appropriate: "One who uses words as a means to crime . . . does not make a contribution to community discussion that is worthy of protection."[2] Admittedly, the urging to commit the crime may be an outlet of self-expression for Alan, but, if he may not enjoy the "outlet" of murdering his uncle, the self-expressive value of a narrow urging that someone else commit the murder is of limited relevance for free speech protection. It is true that Alan's encouragement is different from his committing the act directly, because it requires an independent choice by another person, but if his dominant and deliberate aim is simply to get Betty to perform the act, his communication is not the sort of communicative self-expression that matters for freedom of speech.

If this analysis is accurate, Alan's failure to set an imminent target date or the unlikelihood that Betty will do what he asks should not be relevant. Factors like these might help others to assess whether Alan seriously intended what he said, but, if he did, that should be constitutionally sufficient for punishment. That courts have been sensitive to the difference between much private solicitation and advocacy is shown by the following judicial comment:

> Advocacy is the act of "pleading for, supporting, or recommending; active espousal" and, as an act of public expression, is not readily disassociated from the arena of ideas and causes, whether political or academic. Solicitation, on the other hand, implies no ideological motivation but rather is an act of enticing or importuning on a personal basis for personal benefit or gain.[3]

Concerning seriousness of intent, three questions need be answered: Is serious intent a constitutional requirement? If so, what is the appropriate standard? And what evidence may be used to meet that standard?

As I suggested in Chapters 3 and 6, people often express themselves orally with some ambiguity, and oral imperatives tend to reflect a less firm intent than that which underlies many other actions. The constitutional interest in free discourse exists even when conversation is private and about subjects of narrow interest. Although the point is debatable, I believe that the Constitution should be interpreted to set limits on determinations of intent when liability is imposed for simple private encouragements.

An appropriate standard would be whether the speaker has intended to express and actually has expressed himself in a manner that conveys a fixed and potentially influential determination that the crime be committed. The precise terms of a standard are difficult here because of the variety of situations. One might think of a "considered" or "deliberate" determination instead of a "fixed" one, but those words might preclude liability for the person who on the spur of the moment strongly and seriously urges an immediate assault. What should matter is whether the speaker communicates a desire that the listener will take as meant seriously to endure to the point of commission of the crime; the carefully considered solicitation needs to be distinguished from the comment expressing a momentary intent (e.g., "You should kill that bastard") when no prospect exists for immediate action. The phrase "potentially influential" is meant to preclude liability for persons who may genuinely wish commission of the crime at the moment but have no reason to suppose that what they say will make any difference. A spectator shouting encouragement for a course of action already undertaken or obviously to be undertaken, does not weigh his words as he might if he thought something turned on his expression.

Whether the speaker has intended and conveyed a fixed and potentially influential determination that the crime be committed would be a mixed question of fact and constitutional law. A trial judge should not submit that issue to the jury unless the evidence against the defendant clearly supports such a finding, and appellate judges should carefully scrutinize jury determinations that the standard has been met.

Against my proposal of very little constitutional protection for private non-ideological counseling, it might be urged that the example of urging murder is unfair, that what is called for is some greater degree of protection for solicitation that would carry the day when the crime urged is much less serious. My crucial claims, however, are about the relatively negligible interest in communication of this sort of message and the lack of opportunity for focused countervailing communication, and these points do not depend on the seriousness of the crime.

The principles I have suggested for private nonideological solicitations may seem barred by the literal import of the Supreme Court's test in *Brandenburg* v. *Ohio*, under which "advocacy of the use of force or of law violation" cannot be made punishable "except where such advocacy is directed to inciting or producing imminent lawless action and is likely to incite or produce such action."[4] But it would be astonishing to suppose that the per curiam majority really considered and meant to protect secretive nonideological counseling to crime, and perhaps its talk of advocacy of law violation was meant to suggest ideological advocacy, not every reason that might be given in favor of an act.

One who argues for the application of *Brandenburg* to this setting might claim that little will be lost by immunizing "pure" solicitations and that applying that test generally to "pure" encouragements to crime will obviate the need to undertake troublesome exercises in line drawing. Both these points have substantial merit. The lines I suggest will be somewhat difficult to draw, although the infrequency of having to draw them takes much of the sting out of this worry. Prosecution of "pure" private solicitations is rare, since private solicitations usually propose agreement or offer some inducement within the control of the person soliciting, and the police are not likely to discover many private unsuccessful solicitations. So using the *Brandenburg* test for all "pure" solicitations or for all unsuccessful pure solicitations to crime would not have serious untoward effects. These indeed are strong reasons for legislators not to forbid "pure" solicitations at all, but it would be a mistake to conclude that the reasons support a constitutional standard to that effect.

Perhaps the primary objection to such a constitutional standard is that privileging someone to go around urging murders for the private gain of himself and the person he solicits would misinterpret the significance of free speech and do so in a setting that thoughtful people would find disturbing. If protection were extended that far, the strength of the reasons for constitutional protection when the values of expression are seriously implicated might be missed.

The point can be seen most strongly if Alan's urging to kill their uncle is acted upon by Betty. I assume that First Amendment protection should not depend on whether a communication is in fact acted upon, because that would make constitutional protection turn on what someone not within the speaker's control does after the speaker has communicated. If Alan's urging to kill the uncle is constitutionally privileged, then while Betty would be subject to the most severe penalties, Alan, who put the idea in her mind and strongly urged her to act upon it, would be immune from any punishment. The anomaly of that result is sufficient to call for this departure from the literal terms of the *Brandenburg* test.

Allowing punishment for seriously intended private solicitations appears to conflict with the view of Justices Black and Douglas that the crucial constitutional line is between speech and action. This conflict affords an opportunity to evaluate that position. Thomas Emerson, who has worked out the implications of that position much more thoroughly than the justices had occasion to do, says that

> conduct that amounts to "advice" or "persuasion" would be protected; conduct that moves into the area of "instructions" or "preparations" would not. The essential task would be to distinguish between simply conveying an idea to another person, which idea he may later act upon, and actually participating with him in the performance of an illegal act.[5]

More directly about solicitation he says, "solicitation can be constitutionally punished only when the communication is so close, direct, effective, and instantaneous in its impact that it is part of the action."[6] Presumably what Emerson means by "instantaneous in its impact" is that it produces the action instantaneously.

Under Emerson's principle, one could not be liable for counseling if the crime counseled were not to occur immediately, and this principle would protect successful counseling as well as unsuccessful counseling. It thus would cut significantly into the centuries-old rules of accessorial liability as well as the rules governing solicitation in most modern jurisdictions. Emerson does not really present specific arguments why private nonideological solicitations should enjoy such constitutional protection. His reason seems mainly to be that the broadly appropriate constitutional line is between speech and action and that protection of private solicitation like Alan's is the outcome that that line produces in this context.

A full response to Emerson's position might require examination of all the benefits of the speech-action line compared with alternatives, but perhaps it is enough to say that any line that does not produce a sensible answer to the problem of encouragements to crime, a rather central issue with regard to freedom of speech, cannot be the exclusive touchstone for First Amendment adjudication. In general, Emerson is intensely, and rightly, concerned with abuses that are possible under alternative First Amendment approaches, and he might defend his own position in this context by saying that unless most solicitations are protected, genuinely important communications will be suppressed. But one is hard put to see how a rule that private nonideological solicitations can be punished will put in jeopardy public expressions of values and facts, and even the danger to private communication of controversial ideas seems relatively slight. So an argument based on the impossibility of distinguishing private nonideological solicitations from some other kinds of communications whose protection is warranted is not very persuasive.

The proponent of the speech-action line might take the bull by the horns and argue that private nonideological solicitations in and of themselves do warrant constitutional protection. I have acknowledged that such communications have *some* value as expression which cannot be duplicated exactly by other kinds of communications, but I have suggested that this value is slight in comparison with the dangerous potential of the communications and that punishment of them does not really impinge on the liberty of expression that matters for a liberal society. Thus, if the defender of the speech-action line relies on some sort of balance of communicative value and potential danger, his position has already received an answer.

Conceivably, an advocate of the speech-action distinction might try to accommodate my conclusions about private solicitation, instead of rejecting them, by denying that this sort of communication is really speech in the relevant sense, but, unless one is willing to say that speech does not include any appeals to action on the basis of self-interest, one cannot plausibly exclude such appeals to commit crimes. One could, of course, simply manipulate the distinction between speech and action to define such solicitations as action. Emerson, perhaps troubled by the implications of his basic approach for criminal counseling, makes a start in this direction when he says:

> The more general the communication—the more it relates to general issues, is addressed to a number of persons, urges general action—the more readily it is classified as expression. On the other hand, communication that is specifically concerned with a particular law, aimed at a particular person, and urges particular action, moves closer to action.[7]

From the standpoint of an ordinary understanding of a distinction between speech and other kinds of action, it is hard to understand why urging a large group of people to kill a governor because she is a racist is less action than urging one person to kill her uncle because he is wealthy. Delimiting the boundaries of categories in light of the underlying reasons for their existence is laudable, but the manipulation of ordinary meaning necessary to get the speech-action dichotomy to yield sensible conclusions in this context is so great as to rule out its usefulness here.[8]

A defense of absolute protection for private nonideological solicitation might be grounded in something other than the speech-action distinction. In his article "A Theory of Freedom of Expression,"[9] Thomas Scanlon rejected that distinction as a general approach to liberty of expression but took a position on encouragements to crime that closely resembled Emerson's. Scanlon proposed that one should focus on the possible kinds of justifications a government might have for suppressing communications. An "appeal to the fact that it would be a bad thing if the view communicated by certain acts of expression were to become generally believed" is not legitimate,[10] and an acceptable justification for suppression cannot include "harmful consequences of acts performed as a result of those acts of expression, where the connection between the acts of expression and the subsequent harmful acts consists merely in the fact that the act of expression led the agents to believe (or increased their tendency to believe) these acts to be worth performing."[11] The underlying basis for this conclusion was the view that "the powers of a state are limited to those that citizens could recognize while still regarding themselves as equal, autonomous, rational agents." Since an autonomous person would not without independent consideration accept "the judgment of others as to what he should believe or what he should do," he could not allow the state to restrict expression in order to protect him against "the harm of coming to have false beliefs."[12]

Scanlon's general position is subject to powerful objections which I have explored in Chapters 2 and 6, where I show that rational people, wanting to restrain those who are acting irrationally or who are acting rationally to the detriment of their fellows, might well accept constraints beyond those posited by Scanlon.[13]

Even if Scanlon had been correct that people should be able to have all arguments in favor of doing an act put before them, the application of that view to criminal solicitation would be troublesome. Scanlon acknowledged that, if the speaker changes the circumstances in which the listener chooses, as by giving him an order, then the speaker can be punished, but he said that if all the speaker does is present persuasive reasons, he cannot be punished. One difficulty is that strong efforts at persuasion do subtly change circumstances to some degree, since the listener is aware that others are often disappointed when their persuasion is disregarded. A rational person might perform an act to avoid disappointment of (and possible later rejection by) the speaker, instead of being convinced by the arguments the speaker presents. The attempt to forestall such responses might be an additional reason for constraining the kinds of persuasion available to those who may commit crimes.[14] More importantly, as Harry Wellington has pointed out, constraints on advocacy of illegal conduct do not significantly limit the ideas that may be put before citizens for their deliberation.[15]

Public Ideological Encouragement

Public ideological communication encouraging specific crimes raises substantial First Amendment problems. Contrary to the supposition sometimes made that the basic dichotomy is between remote advocacy of ideas and specific solicitation of immediate action, matters are more complicated. As we have seen in the example employed in the previous section, encouragement can be quite specific but for a crime that is not to be immediate, and sometimes fairly general advocacy can pose an immediate threat of harm, as was illustrated in John Stuart Mill's example of someone telling an excited mob standing outside a corn dealer's house that corn dealers starve the poor.[16] A constitutional standard for public speech must deal both with comments amounting to solicitations of specific crimes and more general advocacy that poses a substantive danger.

For public ideological speech something like the stringent requirements of the *Brandenburg* v. *Ohio* test are most plainly apt. Such public speech should generally be constitutionally punishable if and only if (1) the speaker seriously urges commission of a specific crime within the very near future, and (2) it is reasonably likely that the speech will contribute to the commission of the crime within the very near future. This principle is subject to two qualifications, however. One qualification concerns a class of "open crimes," considered below in this section, for which encouragement should possibly receive more absolute protection than the principle affords. The second qualification involves special instances, explored in later sections, in which public speech urging crimes may be punished even though the demands of the first branch of this principle are not met.

The two branches of the basic standard are drawn largely from *Brandenburg*, but an explanation of their content and a defense against possible alternatives are needed. The first branch is composed of three criteria: serious urging, specific crime, and very near future. Serious intent, as already indicated in respect to private nonideological solicitation, should be understood as a signficant constitutional requirement. The court of appeals in *United States* v. *Spock*[17] observed that people may sign written documents whose explicit terms urge criminal acts without themselves subscribing to the criminal purpose, and some explicit oral encouragements are either not really intended or are not intended in a firm way. Because of the special danger that juries trying defendants who have advocated unpopular social doctrines will find serious intent on the basis of ambiguous evidence, the rule should be that such intent cannot be found of someone engaging in public advocacy unless the believed external facts foreclose other possible constructions of his or her action. *Hess* v. *Indiana*,[18] in which defendant had said in the midst of a demonstration, "We'll take the fucking street later," provides an example of a situation in which this standard would require acquittal. Whether or not Hess had any serious aim to reoccupy the street at a later time was simply not ascertainable from these events. Sometimes a serious intent would be evident from the circumstances of the communication and its content. If a speaker urges young men to turn in their draft cards at a meeting called for that purpose, the inference is irresistible that he seriously intends his listeners to do just that. In other circumstances, if words used by the speaker yield the natural interpretation that he is urging commission of a specific crime, external evidence may demonstrate beyond doubt the speaker's serious intent, evidence of the sort that was available against William Sloane Coffin in the *Spock* case.[19]

The second criterion requires that the speaker urge commission of a specific crime, specificity being judged in terms of whether members of the audience, without further instruction, would know in what behavior to engage. If, for example, the speaker seriously urged that members of the audience shoot police officers whenever they meet them alone, that would be specific enough, but a general plea for force against the police would not be. The main reason for distinguishing between urging to specific crimes and mere advocacy of illegal acts is that the latter, even if clearly constituting urging to action rather than abstract advocacy, lies too close to the expression of general ideas to warrant punishment in any but the most exceptional circumstances. A subsidiary reason for drawing that line is the unreliability of judgments about intent and likely danger in the absence of encouragement to a specific crime. Exactly how specific the crime must be is troublesome. Suppose the speaker names five or six crimes any one of which the listener is urged to commit against a particular person. That seems specific enough; the speaker is urging these crimes in the alternative. Suppose, instead, the speaker said, "Make sure you do something so that the particular victim will feel severe pain and require hospitalization." This language urges at least a serious assault. What of Most's proposal at the turn of the century that his readers murder government officials?[20] It might be doubted whether all officials were meant to be prospective victims, but certainly high officials would be. If the likelihood of acting was high and imminent *and* Most was plainly serious in his urging, perhaps that should be enough to satisfy the constitutional minimum. If that is correct, the requirement of specificity can be seen as closely linked to seriousness of intent and imminent danger. It is arguable whether the requirement of specificity should be viewed as an independent requirement under the First Amendment or as bearing heavily on the presence of other constitutional requisites.

The third criterion of the first branch, "very near future," refers to what the speaker intends. The same criterion in the second branch refers to what is actually likely to happen. "Very near future" is substituted for *Brandenburg*'s "imminent" to avoid any suggestion, possibly to be gleaned from *Hess* v. *Indiana*, that "imminent" always means momentarily. (Recall that the Court said that an urging to "take the street later" did not pose an imminent harm when what must have been contemplated was not more than a delay of a few hours.) If a speaker or writer seriously urges the murder of a specified individual one day hence, then his speech should not be immune from punishment because of the temporal delay. "Very near future" is meant to have a modest degree of flexibility, account being taken of the seriousness of the crime, opportunities for intervening speech, and the likelihood that the audience will have opportunity for critical reflection before the crime is to be committed. I say a modest degree of flexibility; a crime to be committed more than a week or two from the time members of the audience receive the communication would in no event be in the very near future.[21]

"Reasonable likelihood" that the speech will contribute to commission of the crime, the other criterion in the second branch, is also meant to be moderately flexible in relation to the seriousness of the crime. Though the likelihood would have to be substantial for any crime, a more-probable-than-not standard would be too strict for a grave crime, though perhaps appropriate for a petty one. The relevant probability concerns the nexus between the speech and the crime, not just the overall likelihood that the crime will occur.

The requirements of reasonable likelihood and very near future cut into the law of criminal solicitation, and some critics will object that a public speaker should not be immune from punishment if he seriously urges a specific crime in the more remote future[22] or seriously urges an immediate crime that is not likely to occur. The demand that an intended and actual danger be close at hand is partly a further assurance that the speaker seriously intends that a specific crime be committed, but the main answer to this challenge rests on my initial assumption that public ideological solicitation does have substantial value as expression and should be punishable only if it seriously threatens the public interest. If encouragement is given for criminal acts in the more distant future, opportunity exists for countervailing speech and for authorities to take steps to prevent the crime. Moreover, as the future extends, estimation of likelihood becomes too difficult; so some sort of proximity requirement is an essential component of any workable test of likelihood.

Other critics will find this basic standard insufficiently speech-protective. The claim that the proper line is one between speech and action has more plausibility here than in the context of private nonideological communication, because the values of expression are more fully implicated in public ideological speech and the dangers of improper determinations based on abhorrence of underlying ideas are greater. Nevertheless, one who urges commission of a crime when there is a substantial likelihood that it will soon be committed bears considerable responsibility for its actual or probable commission. And requiring people to refrain from such urging is not seriously to erode the ambit of protected speech, since people are left free to communicate their underlying ideas in other ways.

A possible narrower attack on my proposed standard would be that liability should be permitted to attach only if the proposed crime is actually committed, the theory being that it takes actual commission to establish the requisite degree of responsibility and to provide a solid enough basis for concluding that commission was likely when the speech was given.

This attack contains a core of good sense which recommends it as a basis for legislative action, but it would be hard to turn this limitation into an appropriate constitutional principle. If, in two settings, identical speeches are made with identical intents and identical likelihoods that they will be acted upon, allowing one speaker to be punished because his audience happens by chance to have a responsive listener and precluding punishment of the other speaker because his audience lacked such a listener would be anomalous constitutional doctrine.

Perhaps the argument might be that we have no solid basis to assess likelihood in the absence of success. The problem with this argument is that, in some situations, for example, when the police intervene in the nick of time or when similar speeches in closely similar settings have produced crimes, a basis does exist for estimating likelihood though no crime has actually occurred. If it is said that the speaker's responsibility is somehow greater just because the harm occurs, that argument hardly is of constitutional dimension, whatever its relevance for ordinary penal policy. Occurrence is not an acceptable constitutional surrogate for likelihood, and it possesses no other plausible constitutional basis.

There may be a narrow class of public ideological encouragements to crime that should receive absolute protection. The class consists of instances in which persons not in institutional positions of authority in relation to their audience encourage the commission of open crimes that do not threaten persons or property. By *open crimes* I mean crimes committed by actors who are identifiable and accessible to punishment, crimes such as open refusal to pay taxes,[23] open refusal to submit to the draft, and illegal strikes.

This possible immunity derives from the "least restrictive alternative" concept of First Amendment law: that the government must not restrict speech more than is really required; it is related to the notion that if speech is to be suppressed the substantive evil should be serious. For some crimes, action against the actual perpetrators should be sufficient to protect society's interests. The requirement of openness guarantees that public authorities will be able to identify those who have committed the substantive crime, so that punishment of the potential solicitor is not necessary in order to prevent otherwise undetectable criminal acts. When substantial harm is done to individuals or property, detection and punishment come too late to protect all important social interests, but, in respect to crimes without these consequences, society's basic interests may be served by keeping criminal actions to a small number, and successful action directly against perpetrators can often minimize the damage of any particular violation. In regard to First Amendment values it is relevant that, if a crime is to be committed openly and violators are typically punished, the arguments presented to a listener for breaking the law are likely to be strongly ideological, and the listener, unless he is a subordinate of the speaker, is likely to reflect carefully before going ahead. If, however, the speaker stands in an institutional position of authority in relation to his audience, e.g., he is a union leader speaking to his members or a priest speaking to his own congregation, his authority may carry his audience into action without their careful reflection and regardless of the intrinsic persuasiveness of his message. In these settings, even if the speaker stops short of commanding action, his responsibility is too great to bar his punishment.

Private Ideological Solicitation to Specific Crimes

Having first discussed private nonideological solicitation and public ideological solicitation, the categories with the least and most claim to constitutional protection, I now address the more troublesome intermediate situations. Earlier chapters establish that many private communications fall within a political principle of free speech and are plainly protected by the First Amendment, but the possibilities of powerful influence and manipulation, the limited audience, and the absence of countervailing communication provide substantial reasons for affording less protection to private ideological solicitation than to public ideological solicitation.

For these reasons and also because outsiders will be hard put to estimate the likelihood that speech will succeed with a small audience, especially one selected by the speaker, private ideological encouragement to specific crimes should not be subjected to the same requirements of likely success and commission in the near future that apply to public encouragements. That is to say, the approach of *Brandenburg* is inapt for private encouragement, even when that is cast in ideological terms.

On the other hand, somewhat greater protection may be warranted than for nonideological private solicitation. As in the context of public advocacy, strict standards for judging the speaker's intent that a specific crime be committed should apply; the speaker should not be punishable unless his message unambiguously urges commission of a specific crime or his message naturally bears that interpretation and external evidence, if believed, leaves no possible doubt about the matter. Further, a private speaker, like a public one, should probably not be punishable for urging, on ideological grounds, an open crime that does not threaten harm to persons or property.

Part of the function of the standard of serious intent, particularly important in this context, is to distinguish active encouragements from responses to requests for advice. One whose advice is sought should be free to respond with the degree of specificity that is elicited, and a conscientious cool response should not be construed as solicitation. This exclusion should be required as a matter of constitutional law. If a person is not making an effort to cause a result but is merely responding to a question about whether it is right to cause such a result, he should be constitutionally free to state his honest opinion, even though he recommends a specific criminal course of action and hopes that his disinterested advice will be taken. Responsive advice often includes an ideological component, but the seeking and giving of sincere advice are so important for personal deliberation and decision that one who renders requested advice should be constitutionally protected even if his advice is addressed solely to how his listener can most effectively pursue his own ends.

Private ideological solicitation should be subjected to some probability test, though one less stringent than the proposed reasonable-likelihood standard for public solicitation. The idea is that some solicitation is genuinely harmless, very unlikely to eventuate in criminal action. When such solicitation involves the expression of ideas, its immunity should rest on a firmer base than prosecutorial discretion or statutory interpretation. An appropriate principle would be that private ideological solicitation cannot be punished if it presents no significant danger of criminal harm.

Public Nonideological Solicitation

When one person wants to tell others that committing a specific crime is in their self-interest, he is unlikely to do so publicly unless his message is colored by ideological content or his aim is commercial. A noncommercial public plea to people to use proscribed drugs, for example, will almost certainly be cast partly in terms of the general value of these drugs for a healthy or profound inner life or perhaps in terms of the right not to be regulated by society in one's personal choices. The only sorts of situations in which public appeals are frequently made to simple self-interest concern commercial relations, understood broadly to include proposed exchanges that provide specific tangible benefits to each party.[24] Then the speaker stands to profit in some quite specific way if the listener acts as the speaker recommends. Since nonideological, noncommercial solicitation is so rare, all noncommercial public solicitation should be treated the same—that is, should be given the protection afforded explicitly ideological public solicitation.

As the Supreme Court opinions on advertising reflect, informing the public about the availability of goods and services at certain prices enjoys less constitutional protection than the sorts of communications historically covered under the First Amendment. The Court has consistently said that advertisements proposing illegal acts can be banned.[25] Partly because promotion of products and information about them is a less important aspect of social discourse than many other subjects and partly because advertisements, even if they do not amount to offers, look toward contractual arrangements and can be viewed as aspects of those arrangements, constitutional protections like those elaborated in *Brandenburg* are plainly inappropriate for commercial advertisements about one's willingness to enter into criminal transactions.[26] Perhaps the safeguards applicable to private ideological solicitations would be appropriate—a strict test for seriousness of intent and a requirement of some danger that the proposals will produce criminal action. But further protection of straightforward commercial encouragements to commit crimes would not be warranted. When a commercial proposal to engage in criminal acts includes some ideological content (say an advertisement for proscribed drugs incorporates strong libertarian sentiments), perhaps the more stringent probability standard of reasonable likelihood that speech will produce the crime should be applied. But likelihood that the crime will occur in the very near future should not be a condition for punishment. The ideological message carries somewhat less presumptive value in this context because of likely manipulation to serve the enterprise's interests. And since a commercial proposal indicating the future opportunity for a criminal transaction may well exercise a continuing influence, a strict temporal test would be inappropriate.

Judicial Lines between Public and Private and between Ideological and Nonideological Solicitation

The suggestions I have made thus far about constitutional protection for encouragements to specific crimes might require drawing a line in some cases between public and private solicitation and drawing a line in other cases between ideological and nonideological solicitation. As I indicated in Chapter 6, the crucial factor for public speech is that the message be communicated in a way in which its content can become known to a wide audience. Speeches made to moderate-sized groups not selected for sympathy with the message qualify as public, but communication to a specifically selected group with a secret membership and confidentiality requirements would count as private.

The line between nonideological and ideological solicitation is roughly the line between telling somebody simply that some act will benefit him and telling him that it is his duty or his right, or will be of broad benefit, or is warranted within some overall philosophical understanding of human life and social change. For a communication to count as ideological, the speaker must make a serious assertion that what is urged has broader significance in one of these ways.

In view of the Supreme Court concern about distinctions based on the content of speech, the distinction between ideological and nonideological speech may appear somewhat troublesome, because it involves the courts in saying that one kind of speech is more valuable than another.[27] This particular judgment about value, however, does not present the danger of preference for messages that those in authority happen to favor which explains much of the distaste for content distinctions. The Court has in fact embraced something like a distinction between ideological and nonideological speech in the context of offers of legal services, allowing a private lawyer's effort to engage a potential client to be subject to much stricter regulation[28] than would be appropriate for a statement by a lawyer for the American Civil Liberties Union to a woman who may have been sterilized illegally by a state agency that the organization wished to sue on her behalf and would give her free representation.[29] I perceive no decisive reason against employing a similar distinction for criminal encouragements.

Nevertheless, direct practical use of that distinction could be eliminated with little loss. In my suggestions, its precise role is with respect to private encouragements, assigning a stricter standard for findings of intent and supplying a minimal-danger standard for ideological solicitation. If those protections were eliminated in that context or extended to all private solicitations, the changes would affect few situations. The somewhat more important distinction for public encouragements is between commercial encouragements and all others, a distinction that enjoys a more settled basis in existing law.

Factual Disclosures Intended to Produce Specific Crimes

This chapter so far has discussed explicit encouragements to commit specific crimes. I turn now to two sorts of communications that are intended to produce crimes but do not involve explicit encouragements.

I first address disclosures of fact made in order to provide someone else with an incentive to commit a particular crime. As I indicated in Chapter 6, such disclosures are usually made in the context of explicit encouragements, but my example of a neighbor's "letting drop" the information that someone is a police informer shows that occasionally a factual disclosure may stand alone. In terms of penal policy, if the speaker has the purpose that the listener commit the crime, factual disclosures are not sensibly distinguished from encouragements, except perhaps in being more dangerous. The communicative value of such disclosures is relatively slight. As with private nonideological encouragement, a person who in private discloses particular facts in order to cause a crime should be punishable upon proof of his serious intent to cause the crime. But, in the absence of expressed support for the crime at the time of the communication, a serious intent should be found only upon the most clear evidence, such as a statement to others about what one was trying to do.

The problem of constitutional standards is more troublesome for facts—"how to make a hydrogen bomb" or "the names of undercover CIA agents"[30]—that are publicly disclosed and of general relevance. In some circumstances disclosures that harm a public interest represent some breach of confidentiality or involve "theft" of the "property" of the entity that possesses the information;[31] but sometimes information has been acquired by the speaker in a manner involving neither a confidential relationship nor a wrongful act. Because of the breadth of the audience, these communications have substantial value as speech, and the need for a strict rule about finding intent is especially important, lest a jury convict because of outrage over the facts someone has chosen to disclose. A person should not be punishable for encouraging a general crime like murder by publicly disclosing facts unless the prosecution's evidence leaves no possible doubt that his purpose has been to aid or cause that criminal result.

Because the effect of crime-aiding information is unlikely to dissipate itself like the persuasive force of encouragement and because possibilities of counter-vailing communication are much less relevant, there should be no requirement that the crime be intended to be and be likely to be committed in the very near future. One thinks, for example, of disclosing the names of CIA agents, expecting that it will take a month or two for terrorist groups to carry out assassinations. The constitutional standard here should be that a person intend that the crime be committed and that it be reasonably likely that it will be committed in the "near future," that term permitting a period of up to a few months for the most serious crimes but precluding speculation about what will happen years hence.

Communications That Fall Short of Encouragement to Specific Crimes but Are Supportive of Criminal Action

In this section I consider expressions which do not amount to criminal solicitation but which nevertheless encourage specific criminal action. Included are general and vague recommendations of criminal behavior that are not specific enough to amount to criminal solicitation or to meet ordinary constitutional standards of specificity, and some remarks that ostensibly do not encourage criminal behavior at all. I shall focus on the latter.

The basic problem for public speech of this kind can be sharply illustrated by the following hypothetical situation: a respected citizen addresses an emotionally charged mob that is on the verge of assaulting a local jail to lynch a prisoner; he first mildly suggests that it is wrong to take the law into one's own hands, but then passionately urges that the prisoner deserves death and that the system of justice is a mockery in failing to provide that option. Even in their emotional state, members of the audience do not take his words as actually urging the lynching, but his strong sympathy with their outrage strengthens their inclination to go ahead. Should the speaker be constitutionally immune from punishment?

According to *Brandenburg*, one can be punished for advocacy of law violation only if the advocacy is "directed to inciting or producing imminent lawless action." If someone who explicitly urges a violation of law can be punished only when this standard is met, *a fortiori*, more general expression of ideas should be protected unless the standard is satisfied. The language of *Brandenburg* would, therefore, preclude punishment of our hypothetical speaker if he did not intend to produce the lynching, and, even if that was his intent, doubt could be raised whether his words were "directed" to producing the lynching unless listeners so understood them. As with other problems we have considered, however, we should not regard the precise formulation of *Brandenburg*, adopted with different circumstances in mind, as foreclosing an otherwise appropriate approach.

A jury should not be permitted to infer from a speech alone that foolhardy remarks falling short of explicit encouragement to crime must have been uttered with intent to produce a criminal result. But if that intent can be clearly established by external evidence (e.g., the speaker has previously told friends he means to stir up the mob to lynching), if the crime is very serious (involving substantial risk of death or serious bodily harm, for example), and if its commission is likely, imminent (in the sense of immediate, within the next few moments), and subject to the speaker's influence, then constitutional principle should permit punishment for solicitation.

This narrow exception to taking the words on their face or as they would be understood by the audience recognizes the power of spoken words that fall short of incitement to provoke emotionally charged audiences into immediate action. The exception could make a speaker liable for general advocacy of criminal action (e.g., "All rapists should be killed"),[32] other expressions of value ("Public justice is a sham"), and statements of fact ("That prisoner has raped and butchered six women"), when he relies on the power of his words to move his audience to immediate and grave criminal action.

Although it is arguable that the First Amendment should not be read to foreclose *general* encouragements of crime made in private contexts and with no ideological message, I believe the interest in free communications is great enough so that standards of specificity warrant constitutional status for private as well as public speech. And if the state's claim is that remarks that are on their face only general encouragements or judgments about others are in fact designed to produce specific crimes, essentially the same stringent test should apply for determining intent as applies to public speech. For private contexts, the crime encouraged should at least have to be fairly serious, say a felony, but it would not have to be imminent.

Encouragements to Harmful Actions That Are Not Criminal

I now turn to situations in which the act encouraged or assisted by information, and so forth, is not in itself criminal but is thought to cause some social harm. Those who support a particular course of action should generally not be subject to more serious penalties than those who actually perform it.[33] In the absence of some special exception, the First Amendment should bar treating someone as a criminal because he urges a noncriminal act, and it should bar imposing civil liability on someone who urges behavior that is not at all wrongful legally.

This suggested basic principle is not beyond dispute. If the government *could* treat behavior as wrongful,[34] arguably it should be able to treat encouragement of the behavior as wrongful, whether or not it actually makes the behavior subject to penalty and regardless of the comparative severity with which it treats encouragement and behavior. But as long as a speaker's communication involves the values protected by liberty of speech, treating the speaker more severely than the actual performer unduly discourages expression.

Even if the basic principle is sound, it is subject to exceptions, some of which I shall sketch. One involves situations in which the act that is likely to be caused is a decision by an official made because of influence from outside proper channels. Once the official receives the message encouraging him to decide a certain way, he may have difficulty completely dispelling its influence, and if he receives no money or other favor for rendering the decision, establishing that he was actually influenced will be impossible. In these situations, the fact that the law does not forbid the simple act of deciding under external influence does not itself preclude punishment for attempts to influence (although as the contempt cases indicate, there are independent constitutional limits on that).

A related, but a more arguable, exception concerns social fears that certain messages may cause persons to act without any independent reflection on the issues involved. Many people will simply not cross a picket line or a labor picket line, regardless of the dispute involved. Since a person can choose not to shop at a store for virtually any reason, having a rule that no one can make that decision on the basis of a picket line would be impractical. But society may wish to limit the number of such decisions by limiting picketing. Because picketing has an element of action as well as communication, the Court has carved out a particular niche for it, but conceivably the government can regulate other communications that have a "signal" effect while leaving responses to the signals unregulated.

Another exception concerns crimes defined partly in terms of a forbidden motive. By themselves such crimes raise no constitutional problem; society may forbid certain acts done with the ulterior objective to aid an enemy in wartime, though the same acts would not be criminal if done for a different objective. If the act that is to be punished is one of communication, then strict standards of proof of the forbidden ulterior objective, as well as the other First Amendment safeguards, would be applied. But there should be no absolute bar to punishing a union leader who in fact urges a strike because he wants to aid the enemy, though his followers have innocently acted upon his appeal to strike for economic gains.

Some communications interfere with special relationships that society wishes to guard against destructive external influences. Although substantial First Amendment arguments could be mounted against the grounding of civil liability on some kinds of communications that may harm family relationships, the simple fact that a husband who loses affection for his wife is not subject to damages does not conclude the issue of whether someone who encourages him to do so may be liable for damages. In this example, bringing the behavior of the encouraged actor under legal control is impossible or undesirable. In other instances primary actors may be subject to special penalties; a soldier may be court-martialed or a professor fired for failing to perform his duties. If society wants to punish "outsiders" who encourage violations of duty, it may appropriately do so by the ordinary criminal law, which may not govern the main actor because of the presence of an effective alternative scheme of regulation.

A more general exception may be applicable to commercial advertising. If some behavior, like cigarette smoking, is deemed socially harmful, but making that behavior criminal is thought unwise, the government may have the authority to bar encouragements to engage in the behavior by those who directly profit from it. Congress has, indeed, acted on that sort of premise in forbidding cigarette advertising over television and radio. The courts have sustained that restriction against attack by broadcasters.[35] And in a 1986 Supreme Court case upholding a prohibition in Puerto Rico of local advertising of casino gambling, Justice Rehnquist wrote, "It would . . . be a strange constitutional doctrine which would concede to the legislature the authority to totally ban a product or activity, but deny to the legislature the authority to forbid the stimulation of demand for the product or activity through advertising on behalf of those who would profit from such increased demand."[36] Such a limitation on encouragements is one illustration of how commercial speech may be less protected than other speech, since noncommercial assertions that people should smoke cigarettes would certainly enjoy constitutional protection.

Though this list of exceptions and arguable exceptions is not intended to be exhaustive, it does suggest the sorts of reasons that support treatment different from that suggested by the proposed general principle that the legal consequences of an encouragement should not be more severe than the legal consequences of the act encouraged.

Institutional Settings and Special Responsibilities

This chapter has concentrated on relationships between the government and ordinary citizens and on legal liability of the usual sorts. The government's involvement in many activities establishes relationships between it and individuals which are more intensive than the relationship between it and an ordinary citizen. Governments have soldiers, bureaucrats, and students at public universities, to mention only a few special subjects of government concern. Some activities engaged in by such persons can be classed as wrongful behavior subject to punishment or as grounds for dismissal, even though the behavior does not violate any ordinary criminal statute. A student may be expelled for cheating, a bureaucrat demoted or dismissed for failure to work, a soldier put in jail for refusing to obey orders. The penalty usually falls short of a typical criminal sanction, but the military example shows that even such sanctions are sometimes appropriate.

What are the constitutional limits on encouragements of behavior that violates special institutional norms? One commentator has suggested that only communications that meet the *Brandenburg* standard can be punished and has criticized Supreme Court decisions that do not conform to this approach.[37] If the communication is by an outsider, the position is unobjectionable; an ordinary citizen should not be held liable for encouraging a noncriminal breach of duty if he could not be held liable for similarly encouraging crime.[38] But the position is not sound for all "insiders." Those with institutional responsibilities often have a special influence over others in similar positions; their denigration of institutional duties can have a destructive effect on working relationships, whether or not their comments lead to ascertainable violations of duty, and their acceptance of special duties to and benefits from the government renders their claims to liberty of expression to denigrate those duties weaker than the claim of an ordinary citizen. Thus the Court has rightly assumed that a military officer can constitutionally be held liable for urging nonperformance of duty even if his speech would not be punishable under the *Brandenburg* test.[39]

Though any attempt to propose appropriate standards for various special settings is beyond the scope of this book, the following generalizations are apt. The interest in liberty of expression must stand very high, and only powerful justifications should support more relaxed standards for punishment than apply to ordinary citizens. Such justifications will be easier to find when the social setting and duties are quite different from those of ordinary civilian life (as with military responsibilities) than when they resemble those of civilians much more closely (as with student responsibilities to observe ordinary campus regulations).[40]

This is one of the few places in the book in which I mention the relevance of special institutional settings, but they can make a difference for most of the other subjects I cover as well. At no point do I separately discuss how far the principles I discuss apply to prisoners, but the prison context also calls for separate attention.

Notes

1. I assume that constitutional standards for encouragements to conspire, aid and abet, or solicit should be subject to the same constitutional standards as direct encouragement to "act"; so I do not treat those more "remote" solicitations separately in this chapter.

2. *Model Penal Code* § 5.02 Comment, at 375–76.

3. *District of Columbia* v. *Garcia*, 335 A.2d 217, 224 (D.C. App. 1975), certiorari denied, 423 U.S. 894 (1975). I should note that the kind of solicitation involved in the case was not a simple encouragement or request but an offer to engage together in illegal acts of sodomy. In *United States* v. *Buttorff*, 572 F.2d 619 (8th Cir. 1978), certiorari denied, 437 U.S. 906 (1978), the court intimated that specific urging to violate tax laws did not count as advocacy under *Brandenburg* v. *Ohio* even when the urging was ideologically motivated and public. But in that case the speech of the defendants included explanations of how to violate the law on tax withholding by making false claims.

4. 395 U.S. 444, 447 (1969).

5. T. Emerson, *The System of Freedom of Expression* 75 (New York, Random House 1970).

6. Id. at 404.

7. Id. at 405.

8. Emerson's approach is criticized in J. Yacavone, "Emerson's Distinction," 6 *Connecticut Law Review* 49 (1973). See also A. Fuchs, "Further Steps toward a General Theory of Freedom of Expression," 18 *William and Mary Law Review* 347 (1976).

9. T. Scanlon, "A Theory of Freedom of Expression," 1 *Philosophy & Public Affairs* 204 (1972).

10. Id. at 209.

11. Id. at 213.

12. Id. at 215–17.

13. They might also wish to forestall their own yielding to temptations, by forestalling encouragement to attractive but harmful actions.

14. Another feature of Scanlon's approach is his suggested line between urging and dangerous information. Scanlon acknowledged the possible justification for proscribing the dissemination of highly dangerous facts, like a simple method of producing nerve gas, id. at 211–12, but he did not then recognize how far that concession undercut the force of his argument. He drew a distinction between expression that points out "good reasons for action" and expression that provides people "with the means to do what they wanted to do anyway," id. at 212, believing that autonomous decision is impaired if the agent is precluded from examining the reasons for and against action, id. at 215–18, but is not impaired if the agent is simply unable to carry out his desires. But what at one level is a good reason for action may at another level be information about a means by which the listener can do what he wants to do. If *A* urges *B* to cheat on his income taxes, telling him that cheaters are rarely caught and indicating which methods of cheating reduce the possibility of discovery, *A* may be providing crucial information to someone who has previously decided he would happily cheat if he could avoid punishment; but, even if *B* had never thought through that issue, he surely has decided he would like to save money, and *A*'s persuasion indicates a means for his doing so. Besides revealing the great difficulty of making Scanlon's distinction, this example partially illustrates the extent to which our thought about what actions are worth performing is conditioned by our understanding of what realistically is possible. Whether one is defining the requisites of autonomous decision or determining the constraints on expression that a rational, autonomous person might accept, one cannot justify a sharp distinction between information about means of doing things and arguments for and against doing things. Thus if we concede that some information about means is so dangerous it can be suppressed, we cannot rule out on principle the possibility that some dimensions of persuasion may also be suppressed. Apparently Scanlon now agrees with this point. T. Scanlon, "Freedom of Expression and Categories of Expression," 40 *University of Pittsburgh Law Review* 519, 534–35 (1979).

15. H. Wellington, "On Freedom of Expression," 88 *Yale Law Journal*, 1105, 1124–25 (1979).

16. See J. S. Mill, *On Liberty*, in *Three Essays*, 69 (World Classics ed., London, Oxford University Press 1912) (1st ed. of *On Liberty* in 1859).

17. 416 F.2d 165 (1st Cir. 1969).

18. 414 U.S. 105, 107 (1973).

19. 416 F.2d at 177–78.

20. *People* v. *Most*, 171 N.Y. 423, 64 N.E. 175 (1902), summarized in Chapter 11.

21. Some opinions have suggested a flexible notion of imminence, in at least one instance apparently accepting outer limits of time beyond what I have urged, *People* v. *Rubin*, 96 Cal. App.3d 968, 158 Cal. Rptr. 488 (1979), certiorari denied, 449 U.S. 821 (1980) (public offer to pay for murder imminent enough although main focus was event five weeks off). See also *United States* v. *Kelner*, 534 F.2d 1020, 1029 (2d Cir. 1976), certiorari denied, 429 U.S. 1022 (1976) (Mulligan, J., concurring) (one week imminent enough for threat to murder). My statement in text supposes that the effect of public urgings of serious crimes is likely to dissipate if they do not occur shortly before the crimes are to be committed, but one might think that some encouragements, particularly organized and repeated ones, are so dangerous they should be punished even though the feared harm is not "imminent" in even a fairly loose sense. See generally M. Redish, *Freedom of Expression* 186–92 (Charlottesville, Va., The Michie Co. 1984), defending the clear-and-present-danger standard as the best approach to advocacy of unlawful conduct and arguing for a flexible test of determining the level of immediacy.

22. In *Freedom of Speech* 158 (Oxford, Clarendon Press 1985), Eric Barendt points out that the British conviction in the *Arrowsmith* case, approved by the European Commission, for a woman's advocacy that soldiers refuse to serve in Northern Ireland or desert the army, could not have survived under the *Brandenburg* formulation.

23. In *United States* v. *Freeman*, 761 F.2d 549 (9th Cir. 1985), certiorari denied, 476 U.S. 1120 (1986), the court of appeals, in an opinion by now Supreme Court Justice Kennedy, said that advocacy of tax noncompliance as an abstract idea was protected, but that "if the intent of the actor and the objective meaning of the words used are so close in time and purpose to a substantive evil as to become part of the ultimate crime itself" a conviction for counseling would be appropriate. The decision overturned the trial judge's failure to instruct the jury in a First Amendment defense, on the ground that the jury might conceivably have believed only the evidence showing advocacy and not the evidence indicating more active involvement. The court did not intimate any possible defense for open solicitation of an immediate violation of the tax laws. Such solicitation would fit within the possible immunity I suggest. Defendant in *Freeman*, however, urged the filing of false returns, and the special immunity would not cover that. On how *Brandenburg* v. *Ohio* relates to ideological tax cases, see also *United States* v. *Buttorff*, 572 F.2d 619 (8th Cir. 1978), certiorari denied, 437 U.S. 906 (1978); *United States* v. *Moss*, 604 F.2d 569 (8th Cir. 1979), certiorari denied, 444 U.S. 1071 (1980).

24. See, e.g., *United States* v. *Barnett*, 667 F.2d 835 (9th Cir. 1982). In classified advertisements, people may encourage illegal actions that will benefit them in some nonmonetary way. For these purposes, such advertisements would count as commercial solicitation.

25. See, e.g., *Pittsburgh Press Co.* v. *Pittsburgh Comm'n on Human Relations*, 413 U.S. 376, 388 (1973); *Hoffman Estates* v. *Flipside, Hoffman Estates, Inc.*, 455 U.S. 489, 496 (1982); *Brown* v. *Hartlage*, 456 U.S. 45, 55 (1982).

26. See generally D. Farber, "Commercial Speech and First Amendment Theory," 74 *Northwestern University Law Review* 372 (1979). See also T. Jackson and J. Jeffries, "Commercial Speech: Economic Due Process and the First Amendment," 65 *Virginia Law Review* 1 (1979); Comment, "Coercion, Blackmail and the Limits of Protected Speech," 131 *University of Pennsylvania Law Review* 1469, 1479-81 (1983).

27. The distinction is sharply attacked by Redish, note 21 supra, at 83-84, who seems to assume that the distinction is more critical for my practical recommendations than it is.

28. See *Ohralik* v. *Ohio State Bar Ass'n*, 436 U.S. 447 (1978).

29. See *In re Primus*, 436 U.S. 412 (1978).

30. See *Haig* v. *Agee*, 453 U.S. 280 (1981) (upholding revocation of passport for former Central Intelligence Agency employee disclosing damaging information including the names of agents in the field).

31. See Emerson, note 5 supra, at 58, on espionage and military censorship.

32. In context, words of general encouragement to crime ("Citizens should kill rapists if the state does not") might clearly communicate intended support for the lynching of a particular suspected rapist. In that event, no external evidence of intent should be required.

33. Melville Nimmer asserted an aspect of this position strongly in what he called an "anti-ignorance" principle: "Speech may not be restricted because it will disclose facts which may persuade those learning such facts to engage in conduct which is harmful, if such conduct is not itself unlawful." M. Nimmer, *Nimmer on Free Speech* 2-32 (New York, Matthew Bender Co. 1984); see *Bigelow* v. *Virginia*, 421 U.S. 809 (1975). The reason why Nimmer's anti-ignorance principle covers only an aspect of the sentence in the text is that it deals only with factual disclosures.

34. If the behavior itself is constitutionally protected, encouragement of the behavior would always (or almost always) be protected too. See Comment, note 26 supra, at 1480.

35. See Public Health Cigarette Smoking Act of 1969, 15 U.S.C. § 1335; *Capital Broadcasting Company* v. *Mitchell*, 333 F. Supp. 582 (U.S.D.C. 1971) (three-judge ct.). Judge Wright, dissenting, indicates that the cigarette companies actually welcomed the legislation because a previous decision holding the fairness doctrine applicable to cigarette advertising had led to the broadcast of many antismoking messages that had reduced cigarette consumption.

36. *Posadas de Puerto Rico Associates* v. *Tourism Company* 478 U.S. 328, 346 (1986). In similar words Eric Barendt, note 22 supra, at 61–62, has written: "If it is constitutionally open for a government to ban, say, the use of a dangerous drug, such as heroin or cigarettes, it would be bizarre if it could not take the more moderate step of discouraging consumption by outlawing promotional advertising." See also Farber, note 26 supra.

37. Comment, "*Brandenburg* v. *Ohio*, a Speech Test for All Seasons?" 43 *University of Chicago Law Review* 151 (1975).

38. The government may, however, have power to reduce the access of speakers to special personnel. See *Greer* v. *Spock*, 424 U.S. 828 (1976).

39. See *Parker* v. *Levy*, 417 U.S. 733 (1974), whose reasoning is criticized in Comment, note 37 supra, at 181–86.

40. A student's duty to keep peace and order under campus regulations is more nearly analogous to an ordinary citizen's duties than is the student's responsibility not to cheat. It is highly doubtful that a state university would have to tolerate a student who kept urging other students to cheat but whose communications were not punishable under *Brandenburg* or the standards suggested here.

16

Reckless and Negligent Risk
That One's Communications
Will Cause Criminal Harms

The last chapter considered situations in which some social danger lies in the effect a communication is intended to have; here I deal with circumstances in which the speaker does not aim for a crime or similar harmful effect, but makes a communication that generates a substantial risk that such an effect will occur.

We can begin with the premise that punishing speech that is reckless as to a particular result cannot constitutionally be easier than punishing otherwise similar speech that is intended to cause the result. Indeed, since the values of speech are more fully implicated when one is not aiming to accomplish an immediate practical result, the requirements for liability should generally be more stringent when all the speaker does is to risk a result. I shall treat a number of related subjects, all on the basic assumption that speech may infrequently be foreclosed solely because of unintended harms its message may cause.

Dangerous Facts

In the absence of proof that the speaker wished to cause commission of a specific crime or is training people for criminal activities, when, if ever, can accurate disclosures of facts be punished because of the likelihood that they will produce criminal acts or grave immediate harms, like death and serious injury? Reserving for Chapter 18 the risks of mistaken or misleading factual assertions, I distinguish two settings in which accurate information may be thought harmful.

In the first setting the government has made a judgment in advance that certain facts are so dangerous they cannot be published, and it has backed this judgment with criminal penalties for violators. As recent Supreme Court opinions suppose,[1] criminal penalties may be part of a security system that covers information within the government's control, protecting against disclosure that increases the risk of crimes such as the murder of intelligence agents or of noncriminal actions harmful to the country's interests. Criminal penalties may undoubtedly be imposed against those who acquire information as government employees, for at least *some* disclosures in violation of security restrictions. There are limits, however; the government cannot silence government employees forever in connection with all information they acquire as a result of government service. Under the First Amendment, courts must undertake some evaluation of government need against the interests in free speech.[2]

Imposing penalties on those who disclose information they have acquired in some other way is more questionable. If a person has acquired information in a way that is actually criminal, then a prohibition on disclosure may be seen as implementing the original prohibition of acquisition.[3] For a narrow range of information whose disclosure is exceedingly dangerous, such as the names of undercover agents or a highly secret military technology, penalties may be appropriate for those who knowingly violate restrictions on disclosure of clearly specified sorts of information even if they do acquire the information from someone other than the government and in a wholly innocent way.[4]

In the second setting there is no statute, regulation, or judicial order[5] that specifies in advance the kinds of facts that one is forbidden to reveal. If the speaker has a forbidden purpose, such as aiding an enemy, he may be punished for disclosing specific, or even general, facts that risk harm; but what of the speaker who has no improper purpose? Although there is some speech interest in allowing people to say what they believe, requiring them to be silent when they are pretty sure that what they say will be used by their listeners to commit a crime is an acceptable constraint on free speech, when the facts disclosed are not generally and easily discoverable. Thus, the crime of criminal facilitation may constitutionally be applied to the giving of such information with a belief that it will probably be used for a criminal purpose. But it should not be sufficient for punishing someone for criminal facilitation that he believe that at least one person in an audience of millions will use a fact for criminal purposes;[6] for someone to be punished for facilitation of ordinary crimes, the main interest of a large part of the main audience must be in committing a crime. And, even then, disclosure of generally available facts, e.g., the road out of town, should probably be constitutionally protected.

Provocations of Violent Acts

Some expressions may be highly likely to promote a violent response although that is not the speaker's intent. Such expressions have often been punishable under breach-of-the-peace or disorderly-conduct statutes, and the doctrine that "fighting words" are unprivileged *apparently* remains a part of First Amendment law. The 1942 decision in *Chaplinsky* v. *New Hampshire*[7] and dicta in other cases indicate that fighting words—words which are personally offensive to those to whom they are addressed and which are likely to provoke a violent response—do not enjoy constitutional protection. The theory advanced in *Chaplinsky* was that such words have no value as expression and are dangerous. *Cohen* v. *California*[8] and more recent cases undercut any assumption that highly emotive communications have no value as expression and leave unclear whether any words can be punished simply because they deeply offend listeners, a subject I discuss in the next chapter. But the Court, often disposing of cases on grounds of the vagueness and overbreadth of statutory formulations, so far has assumed that some words directed to some people are so likely to provoke assaults that their use in such contexts can be punished. Plainly, the category of fighting words is now thought to be much narrower than traditionally, and Justice Powell has suggested, properly in my view, that, since police officers should be well enough trained not to react violently to epithets that might provoke the average citizen, the range of permissible speech directed to them (and presumably to similar officials) is greater than for remarks directed to others.[9]

Chaplinsky and *Cohen* suggest that fighting words would provoke an "average addressee" or the ordinary citizen to fight. Whether there are now any general expressions that cause *most* people to whom they are actually directed or would cause *most* people to whom they might be directed[10] to fight is highly doubtful, especially if one considers that adults sometimes address abusive words to small children, that slightly more than half of the population is female, and that much of the population is elderly. (Without getting into causal explanations or possible future changes in behavior, I assume that women and older people are on the average less likely than young men on the average to respond to insults with physical violence.) But some expressions would cause a substantial percentage of addressees to fight. If persons using such expressions are warned that they are forbidden, punishment for their use is proper, since fighting words make a relatively small contribution to the exchange of ideas and constitute a substantial danger.

Classifying particularly dangerous offensive expressions is a serious difficulty. Forms of expression vary so much in their contexts and inflections that one cannot specify particular words or phrases as being always "fighting." What is gross insult in one setting is crude humor in another. And what is offensive shifts over time. On the other hand, if a legislature supplies only a statute forbidding some open-ended crime like "breach of the peace," it may give insufficient warning of what is impermissible, especially given the present uncertain ambit of the fighting-words doctrine. Nevertheless, it should be adequate for a legislature to forbid "abusive" or "offensive" language of a sort that would often create a substantial risk of a violent response. (What I mean by such a standard is explored more fully in the next chapter.) Given such a statute, punishment for a narrow category of expressions traditionally understood as fighting words should still be permissible in some contexts.

The lowest acceptable standard of culpability should be recklessness, understood here in a certain way. A person would not actually have to *want* to provoke a fight if he is aware that his words may have that effect. But if the speaker can establish that he was actually *unaware* that words of the sort he used might provoke violence he should be constitutionally protected. Although such a claim of unawareness might not have been a defense under traditional law, the threat to open communication is substantially increased if persons can be punished for uttering words that they are unaware have a potential for causing violence. As far as the Constitution is concerned, it should be sufficient for punishment that the defendant know the propensity of the words he uses, even if at the time of speaking he was in such a rage he did not consider their likely effect. Thus, ignorance about the effect of words would provide a constitutional defense, but a failure to bring one's understanding to bear on the situation would not.

Legislatures should not be free to condemn broad categories of expression because of the general tendency of the substantive message to cause conflict. A broad "group defamation" law of the sort upheld in 1952 in *Beauharnais* v. *Illinois*,[11] a law that forbids publication portraying "depravity, criminality, unchastity, or lack of virtue of a class of citizens of any race, color, creed, or religion [which exposes them] to contempt, derision, or obloquy," should now be held unconstitutional, as most observers have supposed that it would be under more modern doctrines.[12] If racial or religious epithets are to be proscribed it must be primarily because they amount to fighting words or because they do some other immediate harm of the sort discussed in the next chapter.

Audience Hostility to the Speaker's Message

Can a speaker be punished because the audience reacts in a hostile manner to what he says? *Feiner* v. *New York*,[13] in which a speaker was punished for disobeying a police order to stop speaking, posed this issue, although the majority's (implausible) assumption that the speaker had actually incited to illegal action and the dissent's assumption that stopping the speech was probably unnecessary left the most thorny question unresolved in both opinions. We need to imagine speech that would otherwise be protected, but which in the circumstances is likely to lead to violence against the speaker and his supporters. In such circumstances, as subsequent Supreme Court cases suggest,[14] officials must make every possible effort to protect the speaker and to prevent violence without stopping the speech. If, however, the police are genuinely unable to cope with the situation by restraining listeners and serious violence may result, they should be free to demand that the speaker stop. Any punishment would have to be based on the knowing failure to follow a reasonable police order, and the evidence that the police had no alternative should have to be much more convincing than what was presented in *Feiner*.

Literary and Artistic Portrayals Likely to Cause Crimes

Criminal behavior may be caused by portrayals of real or fictional events. Often the main point of portrayals is not to convey information or assert values but to evoke recognition or intensify vicarious experience for the audience. At an early stage in the development of First Amendment law, the Supreme Court suggested that movies were a form of entertainment outside the boundaries of protected expression, but the protection of fictional works by the First Amendment has long been taken for granted; and it is now accepted that movies, television programs, and the products of the fine arts enjoy constitutional protection.

Certain artistic depictions and portrayals may lead some members of the audience to commit crimes, and that possibility exists in connection with work that undeniably constitutes expression as well as work whose status is more arguable. Sex and violence, and particularly violent sex, are the main subjects of concern. One asserted justification for suppressing obscenity is that some of those who see obscene materials may be led to commit sexual crimes. And critics of violence on television claim that it tends to produce violent behavior in viewers.[15]

These asserted connections are plainly an inadequate basis for holding the communicators criminally liable for the crimes that may be committed after exposure to the communication. In any real instance, the most that can be said is that the communicator disregarded a risk that what he said would cause criminal behavior, a risk of which he was aware or should have been aware. Given the extreme difficulty of estimating that in any particular instance the person who receives the communication, or even one of an audience of millions, will commit a crime as a consequence, demonstrating a substantial and unjustifiable risk of the sort needed to establish recklessness or negligence would be very hard. In any event, the First Amendment would preclude liability on those theories because courts and jurors should not be in the business of assessing the unjustifiability of risks by engaging in ad hoc weighing of the expressive value of a particular program or communication against the dangers it creates. Though this conclusion does not necessarily foreclose all regulation of obscenity and of television violence, it does mean that criminal liability for particular portrayals cannot be based on crimes committed by consumers and supposedly caused by the expressive materials, when the materials are not otherwise forbidden. It also means that a crime of reckless endangerment cannot be committed by means of acts of literary and artistic expression.

The dangers of interference with forms of expression are grave enough also to bar civil recovery when victims of crimes by consumers sue those responsible for communications on a theory of reckless or negligent causation. For example, if a viewer "acts out" a violent scene from a television drama, the victim cannot recover against the company that has shown the program.[16]

If portrayals in literature, movies, television, photography, and the fine arts may ever be forbidden or made the subject of civil liability because of a propensity to cause crimes, the great danger of a particular sort of communication must be powerfully shown, and the proscribed communications must be very clearly defined.[17]

Notes

1. See, e.g., *Snepp* v. *United States*, 444 U.S. 507 (1980).

2. So much seems clear from the *Snepp* case, note 1 supra, although I am among the many critics who think that the result in that case was far from sufficiently attentive to free speech concerns and that the failure to have full briefing and oral argument was disgraceful.

3. Some of the individual opinions in the Pentagon Papers case, *New York Times Co.* v. *United States*, 403 U.S. 713 (1971), indicated that though newspapers could not be enjoined from publishing the material involved, criminal sanctions might be appropriate. In *New York* v. *Ferber*, 458 U.S. 747 (1982), the Court upheld a prohibition on selling films that depicted sexual activities of children, thereby sustaining penalties for publication because of a wrong in the way materials were produced.

4. In a case upholding denial of a passport to a former Central Intelligence Agency employee who was disclosing the names of undercover CIA agents, the Court seemed to

suppose that such disclosures were not constitutionally protected speech, however Agee had acquired his information and regardless of whether he actually wanted violence directed against those whose names he exposed. *Haig* v. *Agee*, 453 U.S. 280 (1981).

5. See *United States* v. *Progressive, Inc.*, 467 F. Supp. 990 (W.D. Wis. 1979), request for writ of mandamus denied sub nom. *Morland* v. *Spreacher*, 443 U.S. 709 (1979), case dismissed, Nos. 79–1428, 79–1664 (7th Cir., Oct. 1, 1979), on the appropriateness of injunctive restraint on the publication of information about how to build an H-bomb. See generally Note, "*United States* v. *Progressive, Inc.*: The Faustian Bargain and the First Amendment," 75 *Northwestern University Law Review* 538 (1980). Any judicial order against publication must meet all the extra barriers against prior restraints, a subject not discussed in this book.

In the United States, the interest in having a fair trial has been regarded as insufficient to preclude publication of facts about crimes, the assumption being that other safeguards are available to protect defendants from having biased jurors. See, e.g., *Nebraska Press Association* v. *Stuart*, 427 U.S. 539 (1976). Some other countries strike the balance between fair trial and free publication quite differently. See, e.g., E. Barendt, *Freedom of Speech* 214–32 (Oxford, Clarendon Press 1985).

6. Someone who writes an article in a major publication exposing ways in which young men avoid the draft may be pretty certain that at least one young man will "take advantage" of the information provided. One can imagine a crime so serious, say a terrorist bombing that will kill hundreds, that disclosure of knowledge that will lead to the crime should be punishable even if only a small part of the audience will commit the crime. But then some explicit statutory provision should cover the situation, not a general facilitation section.

7. 315 U.S. 568 (1942).

8. 403 U.S. 15 (1971).

9. *Lewis* v. *City of New Orleans*, 408 U.S. 913 (1972) (concurring opinion). Perhaps there are no general epithets, e.g., "pig," "bastard," "wop," "nigger," that should be expected to provoke officers to violent response, but there remain more pointed personal remarks, e.g., "I know your wife; she's a whore who fucks anyone," to which even well-trained officers might not be expected to remain impervious.

10. Potential addressees for this purpose should be limited to the class to which a particular epithet would be directed. The percentage of actual addressees and potential addressees who would fight might vary for a number of reasons, for example, because epithets are more often directed at young people than at old people and are often directed by people who have been drinking to people who have been drinking.

11. 343 U.S. 250 (1952).

12. See, e.g., *Collin* v. *Smith*, 578 F.2d 1197 (7th Cir. 1978), certiorari denied, 439 U.S. 916 (1978).

13. 340 U.S. 315 (1951).

14. *Gregory* v. *City of Chicago*, 394 U.S. 111 (1969). British law is substantially less protective of speakers faced with hostile audiences. See Barendt, note 5 supra, at 203; R. Stewart, "Public Speech and Public Order in Britain and the United States," 13 *Vanderbilt Law Review* 625 (1960).

15. See generally T. Krattenmaker and L. Powe, "Televised Violence: First Amendment Principles and Social Science Theory," 64 *Virginia Law Review* 1123 (1978).

16. *Olivia N.* v. *NBC*, 126 Cal. App.3d 488, 178 Cal. Rptr. 888 (1st Dist. 1981), certiorari denied, 458 U.S. 1108 (1982), was a highly publicized case dealing with this problem.

17. Various possibilities for regulating violence on television are thoroughly canvassed in Krattenmaker and Powe, note 15 supra.

17

Offensiveness, Emotional Distress, and Diffuse Harms

In this chapter I explore possible reasons for making communications criminal which do not have to do with improper coercion of the listener to perform actions the speaker wants or with the likelihood that the listener will commit a crime or be quickly influenced to perform another antisocial act. The discussion deals with disclosure of information, abusive words, and offensive pictorial representations and writings; the problem of false representation is reserved for the next chapter.

Immediate and Longer-Run Harms

Apart from violence or crime, communications can, as Chapters 5 and 8 suggest, cause a variety of immediate harms: the shock and fear of being threatened, the humiliation and anger of being subject to verbal abuse, the acute embarrassment of hearing secrets about oneself revealed, and the sense of unease at being exposed or having others exposed to words and pictures that are grossly inappropriate. Longer-run and more diffuse harms include the possibility that others will lower their opinions of persons who are objects of humiliation or of the disclosure of embarrassing secrets and that listeners may experience shifts in attitudes that are personally or socially destructive, as when a black is led to feel inferior by racial epithets or when a man exposed to pornography learns to regard women as sex objects.[1] The most general question for this chapter is whether worries about these sorts of effects can, under the First Amendment, permissibly underlie criminal prohibitions or at least civil damages in respect to various forms of communication.

The Supreme Court has never focused carefully on how far speech may be restricted because it threatens these harms or on when, if ever, civil liability is permissible even though criminal punishment is foreclosed. Rather, in cases in which it might have addressed these issues, the Court has either emphasized the companion danger of causing crimes or has categorized the communications as beyond the ambit of speech protected by the First Amendment or done both. Partly for this reason, coming up with plausible standards is difficult. Before I examine particular forms of speech that arguably should not be fully privileged, I suggest two preliminary and general guidelines.

No General Crime Based on Noncriminal Harms and
No General Restrictions of Fully Valued Speech

I start with the obvious proposition that a legislature could not create a crime of "antisocial communication," which would penalize communications that offend or generate other noncriminal harms. Nothing analogous to the crime of criminal solicitation, which includes all attempts to encourage specific crimes, is possible for communications threatening broader and more amorphous harms. A definition of a crime cast in that broad way would restrict much too much communication, would fail to an extreme degree to give fair warning to citizens about what is prohibited, and would provide inadequate guidance for those applying the law. A corollary of any political principle of free speech is that such a broad prohibition would be inappropriate; a corollary of any interpretation of the First Amendment that reaches beyond prior restraints is that as broad a prohibition as this would violate the First Amendment. If offensiveness, emotional disturbance, and other harms are to be the basis for prohibiting speech, then the forms of speech forbidden must be contained more narrowly and indicated with more particularity. Similar reasoning forecloses the permissibility of any general tort of "harmful communication."

My second proposed principle, less obvious and possibly subject to certain exceptions, is that if neither direct criminal harm nor coercive influence is feared, communications that fully implicate the values of free speech cannot be prohibited in all settings. For a prohibition to have a serious claim to constitutionality, it must either cover communications that have substantially less value as expression than ordinary assertions of fact and value *or* be limited to particular aims or settings. Communications might have lower value either because of the way in which they employ language or because what they say is simply not very important.

In the most notable cases holding against First Amendment protection for certain communications, the Supreme Court has declared that obscenity and fighting words are not within the scope of the First Amendment. The position that these forms of communication are wholly outside the First Amendment is not very persuasive, since they do have *some* speech value, as Chapter 8 suggests and as *Cohen* v. *California*[2] strongly intimates in respect to fighting words.

What *is* a plausible position is that the emotional outbursts reflected in most fighting words and the appeal to a straightforward interest in sexual stimulation that explains the sale and purchase of most pornography are much less significant as expression than serious assertions about fact and value.[3] Grounds for suppression that would plainly not suffice for fully valued speech might be adequate for these marginal forms of expression. For example, suppose a legislature decided that two kinds of speech—pornographic materials and serious assertions that genetic endowments make women less aggressive and more suited for nurturing roles than men—are offensive to many women and contribute to patronizing and unhealthy attitudes in men. That determination clearly would not warrant prohibition of the claims about genetic endowments, but arguably it would justify prohibiting pornographic materials.

The legitimacy of restrictions can also depend on objectives, settings, and relationships. As Chapter 15 indicates, a particular aim may render punishable a communication that would otherwise be protected. Speakers may be treated as criminal if they attempt to aid the enemy or to influence officials improperly. Speech that is otherwise protected may be barred as offensive within certain limited settings. A state can make it a criminal contempt to utter crudities during judicial proceedings that it must allow if spoken in a public park or in the home; even the opinion that a judge is extremely stupid is not one a lawyer has a right to express to the judge in open court. The government's limited ability to decide what is appropriate for a particular setting may be regarded as part of its authority to control time, place, and manner.

Another aspect of the government's power to restrict communications derives from relationships that arise out of government activities. I argued in Chapter 15 that the government may penalize or dismiss employees for encouraging behavior that violates special institutional norms though similar encouragements by ordinary citizens might be constitutionally protected.[4] On other occasions, speech may be thought to jeopardize institutional relationships though no improper acts are urged; an employee may sharply criticize a superior, or denigrate those, say the people of a foreign country, with whom the government agency must deal. The Supreme Court has faced this sort of problem when government employees are dismissed. What has emerged is one of the relatively few areas of law in which the precise content of the speech is acknowledged to be of critical importance. If the employee's communication does not involve a matter of public concern, the Constitution permits superiors virtually absolute discretion to decide whether what has been said warrants dismissal.[5] If the employee's comment is of public concern, then the government bears the burden of showing that the efficiency of the public service requires dismissal.[6] What the Court has said and done is subject to criticism on at least two grounds. It has too easily assumed that criticism of superiors which is tied to a particular employment dispute but which also has broader public relevance does not count as comment of public concern;[7] and, in dealing with a passing remark to a fellow employee and friend in private that if "they go for him [try to shoot President Reagan] again, I hope they get him," too much emphasis was placed on the public concern reflected in the comment and not enough emphasis on the need to preserve areas of private spontaneous conversation for government employees.[8] Nevertheless, the Court is sound in supposing that some balance must be struck between effective office operation and freedom of employee expression and that the nature and context of the communications matter for how this balance is struck.

I have certainly not shown that every plausible argument that suppression is permissible because of emotional hurt or offense or unhealthy attitudes necessarily relies on some special setting, relationship, or aim of the speaker, or depends on a claim that the communications involved are *less worthy* of protection than ordinary assertions of fact and value, but perhaps suppression because of these harms should never be upheld in the absence of solid argument of one of those kinds. I now consider four kinds of communications that illustrate these possibilities, and inquire in a fairly summary way about appropriate constitutional principles in light of the relevant arguments. I treat in turn serious "pure" threats, abusive words, including racial and religious epithets, disclosures of embarrassing facts, and pornography.

Pure (Unconditional) Threats

Serious threats to life and bodily integrity can cause shock and fear when the threat is made, and the fear is likely to extend over time so long as the victim thinks the threat may be carried out. A threat does predict a future event and is often expressive of very strong emotional feelings. But the point of most threats is not to give the listener helpful information but to put him in a state of fear, and the emotional outlet of the threat is not so different from the emotional outlet of an actual physical assault.

If fear and related emotional harm are to be the main grounds for suppression of threats, probably the minimum constitutional threshold for a general criminal prohibition is that the threats will cause deep fear for the physical integrity of the listener or of those he loves and that that be their aim. (If the object of the threat is someone other than the immediate listener, it would be sufficient if one plans that the threat be relayed to the person who is its object.) Civil liability might be grounded on somewhat less intense emotional harm, and perhaps recklessness about causing fear should be a sufficient state of mind.

Some threats may be prohibited less because of the emotional damage they cause than because they produce other harms that are not a consequence of a considered reaction to any idea that they implicitly express. When direct threats to high government officials are made, extensive social resources are devoted to ascertaining whether genuine danger exists and preventing actual attacks; such threats may properly be made criminal.

I shall concentrate on criminal liability for threats against ordinary citizens and comment briefly on the tort of inflicting extreme emotional distress. A basic constitutional requirement is that the threat be serious, not a joke or a form of hyperbole or an ambiguous way to let off steam. In *Watts* v. *United States*[9] the Supreme Court held that the comment at a small, informal political gathering, "If they ever make me carry a rifle the first man I want to get in my sights is L.B.J.," was not meant as a genuine threat reached by the federal statute on threatening the president. Reviewing a conviction of a voluntary psychiatric patient who, upon watching "The Day After," a disturbing television portrayal of the aftermath of nuclear war in Lawrence, Kansas, had said to a nurse, "If Reagan came to Sheridan (Kansas), I would shoot him," the Tenth Circuit Court of Appeals held in 1986 in *United States* v. *Crews*[10] that this was a punishable threat. The *Watts* decision was sound and should be understood as constitutionally compelled. Perhaps the psychiatric patient in Sheridan was not just engaging in hyperbole, but this sort of threat should generally also be protected. Crews was not trying to frighten anyone, and, since President Reagan had no plans to come to Sheridan and since you do not expect what you tell a hospital nurse in a moment of upset to end up being reported to federal authorities, there is no reason to suppose Crews really intended to kill the President or intended anyone to be frightened or worried by that prospect. If a sister from Pittsburgh had written him a letter that enraged him and he had said, "If she ever comes to Sheridan, I'll kill her," that alone could not count as a serious threat punishable under the Constitution. Given the need to regard seriously any threat to the president, however bizarre, and the terrible wound to the country that assassination of the president produces, deciding that threats of the president may warrant punishment when other threats do not is reasonable, but generalizing from Crews's remarks to what are ordinarily punishable threats would be gravely mistaken.

In one of the leading federal cases, *United States* v. *Kelner*, the Second Circuit Court of Appeals said that federal provisions on threats should be interpreted to demand that a threat be "so unequivocal, unconditional, immediate and specific as to the person threatened, as to convey a gravity of purpose and imminent prospect of execution."[11] The court explicitly held that apparent determination and ability to carry out a threat are sufficient and that the threatener need not *actually* intend to perform the threat. Since the reasons for punishing threats depend on what listeners believe and reasonably believe and what the speaker aims to have them believe, neither an actual intent nor actual ability to carry out the threat should be needed to meet a constitutional minimum.[12] What counts is how a listener should be and is expected to react at the time of the threat. How immediately it appears a threat may be carried out is usually relevant to the seriousness with which it may be taken and the fear it is likely to cause, and the force of Kelner's threat in a television interview that members of the Jewish Defense League would assassinate Yasser Arafat was certainly affected by the proximity of Arafat's visit to the United Nations. But an ingeniously plotted private threat or combination of threats that leaves the victim believing that he really will be murdered six months from now should be punishable.[13] Threats in this respect are different from public incitements to illegal action; damage depends not only on whether the feared substantive harm occurs, but also on how a vulnerable human being will feel if he must live in the shadow of the threat.

The federal government and many states have laws dealing with harassment over the telephone, and some threats have been punished under these provisions,[14] which also reach other calls made with a purpose to annoy. Since a telephone call intrudes on a private domain of the listener, the government may well have authority to prohibit communications that would be protected in a face-to-face encounter;[15] if so, disturbing telephonic threats may be punishable even if the ordinarily stringent constitutional standard is not met.[16] For example, if someone telephones someone else with a purpose to disturb by threatening violent harm, perhaps the caller may be punished even though the listener might not reasonably believe that the caller will perform the threat.[17]

When recovery in tort for the intentional or reckless infliction of severe emotional distress is based on communication, First Amendment restrictions are applicable. According to the *Restatement* (Second) *of Torts*, "one who by extreme and outrageous conduct intentionally or recklessly causes severe emotional distress to another is subject to liability for such emotional distress."[18] This formulation would cover many serious threats,[19] including many telephonic threats, that actually produce severe distress. If recovery for pure threats of physical harm is limited to extreme and outrageous conduct, that probably satisfies First Amendment concerns.[20] Whatever may be true of some other threats,[21] careful application to these threats of the limits of liability now conceived as an aspect of the common law should not run afoul of the Constitution.

The subject of threats affords an occasion for brief comment on the idea of civic courage, an idea whose significance will loom larger in the next section. As the discussion of autonomy in Chapter 2 suggests, Justice Brandeis's idea of the courageous citizen,[22] independent of mind and hardy emotionally, might be understood in either of two ways for First Amendment adjudication. One might think either that courts should assume that citizens already have these characteristics or that an object of First Amendment doctrine should be to engender that kind of citizen. Whatever the characteristics are of the emotionally hardy person, probably only a rare individual can countenance serious personal threats with equanimity, and the ability to do so would seem to bear little relation to the kind of hardiness that matters for a liberal democracy. If part of the aim of the law is to encourage people to become more hardy in ways that matter, then protecting people from personal threats might contribute to that objective. People may be more likely to espouse and act upon controversial ideas if they are not exposed to serious threats to life and limb as a result. In sum, if civic courage is taken as a central component of First Amendment analysis, it should not constitute a bar to punishing serious threats and might even slightly augment other arguments for punishment.

Abusive Words

The troubling constitutional question of whether extremely abusive words can be prohibited apart from special settings and independent of the likelihood of immediate violence is in part the issue of whether a law restricting expression can guard individuals and society from harms other than immediate physical fear. By extremely abusive words, I mean to include both strong personal insults ("You are a fucking whore"), class-based epithets (like "wop," "kike," "nigger," and "pansy"), and more elaborate slurs of classes of people. When directed at its object, such language can wound and humiliate and may be designed to provoke retaliation, but, like threats, abusive words often express strong emotions and, more than threats, make some vague assertion about facts and values. When directed to third persons ("Tony is a dirty wop") these words are dominantly intended to convey some message, however vague and unenlightened.

I shall offer a few general comments about approaching the constitutional issues, give a brief description of present law and its uncertainties, and then proceed to examine which reasons for suppression should carry weight in a constitutional analysis and which uses of abusive language might permissibly be made illegal.

My basic approach to the constitutional questions fits the analysis of Chapter 8, which suggests that the critical variables are the manner in which abusive speech is employed and the harms that it threatens. The more the abuse is meant to trigger action or inflict immediate wounds, the less its claim to protection; as harms become more grave, more clearly evident, more subject to formulation in legal language, and less dependent on the ideas that abusive words may express, the stronger the argument that the harms may be the basis for restriction. Probably more severe harms are required to justify criminal punishment than to warrant civil liability. Even though substantial civil damages may in fact be more onerous than a minor fine, the basic notion that a person has offended against the entire community by his speech and is, therefore, criminally punishable demands a strong justification. Further, the basic principle that the government should use the "least restrictive alternative" when it curtails speech counsels that, for circumstances in which civil remedies seem adequate, use of criminal punishment should be constitutionally inappropriate. (This supposition is examined in somewhat greater detail in connection with fraud and libel in the next chapter.) Because of the difficulties in defining the class of communications covered, a very significant difference between criminal and civil liability in this context is that the Constitution permits a degree of vagueness and open-endedness in a standard for civil recovery that would be unacceptable for a criminal provision, for which "fair warning" is a vital constitutional safeguard.

I divide my discussion of existing law between "fighting words" and group epithets and slurs. It is important to remember, however, that group epithets can themselves often be fighting words. An account of both branches of this subject is a bit unsatisfactory. Although dispositions that evade certain critical issues and hints thrown out here and there have led most observers to agree about the drift of the Supreme Court's understanding, it has been some decades since the Court has actually attempted to elaborate with clarity what counts as punishable fighting words and whether or not "defamation" of entire classes of people can be punished; even when the Court has spoken to these matters, it has hardly been with systematic rigor.

What is still the leading Supreme Court case on fighting words was decided nearly half a century ago.[23] Chaplinsky, a Jehovah's Witness, annoying some people with his proselytizing and warned by a city marshall to "go slow," called the marshall "a God-damned racketeer" and "a damned Fascist" and said the whole government of Rochester were Fascists. He was convicted under a statute that forbade addressing "any offensive, derisive or annoying word to any other person . . . [or] call[ing] him by any offensive or derisive name." Despite the evident political aspect of the comment and the fact that it was addressed to a law enforcement officer, presumably trained to exercise self-restraint, the Supreme Court upheld the conviction, saying in an often-quoted passage:

> There are certain well-defined and narrowly limited classes of speech, the prevention and punishment of which have never been thought to raise any Constitutional problem. These include the lewd and obscene, the profane, the libelous, and the insulting or "fighting" words—those which by their very utterance inflict injury or tend to incite an immediate breach of the peace. . . . [S]uch utterances are no essential part of any exposition of ideas, and are of such slight social value as a step to truth that any benefit that may be derived from them is clearly outweighed by the social interest in order and morality.[24]

Reasoning that the state court had construed the statute only to cover words that "men of common intelligence would understand [to be] likely to cause an average addressee to fight," the Supreme Court decided that the statute was neither too vague nor an undue impairment of liberty. Left unsettled by the decision was whether words can be punished for wounding even if they are not likely to provoke a fight, and what exactly is the constitutional minimum for the punishment of words because of their capacity to provoke violence.

Two major developments have occurred in the years since *Chaplinsky*. Overturning the conviction of a young man who wore a jacket saying "Fuck the Draft," the Supreme Court in *Cohen* v. *California*[25] emphasized the importance of emotive elements of communication and their protection under the Constitution. After *Cohen*, it is extremely hard (without rejecting *Cohen*) to argue that everything that might amount to fighting words is simply without expressive value and thus falls wholly outside the First Amendment. The second development was a series of per curiam opinions in which the Court invalidated on grounds of overbreadth and vagueness disorderly-conduct and related statutes that reached vulgar or offensive or opprobrious language.[26] Although in one case the Court said that the statute covered words that did not "by their very utterance inflict injury or tend to invite an immediate breach of the peace,"[27] in general the Court's emphasis has been on the absence of any danger of immediate violence. Many observers have concluded that no restriction of abusive speech outside of special settings is constitutionally acceptable unless there is a serious risk of violence.

The history of restrictions of group epithets bears important similarities. In a 1952 case, *Beauharnais* v. *Illinois*,[28] the Court upheld a conviction under an Illinois statute that forbade public exhibition of publications portraying "depravity, criminality, unchastity, or lack of virtue of a class of citizens, of any race, color, creed or religion [in a way that exposes those citizens] to contempt, derision, or obloquy or which is productive of breach of the peace or riots." Beauharnais had organized distribution of a leaflet asking city officials to resist the invasion of the Negro and warning that if "the need to prevent the white race from becoming mongrelized by the negro will not unite us, then the aggressions, . . . rapes, robberies, knives, guns and marijuana of the negro, surely will." The Court's main line of reasoning was to assimilate this speech to group libel, instances in which something defamatory is said about a small group in such a way that the damaging remark falls on members of the group, for example, "The [15-member] firm of Mix and Nix is a bunch of crooks."[29] The Court mentioned the danger of racial riots which a legislature might reasonably think were made more likely by racist speech. And it sustained the refusal of the Illinois courts to entertain truth as a defense, on the ground that a state might, and did, require "good motives" and "justifiable ends" as well as truth, and if these requisites could not be satisfied the court did not need to consider evidence of truth.[30]

In the years since *Beauharnais*, itself a sharply contested 5–4 decision, the Court's developing protection of civil libel, the *Cohen* case, and the sharp restrictions on breach-of-the-peace and disorderly-conduct statutes that lacked reference to immediate danger of violence have cast the continuing authority of *Beauharnais* into grave doubt. Although the case has occasionally been cited by opinions in peripheral contexts, the prevailing assumption has been that any statute as broad as the Illinois statute upheld in that case would now be declared unconstitutional and that the publication in that case would be thought to be constitutionally protected however a statute was cast. In cases that arose out of the intense controversy over whether Nazis might march in uniform in Skokie, a city inhabited by many Jewish survivors of the Holocaust, appellate judges acted on these premises, striking down ordinances designed to keep the Nazis out and indicating that a Nazi march could not be altogether foreclosed.[31]

The common direction concerning fighting words and racial and ethnic slurs has been to demand very narrowly drawn statutory language focusing on imminent violence. This direction fits comfortably both with the general distaste for content-based restrictions and with the modern treatment of the hostile-audience problem,[32] which is to insist that the first duty of government for unpalatable speech is to protect speakers. Because the direction I have described is, however, not based on square Supreme Court holdings, the Supreme Court could with relative ease broaden permissible bases for prohibition if it were persuaded by arguments to do so.[33]

The one proposition the Court is clear about and on which everyone agrees is that the prevention of violence is a legitimate basis for restricting gravely abusive remarks. This concern may be reflected in a statutory formulation, such as the Model Penal Code's section on harassment, which makes it criminal "with purpose to harass" to "[insult, taunt, or challenge] another in a manner likely to provoke a violent or disorderly response."[34] An analogous constitutional standard would make the likelihood of violence the key to whether abusive remarks can be punished. I shall discuss two basic questions: With what breadth is the likelihood of violence to be conceived? And how high must the likelihood be?

If violence is the basis for restriction, the most straightforward approach is that of the Model Code: describe the category of unprotected abusive words in terms of their propensity for violence and make that propensity an inquiry about individual circumstances. As Chapter 8 indicates, there are deeply troubling aspects of this approach which should make one hesitant to embrace it as either a statutory or a constitutional standard. Imagine that in an area of town in which few blacks live[35] a twenty-five-year-old white man of average size and strength is waiting for a bus with a solitary black person; without any other words having been spoken, the white man says to the black stranger: "You're dumb like all niggers are dumb. You should all be sent back to Africa or dropped in the ocean." Does it matter whether the black listener is (1) a strong twenty-year-old man, (2) a seventy-year-old man on crutches, (3) a very small woman of fifty, (4) a child of nine? Only the first setting here presents any real likelihood of violence. Can it be that the same remark is constitutionally unprotected if directed at the one person able to respond and is protected if directed at people who are incapable of matching the speaker physically? To ask this question is for me to suggest two separate but compatible answers. The first is that something more lies behind legal restraint than prevention of immediate violence. The second is that, even if prevention of immediate violence is the primary reason for prohibition, there should be a principle of what I shall call "equalization of victims," under which inquiry would not concentrate on the perceived capacity of a particular victim to respond with physical force.[36] It is appropriate to ask whether the words are spoken in a context and with a force that would cause many addressees to respond with physical force, but it should not be a constitutional requisite that a particular addressee be or appear to be likely to respond in that way.

Whether the focus is on the particular addressee or more broad, the issue arises of how likely a violent response needs to be to cause words to be unprotected. A phrase found in the *Chaplinsky* opinion and often repeated is "words likely to cause an average addressee to fight." This phrase has some powerful ambiguities and is probably not to be taken literally however it is plausibly construed. The first ambiguity is who counts among potential addressees, everyone or only people to whom a phrase "applies"? A white person may react very differently from a black person to being called a "nigger." I assume that average addressees include only those people to whom a denigrating expression might apply.[37] The next and more serious problem is how an "average addressee" is to be understood. A class epithet of the sort used in my bus-stop example can be directed at any member of the class, including women and children. It would plainly be arbitrary just to say that only men count as addressees, though I believe that the *Chaplinsky* language is one of the innumerable pieces of evidence that traditionally the imagined actors for most legal problems have been male. But it may be the case that, outside of quarrels among intimates, abusive words are very often spoken by and to young men, often after alcohol has been drunk. In that event the average person to whom the words are actually addressed may differ from the average *potential* addressee to whom the words might be spoken, and it is possible that some words that would not cause the average potential addressee to fight would cause the average actual addressee to fight.[38] Even if one focuses on the actual addressees, I am dubious that there are any words that now cause the average addressee to respond with violence. In any event, that seems too stringent as a minimum constitutional test. Suppose a social science study somehow showed that, when certain words are spoken in certain contexts, thirty percent of the addressees respond by fighting. That should be a high enough percentage to restrain the words in these contexts. If the focus is on the individual to whom the words are addressed, the standard should be whether there is a substantial probability that violence may be provoked. If, instead, as I have proposed, the focus should be on words and context but not on the capacity of particular victims to respond, the standard should be whether, when words of that sort[39] are spoken in that context, a substantial proportion of addressees would be provoked to violence.

There is no doubt that abusive words can be deeply wounding to people at whom they are addressed, amounting to a kind of psychic assault;[40] but can concern about that constitutionally underlie criminal penalties or civil liability? Since much language that is abusive in one way or another is a part of heated personal exchanges and strong disagreements about ideas and policies, most of us having an incapacity or disinclination to modulate our discourse to the magnitude of our subject, the First Amendment must be understood to require legal toleration of many words that hurt, and the Supreme Court's invalidation of statutory provisions that reach broadly to offensive or opprobrious language has been sound.[41] If any abusive words can be punished because they wound, they must be a small subcategory, narrowed in terms of the aims of the speaker, damage to the listener, the nature of the language used, or some combination of these three criteria. Suppose that four men think it would be "fun" to humiliate a Hispanic woman standing alone at a bus stop. They say to her, "You spic whore," and similar things. The words wound deeply. Because utterances whose dominant object is to hurt and humiliate, rather than to assert facts or values, have limited expressive value and because the harm in such cases can be serious, I believe that an instance like this, viewed in isolation, should not be constitutionally protected against criminal punishment.[42] This conclusion fits well with the actual language of *Chaplinsky*, which talked of words "which by their very utterance inflict injury *or* tend to incite an immediate breach of the peace."[43] But line-drawing problems are severe. Many words inevitably inflict some injury, but also have another point. Motives will usually be mixed, and separating an intent to humiliate from an honest but crude statement of one's views about individuals or classes of people is extremely difficult. It is doubtful whether a criminal statute framed generally to reach the use of abusive words to hurt and humiliate should be judged constitutional,[44] although criminal penalties may be appropriate when the pattern of behavior involves initiating contact with a person just to harass him or her, as in my last example,[45] or a clear intent is shown to intimidate a person from exercising legally protected rights.[46] Further, my suggestions about fighting words should be understood partly as an implicit recognition of the legitimacy of protecting against deep hurt. Whether words would cause many addressees to fight is an excellent test for whether the words have passed the boundaries of what innocent citizens should be expected to tolerate. The hurt in a particular instance may not be correlated with a capacity and willingness to fight, but those words about which people do fight are those words which hurt the most. Indeed, it is not unlikely that they hurt those victims who feel defenseless and unable to fight more than those who actually strike back. If the propensity to generate a violent response is seen as a measure of the intensity of hurt, then there is good reason to adopt what I have called a principle of equalization of victims, under which apparent capacity to fight back is not critical to whether a crime has been committed.

If that principle makes sense, it requires a little further development. Some other features of the situation should be disregarded besides the character of the particular victim. For example, the number of people supporting the person using the abusive words or the presence of bystanders who might support the victim should be irrelevant. Perhaps an addressee will rarely fight back if he is alone and insults are directed to him by members of a large group that seems eager for an excuse to gang up on him.[47]

A more subtle concern involves words that intrinsically apply to classes whose members are less likely to fight. Suppose members of some ethnic group, or women, are much less likely to respond with physical violence than other members of society. That does not mean they are less hurt than others when insulted. Under the approach I have taken so far, this difference does not create a problem for words that could be applied generally; but what of words of abuse that peculiarly apply to the group in question? If the class of addressees generally is less likely to fight, does that mean that otherwise equivalent abuse is more protected? The answer should be "no." An ethnic slur should be treated like similar ethnic slurs.[48] Calling a woman a "cunt" should probably be treated like calling a man a "prick." Thus, when it is asked whether words "of this sort" would lead many addressees to fight, the inquiry should abstract from the particular inclinations to fight of the class of potential addressees of these exact words.

Civil liability is also a difficult problem. The standard for possible civil liability damages may be vaguer than is acceptable for criminal liability. The tort of intentional infliction of emotional distress has been said to require extreme and outrageous conduct and severe emotional distress.[49] When these conditions are met, liability for abusive words is appropriate. However, there should be an absolute privilege for communications that have general public significance, as the Supreme Court held for parodies of important public figures.[50]

Another possible basis for punishing abusive words is the offense they cause to the audience at hearing them. People can be disturbed by hearing words like "fuck" and "nigger," even when they are not the object of the words. *Cohen* v. *California* and other cases intimate strongly that the offensiveness of language alone cannot be the basis for a general prohibition. The disquiet most people may feel about hearing certain words and expressions is not nearly of the magnitude of what they feel when they or their loved ones are the direct object of the humiliating language. The offense of some people at simply being exposed to certain forms of expression or at knowing what other people are saying cannot be a substantial reason for suppression of speech that is otherwise protected by the First Amendment. If people strongly wish not to be exposed to coarse language it is up to them to try to avoid settings where such language is likely to be used.

If offense cannot be the basis for a general prohibition, it can be the basis for restriction in some settings. Certain language may be forbidden to lawyers who are handling cases in courts, for example. The Supreme Court has upheld both discipline of a high school student for offensive remarks at a school assembly[51] and federal restrictions on the use of coarse words on daytime radio.[52] The latter decision may be challenged on the grounds that people are free to switch the dial and that few children are listening to daytime radio, the former decision because it concerned a campaign speech for student office which exceeded good taste but which was less than shockingly abusive or extremely coarse, but the Court's general point is sound that, in some settings, especially where there are captive audiences, some regulation against offensive speech is permissible.

Finally I address the most elusive of the possible reasons to prohibit insults, epithets, and slurs, the worry about long-term harms. In reality, as Chapter 8 indicates, one can think of a number of long-term harms, and their constitutional status may be different. I shall say a brief word about the quality of public discourse before concentrating on closely related harms that relate to social resentment and inequality. Some respected authors have argued that the opinion in *Cohen* v. *California* gave insufficient weight to maintaining a civil quality to public discourse.[53] Worry that coarseness and abuse may have a negative effect on reasoned discourse is understandable, but it is highly doubtful that government should be in the business generally of setting standards of acceptable expression,[54] and it is not a coincidence that those less privileged culturally or more radical politically are likely to use words and phrases that might be judged to impair civil discourse. On top of this, drawing distinctions between what is acceptable and what is not is exceedingly difficult. For all these reasons, the Court's assumption that outside of special settings the government cannot constitutionally decide upon the proper terms of discourse makes sense.

The more troubling question involves the long-term effects of reinforcement of feelings of prejudice and inferiority and of social patterns of domination. Although certain insults of individuals, for example, "You fat slob," may be repeated and may cause continuing psychological damage, that is an insufficient basis for restrictions of any one infliction of the insult. I assume that the argument that long-term effects should permit restrictions on speech is plausible only for epithets and slurs directed at membership in classes defined in terms of race, ethnic or national origin, religion, gender, or sexual preference.[55] As Chapter 8 indicates, when epithets and slurs are about less privileged groups, they may well have seriously damaging effects on the self-respect of members of the group and on the way they are viewed by others.

Any such singling out of types of expression is undoubtedly a form of content discrimination. Words are made illegal because they place people in certain categories and are critical of members of those categories.[56] Words that classify in other ways ("graceful" or "awkward") are not potentially subject to a penalty even if it hurts to be called a "clumsy oaf," and positive words about members of groups ("I love Yugoslav-Americans") are not penalized. (A further content discrimination would be involved if negative comments only about underprivileged or despised groups were punished, but I shall assume that, at least in terms of the definition of the crime or tort,[57] no such distinction is explicitly involved.) In answer to the worry about content discrimination, it can be argued that these sorts of abusive words have peculiarly harmful effects, many of which do not derive from any conscious consideration of the message involved. Further, if one is left free to express in less obnoxious words any facts or values about members of the group, the cognitive substance of the message is not foreclosed.

Nevertheless, it is hard to avoid the conclusion that, if the law forbidding denigrating remarks covers comments made generally or to third persons about members of these groups and if it covers the "ordinary" language of the publication in *Beauharnais* as well as particular epithets, what is really being suppressed is a message whose content and intensity are judged particularly hurtful and obnoxious. In any taxonomy of uses of language in context, it is hard to characterize this as "low value" speech, except by virtue of a judgment about its substantive message. Some proponents of laws of this type have argued that, if such speech is tolerated, the government is implicitly endorsing a message contrary to fundamental values of our social order,[58] but, at least on superficial analysis, this is not so. The government permits all kinds of speech that is contrary to the dominant and constitutional values of society; that is an aspect of freedom of speech. By its own actions, by regulating the noncommunicative behavior of private citizens, by education and advocacy, the government can promote equality; its allowing of racist rhetoric does not establish its support of racism. Of course, it is possible that in a society in which less privileged members of minorities identify the majority with the government and the government stands by in the face of such disturbing communication, the passivity of the government will be perceived as support, but, if that were the case, more emphasis on the government's direct commitment to positive values of equality and more education about the nature of free speech would seem preferable to suppression of the hated message.

As far as political judgment is concerned, it would be reasonable to conclude, as have many countries,[59] that suppression of this sort of message at some cost to free speech is warranted because the values of equality and dignity are so central and so vulnerable, and the support for these constitutional values of the community here overrides a claim to freedom of expression. For constitutional adjudication, it is hard to know how the line would be drawn once this step was taken and this basis for suppression was deemed sufficient; my own judgment coincides with the dominant present assumption that a law like that in *Beauharnais* is unconstitutional.

One way of meeting these objections would be to say that only "false" speech about members of groups could be punished.[60] Such speech would lack "full value" because of falsity, and prohibiting it would not open the door for broad prohibitions of speech. Aiming at false speech of this particular sort seems either an ineffectual course or one sown with drawbacks. Suppose that the "false" remarks to be criminalized were those which asserted definite facts about members of groups that were demonstrably false and were known to be false by those making the assertions, for example, "Every single black person in this country scores lower on standard intelligence tests than the worst-scoring white person." No doubt such false remarks are sometimes made and are meant to be taken literally rather than as rhetorical flourishes, but punishing these would have a very slight effect on hate literature. To have any bite, the law's coverage of punishable false statements would have to include matters of opinion or much vaguer and more ambiguous factual assertions. I have said that, as far as free speech is concerned, opinions are not to be labeled as true or false. With respect to factual assertions, the publication involved in *Beauharnais* is instructive about difficulties. It asserted among other things that, if the need to prevent being mongrelized by the Negro did not unite white people, the "rapes, robberies, knives, guns, and marijuana of the Negro, surely will." The *desirability* of white people uniting is a matter of opinion; the likelihood that that will happen is a prediction of vague and uncertain future facts that cannot be punished. Exactly what Negroes are said to be doing to bring about "mongrelizaton" is much too unclear to amount to a punishable assertion of facts. That leaves the statement about the "rapes, robberies," and so forth. What exactly is being asserted here: that all Negroes engage in these bad acts, that most do, that a higher proportion of Negroes than whites do? The first proposition is absurd and the second is probably demonstrably false, but Beauharnais might say at his trial: "Well, all I meant factually is that the percentages are a lot higher among Negroes and that, for this reason, the safety of neighborhoods will deteriorate if Negroes move in." I do not know what was true in Chicago around 1950, but we do know that Beauharnais offered to prove truth, and that, around 1989, at least judged by convictions, the percentage of blacks who commit many serious crimes is higher than the percentage of whites who do so. What will be the benefits to underprivileged groups if obscure merchants of hate are prosecuted and given the public forum of a trial to present in the most unsympathetic way possible all the damaging facts they can find about the group they hate? Two conclusions emerge.

Since the factual assertions of hate literature are often highly vague and since, if falsity is an aspect of liability, people should be punishable only for facts they clearly assert, much denigrating comment and hate literature would escape if falsity had to be proved. The trials over truth could easily do much more harm than the original communications. Whatever the constitutional status of a law precisely limited to false assertions of fact, it would be senseless to adopt such a law.

If racial and ethnic epithets and slurs are to be made illegal by separate statutes, the focus would have to be on face-to-face encounters, targeted vilification where members of the audience are the objects of venom.[61] For these, I have said that expressive value is often slight, because the very aim is to wound and humiliate or to start a fight. Since fighting words are already punishable and since the tort of extreme emotional distress is available, what would be the significance of separate provisions for the language of group vilification? They could stand as a symbolic statement that such language is peculiarly at odds with our constitutional values, and they might relieve prosecutors or plaintiffs of having to establish all the prerequisites that the more general offense or tort contains.[62] Against such special provisions, it can be argued that the class of utterances to be covered is too difficult to determine[63] and that, under laws of this type, it may actually be angry members of the underprivileged groups that end up being prosecuted most often.[64]

Constitutionality is a close question. If a *purpose* to initiate contact in order to humiliate can be shown or an attempt to intimidate, I believe criminal punishment under a narrowly defined statute should be acceptable. Otherwise, the criminal law should have to focus on immediate wounding and propensity for violence; though perhaps as an adjunct of a more general law, there might be established some presumption that serious racial and ethnic and perhaps other epithets are words to which many addressees would respond with physical force.[65]

As far as tort law is concerned, I think the longer-term effects of class-based insults are grave enough to allow recovery even if extreme emotional distress cannot be shown in a particular case. When an intent to demean is present[66] and the kinds of words are used which have inflicted grave humiliations and damage to an ideal of equality throughout our history and which continue to do severe harm, recovery may be allowed on some lesser showing of immediate injury than might otherwise be required. Of course, special treatment for class-based insults would be a modest exception to "content-neutrality," but an exception that, I believe, is warranted in light of the values involved.

In closing this section, I want briefly to consider the impact of an ideal of civic courage for abusive words. If an aspect of a belief in free speech is an assumption that people are hardy or an aim that they become so, the argument is strengthened that coarse and even hurtful comments should be protected in the rough and tumble of vigorous dialogue. But epithets and slurs meant to hurt listeners are another matter. It is much easier to be impervious to epithets when one is a member of a privileged majority than when one is a member of a reviled minority, and a general encouragement of civic courage may be more likely if targeted racial and religious abuse is not allowed. As with direct personal threats, it is doubtful whether "courageous citizens" should be expected to swallow such abuse without deep hurt, and it is also doubtful whether being the victim of such abuse contributes to one's hardiness in ways that count positively for a democratic society.

Embarrassing Disclosures of True Facts

Is the disclosure of truthful, factual information absolutely privileged under the First Amendment, in the absence of some serious threat to public welfare and in the absence of a confidential relationship or some illegal behavior by which the speaker acquired the information? That question is posed by the branch of the tort right of privacy, a "branch" based on relatively few cases, that permits recovery for general and outrageous publication of highly embarrassing information that is not a subject of public concern. At least in the United States, there is no criminal liability for such disclosure, and criminal liability might well be unconstitutional. But it is somewhat doubtful whether even tort liability is permissible,[67] an issue the Supreme Court has thus far stopped short of resolving decisively. It did say in *Cox Broadcasting Corporation* v. *Cohn*[68] that the "states may not impose sanctions for the publication of truthful information contained in official court records open to public inspection," but it intimated that liability for truthful disclosures about matters that are not of public record might be acceptable.

So long as every matter of public concern is protected and the scope of legitimate "public concern" is broadly construed here in favor of publication, it should be regarded as constitutionally permissible to allow damages for general publicity that reveals highly embarrassing secrets.[69] No doubt protecting truthful information is part of the core of the First Amendment. Although those disclosing embarrassing secrets may not always have the noblest of motives, they are not typically aiming to humiliate, and the disclosure of embarrassing secrets does not have the same sort of long-term negative impact on the broader society as some kinds of abusive words. Nevertheless, conventional respect for boundaries of privacy is very important, and maintaining some sense of what is of public concern is vital for a society, whether the primary agency of maintenance is customary practices or law.[70] The public loss if reports of matters of private concern are actionable is slight; people have no legitimate interest in whether a woman was raped twenty years ago[71] or has an ugly scar across her abdomen. Privacy matters, and the law properly helps to preserve it.

Pornography

One can say that over time a prevailing assumption about the First Amendment has been that it does not protect obscene or pornographic materials, but the practical significance of that premise has shifted radically. The leading decision in this development was *Roth* v. *United States*,[72] a 1957 case in which the Supreme Court reviewed the validity of the federal and California obscenity statutes. The federal law forbade mailing of material that was "obscene, lewd, lascivious, or filthy . . . [or] of indecent character"; the material had "to stir to sexual impulses and lead to sexually impure thoughts." The California statute made it punishable to sell or keep for sale material that was "obscene or indecent," having a "tendency to deprave or corrupt its readers."

Although holding that the statutes were constitutionally acceptable and stating that the First Amendment did not protect obscenity, the Court made clear that what *constituted* obscenity was a First Amendment problem, and it defined obscenity in a manner that provided significant constitutional protection. The Court rejected the older approach of *Regina* v. *Hicklin*[73] that material could be judged obscene on the basis of how especially susceptible people might react to isolated passages. Drawing from later decisions of American courts, it formulated the standard as "whether to the average person, applying contemporary community standards, the dominant theme of the material taken as a whole appeals to prurient interest."[74] Justice Brennan's opinion for the Court perceived no difference between its own test and that of the Model Penal Code, which provided that material judged obscene must have a predominant appeal to the prurient interest and go "substantially beyond customary limits of candor." According to the Court, obscenity is "utterly without redeeming social importance." Acknowledging that obscenity law was not fully developed at the time of the First Amendment, the Court found sufficient historical evidence that obscenity, along with libel, was not meant to be protected.

After *Roth*, it was apparent that serious works of literature like D. H. Lawrence's *Lady Chatterly's Lover*, James Joyce's *Ulysses*, and Edmund Wilson's *Memoirs of Hecate County* could not be banned. As the Supreme Court proceeded to overturn determinations of obscenity in per curiam opinions, it was also evident that the justices had divergent views about what might be suppressed. In the 1966 case *Memoirs* v. *Massachusetts* a measure of clarity was attained.[75] The Court overturned a ruling that John Cleland's *Memoirs of a Woman of Pleasure* (*Fanny Hill*) might be treated as obscene. Justices Black and Douglas argued that obscenity could not be suppressed under the First Amendment.[76] Justice Stewart urged that only "hard-core" pornography could be prohibited. In a statement often quoted, Stewart had said in an earlier opinion "perhaps I could never succeed intelligibly in defining [hard-core pornography] . . . [b]ut I know it when I see it." In a case decided with *Memoirs*, he indicated more explicitly what he had in mind: photographs with no pretense of artistic value graphically depicting acts of sexual intercourse and similar cartoon strips and verbal accounts.[77] Justice Harlan, in *Memoirs*, agreeing with Justice Stewart's position about the appropriate federal standard but wishing to afford the states much wider latitude, would have upheld the state's finding of obscenity,[78] as would Justices Clark and White, who thought that predominant appeal to prurient interest should alone remain the critical test.[79] This left a plurality of Justices Brennan, Warren, and Fortas. Brennan's opinion for them turned the three elements mentioned in *Roth* into an explicit three-part test: for material to be classed as obscene, "it must be established that (a) the dominant theme of the material taken as a whole appeals to a prurient interest in sex; (b) the material is patently offensive because it affronts contemporary community standards relating to the description or representation of sexual matters; and (c) the material is utterly without redeeming social value."[80] In a companion case, the Court indicated that how material is advertised and marketed could affect its classification if it is otherwise on the border between the obscene and not obscene.[81] Because the *Memoirs* plurality made up the "center" of the Court, its opinion represented the prevailing approach for the time being, as the Court continued to deal with most obscenity cases by per curiam reversals.

After the Court in 1969 held that some combination of principles of free speech and privacy precluded states from punishing the possession of obscenity in one's home,[82] some expected the Court to go farther and say that all transactions in pornographic materials between willing buyers and willing sellers are constitutionally protected. In two 1973 decisions, the Court, in opinions by Chief Justice Burger, declined to take this step by a 5–4 margin. In *Miller* v. *California*,[83] a majority of the Court set out revised standards for scrutiny of obscenity determinations. To avoid difficulties of vagueness and overbreadth, it required that statutes be written or construed to be confined to works depicting or describing sexual conduct which is "specifically defined" and which, "taken as a whole, appeal to the prurient interest in sex, . . . portray sexual conduct in a patently offensive way, and . . . taken as a whole, do not have serious literary, artistic, political, or scientific value."[84] In a companion case, *Paris Adult Theater* v. *Slaton*,[85] the Court wrote of the interests that justify prohibiting consensual transactions in obscenity: protection of the quality of life and community environment against the crass commercial exploitation of sex, and a reasonable fear of a correlation between obscene material and crime. Both *Miller* and *Paris Adult Theater* were decided over dissents by Justice Brennan, who had authored the Court's opinion in *Roth* and the plurality opinion in *Memoirs*. Brennan had come to believe that the difficulties of determining what is obscene were so great that all material for consenting adults should be deemed constitutionally protected, leaving the states free to regulate only in order to safeguard the interests of minors and nonconsenting adults.[86]

The basic constitutional standards have remained those of *Miller*. Although the formulation of *Miller*, particularly in its third criterion, seems marginally more favorable to a suppression than the plurality formulation of *Memoirs*, in practice the category of what can now be successfully suppressed may be no broader than the "hard-core" pornography of which Justice Stewart wrote.[87] It remains open to suppress some writing as well as pictorial materials, but works of writing alone are rarely proceeded against and treated by courts as obscene.

Under present American constitutional law, then, statutes to suppress obscenity must, roughly, be aimed at "hard-core" pornography. I shall inquire whether there is an adequate theory regarding the nature of such communications and their harms to warrant the Court's conclusion that prohibition of this matter is permissible. I shall also inquire whether some material other than hard-core pornography may be forbidden because it presents women in a degrading way.

The question of the nature of pornographic material has been discussed in Chapter 8. There may be material which is exclusively designed to stimulate a physical response and which has neither any message about facts and values nor any aesthetic value, but it is far from clear that such a category can be identified or that materials in it belong wholly beyond the pale of the First Amendment. Saying when a thin plot about sexual freedom and pleasure has no value as expression or drawing the line between aesthetic expression and portrayals without aesthetic aspiration or effect is difficult. If aesthetic expression involves a degree of detachment by the consumer, what is the status of communications that seek to provide intense emotional experience for the consumer by breaking down distance between him and what is communicated? It may be said of some rock music and popular literature that it succeeds most when the consumer loses a sense of distance from the work. Though an argument can be made that a free speech principle and the First Amendment reach only work that aims at the intellect in some sense,[88] that conclusion is by no means obvious, especially since in the longer run one's intellect will be affected by intense nonintellectual experience. In accord with judicial protection of nude dancing that is not obscene but lacks aesthetic ambition,[89] the First Amendment may also cover expressive attempts to create intense emotional experience that does not involve detachment. Insofar as the Supreme Court has claimed that original understanding places obscenity outside the First Amendment, its historical evidence that, at the time of the Bill of Rights, pornography was viewed as a distinct category of material is dubious. In any event, I have asserted that historical intent is not dispositive on an issue of this sort. In summary, as most scholars have thought, the Supreme Court's formal position that what really amounts to obscenity is altogether outside the First Amendment is too simplistic.

If "hard-core" pornography deserves at least some preliminary protection under the First Amendment, the inquiry turns to whether the reasons for suppression are strong enough to justify the restriction on expression that a criminal statute entails. Chapter 8 has surveyed the possible bases for prohibition, and we need to ask whether, singly or in combination, they are ample. I conclude that claimed justifications for prohibiting pornography either are inappropriate bases for restricting speech or are powerful enough to proscribe only low-value expression.

The argument that pornography causes "offense" is, at least in its superficial form, most out of place for First Amendment analysis. I assume that protecting children and nonconsenting adults from pornography are legitimate objectives;[90] these objectives might warrant regulation of pornography that make obtaining materials marginally harder for willing adult consumers, but they cannot support complete prohibition of pornographic works. The offense that some people feel that *others* are looking at obnoxious materials is not a ground for prohibition consistent with the First Amendment. The principle of freedom to express oneself in ways that others dislike bars using this justification as a basis for restriction.

Contrary to the import of Chief Justice Burger's opinion in *Paris Adult Theater*, the concern about pornography's driving out good literature, by itself, should be regarded similarly. By its control over much education, by its own advocacy, and by financial support of "better" literature and art, the government can promote what it deems worthwhile, but, in the absence of other harms, it should not be able to decide that people not partake of forms of expression they prefer. That is an impermissible form of control of content.

The worry that perusing pornography leads to crime is of a different order. A clear and strong enough connection between viewing pornography and committing crime could warrant suppressing pornography. But one must proceed with caution. If there are discrete subcategories of pornography and only some of them pose a threat of crime, then First Amendment standards of overbreadth would preclude suppressing all pornography because of a harm caused by identifiable subcategories. The idea that pornography leads to crime is most powerful in respect to portrayals of violent sex in which the violence is presented in a positive light; for example, a man rapes a woman and she then "enjoys" it. The 1986 Report of the Attorney General's Commission on Pornography concluded, on the basis of social science research and common sense, that exposure to sexually violent materials increases the likelihood in men of aggression toward women and that this "bears a causal relationship to antisocial acts of sexual violence and, for some subgroups, possibly to unlawful acts of sexual violence."[91] The Commission went on to say, in respect to nonviolent materials depicting degradation, domination, subordination, or humiliation of women, "It appears that effects similar to although not as extensive as that involved with violent material can be identified with respect to such degrading material, but that these effects are likely absent when neither degradation nor violence is present."[92] If the Commission's views are sound, then the concern about violence is a good reason to prohibit only violent and degrading pornography.[93]

What the Commission believes about violent pornography almost certainly would not support suppression of full-value speech. Its causal assumption is of the following sort: that among those people who view violent pornography, a small percentage of persons, not themselves individually identifiable, who would not otherwise commit particular violent acts do so because of their exposure to the pornographic materials. Suppose that a convincing statistical correlation of this low order were made about publicly expressed opinions that violence is cleansing or that most women strongly prefer dominant and aggressive men. The First Amendment would not allow prohibition of such serious claims of fact and value that happen indirectly to lead a small segment of the population to commit crimes. The Commission in effect acknowledges this. It takes pains to argue that pornography does not get over a low threshold of cognitive appeal.[94] It also does not recommend suppression of violent material that is not pornographic, although it grants that the crime-causing potential of violent portrayals of sex does not depend on whether material is hard core.[95]

Another argument for suppression is that pornography causes unhealthy sexual acts. Part of this concern is the use of children and coerced adult actors in pornographic movies. The Supreme Court has held that it is permissible to ban showings of pornographic movies in which children appear as actors in order to bolster a prohibition against children's being used in this way and to avoid the further harm that can be caused if children know that their sexual acts are being viewed by others.[96] But all showings of all pornographic movies could not be foreclosed in order to prevent some adults from being coerced to perform. When one focuses on consumers, the concern is that they may engage in less than desirable sexual acts, such as adultery, group sex, or masturbation. That pornography increases the incidence of this behavior is doubtful; any plausible supposed connection would not be of a high enough order to warrant prohibition of full-value speech and might well be insufficient for prohibition of low-value speech. Insofar as the worry is that pornography causes violent sex or dominating sexual relationships, it is dealt with in the preceding and succeeding paragraphs.

The most elusive of the arguments for suppressing pornography is that it has a harmful effect on attitudes about sexual relations, family, and gender. Explicit advocacy of these destructive attitudes, say in a pamphlet arguing openly that sex is most healthy if treated as a temporary pleasure without emotional involvement or the institutional ties of family, would be constitutionally protected even if it led some people to develop the undesirable attitudes advocated. It follows that worry about such attitudes cannot underlie a prohibition of pornography, unless pornography is less than full-value speech.

I shall concentrate on the harmful effect on attitudes most recently emphasized by feminists: namely that pornography portrays women as objects for men's pleasure and as degraded and, thus, reinforces the mental attitudes that support patterns of male domination.[97] As Catherine MacKinnon has put it, the issue is not morality but power.[98]

Someone who thinks that the main reason for suppressing pornography is the protection of women from attitudes of male domination might see this rationale as working in one or more of three ways. First, it could support a prohibition that reaches only "hard-core" pornography[99] and does not define what is prohibited explicitly in terms of gender. Second, it could justify suppression of some material that might not qualify as "obscene" under the prevailing standards of *Miller* v. *California* (which I have taken as amounting to a restriction of hard-core pornography only). Third, it could undergird a statute in which how a work treats females is one of the explicit criteria of the offense. The highly publicized Indianapolis ordinance, struck down by a three-judge district court,[100] whose decision was affirmed by the Supreme Court,[101] followed both the second and third courses, expanding the categories of materials covered in some respects and making the manner in which material treats women an explicit component of what is illegal. The ordinance covered only "sexually explicit" works, but in the final version that term was left undefined; the ordinance did not refer to prurient interest, patent offensiveness, or literary, artistic, political, or scientific value; it did not make illegality depend on the work as a whole rather than isolated passages; it prohibited works in which "women are presented as sexual objects who enjoy pain or humiliation" or "are presented in scenarios of degradation, injury, abasement" or "are presented as sexual objects for domination, conquest, violation, exploitation, possession, or use."

The court in *American Booksellers Association* v. *Hudnut* held the ordinance invalid because it engaged in viewpoint discrimination. Without doubt the status of materials under the ordinance depended on the viewpoint the material explicitly or implicitly conveyed. Sexually explicit material in which no one was degraded or men were degraded was allowed; only material degrading women was forbidden. The question whether this particular viewpoint discrimination can be defended bears resemblance to the question whether a statute might forbid only those racial and ethnic slurs directed at an underprivileged group. The argument for the form of content discrimination found in the ordinance is twofold: that, given pervasive social structures and messages that support male domination over females, there is no need to proscribe sexually explicit materials in which no one dominates or women dominate, and that the messages of domination are conveyed surreptitiously, not leading to considered acceptance or rejection.[102]

This argument has substantial force, but its implications for First Amendment analysis are disturbing. As the *Hudnut* court notes,[103] many messages influence people in unconscious ways. Pornography is not like subliminal advertising in which the important message is one that the viewer does not even perceive at the conscious level. People can understand how pornography portrays women, and if countervailing speech cannot eliminate the force of continued exposure to pornographic materials, it can alert people to their danger and keep them from becoming unwitting consumers of a message of male domination. Unless sharply contained, the idea that the government can restrict communications that reinforce positions of privilege and domination is a potential threat to free speech. Many restrictions could be justified as counteracting domination and promoting equality.[104] On balance, the worries about viewpoint discrimination should be sufficient to invalidate any statute drawn explicitly in terms of how women, as compared with men, are portrayed. My conclusion is different, however, when worry about effects of this sort supports a statute with other justifications and drawn in different forms. A court, of course, will not ordinarily examine why legislators voted for a measure; but when a pervasive message both is highly destructive and operates mainly at a nonconscious level, legislators should regard themselves as able to take that into account, so long as they do not actually discriminate among materials in terms of the viewpoint conveyed.

The Indianapolis ordinance is also to be faulted for the extent of its reach to materials not qualifying as obscene under Supreme Court doctrine. Barring a radical shift away from free private expression toward suppression in favor of social ideals, works should be judged as a whole and should be protected if they have serious literary, artistic, political, or scientific value. The failure to provide these safeguards is a fatal flaw in the ordinance. The appropriate fate of predominant appeal to prurient interest and patent offensiveness is more doubtful. If the main harm of pornography lies in its relation to violence and domination of women, it is arguable whether these established indicia of obscenity should be critical. There can be little question that many nonpornographic communications, including action movies and television advertisements, reinforce ideas of male domination. The significance of dominant appeal to prurient interest lies not really in a special connection to this feared harm, but mainly in its indication of low-value speech. That test deserves retention for this purpose.

When one has viewed the main arguments for suppressing pornography, one must conclude that the premise that suppression is permissible depends upon an assumption that pornography is less than full-value speech. In view of the dominant aims and effects of pornographic materials, that assumption is sound. The gist of much of the analysis in this book is that material that has some expressive value and deserves some protection under the First Amendment may yet warrant less protection than ordinary claims of fact and value. Although the question is close, "hard-core" pornography is sufficiently identifiable and has little enough expressive value to warrant the conclusion that the Supreme Court's treatment of it as unprotected is defensible.

Summary

This chapter has examined the possibility of grounding criminal or civil liability on harms other than coercion or the sorts of immediate damage at which the criminal law has mainly aimed. Of course, more diffuse harms may provide extra support for prohibitions mainly designed to prevent crime and violence, but we have also considered utterances unlikely to produce crimes or physical harm directly. I have concluded that a persuasive argument for prohibition must show that the utterances involved have less than full value as speech. Beyond that, a delicate examination of expressive value, social harm, and administrable distinctions is needed to yield sensible constitutional guidelines.

Like Chapters 7 and 9, this chapter is more modest in its aspirations than most in the book. The issues I discuss throughout are difficult, and readers can reasonably reject many of my suggestions about constitutional approaches, but, at least for coercion and criminal encouragements, my discussion is as exhaustive as any in the literature. That is not true about this chapter or about the two that follow. Here I have tried to apply my perspectives to highly controversial issues on which they bear, but one would need to digest a great deal of what is to be found in judicial opinions and scholarly analysis before reaching firm considered judgments on these issues. For such judgments, my discussion here is essentially schematic and introductory.

Notes

1. Perhaps, in light of all the influences on attitudes, it would be more realistic to suppose that epithets and pornography might reinforce unwholesome attitudes.

2. 403 U.S. 15 (1971).

3. For the position that no assessment of the comparative value of kinds of speech is proper in constitutional adjudication, see M. Redish, *Freedom of Expression* 13 (Charlottesville, Va., The Michie Co. 1984).

4. In the military context, see *Parker* v. *Levy*, 417 U.S. 733 (1974).

5. See *Connick* v. *Myers*, 461 U.S. 138 (1983).

6. See *Rankin* v. *McPherson*, 107 S. Ct. 2891 (1987).

7. See *Connick* v. *Myers*, note 5 supra.

8. See *Rankin* v. *McPherson*, note 6 supra.

9. 394 U.S. 705 (1969).

10. 781 F.2d 826 (10th Cir. 1986). Anyone who actually watched this program may be a little surprised that it was considered good fare for patients in a psychiatric hospital, especially since reviews gave ample warning how disturbing it might be.

11. *United States* v. *Kelner*, 534 F.2d 1020, 1027 (2d Cir.), certiorari denied, 429 U.S. 1022 (1976).

12. Construing a harassment statute in light of the state constitution, the Oregon Supreme Court said, "the statute could constitutionally be applied only if the threat is objectively likely to be followed by unlawful acts." *State* v. *Moyle*, 299 Or. 691, 705, 705 F.2d 740, 749 (1985). See id. at 709, 705 P.2d, at 752 (concurring opinion of Linde, J).

13. This is one of the numerous instances in which courts may look to *Brandenburg* v. *Ohio* although the problem with which they deal is significantly different.

14. See, e.g., *United States* v. *Lampley*, 573 F.2d 783 (3d Cir. 1978); *Gormley* v. *Dir. Conn. State Dept. of Prob.*, 632 F.2d 938 (2d Cir. 1980), certiorari denied, 449 U.S. 1023 (1980).

15. The court, in id. at 941–42, talks unhelpfully of the statute's regulating the *conduct* of making the telephone call with the requisite intent and in a specific manner. But, on this view, any statute prohibiting specific communications could be said to regulate conduct, since one opens one's mouth and communicates with the requisite intent and in the specified manner.

16. The Model Penal Code treats as harassment making "a telephone call without purpose of legitimate communication." § 250.4(1). Under such a provision, it might matter whether a threat emerged as part of an angry conversation or was the only reason for a call's being made.

17. Conceivably, the approach to telephone conversations might have relevance when someone persistently keeps talking to another person who walks away and clearly does not want to talk any longer, but probably this special approach for criminal cases should be limited to telephones and other similar modes of communication.

18. § 46 (1965), Vol. 1, Ch. 2, at 71.

19. See, e.g., *Knierim* v. *Izzo*, 22 Ill. 2d 73, 174 N.E.2d 157 (1961).

20. See, generally, Note, "First Amendment Limits on Tort Liability for Words Intended to Inflict Severe Emotional Distress," 85 *Columbia Law Review* 1749 (1985).

21. One might imagine threats regarding political matters or personal relationships that could be outrageous and highly disturbing but protected by the First Amendment.

22. *Whitney* v. *California*, 274 U.S. 357, 377 (1927); see V. Blasi, "The First Amendment and the Ideal of Civic Courage: The Brandeis Opinion in *Whitney* v. *California*," 29 *William and Mary Law Review* 653 (1988).

23. *Chaplinsky* v. *New Hampshire*, 315 U.S. 568 (1942).

24. Id. at 571–72.

25. 403 U.S. 15 (1971).

26. See, e.g., *Gooding* v. *Wilson*, 405 U.S. 518 (1972); *Lewis* v. *City of New Orleans*, 415 U.S. 130 (1974). See also *Rosenfeld* v. *New Jersey*, 408 U.S. 901 (1972).

27. *Lewis* v. *City of New Orleans*, note 26 Supra, at 133.

28. 343 U.S. 250 (1952).

29. See generally Note, "Group Defamation: Five Guiding Factors," 64 *Texas Law Review* 591 (1985).

30. This aspect of the Court's opinion is unsatisfying, because the trial court did not indicate that it would consider truth if Beauharnais also made a showing of "good motives" and "justifiable ends." I assume that courts cannot reject motives and ends as unjustifiable because they disapprove of the political program that is urged.

31. See especially *Collin* v. *Smith*, 578 F.2d 1197 (7th Cir. 1978), certiorari denied, 439 U.S. 916 (1978). See also D. Richards, *Toleration and the Constitution* 191–92 (New York, Oxford University Press 1986).

32. See L. Bollinger, *The Tolerant Society* 180–81 (New York, Oxford University Press 1986); D. Downs, "Skokie Revisited: Hate Group Speech and the First Amendment," 60 *Notre Dame Lawyer* 629, 632–35 (1985).

33. That is to say, it would not actually need to overrule cases to do so. It could say "this precise issue has not been presented."

34. §250.4.

35. I add this detail to reduce the possibility that a defenseless black might call on others on or off the next bus for retaliation.

36. In a subsequent passage, I also discuss the relevance of bystanders and their attitudes.

37. Of course, sometimes it can be an insult to place a person in a category which both speaker and listener know is literally inappropriate. Calling a boy or man "a little girl" may be a way to impute cowardice or other "weakness."

38. To quantify this crudely, if 80 percent of young men respond by fighting and only 20 percent of the much larger remaining pool of potential addressees respond in that way, and if the abusive words are addressed to young men more than to the remaining pool together, then the average potential addressee (from the whole pool) would not fight, but the average actual addressee would fight.

39. I subsequently say more about "words of that sort."

40. See generally Bollinger, note 32 supra, at 198.

41. See also *State* v. *Harrington*, 67 Or. App. 608, 680 P.2d 666 (1984).

42. See, e.g., Downs, note 32 supra; R. Delgado, "Words that Wound: A Tort Action for Racial Insults, Epithets, and Name-calling," 17 *Harvard Civil Rights—Civil Liberties Law Review* 133 (1982) (on civil liability).

43. 315 U.S. at 372 (emphasis added).

44. See *State* v. *Harrington*, note 41 supra.

45. This behavior bears some resemblance to making a telephone call in order to harass. It has been assumed that that behavior can be punished in the absence of any prospect of immediate violence.

46. Intimidation involves a kind of conditional threat, although one that may not be explicit and may be rather vague in content.

47. No doubt, self-control is lessened when one is victimized by abusive words, but I think it is misleading to describe a physical response as "an automatic reaction." See S. Ingber, "The Marketplace of Ideas: A Legitimizing Myth," 1984 *Duke Law Journal* 1, 32.

48. It is, of course, tremendously difficult to decide what are equally strong slurs or epithets, since some informal group characterizations are milder than others.

49. See generally Note, note 20 supra.

50. *Hustler Magazine* v. *Falwell*, 108 S. Ct. 876 (1988).

51. *Bethel School District* v. *Fraser*, 478 U.S. 675 (1986).

52. *FCC* v. *Pacifica Foundation*, 438 U.S. 726 (1978).

53. See A. Bickel, *Morality of Consent* 72–73 (New Haven, Yale University Press 1975).

54. See, e.g., D. Farber, "Civilizing Public Discourse: An Essay on Professor Bickel, Justice Harlan, and the Enduring Significance of *Cohen* v. *California*," 1980 *Duke Law Journal* 283.

55. See generally Delgado, note 42 supra.

56. The second distinction involves viewpoint discrimination; the first seems to me to fall somewhere between viewpoint and subject discrimination. See the discussion in Chapter 12.

57. A general definition requiring a certain amount of expected humiliation might in fact most often reach slurs of the underprivileged. See Delgado, note 42 supra, at 180.

58. See, e.g., Note, "A Communitarian Defense of Group Libel," 101 *Harvard Law Review* 682, 690–91 (1988).

59. See the discussion in Chapter 8.

60. See, e.g., Note, note 58 supra.

61. See Delgado, note 42 supra; Downs, note 32 supra.

62. See Delgado, note 42 supra, at 151–57.

63. The difficulties involve both what classes are to be covered—e.g., what of insults to religious groups?—and how severe the abuse must be.

64. That, in fact, has been the experience in England. See E. Barendt, *Freedom of Speech* 163 (Oxford, Clarendon Press 1985).

65. Whether the presumption was only a "permissible inference" or required rebuttal by a defendant would have to be decided if this general option were pursued.

66. See Delgado, note 42 supra. The standard of liability he proposes is that a plaintiff must prove: "Language was addressed to him or her by the defendant that was intended to demean through reference to race; that the plaintiff understood as intended to demean through reference to race; and that a reasonable person would recognize as a racial insult." Id. at 179.

67. In *Time, Inc.* v. *Hill*, 385 U.S. 374 (1967), the Court applied the standard of liability of *New York Times* v. *Sullivan* (see Chapter 18 infra) to a "false light" privacy case, i.e., a privacy case in which what is said that is derogatory or embarrassing is not true. The constitutionality of recovery for false but not defamatory statements about individuals remains clear, although it is now doubted whether the Court would still require that the speakers have acted in reckless disregard of truth or falsity.

68. 420 U.S. 469 (1975). See generally A. Hill, "Defamation and Privacy under the First Amendment," 76 *Columbia Law Review* 1205 (1976).

69. See e.g., id. at 1255–70, 1286–90; L. Tribe, *American Constitutional Law* 887–90 (2d ed., Mineola, N.Y., Foundation Press 1988); K. Greenawalt, "New York's Right of Privacy—The Need for Change," 42 *Brooklyn Law Review* 159, 177–82 (1975).

70. Assuming that the primary safeguard is customary respect, the law may still be needed to stop the few people who see a profit in breaching customary limits.

71. One can imagine, of course, circumstances in which it might be relevant whether someone had been raped twenty years before. Such a report, for example, about a woman who was leading a movement to reinstitute the death penalty for rape would be constitutionally protected.

72. 354 U.S. 476.

73. [1868] L.R. 3 Q.B. 360.

74. 354 U.S. at 489.

75. 383 U.S. 413 (1966).

76. Id. at 424 (concurring opinion of Douglas J.); dissenting opinion of Black J. in companion case of *Ginzburg* v. *United States*, 383 U.S. 463, 476 (1966).

77. Id. at 499. The earlier quote of Justice Stewart's in the text is from his concurring opinion in *Jacobellis* v. *Ohio*, 378 U.S. 184, 197 (1964).

78. 383 U.S. at 455.

79. Id. at 441 and 460 (respectively).

80. Id. at 418.

81. *Ginzburg* v. *United States*, 383 U.S. 463 (1966).

82. *Stanley* v. *Georgia*, 394 U.S. 557 (1969).

83. 413 U.S. 15 (1973).

84. Id. at 24.

85. 413 U.S. 49 (1973).

86. Id. at 83–103.

87. When Justice Stewart wrote in 1966, "hard-core" pornography seemed a somewhat narrower category than what might be suppressed under the standard of the *Memoirs* plurality.

88. See generally J. Finnis, "'Reason and Passion': The Constitutional Dialectic of Free Speech and Obscenity," 116 *University of Pennsylvania Law Review* 222 (1967). For some views on the relationship between pornography and art, see J. Feinberg, *Offense to Others* 129–38 (New York, Oxford University Press 1985).

89. See *Schad* v. *Borough of Mt. Ephraim*, 452 U.S. 61 (1981).

90. On nonconsenting adults, however, see the interesting observations by Thomas Scanlon in "Freedom of Expression and Categories of Expression," 40 *University of Pittsburgh Law Review* 519 (1979).

91. §5.2.1, at 326.

92. §5.2.2, at 330–31.

93. I discuss below the possibility that some viewpoint distinctions are unacceptable. It is conceivable that the class of restricted materials might be expanded to avoid viewpoint classifications.

94. §3.3 at 264.

95. §5.2.1, at 323–29.

96. *New York* v. *Ferber*, 458 U.S. 747 (1982).

97. See, e.g., A. Dworkin, *Pornography: Men Possessing Women* (New York, Putnam 1981); C. MacKinnon, "Pornography, Civil Rights, and Speech," 20 *Harvard Civil Rights—Civil Liberties Law Review* 1 (1985). A thoughtful attempt to relate this challenge to pornography to more traditional "conservative" opposition is found in Comment, "Feminism, Pornography, and the First Amendment: An Obscenity-based Analysis of Proposed Antipornography Laws," 34 *University of California in Los Angeles Law Review* 1265, 1286–97 (1987).

98. See C. MacKinnon, "Not a Moral Issue," 2 *Yale Law and Policy Review* 321, 322–25 (1984).

99. Such a prohibition might be limited to violent pornography or pictorial pornography.

100. *American Booksellers Ass'n* v. *Hudnut*, 771 F.2d 323 (7th Cir. 1985).

101. 475 U.S. 1001 (1986) (with three justices dissenting). A summary affirmance is in theory a decision on the merits, whereas a denial of certiorari is only a discretionary determination not to review.

102. See the careful analysis in C. Sunstein, "Pornography and the First Amendment," 1986 *Duke Law Journal* 589.

103. 772 F.2d at 328–29.

104. Someone who believes that state support of equality and social solidarity matter much more than free speech may be undisturbed by this implication.

18
Falsity

This chapter considers in a summary way how far the First Amendment precludes liability for statements because they are untrue or insincere. I begin with the assumption that, in general, for claims of value and other matters beyond demonstration as true or false, neither falsity nor insincerity can be the basis of liability. That the government may not penalize falsehoods on these subjects is evident. Though some argument might be made that insincere assertions about values or complex interpretive conclusions should be punishable, insincerity on these subjects will usually be very hard to establish. I assume that insincerity does not deprive assertions about these matters of the First Amendment protection they would otherwise have. When the Supreme Court said in *Gertz* v. *Robert Welch, Inc.* that "there is no such thing as a false idea,"[1] it did not quite say that insincere statements of ideas are protected, but it implied that the law has no business reviewing "ideas" in terms of truth or sincerity. Thus I suppose that neither penal nor civil liability can be premised on assertions like "Saluting the flag is ridiculous" or "In the origins of World War II, England was much more to blame than Germany."[2] I shall concentrate on false statements of fact.

What constitutional status do false statements of fact enjoy? We might place at the extremes the belief that false statements have as much value as speech as true statements and that, as the *Gertz* Court said, "there is no constitutional value in false statements of fact."[3] Since people can learn by having to test statements that are untrue, untrue assertions of fact can have some value for the audience. The speaker can also learn from having his untrue statements answered, and, if he makes the statements believing they are true, the aspect of speech as expression of personal opinions and feelings is also served. In ordinary discussion, sincere untrue statements are a critical part of the give and take. On the other hand, untrue statements contribute less to understanding than do true statements, and a knowingly false statement does not usually enhance the speaker's search for truth or express his honest feelings. Chapters 3 and 7 have discussed the possible speech value of false statements believed to be false by the speaker. The value is generally slight except when they initiate an exploratory conversation about what really is true.[4]

With these background premises, I focus on some narrower aspects of liability for falsehood. I first comment briefly on false statements as part of a course of behavior that violates an ordinary penal provision. I then consider crimes for which a prescribed element is intentionally telling a falsehood, examining in some detail the possibility of fraud prosecutions for claims of truth regarding matters of public importance. I next address liability for false statements of fact when the speaker may be unaware of falsity, a liability that is especially important in regulation of commercial speech. Finally, I treat defamation. As far as commercial speech and defamation are concerned, my brief discussion pales beside the extensive examination given by courts and writers. Here, as with much of Chapters 17 and 19, my treatment should be viewed as an attempt to summarize the law for those unfamiliar with it and to tie my other claims to these important subjects; what I say does not represent an independent and original contribution that could stand on its own.

The precise place under the First Amendment of intentional falsehoods, taken in and of themselves, is difficult to ascertain, partly because in actual cases courts have focused on the deterrent effect that liability for falsehoods would have on sincere and true statements. The quote from *Gertz* suggests that falsehoods have no constitutional value. If that is correct, it follows that a puritanically inclined government could actually penalize all lies, subject only to (huge) concern that such a law would deter honest and true utterances.[5] Given the place of lies in much common discourse, perhaps a better view is that lies are part of the speech reached by the First Amendment, but speech with a very low value. On this view, the government could forbid falsehoods only when falsehoods of a given sort cause some specific social harm. As one federal court has indicated, the speech and press clauses may set some threshold of harm before lies can be prohibited.[6] Respect for this low threshold would be in addition to the more significant constraints set by the need to protect true statements from being deterred by punishment of false statements.

Ordinary Crimes

I have indicated in Chapter 7 how an ordinary crime, which does not have telling a falsehood as an element, may be committed by someone who states an untruth. If Sadie tells her companion on the mountain path that it is safe to step to the right, hoping he will do so, she is guilty of murder if he dies from the fall. If a dispatcher carelessly tells an engineer that it is safe to proceed and people are killed in the accident that results, the dispatcher is guilty of reckless or negligent homicide.

The First Amendment has no significant bearing on criminal liability in these contexts. The speech value of a factual assertion whose aim is an immediate practical objective is very slight. Certainly when someone intentionally lies about facts in a way that leads another appropriately to rely without checking on what he has said, he may be criminally punished for a harm the lie predictably causes. Even when the speaker does not intend a harm and is only reckless or negligent about the truth of what he says, his careless giving of incorrect information should not be treated differently from his careless flipping of a switch.

In at least some situations, the First Amendment should properly be understood to bar liability for misinformation. Punishment should be barred if the speaker lacks any criminal objective, has no special relationship to the listener (he is not the listener's nurse or railroad dispatcher), and states what he honestly believes, *and* if a proper response by the listener would not result in harm, either because the listener should check the information elsewhere or because what the listener decides to do is an independent wrong that he should not commit whatever the truth of the speaker's statement. Suppose, sitting in New York, I am asked whether a named run at the Arapahoe Basin Ski Area in Colorado is safe for novices. I say, "It sure is." In fact the trail is terribly difficult, and my friend has an accident skiing on it. If I know that the person asking the question relies heavily on my judgment and if I have not been to that ski area for five years, I may be reckless or negligent in speaking with such confidence instead of reflecting carefully or admitting uncertainty. But, if I am careless, my friend is even more careless. You do not take one person's say-so about the safety of a ski trail when you can ask others, check trail maps, and look at signs. Given the interest in free discourse, people in ordinary conversations who express their views about important facts to listeners who should be expected to do further checking should not be subject to potential liability for recklessness or negligence. A hypothetical example of independently wrongful action is provided by a variation on my example of Carla's telling her neighbor David, who occupies a high position in organized crime, that an employee of his is helping the police. Suppose that Carla has refused to believe indications of her neighbor's true vocation and is carelessly wrong about the employee's actually helping the police. If David acts wrongfully and the employee gets killed because of misinformation, Carla should be constitutionally protected from liability for reckless or negligent homicide. Not only should liability for the resulting harm be barred in such contexts; so also should liability for risking the harm as provided by statutes on reckless endangerment.

The subject of the last paragraph is close to the discussion of liability for recklessness and negligence in Chapter 16, and the conclusions are compatible. There I urged some protection for innocently uttered true statements that risked harms. Although it might be argued that false statements deserve less protection than true ones, serious criminal liability should not turn on actually getting things right when an appropriate response by the listener, including reasonable checking and lawful objectives, would not yield any harm.[7]

Crimes for Which Conscious Falsehood Is an Element

Some crimes, such as perjury, forgery, false impersonation, and fraud, contain intentional misrepresentation as an element. In the typical instances of a conscious lie or misrepresentation about some plain factual matter, the falsehoods involved have virtually no value as expression. Traditional criminal statutes dealing with crimes like these, as drafted and as applied in typical instances, do not raise a serious First Amendment problem. The "lies" with which they concern themselves are socially harmful, no "approver" contemplated that some constitutional protections would apply to them, and the arguments for freedom are weak.

When, however, prosecution or drafting extends beyond typical instances, substantial First Amendment questions may emerge. I shall comment on a few of these, concentrating on an interesting problem raised by a 1985 case concerning fraud about a subject of public interest.

Perhaps some limit exists on how broadly false statements may be made criminal. Punishing lying under oath or on documents seeking specific information may do relatively little to threaten free discourse, but a law that criminalized a factual lie to any public official in all circumstances would be a different matter. We can imagine that such a law would inhibit free conversation between citizens and officials, say about conditions in one's neighborhood, and the possibility that an official who does not happen to like you might misinterpret or "make up" parts of a conversation in a manner that could make you criminal would be worrisome indeed. The danger of arbitrary selective enforcement concerns due process in the sense of fairness, but it also touches free speech, since the prospect of such enforcement casts a chilling pall over candid, antagonistic comments made to officials. The First Amendment should be conceived as setting some threshold for the seriousness of harm caused by the categories of lies made criminal[8] and as limiting the extent to which crimes like perjury can be stretched beyond their traditional boundaries.[9]

A different kind of First Amendment restraint involves the kinds of falsehoods that may be made criminal. As the first paragraph of this chapter indicates, punishment, in the absence of close regulation of commercial speech, cannot be imposed for "false" statements of opinions or complex interpretations of facts that are not subject to definitive judgments of truth or falsity. The punishment of such statements under the Espionage Act of World War I should—and would— now be regarded as constitutionally unacceptable.

A more interesting question is posed by the assertion of evident historical falsehoods in public. We have a poignant and most disturbing example ready at hand: the denial that millions of Jews were exterminated during World War II. The damage that such statements may cause is not an immediate loss of property or deception worked on government officials trying to apply the law, but a contribution to seeds of discord in social relations. The ultimate harm that such discord can do is evidenced by the very historical fact that is being denied, and it is not surprising that falsehoods of this type have caused concern in the Federal Republic of Germany.[10] Typically, this reconstruction of history is found in the midst of scurrilous anti-Semitic diatribes, and in Germany efforts to punish have relied on laws forbidding incitements to class or race hatred and insults to personal honor.[11] These bases for criminalization have been discussed in the last chapter. They do not easily reach an imaginary and apparently sympathetic observer of history who writes:[12]

> I admire the Jews. They have made great contributions to Germany, and no one should ever deny them a full measure of human dignity and equal treatment. Unfortunately, a mistaken conception has grown up, perhaps spread by Communists and actually believed by much of an unsophisticated public, that Germans have treated Jews unequally in the past. Such a view is pure historical fantasy, which reaches absurd proportions in the claim that Hitler's government actually had a policy of killing Jews. No doubt much was bad, even evil, about the Nazis, but stories about their mistreatment of Jews lack a basis in historical fact.

During this decade, proposed laws that would explicitly have made such statements criminal have been considered but not adopted.[13] The question I want to pose is whether any such law would be constitutional in the United States. The answer almost certainly is "no," even if the law reached only those who lied intentionally. Assertions about important historical events of this sort fall squarely within the core of the First Amendment. Were intentional falsehoods of this sort punished, those who innocently repeated the same falsehoods would be at risk, as would those who take controversial positions on facts whose truth is more difficult to establish. Blatant lies about history or present events can do serious harm, but the risk of harm is one that liberal democracies in general should tolerate. I say "in general" because this is one of those aspects of free speech whose application should take into account special historical experience. In the absence of terrible events of the sort that took place in Germany in the relatively recent past,[14] our First Amendment should be construed to protect such speech.

The constitutional limits on what can be punished as fraudulent speech were tested in an interesting 1985 case decided by the Third Circuit Court of Appeals en banc.[15] Antoni Gronowicz had written a book, *God's Broker*, published by Richardson & Snyder, about the life of Pope John Paul II; the book is largely made up of supposed quotations from private conversations the author had with the Pope and other high Roman Catholic officials. When it subsequently appeared that the conversations had never taken place, the publisher withdrew the book and sued Gronowicz for civil fraud. A federal grand jury investigated whether Gronowicz had violated the federal mail-fraud statute by defrauding the publisher,[16] and sought various documents from Gronowicz. Gronowicz refused to produce the documents, claiming a constitutional privilege. I shall disregard the special wrinkle in the case, that what actually was at stake was the production of documents, not the constitutionality of a conviction for the alleged behavior,[17] and I shall also disregard the fact that the federal statute does not actually necessitate completion of fraud, requiring only a scheme to defraud plus some use of the mails.[18] The question on which I want to focus is whether someone may be punished for falsely claiming that interviews took place when: (1) the claim was obviously to be taken on its face and not as a literary device; (2) the interviews were undoubtedly critical to the value the publisher placed on the manuscript; (3) the publisher believed that the interviews had taken place; (4) the author knew they had not; (5) the subject of the manuscript was of undoubted public importance; (6) proof of the fraud is largely inseparable from proof of the falsity of parts of the book. Put in this way, the question appears to capture the allegations in *Gronowicz* and to be a question about which most of the court took a view sharply different from that of two dissenters.[19]

Judge Gibbons, writing for the court, says that, in fraud as in libel, the balance of free expression and social harm is struck in terms of scienter (knowledge) requirements: "false statements made intentionally receive no first amendment protection in the post-publication sanctioning context."[20] The dissenters urge that government interference with speech is justified only by a compelling state interest[21] and that protecting the publisher's economic interest is not enough to warrant a criminal penalty, especially since the remedies of civil fraud adequately protect that interest. Judge Sloviter concludes, "I would hold that a criminal prosecution focussing on the truth of the contents [of the book] would be incompatible with the First Amendment."[22]

Two fundamental disagreements concern whether First Amendment values are sufficiently safeguarded by stringent scienter requirements, and whether criminal prosecutions are to be assimilated to civil suits in terms of limits on liability. If one addresses scienter requirements *in general*, the answer must be that they do not *always* provide sufficient constitutional protection. We need only revert to the "historical lie." Suppose a criminal statute were based on the premise that any significant conscious falsehood an author tells defrauds the public. Even if prosecutions were limited to statements whose falsity could be demonstrated beyond doubt, an author's state of mind would not be easy to show. Any author who has reported the thoughts of others or who has had others report his or her thoughts, any cite checker who has carefully gauged whether one author has accurately reported what another has said, knows how easily and how often inaccuracies creep into the work of conscientious writers, not just mistakes about subtle nuances but blatant errors that are easily refutable from the original text.[23] Human beings have a powerful tendency to fit the facts to their own preconceived notions, and it takes strenuous discipline to try to "get things right." If all that stood in the way of prosecution for significant errors was one's own good faith, the chilling effect on authors would be substantial. Even assuming that only charlatans would end up being convicted, the prospect of investigations and possible charges would be worrisome enough. One would be hesitant to tackle controversial subjects that would lead opponents to be "on the lookout" for factual errors. Thus I conclude that, despite whatever support it may seem to derive from occasional Supreme Court dicta in libel cases, Judge Gibbons's suggestion that false statements made intentionally receive no First Amendment protection from post-publication liability is definitely not sound as applied to conceivable fraud prosecutions for some kinds of errors.

The *Gronowicz* court assumes that First Amendment limits do not depend on whether liability is civil or criminal. As far as present law is concerned, perhaps the most important point is that the Supreme Court has yet to address carefully any argument to the effect that, although a particular activity is undoubtedly subject to civil liability, a criminal penalty for that activity would violate the First Amendment. Occasional stray comments have intimated the appropriateness of criminal punishment for defamation or fraud involving public speech of general concern,[24] but the most important case, *Garrison* v. *Lousiana*,[25] looks in two directions. The Court overturned a conviction for criminal libel, holding that the civil standard of reckless disregard of falsity, newly established in *New York Times* v. *Sullivan*, had not been met. The case clearly established that whatever protections constitutional standards afford in civil cases are also available in criminal cases. But Justice Brennan's opinion also goes on to indicate that concerns with public peace may have underlain the original crime of libel, and Justice Brennan expresses some approval of the Model Penal Code's elimination of libel as a criminal offense. On my reading, it is neither correct that "*Garrison* itself rejects"[26] a distinction in standards between civil and criminal liability nor that Justice Brennan "strongly suggested that criminal libel must be limited to speech that has a clear and present danger of leading to public disorder."[27] I think an accurate statement is that *Garrison* establishes that any civil protections apply to criminal cases, that it leaves open the possibility of more stringent constitutional limits on criminal libel, while expressing approval for movements to eliminate criminal libel or sharply reduce its scope. On this view, neither *Garrison* nor any other case really settles the question whether, for fraud, more powerful First Amendment restrictions apply to criminal cases than to civil ones.

The right answer to this question is "yes," or at least "possibly." In various contexts the Supreme Court has indicated that, in regulating speech, the government must choose the least restrictive alternative. Sanctioning what is said on matters of public concern is a serious enough regulation of speech to bring this concept into play. If civil remedies are really adequate to protecting whatever interests are at stake, then criminal punishment should be foreclosed.

If these general observations are sound, the crucial inquiries in a case like *Gronowicz* are how great is the threat to expression, and whether the undoubted social desirability of reducing outright fraud is adequately served by civil remedies. A helpful approach to resolution is to move to the facts of *Gronowicz* from hypothetical cases on "either side." Suppose that an author intentionally misstates ascertainable historical facts or what other people have said in writing. These are matters a publisher can check, and I have argued in this chapter that criminal liability for such speech would significantly inhibit discourse. I am indeed doubtful whether a publisher should be able even to recover for civil fraud when an author has been inaccurate about what is already on the public record. On the other hand, if someone simply forged a document, say a diary of Napoleon, and persuaded a publisher to buy the document for publication, this would be fraud in the same manner as would consciously selling a copy of a Giotto painting as an original. One would not need to look at the book itself to show that the diary was a fake. If someone sold faked tapes of a series of interviews with President Bush, the result should be the same. The tapes would be shown to be fraudulent without respect to the content of the book, and punishment would be permissible under the First Amendment.

We move to somewhat more debatable facts. Suppose a well-known expert (who has decided to earn a fast buck by fraud) sells the publisher only a manuscript that purports to translate Napoleon's diary, whose genuineness the author guarantees. One must now look at the manuscript to see what is claimed, but proof of fraud requires only a showing that the purported diary is a fake or that it has never even existed. I think the same conclusion applies if all the expert does is sell the publisher the transcription of the supposedly taped Bush interviews. Again, punishment is permissible. Matters become more difficult if the interviews are interwoven with other materials and not claimed to be backed by objective evidence like a tape. It remains true that one need not scrutinize what was supposedly said in an interview if the claim of fraud is that no such interview ever took place, but one needs to look at the manuscript to determine just what interviews were claimed, and whether the "interviews" could possibly be a "literary device." Given opportunities for personal or telephone interviews at various places and times and the fact that sometimes people who were interviewed and regret what they actually said or think it has been misinterpreted will deny that the interview ever took place,[28] it will be hard to show conclusively that claimed interviews never occurred. Popes and presidents may be exceptional in this respect since their movements are so carefully monitored, but no special rule should be created for claimed interviews with them. Though *Gronowicz* is a borderline case, I am inclined to think, especially since cases like this are rare and publishers are adequately protected by their own expert judgment and by the law of civil fraud,[29] that prosecution for criminal fraud should be foreclosed for such publications, unless the fraud can be shown by proving that some crucial document separate from the manuscript is either itself faked or does not exist. Thus, on the facts of *Gronowicz* I agree with the dissenters. The more general point is that fraud prosecutions in the circumstances of books of public interest warrant careful scrutiny under the First Amendment.

Restriction That Does Not Depend on the Speaker's State of Mind: Commercial Speech

One general if subdued theme of the preceding sections is that innocent falsehoods cannot generally be restricted. Apart from information provided by people to others who are expected to rely without independent judgment, I have suggested that strict liability and liability for negligent misstatements violate the First Amendment. Yet the regulation of advertising is based almost entirely on the content of what is said without respect to any particular person's, or company's, state of mind.

That much closer regulation of factual assertions is allowed for commercial speech than for other speech is one manifestation of the special, inferior status that such speech has under the First Amendment. During the 1970s the Supreme Court abandoned its former position[30] that commercial speech is not reached at all by the free speech and free press clauses,[31] but it continues to permit forms of regulation that would be unthinkable in other areas. Chapter 7 has already suggested a number of reasons why commercial speech is special. Although informational speech about products and services helps readers to make intelligent judgments in matters they care about, such speech does not represent the personal feelings or choices of individuals, it may generally be both more easily verifiable and more durable in the face of regulation than other speech,[32] it is closely related to contractual undertakings, and it deals with subjects of less overall public importance than speech on a great variety of other topics.[33] Almost everyone who agrees with the Supreme Court that commercial speech should have some protection under the First Amendment also agrees that less than full protection is appropriate.

Drawing the line between commercial and other speech is no doubt difficult. A company might rely on glowing assumptions about political events to predict its future, advertisements for a brand of condoms may contain warnings about the need to use condoms to prevent AIDS,[34] a magazine like *Consumer Reports* may offer disinterested information about commercial products. In all probability it is a mistake for courts to assume that the same dividing lines between speech that is "commercial" and speech that is not will work for all cases. Rather, in the context of specific forms of regulation, courts should ask whether the reasons for a relaxed standard of review apply, and, as Steven Shiffrin has emphasized, one critical inquiry is about the dangers of government bias in that kind of regulation.[35]

Without attempting to describe in detail the First Amendment law relating to freedom of commercial speech, I shall mention some leading features. Advertisements that are deceptive or misleading as well as those which are false may be forbidden.[36] Vague claims about present benefits or likely future benefits or competence may be foreclosed, although they would count as "opinion" if the subject of the speech were history or politics.[37] Advertisements and labels may be required to provide particular information,[38] including warnings of danger. Prescreening of a sort generally unacceptable as a "prior restraint" may be allowed.[39] State licenses are required of people who wish to provide information on certain topics, such as law and medicine. Those who provide some services may be stopped from soliciting business in person if the dangers of misleading or overbearing potential users of the services are serious.[40] All these doctrinal exceptions to normal First Amendment approaches show how much greater is the power of the state to control how and what information is provided if the aim is to persuade a consumer to enter into some kind of business transaction (broadly understood to include the purchase of legal and medical services).

Defamation

One traditional basis for liability concerns falsehoods that injure another's reputation in the community. Written falsehoods are *libels*; spoken falsehoods are *slanders*. For some time the Supreme Court said that defamation was outside the First Amendment, and civil libel was mainly governed by common law rules, with complicated origins.[41] These allowed recovery for falsehoods damaging enough to be defamatory—for example, "she stole money from the bank," "he is a terrible coward," "she just returned from a mental institution." If the speaker could not establish the truth of what he said, he was liable regardless of his state of mind. In many states there was also provision for criminal libel, but the crime fell into increasing disuse in the twentieth century.

There is little doubt that defamations can harm. Standing in the community is of economic value, and, quite apart from economics, most people want to be well regarded. Moreover, having bad things said about oneself is immediately upsetting. In this respect, defamation lies close to many fighting words, and, indeed, in the face-to-face setting many defamatory comments can amount to fighting words. Centuries ago defamatory remarks could lead to duels, and legal remedies, by providing an alternative way to prove one's honor, help to preserve the peace.[42]

Presented with a $500,000 damage assessment against the New York Times for carrying an advertisement placed by supporters of Martin Luther King, Jr. that contained minor errors about how Alabama law enforcement officials had acted, the Supreme Court, in *New York Times* v. *Sullivan*,[43] declared that the First Amendment restricts recovery for libel when public officials are criticized. Drawing from the judgment that the First Amendment renders invalid any crime of seditious libel, the Court held that a public official may not recover damages for "a defamatory falsehood relating to his official conduct unless he proves that the statement was made with 'actual malice'—that is, with knowledge that it was false or with reckless disregard of whether it was false or not."[44] The proof presented to show actual malice had to establish it with convincing clarity.[45] The Court subsequently extended the *New York Times* rule to libels of public figures,[46] and a critical plurality held in a later case that it also reached any matter of public and general interest.[47] In *Gertz v. Robert Welch, Inc.*,[48] the Court backed away from this last innovation, deciding that actual malice need be proved only when public officials and public figures are defamed. It did say that, at least for media defendants, states could not impose liability without fault and could allow punitive damages only upon a showing of reckless disregard of truth. By a narrow margin and without a majority opinion, the Court in 1985 held that the *Gertz* limit on punitive damages did not apply to a false report by a credit-reporting agency to five subscribers.[49]

What I have argued in this book strongly supports the idea that damaging remarks about individuals are within a principle of free speech and are a proper subject of First Amendment concern. Because of the harm defamations can do and because countering their effects is extremely difficult (and would be made more so if they were absolutely privileged), a rule of complete constitutional protection would be misguided. Some balance needs to be struck between expressive freedom and the need to protect feeling and reputation from unwarranted attacks, and the Supreme Court has attempted that, choosing categorical rules for drawing distinctions in this domain. There are certainly alternative categorical rules that might reasonably be chosen—perhaps, for example, more emphasis should be placed on the content of speech and less on who is defamed[50]—but, taken as a whole, the Supreme Court's standards are responsive to competing concerns.

Unfortunately, the rules are not working very well in practice. The costs of litigation, increased by the investigation needed to determine whether someone has been reckless about truth or falsity, and uncertainties of application of the rules leave publishers vulnerable, even when they may ultimately succeed. Who exactly is a public figure is hard to say, and the now well-established distinction between constitutionally protected opinion and factual mistakes for which one may be liable can be difficult to apply in practice. The latter point is illuminated by the various opinions in the United States Court of Appeals for the District of Columbia when it had to decide the status of a statement that a political scientist had "no status within the profession."[51]

There is a lot of room for reform in the civil law of defamation, but most of it is not in the realm of constitutional law. Inexpensive ways to establish falsity should be provided for persons who care more about the falsehood's being corrected than about getting money. When falsity is determined, those responsible for the libel should have to print corrections.[52] Certainly one lesson to be learned from the law of defamation is that relative theoretical soundness of a branch of law under the First Amendment does not guarantee overall effectiveness and fairness in practice.

The fate of criminal libel is both not clear and not important. The Supreme Court has never declared that criminal libel is unacceptable or even that it must satisfy more stringent standards than those for civil libel. But, as I indicated in the last section, the Court's opinion in 1964 in *Garrison* v. *Louisiana*[53] regarded the withering away of criminal libel with some approval. Were the Court to address the problem, the fate of criminal libel should be subject to inquiry into whether it serves any real need not adequately met by civil libel; if not, it should be struck down as not satisfying "the least restrictive alternative" requirement.[54] If criminal libel survives at all, it should probably be only for libels that are knowingly false and so serious that they pose threats to public peace as well as damage to individual reputations.

Notes

1. 418 U.S. 323, 339 (1974).

2. This position represents some shift from the treatment of prosecutions under the Espionage Act in World War I. The Supreme Court sustained a conviction in *Pierce* v. *United States*, 252 U.S. 239 (1920), in which a section of the act forbidding "false reports" was read to proscribe particular interpretations of complex historical events and predictions of future events. See also *United States* v. *Burleson*, 255 U.S. 407 (1921). An analogous problem is posed by treating religious claims as false or insincere. See *United States* v. *Ballard*, 322 U.S. 78 (1944).

3. 418 U.S. at 340. See also *Keeton* v. *Hustler Magazine, Inc.*, 465 U.S. 770 (1984). I assume that, in contrast with the traditional law of defamation, if one truly reports in a matter of public concern what someone else has falsely stated, one is protected. I assume, therefore, that the doctrine of "neutral reportage" is required by the First Amendment. See *Lasky* v. *American Broadcasting Company, Inc.*, 606 F. Supp. 934 (S.D.N.Y. 1985).

4. In Chapter 3, I used the example of a statement like "Of course, I don't believe that Janet would take money from the bank, but I heard someone say she did. What do you think?" said by someone who really does think Janet has stolen.

5. The *Gertz* Court was, of course, not focusing on this problem; so its language is hardly dispositive.

6. *American Postal Workers* v. *United States Postal Service*, 598 F. Supp. 564, 570 (U.S.D.C. 1984). The context of the court's treatment is discharge for the speech of public employees, and the court talks of trivial lies that might amount to harmless fictions or apocryphal stories; so its view of the constitutional status of a fully serious but insignificant lie is not entirely clear.

7. It is a closer question whether civil liability for negligence should be regarded as acceptable, but I believe that should be barred as well.

8. If the category of lies made criminal causes some substantial harm, it should not be a constitutional defense that one's own lie within that category was trivial.

9. See *State* v. *Huntley*, 82 Or. App. 350, 728 P.2d 868 (1986), concluding that criminal penalties for candidates' misstatements about their backgrounds in forms that go to voters were a "contemporary variant" of perjury, since the facts (candidates' degrees) were not open to debate, candidates had ample opportunity to present other facts relevant to the election, and false information on the forms would mislead voters and undermine the electoral process.

10. See E. Stein, "History against Free Speech: The New German Law against the 'Auschwitz'—and other—'Lies,'" 85 *Michigan Law Review* 277 (1986).

11. See id. at 281–305, for the statutory provisions and their treatment in courts.

12. One might, of course, argue that any denial of the "Holocaust" is itself an insult to

Jews and an implicit encouragement to hatred of Jews, but that would be a troubling extension of the idea that hate literature about ethnic or religious groups can be punished.

13. See id. at 305–12.

14. I recognize that I am making here a somewhat debatable judgment. A critic might say that treatment in this country of Native Americans and blacks is analogous to German treatment of Jews and, even if not quite so bad, at least in this century, has been bad enough to warrant prohibition of historical lies that deny mistreatment. That is the argument by analogy that the text rejects.

15. In re Grand Jury matter, *Gronowicz*, 764 F.2d 983 (3d Cir. 1985), certiorari denied, 474 U.S. 1055 (1986). Prior to the denial of certiorari Gronowicz died.

16. 18 U.S.C. §§ 1341 and 1343.

17. The point is emphasized in Judge Higginbotham's dissenting opinion, 764 F.2d at 994–98.

18. See J. Coffee, "The Metastasis of Mail Fraud: The Continuing Story of the 'Evolution' of a White-collar Crime," 21 *American Criminal Law Review* 1, 10–13 (1983); Note, "Mail Fraud and Free Speech," 61 *New York University Law Review* 942 (1986).

19. Compare 764 F.2d 983–89 (court's opinion) with id. at 992–94 (dissent of Hunter, J.) and 1000–1002 (dissent of Sloviter, J.). Judge Higginbotham's dissent, note 17 supra, evidences considerable sympathy for Gronowicz's constitutional position on this question, but believes that it is too far at odds with what the Supreme Court has said. Two academic comments on the case assert that such a conviction would violate the First Amendment: Note, "Mail Fraud and Free Speech," note 18 supra; and Note, "Crime of the Century: Use of the Mail Fraud Statute against Authors," 67 *Boston University Law Review* 507 (1987).

20. 764 F.2d at 988.

21. 764 F.2d at 993 (dissent of Hunter, J.).

22. 764 F.2d at 1002.

23. According to an article in the *New York Times*, a study of medical journals "showed that the original author was misquoted in 15 percent of all references and that most errors would have misled readers who did not look up the original reference." L. Altman, M.D., "A Flaw in the Research Process: Uncorrected Errors in Journals," *New York Times*, May 31, 1988, Section C, p. 3, col. 1.

24. *Branzburg* v. *Hayes*, 408 U.S. 665, 683 (1972) (defamation); *Cantwell* v. *Connecticut*, 310 U.S. 296, 306 (1940) (fraud).

25. 379 U.S. 64 (1964).

26. *Gronowicz*, note 15 supra, at 988 n. 4 (opinion of court).

27. Id. at 1000–1001 (opinion of Sloviter, J.).

28. Note, "Crime of the Century," note 18 supra, at 510, for some fascinating hypothetical situations drawn from the *Gronowicz* circumstances and suggesting possibilities of abuse.

29. Fraud is different from defamation in one important respect. If a defamation profits a speaker at all, it will rarely do so to the extent of the damages he might pay if he is liable. The balance will be much closer in fraud; that is, gain will be approximately as great as likely possible loss. Therefore, one might suppose that the "extra" criminal sanction is needed to discourage the wrongful behavior. An effective answer to this abstract analysis is that publishers seem rarely to be defrauded by this sort of hoax, which certainly would be sufficient to ruin an author's credit in the publishing business. See id. at 530–31.

30. See *Valentine* v. *Chrestensen*, 316 U.S. 52 (1942).

31. *Virginia State Board of Pharmacy* v. *Virginia Citizens Consumer Council*, 425 U.S. 748 (1976).

32. Id. at 771–72, n. 24.

326   Constitutional Limits on Prohibiting Speech

33. See *Ohralik* v. *Ohio State Bar Ass'n*, 436 U.S. 447, 456 (1978); *Central Hudson Gas & Elec. Corp.* v. *Public Service Comm'n*, 447 U.S. 557, 562, n. 5 (1980); S. Shiffrin, "The First Amendment and Economic Regulation: Away from a General Theory of the First Amendment," 78 *Northwestern University Law Review* 1212, 1218–20 (1983).

34. See *Bolger* v. *Youngs Drug Products Corp.*, 463 U.S. 60 (1983).

35. See Shiffrin, note 31 supra, at 1261–76.

36. *Virginia State Board of Pharmacy* v. *Virginia Citizens Consumer Council*, note 31 supra at 771–72.

37. See *Bates* v. *State Bar of Arizona*, 433 U.S. 350 (1977); *Zauderer* v. *Office of Disciplinary Counsel*, 471 U.S. 626 (1985).

38. See, e.g., id.

39. *Central Hudson Gas & Elec. Corp.* v. *Public Service Comm'n*, note 33 supra, at 571, n. 13.

40. *Ohralik* v. *Ohio State Bar Ass'n*, note 33 supra.

41. See W. Keeton et al., *Prosser and Keeton on Torts* 771–73 (5th ed., St. Paul, Minn., West Publishing Co. 1984).

I consider defamation of individuals, but what I say also applies to genuine group defamation, where the damaging statement is about members of a discrete group and could reasonably be taken probably to apply to an individual in the group, e.g., "The members of the Columbia tennis team sniff cocaine."

42. In many instances, at least, the threat that a defamation will disturb the peace is not immediate. *A* defames *B* to *C*, and the remark eventually gets back to *A*, who then "defends his honor."

43. 376 U.S. 254 (1964).

44. Id. at 279–80.

45. Id. at 284–86. *Bose Corp.* v. *Consumers Union of United States, Inc.*, 466 U.S. 485 (1984), indicates that appellate courts must exercise independent judgment about whether the requirement of convincing clarity has been met. The relevance of the requirement for summary judgment is addressed in *Anderson* v. *Liberty Lobby, Inc.*, 477 U.S. 242 (1986). In *Philadelphia Newspapers, Inc.* v. *Hepps*, 475 U.S. 767 (1986), the Supreme Court held that when speech is of public concern, a private-figure plaintiff has the burden of proving falsity.

46. *Curtis Pub. Co.* v. *Butts*, 388 U.S. 130 (1967).

47. *Rosenbloom* v. *Metromedia, Inc.*, 403 U.S. 29 (1971).

48. 418 U.S. 323 (1974).

49. *Dun & Bradstreet, Inc.* v. *Greenmoss Builders, Inc.*, 472 U.S. 749 (1985).

50. See M. Franklin, "Constitutional Libel Law: The Role of Content," 34 *University of California in Los Angeles Law Review* 1657 (1987). One basis for the Court's differentiations is that public officials and public figures have access to the media to answer attacks. But that is not always true, and there is something paradoxical about the possibility that a story about a named private individual's bribing a named judge would be subject to one constitutional standard when the individual sues and to another when the judge sues.

51. *Ollman* v. *Evans*, 750 F.2d 970 (D.C. Cir. 1984) (en banc), certiorari denied, 471 U.S. 1127 (1985).

52. The notion that having to print replies or determinations of falsity is an interference with editorial judgment, see *Miami Herald Pub. Co.* v. *Tornillo*, 418 U.S. 241 (1974), is overdrawn, so long as the editors are free also to say that they do not find a reply persuasive and that they think a determination was erroneous.

53. 379 U.S. 64 (1964).

54. It might be objected to this "least restrictive alternative" approach that criminalization reflects a judgment of community condemnation for which civil remedies can never

substitute. Of course, the whole law of intentional torts and certainly that of punitive damages can be said to reflect ideas about wrongful behavior, but criminal sanctions may express a stronger notion of wrongfulness than they do. If this reason for using a criminal sanction is appropriate—and I think it is—then the ability of courts to reject the criminal alternative depends on their capacity to estimate how wrongful behavior is and how it is regarded. The assumption in the text is that, if other interests are adequately served by civil remedies, the "interest" in strong condemnation could be employed to justify criminal penalties for speech only if the behavior is regarded as truly abhorrent, something that is not true about most defamation or most fraud.

19

Prohibition Not Ostensibly Directed at the Content of Communications

This chapter takes up the constitutional dimension of subjects discussed in Chapter 9, prohibitions of expressive activities for reasons unrelated to what is communicated and prohibitions of activities that themselves need not be expressive but in which some people engage for reasons of expression. These subjects are a very important and complicated aspect of First Amendment law, and I shall barely scratch the surface. I consider in turn legislation that largely affects communicative activities, legislation that interferes with some communicative acts, and the ways courts determine whether legislation is designed to suppress messages or not.

If the evident purpose of a scheme of prohibition is to suppress a particular viewpoint—for example, demonstrations against draft registration are prohibited—the prohibition is invalid unless it falls within a permissible basis for restriction of the sort discussed in earlier chapters, but this possibility does not meet all the concerns about viewpoint discrimination. A prohibition serving an interest not related to communication—for example, demonstrations are forbidden because they slow traffic—may have an *exception* for a particularly valued point of view—for example, demonstrations in favor of war efforts—or a prohibition may be cast in such vague and general terms that administrative officials are left free to engage in viewpoint discrimination.[1] I subsequently say a bit more about deciding when viewpoint discrimination exists if it is not transparent, but when a statute undertakes or authorizes such discrimination, it is presumptively invalid.[2]

When legislatures avoid content discrimination and act for reasons unrelated to the message involved but interfere with what are undoubtedly expressive activities, such as demonstrations, courts applying constitutional principles must see that a reasonable balance is struck. Categorical rules are not well suited to the great variety of cases, but ordinarily the interest in speech is given substantial weight, and courts must determine that an approach less restrictive of speech would not adequately serve the government's need. It will be very important whether the restraint is only one of time and location, leaving people free to engage in the same expressive activity at another time or place.[3] It will matter whether what is restricted is a traditional form of public communication.[4] Also important, though often not mentioned by courts, will be substitutability if a particular form of communication is substantially foreclosed: Can the people who would have engaged in this activity communicate their message with something like similar effectiveness in some other way?[5]

When a legislature restricts demonstrations, sound trucks, or billboards, it knows it is curbing one form of communication, even when it has no aim to curtail the messages expressed. In other circumstances it can adopt laws—for example, forbidding sleeping overnight in public parks or public nudity or requiring possession of draft cards—which do not directly concern communication at all but which end up precluding some communicative efforts. What the judicial approach should be to these latter cases, and their relation to the former cases, are difficult questions.

We may start by rejecting one possible constitutional approach: that one's rights turn largely on one's private motives. Under this approach the government would have to meet a much higher standard to punish someone with a communicative motive than to punish others. To draw from an example in Chapter 9, suppose that the law forbids appearing nude on a public beach. If subjective motivation were crucial, a person lying nude on a beach towel who feels that appearing nude makes an important antipuritanical statement would be treated differently from the person lying nude next to him who just likes the sensation of being without clothing.[6] As I suggested in the earlier chapter, making punishment possibly depend on each person's "dominant" or "subordinate" motive to make a "statement" in favor of nudity is not feasible, and no one has suggested that private motive should determine the standard of review for these situations.[7]

The harder problem involves circumstances in which a person's actions obviously show an aim to communicate a message. An example is afforded by burning a draft card in public during an antiwar rally. This is not an act that people perform unless they are trying to say something. We need to imagine that the criminal statute is not ostensibly directed at communication and that, at least as far as the courts are concerned, no aim to suppress communication is discernible. This is how the Supreme Court characterized the new statute forbidding destruction of draft cards which it considered in *United States* v. *O'Brien*.[8] If the Court's failure to say that Congress aimed to restrict communication was a misstep, as I shall suggest below, its characterization would certainly have been accurate for the combination of earlier statute and selective service regulations that preceded the challenged law. Under these, which were aimed not at communication but at ensuring that people keep their draft cards, O'Brien's burning of his draft card generated a punishable knowing failure to possess his draft card. What is the significance of the communicative aspect of O'Brien's behavior in the face of such a "neutral" statute and regulations not aimed at communicative activity?

We can imagine at least two ways in which this communicative aspect might make a difference; ways in which it might affect the test for evaluating the statute itself or the test for deciding whether O'Brien's behavior was itself constitutionally protected from punishment under the statute. I shall briefly consider the first possibility. When legislatures regulate noncommunicative matters that do not involve independent constitutional rights, they have almost absolute discretion to decide what needs to be done. The only constitutional review involves the "relaxed" rational-basis standard under which virtually all legislative choices survive. If that standard were otherwise appropriate for judging a statute, it could not be rendered inappropriate because one violator was obviously trying to communicate. For example, judicial review of parking regulations would not be altered because one person who parked illegally did so in a manner that clearly evidenced an aim to communicate. Thus, O'Brien's behavior alone could not affect the standard of review for a statutory provision. If it could be shown, however, that a high percentage of actual violators and potential violators[9] did and would have communicative aims, that conceivably should affect the standard of review, even apart from what the aims of most violators might indicate about legislative purpose.[10]

The second way in which the communicative aspect of O'Brien's behavior might matter is in affecting the standard for determining whether his own conduct can be punished under the statute. Although, once it determined that the law against destruction of draft cards was not aimed at communication, the *O'Brien* Court was not entirely clear whether it was reviewing the statute itself or the application of the statute to O'Brien's situation,[11] that part of the opinion should be regarded as directed to the latter question.[12] On this problem, the Court equivocated a bit. It said:

> We cannot accept the view that an apparently limitless variety of conduct can be labeled "speech" whenever the person engaging in the conduct intends thereby to express an idea. However, even on the assumption that the alleged communicative element in O'Brien's conduct is sufficient to bring into play the First Amendment, it does not necessarily follow that the destruction of a registration certificate is constitutionally protected activity.[13]

The Court then went on to elaborate a First Amendment test for such circumstances: a government regulation otherwise within constitutional power is sufficiently justified "if it furthers an important or substantial government interest; if the governmental interest is unrelated to the suppression of free expression; and if the incidental restriction on alleged First Amendment freedoms is no greater than is essential to the furtherance of that interest."[14] In requiring a substantial interest, not any plausible interest, and in demanding that the restriction of expression be no greater than is essential to furthering the interest, the Court seemed to announce a fairly stringent balancing test, which goes well beyond "rational basis" review and which might also be appropriate for government regulation of demonstrations or leafleting. As applied in *O'Brien*, however, the standard is very relaxed, with the Court accepting some rather thin claims about why granting those like O'Brien a right to burn their cards would interfere with the effective administration of the draft.[15]

The *O'Brien* formulation continues to be used. In no subsequent case has the Supreme Court actually held that application of an otherwise permissible prohibition not directed at communicative activity was impermissible because the defendant's behavior on its face was communicative. For reasons of administrability and evenhandedness among violators, it may be argued that no serious balancing test is called for when legislation does not itself concern evidently communicative activities. Since it is clear that no categorical test can cover all the circumstances in which neutral regulations impinge on communicative efforts,[16] the three reasonable choices are: (1) no review beyond rational basis,[17] (2) a slightly more stringent but still rather weak review, that is, what *O'Brien* has amounted to in practice for these kinds of cases, (3) a more stringent test, applied more the way the *O'Brien* formulation reads. Without canvassing all the relevant situations, I am inclined to the view that the interest in free communication is strong enough to warrant a more demanding test than *O'Brien* has proved to be in practice. At least when communicative violations are fairly common and are not motivated by a desire to do something because it is illegal,[18] the Court might try to achieve an accommodation of expressive aims not unlike the accommodation that is made in some areas for strong religious reasons for refusing to do what the law requires.[19]

In respect both to regulation of forms of communication like demonstrations and leaflets and to prohibitions not ostensibly concerned with expression at all, a judicial review of constitutionality must assess whether legislation is really suppressing the content of messages. That judgment might be made on the basis of the language of a statute, on a consideration of the statute in the context of other legal rules, or on a review of legislative history. The consequence of the judgment that suppression is really of particular messages is to render a statute presumptively invalid, unacceptable unless it meets the standards for suppression set out in earlier chapters or fits within some other exception to First Amendment protection.[20] If courts do not decide that the statute is directed at messages, its application will be subjected to some form of balancing along lines indicated in this chapter.

The easiest instances are those in which the face of a statute reveals its direction. As Chapter 9 suggests, a statute that forbids "defiling" the flag is aimed at those whose physical acts communicate some negative message in relation to the flag;[21] the language of the statute reveals a design to stop one kind of show of disrespect for this symbol of the country. This alone is enough to trigger a more stringent standard of review than ordinary balancing. Although an argument can be made that preserving the power of the flag as a symbol warrants the slight impediment of not permitting the particular expressive action of disrespectful destruction or mutilation, the general interest in free expression and the undesirability of viewpoint discrimination support the conclusion that desecration cannot permissibly be punished in the absence of a serious potential for violence.[22]

Matters are a little more complicated in regard to statutes aimed at preventing "improper use" of the flag. These forbid such acts as placing "any word, figure, mark, picture, design, drawing or advertisement" on a flag. Such provisions are neutral about the content of any message being conveyed by the forbidden behavior and, indeed, about whether any message at all is being conveyed—one might choose to wear a flag design on a vest because it looks attractive.[23] Nevertheless, the flag is itself an important communicative symbol, and the *special protection* of that symbol from interference is itself probably a form of content discrimination that calls for review more stringent than an ordinary balancing test.[24]

The most difficult cases are those in which the face of the statute and implications that can be drawn from it[25] yield no conclusion that it is either aimed at communication of messages or designed to provide special protection for particular symbols that convey messages. The provision forbidding destruction of draft cards is an example. The simple aim to keep draft cards intact has nothing obvious to do with communication. Yet it was readily apparent in 1969 that Congress had added a new statute dealing directly with draft-card destruction, an activity already adequately covered by a more general statute and by selective service regulations,[26] because it was disturbed by the opposition to the Vietnam War manifested in public burnings of draft cards.

I shall not undertake analysis of the complicated question of how far courts should try to assess legislative motives,[27] but, if the most plausible explanation for a statute is that it was aimed to discourage a particular sort of message, if, as Lawrence Tribe suggests, a complainant proved that the legislature was motivated in substantial part by an illicit motive and if the government cannot establish that the statute probably could have been enacted anyway,[28] then the courts should treat the statute as an attempt to control expression. Contrary to the conclusion the Supreme Court reached in *United States* v. *O'Brien*, this threshold was crossed for the statute that forbade destruction of draft cards. Once the determination is made that in context a statute was aimed at expression, review more stringent than the balancing test of *O'Brien* would follow.

Notes

1. *Cox* v. *New Hampshire*, 312 U.S. 569 (1941).

2. See L. Tribe, *American Constitutional Law* 794–804 (2d ed., Mineola, N.Y., Foundation Press 1988); J. Ely, "Flag Desecration: A Case Study in the Roles of Categorization and Balancing in First Amendment Analysis," 88 *Harvard Law Review* 1482 (1975). In *Chicago Police Dept.* v. *Mosley*, 408 U.S. 92 (1972), the Court reached a similar conclusion about subject-matter discrimination for picketing. See K. Karst, "Equality as a Central Principle in the First Amendment," 43 *University of Chicago Law Review* 20 (1975).

3. See generally *Schneider* v. *Irvington*, 308 U.S. 147 (1939); *Cox* v. *Louisiana*, 379 U.S. 559 (1965); Ely, note 2 supra. Ely notes ambiguity in the less-restrictive-alternative standard. Is the question whether the government's interest will be *equally well* served by a less restrictive alternative (in which event it might be said that prohibitions of leafleting *and* littering will work better than a prohibition of littering alone), or is the question whether the government's interest will be *adequately* served by the alternative (in which event a prohibition of littering will suffice)?

4. See Ely, note 2 supra, at 1488. One of the factors that has figured prominently in recent Supreme Court litigation is whether expression takes place in a "public forum." See, e.g., *United States* v. *Albertini*, 472 U.S. 675 (1985); Tribe, note 2 supra, at 986–97.

5. See *Los Angeles City Council* v. *Taxpayers for Vincent*, 466 U.S. 789 (1984).

6. This is not to say that the final constitutional outcome would necessarily be different. The state's interest might be strong enough to punish even the person whose nudity is aimed at communicating.

7. A stronger argument would be that, because most people with a wish to engage in the behavior do have a communicative motive, the provision and its application generally should be subject to stricter review. I discuss something close to this contention in the text below.

8. 391 U.S. 367 (1968).

9. The potential violators are very important. Suppose that (1) 1000 people were inclined to commit a certain act, and only 10 of these were inclined to do so for an expressive purpose; and (2) once a law was passed making the act illegal, all but those with the expressive purpose were deterred. The only actual violators of the law would have an expressive purpose, but the law would effectively be controlling a great deal of nonexpressive behavior.

10. If virtually all those inclined to engage in the behavior that the law forbids had an expressive purpose, it would be hard to suppose that the legislature did not understand at least that its restriction would fall heavily on expression. But it might understand this and still not be aiming to suppress messages, as, for example, if it established a maximum sound level, knowing that sound trucks would be mainly affected.

11. In fact, since few people would be prosecuted for destroying draft cards who did not have a communicative purpose, it made little practical difference whether the Court's review was of the provision in general or of its application to O'Brien.

12. As the text above indicates, that one defendant had a communicative purpose should not have been enough to trigger a more stringent review of the provision in general.

13. 391 U.S. at 376.

14. Id. at 377.

15. To defend this claim, I would have to analyze in some detail what the Court said about the government's interests in administering the draft. The characterization in the text is widely shared by constitutional law scholars, but a skeptical reader would do well to examine the opinion.

16. See, e.g., Tribe, note 2 supra, at 977–86; Ely, note 2 supra.

17. This option is intimated in the Court's initial suggestion in *O'Brien* that it does not "accept the view that an apparently limitless variety of conduct can be labeled 'speech.'"

18. Chapter 9 explains why it does not make sense to make legal, by a constitutional privilege, an act that is performed *because* it is illegal.

19. See, e.g., *Wisconsin* v. *Yoder*, 406 U.S. 205 (1972).

20. See generally Tribe, note 2 supra, at 794–825; Ely, note 2 supra.

21. This may be a bit less obvious about other common verbs used, like "deface," but the aim probably is not to reach people who carelessly spill paint on their flags. See id. at 1502–3.

22. See A. Loewy, "Punishing Flag Desecrators: The Ultimate in Flag Desecration," 49 *North Carolina Law Review* 48 (1970).

23. See *Cowgill* v. *California*, 396 U.S. 371 (1970) (per curiam) (dismissed for want of substantial federal question). It may be argued that one's choice of clothing, hair style and length, etc. are inevitably communicative because they reflect the way we want to present ourselves. See, e.g., M. Nimmer, *Nimmer on Freedom of Speech* 3–65 to 3–71 (New York, Matthew Bender Co. 1984). I am assuming, to the contrary, that such choices count as communicative only if one is consciously trying to communicate some particular message.

24. See Ely, note 2 supra, at 1503–8. Although Ely's analysis on this point seems correct, regulation that chooses some symbolic messages to protect from every sort of interference, including notably trivialization, strikes less fundamentally at free speech than regulation that suppresses some messages in favor of others. Thus, I remain open to the possibility that "improper use" statutes can be more easily justified than "desecration" statutes.

25. If a school forbids the wearing of armbands, but the main reason for wearing armbands in this culture and the only reason for the prohibition have to do with communication, then the regulation is clearly directed at expression. See *Tinker* v. *Des Moines School District*, 393 U.S. 503 (1969).

26. The new law did make it illegal to destroy someone else's draft card, but it seems unlikely in the extreme that Congress was especially concerned with that behavior.

27. As David Bogen has suggested, many doctrines formulated by the Court can be seen as attempts to forestall legislation based on forbidden purposes, without the necessity of judicial determinations of forbidden purposes in individual instances. See generally D. Bogen, *Bulwark of Liberty: The Court and the First Amendment* (Port Washington, N.Y., Associated Faculty Press 1984).

28. Tribe, note 2 supra, at 823.

20

Agreement to Communicate

Agreements to engage in communication raise special problems not presented by agreements to commit ordinary criminal acts like murder and burglary. Our review of Supreme Court cases has indicated how frequently those engaged in subversive advocacy have been punished as conspirators. The issue that has usually occupied the Court is whether the communications are punishable, it being assumed that if the answer to this question is "yes," punishment for conspiracy is also appropriate. Yet Judge Coffin in the *Spock* case and some commentators have urged that, when the subject of agreement is communication, punishment for conspiracy may not be acceptable, even if punishment on another basis is.[1] I shall address this troublesome issue shortly, but it can be clarified by analysis of two related questions.

The first question is whether punishment for conspiracy is ever appropriate when punishment for the individual communications would be precluded because the relevant communications are constitutionally protected. The short answer to this question is "no." Because of the size and nature of a conspiracy, a particular communication may pose a risk of imminent evil that would not be present if the communication had been made by a "loner." But if that were true, the existence of the conspiracy could be introduced as a relevant circumstance in a prosecution for the communication itself. The prosecution should never be able to convict for an agreement to communicate unless it could also convict for what is communicated as a product of the agreement.

Justice Harlan's majority opinion in *Yates* v. *United States*[2] raises the second question by indicating uncertainty whether or not punishment under the Smith Act would be appropriate if the conspirators had not yet engaged in any advocacy. Can conspirators ever be punished for agreeing to communicate, when no communication has yet taken place? The proper constitutional approach to this kind of case depends upon whether the punishability of the proposed communications requires reference to their precise content and to the actual conditions in which they are uttered.

Suppose *A* and *B* agree that each will separately make specific coercive threats to *C* or will urge *C* to kill their uncle. What is contemplated is communication in private threatening *C* or encouraging *C* to commit a particular murder. If made, the coercive threats would fall outside the First Amendment, and the encouragements would be subject to the standard suggested in Chapter 15. Each would properly be punished if the speaker evidenced a serious intent to carry out the threat or have the crime committed. If A and B were prosecuted for the actual threats or encouragements, their advance agreement would constitute powerful evidence of serious intent; indeed the agreement would support such a finding in the absence of the communications. Even if the exact circumstances and precise language of the communications are not fixed, A and B have agreed that communications that would undoubtedly be criminal will take place. Unless some general principle exists against any punishment for conspiracy to communicate, little reason appears for distinguishing their liability from liability under an agreement to commit any other sort of criminal act.

Suppose instead that A and B agree that they will try to pressure C or give public speeches urging violence against the police. Now the precise language and context are critical. One cannot know whether the communications themselves are punishable until they actually take place or until planning advances to a further stage, and punishment for conspiracy should not be allowed on the basis of uncertain speculation about what would be said. Barring virtual certainty about the actual message and circumstances of delivery, the proper constitutional test for public speech, which emphasizes specific content and context, indirectly bars conviction for unfulfilled plans to engage in such speech.

I now tackle the most perplexing issue. If communication has already taken place, should the government be able to charge a defendant with conspiracy, or should it charge him only as a principal or accessory for the communication itself? In the *Spock* case, Judge Coffin in dissent objected to the use of a conspiracy charge. He argued that the First Amendment should be read to bar prosecutions for conspiracy when "(1) the effort was completely public; (2) the issues were all in the public domain; (3) the group was ill-defined, shifting, with many affiliations; (4) the purposes in the 'agreement' are both legal and illegal; and (5) the need for additional evidence to inculpate . . . is recognized."[3] His careful description of the kind of public conspiracy involved was designed in part to counter the majority's criticism that conspiracy convictions would be appropriate for public agreements to violate laws against restraint of trade or laws forbidding the sale of certain commodities, and would also be appropriate for a group of vigilantes in a public square agreeing to call out a lynch mob. Some commentators have gone farther than Judge Coffin and suggested that conspiracy convictions should never be allowed for agreements to engage in expression; having in mind political expression like that involved in *Spock*, *Dennis*, and *Yates*,[4] these writers do not explicitly address whether their theories would also bar agreements to engage in private criminal solicitation.

In considering punishment for agreements to communicate, I shall initially concentrate on the substantive theory of conspiracy liability. As I indicated in Chapter 4, a substantial overlap exists between a person's liability for conspiracy and his liability as an accessory if the acts planned are carried out by another conspirator. In the ordinary case, one who is liable as an accessory will have been a conspirator, and conspirators will be liable as accessories after the crime is committed. To bar conspiratorial liability for communication without touching accessorial liability would have very limited effect as far as substantive liability is concerned.[5] So we need first to ask whether accessorial liability for communication is constitutionally permissible.

The answer must be "yes" in the private context. Say *A* has paid *B* to encourage *C* to murder his uncle and *B* has done so; or *A* and *B* have agreed that each will encourage *C*, and the police interrupt their plans only after *B* has acted. Surely it is appropriate to punish *A* for *B*'s solicitation in both instances.

Should it matter if the speech is public and ideological? *A* has paid *B* to stir up a mob to riot, or *A* has agreed with *B* that if *B* stirs up a mob on one day *A* will do so on the next. Again, if *A* has clearly endorsed *B*'s communication and by inducement or agreement has enhanced the likelihood that it will take place, it is difficult to understand why the First Amendment should bar liability. Of course, *A* should not be punished unless he has displayed the same firm intent to have *B* make a criminal communication that *B* himself must have.[6] The key to *A*'s protection when he is a participant in an agreement to communicate is that the basic stringent constitutional standards for punishment of public speech must be applied independently to him.

In sum, accessorial liability for communications should not be barred under the First Amendment and, subject to a strict test, may even be appropriate for some public speech. If communication has taken place, those who are liable for conspiracy may also be liable for the substantive offense, and conspiracy does not add significantly, or at all, to the range of substantive liability.[7]

Prosecutors sometimes employ a conspiracy theory in order to attain procedural advantages relating to joinder, venue, hearsay evidence of conspirators, order of evidence, and the like.[8] In fact, many of these advantages would also be available for prosecution of accessories; so conspiracy is less crucial to their employment than is often supposed. Although these tactical advantages and perhaps even the sinister connotations of the word "conspiracy" may lend themselves to occasional prosecutorial abuse in political cases, this danger bears a rather tenuous connection to First Amendment analysis. It can be argued that, since prosecution on a conspiracy theory is not really necessary in any case in which punishable communications have been completed, use of that theory should be constitutionally barred because a less drastic means—other bases of criminal liability, including accessorial liability—is available to serve the government's interest. But treating one basis for criminal liability as less drastic than another because of its supposedly smaller potential for abuse in practice involves a strained sense of "less drastic" means, and although the argument along this line is not wholly implausible, neither is it finally convincing. The more appropriate constitutional safeguard is to impose very strict standards for punishment for communication, whatever the general penal theory of liability.

Notes

1. See 416 F.2d 165, 184 (1st Cir. 1969) (Coffin, J., dissenting); D. Filvaroff, "Conspiracy and the First Amendment," 121 *University of Pennsylvania Law Review* 189 (1972); Note, "Conspiracy and the First Amendment," 79 *Yale Law Journal* 872 (1970).
2. 354 U.S. 298, 324 (1957).
3. 416 F.2d at 186.
4. Filvaroff, note 1 supra; Note, note 1 supra.

338   Constitutional Limits on Prohibiting Speech

5. There are some situations in which remote conspirators in a far-flung criminal organization may not be accessories for particular acts. In those cases it might ordinarily matter whether a conspiracy theory was employed, but the test I suggest below for any defendant's liability would preclude punishment for such remote participants.

6. If A and B have agreed that B will accomplish a particular criminal objective and the means are left to B's discretion, say B is to get C killed by some means, A can be liable if B chooses to proceed by a form of communication, say soliciting D to kill C.

7. See note 5 supra.

8. See generally P. Johnson, "The Unnecessary Crime of Conspiracy," 61 *California Law Review* 1137 (1973).

21

Conclusion

In this book, I have offered an approach to political and constitutional issues of free speech. The approach is modest in three important aspects. It assumes that not every human action that "expresses" something about the actor qualifies as speech that is covered by a principle of free speech. It concentrates on what is special about communicative acts, suggesting criteria for evaluation that do not depend on an overall theory about appropriate domains of liberty. Legislators are often called upon to consider speech-restrictive legislation that deals with many discrete activities, for example, forbidding solicitation of crimes in general. Judges must review punishments of particular expressive behavior. Neither for legislators nor for judges acting in these contexts is it very helpful to say that communications relating to one activity or another should be permitted because the underlying activity ought to be allowed, even though as things stand now it is forbidden, its prohibition has been declared constitutional, and there is no chance of repeal in the foreseeable future. Without doubt, analysis of free speech does depend on some, largely liberal, assumptions about a just and desirable polity, but that analysis can leave unresolved other independent questions about liberty. The third sense in which my approach is modest is in not proposing any single *key* to First Amendment interpretation. Attempting to rely on one key produces either grave distortion of concepts or highly inappropriate results.

Sensible interpretation of the First Amendment requires evaluation of the values of liberty of speech and of the dangers of particular kinds of communications. Initial determinations of whether the ambit of the amendment touches certain kinds of communications should rest on the expressive value of the communications; decisions about appropriate tests for communications to which the amendment is relevant should rest on both expressive value and danger.

Language serves a variety of functions, only some of which are covered by the special reasons for freedom of speech. Drawing constitutional lines of inclusion and exclusion is vastly complicated by the multiple purposes and effects that particular communications can have, but we can identify utterances that have much less claim to protection than do the claims of fact and value that the amendment obviously embraces. Words are sometimes used to alter normative or other relations, the utterances themselves establishing new duties and rights, or prospects of unfavorable or favorable consequences. I have suggested that, although such situation-altering utterances as orders, agreements, offers, and most conditional threats may involve implicit assertions of fact and value, their dominant purpose to change reality puts them outside the First Amendment. This is a point not much addressed in the cases and literature on freedom of speech, but the conclusion coincides with the long-standing assumption that punishment of agreements to commit ordinary crimes and the crime of extortion do not raise constitutional difficulties.

Weak imperatives whose dominant purpose is to induce others to action present more difficult analytical problems. Although simple imperatives are plainly distinguishable from assertions of fact and value, most requests or encouragements contain explicit or implicit valuations, and frequently these valuations could not easily be reformulated in a different way. Yet the inducement element of these utterances seems largely outside the rationales for liberty of speech. My basic conclusion is that, for encouragements to specific crimes, the level of constitutional protection should depend on their general value and harmfulness in various contexts. The major distinction is between public and private encouragements, the latter enjoying less protection because of their relatively slight expressive value, the unlikelihood they will be met by direct countervailing communication, and the special dangers they create. Public encouragements are the sorts of utterances for which something like the test of *Brandenburg* v. *Ohio* is appropriate, and I have indicated what the dimensions of such a test should be.

Concentrating on the uses of language and the values of expression, I have canvassed a number of other problems of legislative wisdom and constitutional principle. Although I have focused in my constitutional analysis mainly on judicial standards for the application of adequately drawn statutes, both that analysis and the treatment of a political principle of free speech have clear implications for development of common law doctrines of civil liability, as well as for the kinds of legislation that should be adopted. With very limited exceptions, legislatures should not be able to punish communications because of their tendency to cause criminal behavior by others, except when those communications are directed to producing specific criminal actions. They should not, for example, be able to proscribe revolutionary or subversive advocacy in some general way.

Perhaps the major lesson of the book is the complexity of the issues it addresses. Anyone who supposes that the protection of the First Amendment can be reduced to one justification or to one all-purpose test of coverage is either deluded or willing to sacrifice a great deal in the interests of theoretical neatness and actual or apparent simplicity of administration.

The time has come to recognize that, even for a single problem like encouragements to crime, something more than the single formula of *Brandenburg* is needed. And, for other areas, such as coercive threats, defamation, or control of demonstrations, quite different analytical techniques may be appropriate. The variety of the approaches the Supreme Court has taken in interpreting the First Amendment may more accurately reflect sensible judicial responses to disparate problems than some fundamental failure of theory,[1] and those who engage in scholarly efforts to link those problems and responses together would do well to begin with the assumption that no single analytical device is likely to serve the courts well in all areas. Aspects of life or law rarely yield to simple dichotomies, and constitutionally protected liberty of speech is no exception.

Note

1. This point has been persuasively argued in Steven Shiffrin's writings. See, e.g., S. Shiffrin, "Defamatory Non-media Speech and First Amendment Methodology," 25 *University of California in Los Angeles Law Review* 915 (1978); S. Shiffrin, "The First Amendment and Economic Regulation: Away from a General Theory of the First Amendment," 78 *Northwestern University Law Review* 1212 (1983).

Index

disinterested advice, 122–23; recklessness and negligence, 123–26, *see also* Reckless or negligent behavior; and weak imperatives, 110–18, 226, 260, *see also* Situation-altering utterances; and weak agreements, 240, *see also* Weak agreements; factual information, 119–20, 272–73; provocations, 120–21, 282–84; other incentives, 273–74; and free speech, 113–15; and other wrongful actions, 274–77; and the First Amendment, 206–9, 260–77

Epstein, R., 105n

Epton v. New York, 248n

Espionage Act, 188, 190, 192, 317, 324n

Extortion: and threats, 93, 100–101, 103

FCC v. Pacifica Foundation, 217n, 311n

False and insincere statements, 130–38; the punishment of, 130, 132–34; and free speech principle, 48–51, 132–34; and defamation, 322–24, *see also* Defamation; the constitutional status of 316–21; and commercial speech, 321–22, *see also* Commercial speech

False ideas: the value of, 16; governmental suppression of, 11, 17, 19; possible governmental promotion of, 20. *See also* Liberal democracy

False imprisonment, and threats, 92

Farber, D., 7n, 73n, 127n, 140n, 156n, 237n, 279n, 280n, 311n

Father of Candor [pseud.], 174–75, 184n

Feinberg, J., 35n, 36n, 155n, 156n, 162n, 312n

Feiner v. New York, 197–98, 284

Fifth Amendment, 168, 169, 172–73, 185n

Filvaroff, D., 337n

Finnis, J., 55, 72n, 156n, 312n

First Amendment adjudication: the standards of, 219–35; the libertarian position, 220; reasonableness and dangerous tendency tests, 221–22; ad hoc balancing, 222–24; categorical balancing, 223–24; evil discounted by improbability, 224–25; content regulation, 225–27, *see also* Indirect regulation of speech; review of legislation, 227; clear and present danger and incitement, 227. *See also* First Amendment interpretation; First Amendment protection

First Amendment interpretation: the standards of, 167–81; the constitutional language, 167–69; the original intent, 169–77; the constitutional structure, 177–79; precedent and other law, 179; deference, 179–80; justice and welfare, 180–81; views of fellow judges, 181. *See also* First Amendment adjudication; First Amendment protection

First Amendment law: the development of,

186–214; early stages, 178–88; the clear and present danger formula, 188–94, *see also* Clear and present danger test; and subversive advocacy, 194–96; and public order, 196–99; and contempt of court, 199–200; and labor relations, 200–201, 212, 257; the advocacy of action and ad hoc balancing, 201–4; the Warren Court, 204–9; the Burger Court, 209–14; and commercial speech, 211. *See also* First Amendment adjudication; First Amendment interpretation

First Amendment protection: the scope of, 4, 228–35; expression-action distinction, 228–30, 239, 263–65, 268; communicative or expressive behavior, 230–31; reliance on history, 232, private communications, 232–33; nonpolitical speech, 233; crimes and revolutionary activity, the social contract, 233–34; simplicity and complexity, 234–35; and the press, 4. *See also* First Amendment adjudication; First Amendment interpretation

Ford, C. (et al.), 139n

Ford, W. C., 184n

Founding Church of Scientology v. United States, 139n

Fourteenth Amendment, 4, 168, 169, 172–73, 176–77, 221, 232

Fox's Libel Act (1792, U.K.), 184n

Franklin, M., 326n

Frantz, L., 236n

Free speech principle: essential requisites of, 3; understanding of, 4, 11; plausible reach of, 3, 5, *see also* Boundaries of free speech; relationship with a minimal principle of liberty, 9–14, 97, 107n; and justifications for free speech, 40–43, *see also* Justifications for free speech; and bases for criminal punishment, 79–162; and speaker's objectives and motives, 47; and falsehood and insincerity, 48–50, *see also* False and insincere statements; and audience response, 50–51, 54; and situation-altering utterances, 58–71, *see also* Situation-altering utterances; and weak agreements, 81–82, *see also* Weak agreements; and conditional threats, 67–68, 94–99, *see also* Conditional threats; and unconditional threats, 91, *see also* Unconditional threats

Freedom of speech: constitutional standard and a political principle, 3–5, 42; the broad sense of, 4; and scientific research, 21, 22; relation to liberal government, 4, 11, 16, *see also* Liberal government; Liberal democracy; relation to underlying institutions, 16; effect without constitutional status, 4; principle behind the constitutional guarantee of, 4;

Locke, J., 30, 38n, 174, 175, 184n
Loewy, A., 161n, 162n, 333n
Lovell v. City of Griffin, 196
Lusky, L., 185n

Mackie, J., 75n
MacKinnon, C., 157n, 313n
Malamuth, N. (and Billings, V.), 156n
Masses Publishing Co. v. Patten, 193-94
Maxwell v. Dow, 182n
Mayton, W., 183n, 184n
McCarthy, J., 180
Meiklejohn, A., 38n, 45, 135, 140n, 177, 178,
    185n
Memoirs v. Massachusetts, 303, 304, 312n
Mendelson, W., 236n
Miami Herald Pub. Co. v. Tornillo, 326n
Mill, J. S., 16-17, 20, 24, 36n, 38n, 48, 127n,
    266, 278n
Miller v. California, 304, 307
Milton, J., 16, 36n, 174
Minimal principle of liberty, 9; and a principle
    of free speech, 10-12. See also Free speech
    principle
Mollan, R., 216n
Monaghan, H., 216n
Moral philosophy: relation between
    consequentialist and nonconsequentialist
    reasons, 14-16. See also Consequentialist
    reasons for free speech; Nonconsequentialist
    reasons for free speech
Montague, A., 155n
Munro, D., 128n
Murphy, J., 105n

NAACP v. Claiborne Hardware Co., 212, 259n
NLRB v. Gissel Packing Co., 212, 259n
Nagel, R., 181n, 185n, 236n
Nally v. Grace Community Church of the
    Valley, 128n
Nebraska Press Association v. Stuart, 286n
Newman, J., 71n
New York Times v. Sullivan, 184n, 205, 210,
    312n, 319, 322-23
New York Times Co. v. United States, 285n
Nimmer, M., 7n, 72n, 127n, 140n, 155n, 250,
    279n, 333n
Ninth Amendment, 172, 185n
Nonconsequentialist reasons for free speech,
    14-16, 29-34; social contract theory, 30-31,
    43; autonomy and rationality, 31-33, 43, 96-
    99; dignity and equality, 33-34, 43;
    marketplace of ideas, 17, 19-20, 22, 34; and
    consequentialist reasons, 14-16. See also
    Consequentialist reasons for free speech;
    Justifications for free speech

Nonverbal communications, and freedom of
    speech, 51-56. See also Boundaries of speech
Noto v. United States, 204
Nowak, J. (et al.), 155n
Nozick, R., 258n

Offensive words: and diffuse harms, 141-54; the
    fighting words doctrine, 197, 210, 283-84,
    286n, 288, 292-98; the tort right of privacy,
    142-43, 402, see also Defamation; group
    epithets and slurs, 143-48, 295-301; and
    obscene literature, 149-54, see also
    Pornography; and civil liability, 298-301; and
    constitutional limits on punishment, 287-309
Offers: and crimes, 82-84, 249-51; the free
    speech concerns, 83-84; and the
    constitutional status of, 241-43
Ohralik v. Ohio State Bar Association, 211,
    217n, 279n, 326n
Olivia N. v. NBC, 286n
Orders: and crimes, 84-85; and free speech
    concerns, 85; and requests, 85; the
    constitutional status of, 243-44
Orwell, G., 10, 35n

Paris Adult Theatre v. Slaton, 304, 305
Parker v. Levy, 247n, 280n, 309n
Pedersen v. City of Richmond, 246n, 247n
Pennock, R. (and Chapman, J.), 258n
People v. Most, 187, 267, 278n
People v. Rubin, 106n, 250, 258n, 278n
Philadelphia Newspapers, Inc., v. Hepps,
    326n
Pierce v. United States, 324n
Pittsburgh Press Co. v. Human Relations
    Commission, 108n, 253, 279n
Plamenatz, J., 174, 184n
Political philosophy, force of
    nonconsequentialist reasons, 15
Pope, J., 259n
Pornography, 149-54, 288; public nudity, 56,
    161; the Attorney General's Commission on,
    306; and liberty of self-regarding acts, 149;
    and application of free speech principle, 149-
    50; and legislative judgment to suppress, 150-
    54; and First Amendment, 205, 210, 302-9
Posadas de Puerto Rico Associates v. Tourism
    Company, 276, 280n
Posner, R., 105n
Powell, J., 176, 177, 182n, 185n
Preventing harm, only legitimate basis for
    speech prohibition, 11, 31
Pryor v. Municipal Court, 247n
Public Health Cigarette Smoking Act (1969),
    280n
Public Order Act (1986, U.K.), 154n